Daily Life

A Sourcebook

Daily Life in Ancient Rome

A Sourcebook

Edited and Translated, with an Introduction, by
Brian K. Harvey

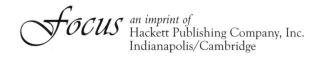 an imprint of
Hackett Publishing Company, Inc.
Indianapolis/Cambridge

A Focus book

Focus an imprint of
Hackett Publishing Company

For further information, please address
    Hackett Publishing Company, Inc.
    P.O. Box 44937
    Indianapolis, Indiana 46244-0937

    www.hackettpublishing.com

Cover design by Rick Todhunter
Interior design by Elizabeth L. Wilson
Composition by Aptara, Inc.

Library of Congress Cataloging-in-Publication Data
Names: Harvey, Brian K.
Title: Daily life in ancient Rome : a sourcebook / edited and translated,
    with an introduction, by Brian K. Harvey.
Description: Indianapolis : Focus, an imprint of Hackett Publishing Company,
    2016. | Includes bibliographical references and index.
Identifiers: LCCN 2015035374 | ISBN 9781585107957 (pbk.)
Subjects: LCSH: Rome—Civilization—Sources.
Classification: LCC DG78 .D135 2016 | DDC 937—dc23
LC record available at http://lccn.loc.gov/2015035374

For My Wife, Sarah

Contents

Preface

Over the course of a millennium, the Romans expanded from their small village on the banks of the Tiber River to eventually become the dominant culture in the Mediterranean basin. Even more than fifteen hundred years after their collapse, the Romans continue to captivate the imagination. Great works such as Vergil's *Aeneid* and the Colosseum in Rome continue to inspire new generations with a desire to learn more about the Romans and their lost culture. Indeed, in modern popular culture, Rome is a frequent topic of television documentaries, historical fiction, and movies for the big and small screen. "Gladiator," "Caesar," "Ides of March," and "Romulus and Remus" are household words.

This book is first and foremost about the Romans themselves: who they were, how they defined themselves, where they lived and what they did to live their lives. There is no better way to study the Romans than to examine the material they left behind. The current volume is a sourcebook, a collection of evidence from the Roman world in the form of primary sources: texts, artifacts, and architecture that were created by the Romans themselves. Each source tells us something about the Romans and how they lived their lives. No single source will tell us everything about Roman culture. Instead we must bring together numerous sources of different types to better understand some facet of ancient Roman life. Literary sources, for example, describe what a Roman child might do with his or her day. Archaeology preserves examples of children's toys and dolls. Sculpture shows us what Roman children looked like and what they wore. Tombstones give us their names and some details about their family lives. Taken individually, each of these sources looks at the bigger picture from a particular angle. By using all of these sources together, we can begin to gain a better understanding of the life of a Roman child as a whole.

The scope of this book is very large so it has been necessary to limit the number of topics as well as the sources provided for each topic. For every source I have included, it was necessary to omit dozens of others. The same is true for the topics discussed. There are many areas of Roman life that I have had to omit to keep the length of this book under control. I have also tended to stress evidence from Rome's most prosperous period: the first century BC to the second century AD. Evidence from Rome's earliest period (the eighth to the second centuries BC) is very limited and often fragmentary. Although there is abundant evidence for the later empire (third to the fifth centuries AD), political and social change had transformed much of Roman life. When material useful for a topic is lacking, I have included evidence from the earlier and later periods, most notably the late imperial law codes of Theodosius and Justinian who drew extensively upon earlier evidence in their compilations and for whom no parallel from the earlier periods has survived. I have also chosen to focus as much as possible on Rome and Italy. By the second century AD, the empire contained a very large and diverse population, and it is necessary to set a geographical limit to better focus the collection and allow the reader to better see connections between different pieces of evidence.

I have aimed this sourcebook primarily at the non-specialist and those with a casual interest in learning about the Romans. Sourcebooks can be difficult for such an audience because the sources were written or created in another time and culture for a Roman audience. As such, the sources tend to omit background information that would have been known to its original audience. For that reason, it is often best to use a sourcebook in tandem with another book or academic course that can help the reader interpret the included sources. Seeing the sources for oneself, however, has tremendous advantages as it allows the reader to observe how scholars have reached their hypotheses and gives a privileged glimpse into the mind of an ancient Roman. Having a scholar tell you how the ancient food supply to Rome worked is important information, but it is also interesting to read documents with receipts for transported goods, to see an ancient warehouse, and to look at a mosaic depicting dock workers unloading cargo from a transport ship in a Roman harbor. Of course, even the sources have been modified to some degree. Archaeological remains and inscriptions are usually damaged by the passage of time. Literary sources, too, have been passed down via manuscripts that have been copied and re-copied over the centuries. Because the non-specialist cannot be expected to know Latin and Greek (about half of the Roman world spoke Greek as its primary language), it is also necessary to translate the original languages into English. All translations provided in this book are my own. Often, I have slightly adapted these translations to include necessary background information to make them easier for the non-specialist to read.

This book includes many sources from the Roman world. Many of the sources are literary works of fiction and non-fiction. There are selections from poems, works of history, speeches, published letters, novels, and even how-to manuals on farming. Other sources are documentary. In addition to such day-to-day items like bills of sale, most of the documents included here are legal texts either preserved in the law codes of the late Empire, or on stone or tablets of bronze. I have also included many examples of epigraphy: texts inscribed on some kind of durable material, usually stone. There are building inscriptions, honorary statue bases, religious dedications, and tombstones. I have also selected a number of examples of material culture: archaeological, artistic, and architectural sources that are more visual in nature. There are descriptions and plans of houses and temples, works of art, and even small finds from archaeological excavations that illustrate what life was like in the Roman world. For details on the individual authors and works quoted, see the section Works Quoted at the end of the book.

Chapter 1: A Short History of the Empire

The Romans broadly organized their history according to changes in their system of government. Officially, they believed that the mythical figure Romulus founded Rome and became the first of its seven kings. The monarchy endured until 509 BC, when the last king was expelled because of his brutal and tyrannical rule. The political mythology then tells how the aristocracy that started the coup against the last king created the Republic, an aristocratic system of government centered on the senate, a body of wealthy magistrates and ex-magistrates. The Republic, too, eventually succumbed to a long period of civil wars in which members of the aristocracy tried to usurp power for themselves. The Republic ended in 27 BC when the winner of one of the civil wars, a man named Octavian, reformed the state and put himself into the equivalent of a monarchical position, using the name Augustus.

These changes signaled the beginning of the Empire, Rome's third major political system. The emperors continued to rule until AD 476, when the last emperor in the west, the appropriately named Romulus Augustulus was forced to give what was left of the Roman Empire in Europe to a barbarian chieftain named Odoacer. The eastern Roman Empire, however, continued to exist under the name of the Byzantine Empire until the sixteenth century.

What follows is a very brief outline of Roman history. It is intended to give an introduction to undergraduates and other people without specialized knowledge a general historical framework in which to contextualize the other sources in this collection. It is not intended to be an exhaustive history and cannot replace more detailed accounts.

The Monarchy

The most difficult part of studying Roman history is the fact that the Romans had no written history until the third century BC. Until that time, history was recorded orally or was reflected in public documents. The lack of a written history opened the possibility of manipulation of historical memory. What has come down to us about Rome's earliest history is a compilation of memory that was only organized into a coherent narrative in the third century BC or shortly before. This narrative, however, is a simplification of reality and plays into the Roman wish to give their city an origin that matched its later glory. Early Roman historians also preferred to see their history as a series of important moments and turning points rather than a slow process of change. In Rome's political mythology (the way later Romans remembered their own, unrecorded past) Romulus founded the city in 753 BC. Kings ruled the city until the Roman aristocracy expelled the kings and established the Republic (in 509 BC).

Very little of Rome's earliest history is certain. While it does seem probable that kings originally ruled Rome, it is unlikely that there were seven with the names that are preserved in the traditional history. It is very likely that what we have preserved is another simplification of history in order to explain how Rome grew into an important city. Archaeology, however, has proven to be both an important corroborative and corrective tool. Excavations in Rome have shown that people were living on the site of Rome from about 1000 BC. The location of the Tiber River was one of the most important factors in the appearance of the city in that location. The settlement developed into a city during the seventh and sixth centuries BC, the period during which Rome's political mythology asserts the city was ruled by kings.

The Early Republic

According to the historical tradition, in 509 BC, the aristocracy expelled the last king of Rome, a tyrant named Tarquinius Superbus (Tarquin the Proud). The Romans then developed a system of government centered on the wealthy aristocracy: the senate. From this aristocracy were elected magistrates who administered justice, led armies, and created legislation. The wealthy held the majority of power, and it was their money that kept the government running.

Rome also vigorously expanded during the Republic. Between its foundation and the middle of the third century BC, Rome conquered the entire Italian peninsula. Rome's remarkable success can mainly be attributed to its superior system of fighting (the legion) and vast supply of manpower that continued to grow as Rome annexed neighboring territories. The conquered peoples were quite loyal due to the promise of receiving a share in Roman citizenship if they remained loyal and continued to supply soldiers for Rome's armies.

After they completed the conquest of Italy, the Romans fought three wars (the so-called Punic Wars) against the Carthaginians of North Africa. While the Romans were uniting Italy, the Carthaginians had grown into a major sea power in the western Mediterranean. Rome first went to war with them in 264 BC over the island of Sicily. Despite being primarily a land power, the Romans quickly developed a navy to counter Carthage's superior navy. The First Punic War ended in 241 BC when Carthage yielded and gave up claims to Sicily and Sardinia. The Second Punic War began in 217 BC when a Carthaginian general named Hannibal marched an army into Italy and lived there for more than a decade. Despite crushing victories over several Roman armies in Italy, Rome's allies remained for the most part loyal. Eventually, Hannibal was forced to return to North Africa when a Roman army under Scipio Africanus threatened Carthage. Hannibal was defeated at the Battle of Zama in 202 BC and Carthage was forced to surrender.

Despite Rome's frequent wars, the empire expanded slowly after the conquest of Italy. Rome added Sicily, Sardinia, and part of Spain as provinces during the Punic Wars but did not annex Carthage or North Africa. The aristocrats saw war as monetarily and politically profitable but control of foreign territory as difficult and expensive. The trend intensified during the second century BC as Rome became embroiled in the complicated political situation of the Hellenistic kingdoms in the Greek East. In 146 BC, Rome won major wars against Carthage (in the Third Punic War) and Greece (with the sack of Corinth). In the aftermath of these wars, Rome annexed the provinces of North Africa and Greece and nearly doubled the size of their empire in one year.

The Fall of the Republic

War and the profit it brought became major motivators for aristocrats to go to war. At home, the manipulation of the lower classes became another way for the ambitious to achieve power. Radical aristocratic reformers such as Tiberius and Gaius Gracchus tried to win power by making grand promises to the lower classes. Such reformers posed a serious threat to the wealth, prestige, and power of the older and more conservative aristocrats. As a result, the more traditional, conservative elements sometimes struck out against such reformers, often in violent ways. In 133 BC, a mob led by conservative aristocrats murdered Tiberius Gracchus and in 122 they did the same thing to his brother Gaius.

In the first century BC, the struggle between political rivals erupted into all-out civil war. Ambitious politicians learned that war was the quickest way to accumulate the funds, supporters, and armies necessary to dominate the state. The general Marius won enormous popularity from his military victories but his monopolization of the consulship caused the more traditional elements of the state to back his rival Cornelius Sulla. Sulla defeated Marius in a bloody civil war. As victor, Sulla attempted to completely reform the state and put the majority of power into the hands of the senate. Few of his reforms survived his death, however. Pompey the Great won support from the lower classes by working against the reforms of Sulla only to be undermined in turn by Julius Caesar who was much better at winning popular support. In the end, however, it was Caesar's better armies that won him the victory. The empire grew quickly during this period as these men achieved their goals through military conquest.

Julius Caesar was assassinated on the Ides of March, 44 BC. The number and influence of his political supporters, however, was so high that the assassins were unable to completely eliminate Caesar's influence. Soon, a new civil war broke out between the young Octavian, who was Caesar's heir, and Marc Antony, Caesar's top general. Both sought to control Caesar's political party. The eventual winner was the young Octavian, who proved to be a shrewder politician and manipulator of public opinion than Antony. Antony's indiscretions with Cleopatra, the queen of Hellenistic Egypt made Octavian's job even easier.

The Empire

Octavian returned to Rome after the civil war as the undisputed head of the Roman world. Worn out by more than a century of civil war, the Romans were willing to accept Octavian's leadership. In 27 BC, Octavian was granted extraordinary power in the state and a new name: Augustus. He used his position to reform the state and society and is remembered as the first Roman emperor. Many of these reforms sought to update the government and make it run more efficiently. The reforms also, however, put a monarch at the head of Roman government. Augustus' system proved to be remarkably successful and would survive the rest of Roman history.

Augustus died in AD 14 and the empire passed to his son-in-law Tiberius. Augustus and the next four emperors were all derived from the inter-related families of the Julians (from the family of Julius Caesar) and the Claudians (the family of Augustus' wife Livia). The men who followed Tiberius on the throne are among the most famous (and notorious) in Roman history: Gaius Caligula (AD 37–41), Claudius (AD 41–54), and Nero (AD 54–68). Nero committed suicide when the senate and his personal bodyguard sided with Sulpicuis Galba, a usurper with the backing of the legions in Spain. Nero's death ushered in a year of civil war in which the armies on the major frontiers (Spain, Germany, the Danube, and the east) each fought to achieve the throne for their own commander. The civil war of AD 69, the so-called "Year of the Four Emperors," ended with the rise of Vespasian, the general in charge of quelling a rebellion of the Jews in the Roman province of Judaea. Vespasian (AD 69–79), the first of the Flavian emperors, was succeeded by first his elder son Titus (AD 79–81) and then his younger son Domitian (AD 81–96).

Domitian was assassinated in a palace conspiracy, and the elderly Nerva (AD 96–98) was chosen as a kind of transitional emperor to help smooth the shift from one dynasty to the next. The state did (barely) avoid a new civil war like that of AD 69. Because he had no children of his own, Nerva adopted Trajan as his successor. Adoption was a useful method of appointing a successor and was heralded as a way of having the most competent ruler on the throne. Trajan (AD 98–117) adopted Hadrian (AD 117–138) who adopted Antoninus Pius (AD 138–161) who adopted Marcus Aurelius (AD 161–180). As the only "adoptive" emperor to have a natural son, Marcus departed from the adoptive method of succession and designated that son, Commodus (AD 180–192), as his successor.

The reigns of these adoptive emperors was the period of the Roman Empire's greatest prosperity. Political and military stability and success resulted in tremendous population growth and economic development. The empire grew steadily as well during this period, mainly as emperors sought to legitimate their power through military conquest.

The later second century was a period of major transition as the economy showed signs of trouble and the empire began to suffer from more serious threats along its frontiers. The emperor Septimius Severus (AD 193–211) came to the throne after a new civil war that broke out after the assassination of Commodus in 192. Severus emphasized the military over every other part of society, an omen of the dominance the army was to have in the coming century. The Severan dynasty lasted until the death of Alexander Severus in 235.

Political and military instability characterized the second half of the third century. A steady stream of usurpers seeking the throne led to nearly constant civil war.

Almost every emperor (and usurper) in this period died in civil war, usually at the hands of their own soldiers who believed they had a better chance of survival if they shifted their allegiance. These civil wars also weakened the empire's ability to face foreign invasion. Tribes like the Alemanni on the Rhine, Goths on the Danube, and the reborn Persian Empire in the east frequently harassed Rome's frontiers. The emperor Decius (AD 249–251) was killed in battle with the Goths in 251 and the Persian king Sapor captured the emperor Valerian (AD 253–260) alive in 260.

The Late Empire

The emperor Diocletian (AD 284–305) managed to temporarily put an end to the downward spiral of the empire. To alleviate the pressure on one emperor and eliminate some of the problems with usurpers, Diocletian created what is called the tetrarchy, the rule of four emperors. There was an emperor for each major part of the empire: the Rhine, Italy and North Africa, the Danube, and the east. He also began an ambitious program of reform to the government, army, and society. The tetrarchy was remarkably successful as long as Diocletian remained in office. After his retirement (he was the first emperor to leave office while still alive), the remaining emperors began to argue and finally fight with one another and the system collapsed. The eventual winner was Constantine (AD 306–337), the son of one of Diocletian's original tetrarchs. He continued the reforms to the state and promoted Christianity and helped to develop, unify, and enlarge the early church.

Constantine died in 337 and the empire was divided among his three sons who immediately began to fight amongst themselves. Constantius II (AD 337–361), Constantine's middle son, was victorious and later promoted his cousin Julian to the rank of Caesar in the west. Julian (AD 361–363) later usurped the throne, but Constantius died, seemingly of natural causes, while Julian was marching east. Julian attempted to return paganism to its former place as the dominant religion. His successor Jovian (AD 363–364) continued this policy after Julian was killed during an invasion of Persia. Christianity returned to its earlier prominence under the brother co-emperors Valentinian (AD 364–375) and Valens (AD 364–378).

The peoples beyond the frontiers, most notably the Goths, continued to harass Roman territory. At the Battle of Adrianople in 378, the Goths killed Valens, who was succeeded by Theodosius (AD 378–395) in the east. In 394, Theodosius defeated a usurper who had seized control of the western empire and briefly united the two halves of the empire. After his death, the empire was split between his two sons, Honorius in the west (AD 395–423) and Arcadius in the east (AD 395–408). In 410, a massive army of Goths invaded Italy and even sacked the city of Rome itself. Honorius' successor Valentinian III (AD 425–455) faced the Huns under the leadership of Attila, who invaded Italy in 452. Similar invasions by the Franks, Saxons, Vandals, and Alemanni carved out kingdoms for themselves in the heart of the western empire. In AD 476, the last emperor of the west, Romulus Augustulus (AD 475–476), gave up his throne to the barbarian chieftain Odoacer, thus ending the history of the Roman Empire in the west.

The eastern empire, however, would go on for another millennium under the name of the Byzantine Empire. Justinian I (AD 527–565) is perhaps the most famous Byzantine emperor. He hoped to restore the glory of the old Roman Empire by re-conquering the west. His hope was only partially realized when he conquered parts of North Africa and Italy. Unfortunately, the territory he reacquired did not remain long under the control of Constantinople (the capital of the empire). Justinian I is also famous for his work to reform the corpus of Roman law and the publication of a number of collections of legislative precedent going back to the second century AD. The Byzantine Empire officially fell when the Ottoman Turks conquered Constantinople in 1453.

Chapter 2: The Structure of Society

Ancient Rome had a rigid class system for free persons, determined by three basic criteria: citizenship, birth (i.e., lineage), and relative wealth. A person had legal rights and responsibilities based on social status. Status based on citizenship, birth, and wealth presupposed that a person was freeborn or a freed slave, as the Roman state considered slaves to have no status at all.

Citizenship

According to the Roman model of an ancient city-state, the free native inhabitants of a particular city-state (their *patria*) were considered to be its citizens. Citizen status granted by the *patria* to its native inhabitants entailed a responsibility in terms of ensuring the continued well-being of the city-state by partaking in civic and political functions; these offices were thus unavailable to non-citizens. Indeed, throughout Rome's history, having citizen status became essential for scaling the social ladder. It also provided special privileges not enjoyed by non-citizens. Citizens had the right to vote for political candidates in elections or run for office themselves (provided they met the financial criteria to be a member of the local aristocracy).

During the Republican period, male citizens of Rome were required to offer themselves for military service, but, in the professional army of the imperial period, service was almost exclusively voluntary. Citizens also enjoyed special legal privileges. They had the right of legal appeal to the people (or, later, the emperor). They were exempt from the jurisdiction of Roman governors in the provinces. They were also protected from torture and the more severe forms of execution, such as crucifixion (see passages #6, #8, #9). Also, citizens were not required to pay certain taxes.

Many of the texts in this section exemplify the development of Roman citizenship. Ancus Martius' grant of citizenship to a city the Romans conquered during the regal period (#1) shows the liberality of the extension of the citizenship early in Rome's history. Further grants of citizenship in 188 BC (#2) testify to a continuation of that policy. A passage from Augustus' *Res Gestae* (#3) gives the number of citizens in the first century BC. One of those citizens was Mygdonius, a former Parthian prisoner of war (#4). Wide-scale grants of citizenship outside of Italy took place under the emperors. Claudius granted citizenship to towns in the Italian Alps (#5). In the early third century AD, the emperor Caracalla granted citizenship to all freeborn inhabitants of the empire (#7).

#1: Ancus Martius Grants Roman Citizenship to the Latins of Politorium

Livy, *Histories* 1.33
Written in the First Century BC Describing
Rome's Mythical Early History

Children became citizens at birth if both parents were citizens, but it was also possible for the government to give citizenship to anyone not already enfranchised. One of early Rome's greatest achievements, however, was the liberality with which they extended the citizenship to outsiders. As Rome conquered Italy in the sixth to the third centuries BC, they also meted out citizenship to conquered cities after years of loyal service to Rome (exemplified by a city's contribution of allied soldiers for Rome's wars against her enemies). The following passage from Livy describes the king Ancus Martius' grant of Roman citizenship to the Latin city of Politorium. Like much of the memory of Rome's earliest history, this passage (and the king it describes) is very likely fictitious, but it nevertheless reflects the city's willingness to extend its citizenship as its sphere of influence spread first through Latium and then the rest of Italy.

King Ancus forcibly captured Politorium, a city of the Latins. Following the precedent of earlier kings who had increased Rome's kingdom by co-opting the enemy into Roman citizenship, Ancus brought the whole population to Rome. Because much of the center of Rome was already inhabited (the Romans had from ages past inhabited the Palatine Hill, the Sabines the Capitoline with the Citadel, and the Albans the Caelian), Ancus assigned the Aventine Hill to the new population. Not much later, even more people were added to the numbers of Roman citizens after the capture of Tellenae and Ficena.... [After even more fighting against the Latins,] he once again granted many thousands of Latins Roman citizenship and settled them in the district of the altar of Venus Murcia in order to connect the Palatine and Aventine districts.

#2: New Citizens and a Census in 188 BC

Livy, *Histories* 38.36
Written in the First Century BC Describing 188 BC

At the beginning of his account of the year 188 BC, Livy describes how the people of Campania sought permission to marry Roman citizens. The children from such marriages would hold Roman citizenship. In the passage, Livy also records a further extension of citizenship to the remainder of Latium as well as a count of all Roman citizens.

While taking a census of the territory of Campania at the request of the senate, the people of Campania petitioned the state that they be allowed to marry women who were Roman citizens and that anyone who had previously married a Roman woman should be considered legally married under Roman law and that any children born before then should be considered legitimate and capable of inheriting property as Roman citizens. The senate granted these requests. In addition, one of the tribunes of the plebs, Gaius Valerius Tappo, proposed a bill that full citizenship be granted to the remainder of Latium (previously, some towns had only the citizenship without the right to vote). Four other tribunes of the plebs opposed this bill on the technicality that it had not been proposed without the sanction of the senate. They dropped their opposition, however, when they were told that the right to vote did not rest with the senate but the people, and so the bill was passed. The people of Formiae and Fundi were enrolled in the Aemilia tribe and Arpinum in the Cornelia tribe.... The final count of Roman citizens at this time was 258,318.

#3: Number of Citizens in the Reign of Augustus

Augustus, *Res Gestae* 8
Early First Century AD

The number of citizens continued to grow throughout the Republic. In 90 BC, the senate granted Roman citizenship to all of the people with the rank of ally (*socius*) in Italy. Much of the rest of Italy received citizenship from the generals who sought political and military support in the civil wars that brought down the Republic. The first emperor, Augustus, records in his account of his life (the *Res Gestae*) how he conducted three counts of Roman citizens during his reign. The document shows how the number of citizens continued to grow as the new emperor sought to gather support to his new regime.

In my sixth consulship (28 BC), I made a census of the people with my colleague Marcus Agrippa. During this census, I made a count of citizens (the previous count had been made 41 years earlier). In this count, I found 4,063,000 Roman citizens. Later, when Gaius Censorinus and Gaius Asinius were consuls (AD 8), I conducted a second count. At that time, I found 4,233,000 citizens. By virtue of my consular power, I conducted a third count with my son and colleague Tiberius Caesar while Sextus Pompeius and Sextus Appuleius were consuls (AD 14). At that time, the number of Roman citizens was 4,937,000.

#4: A Former Prisoner of War

CIL 11.137; *ILS* 1980
Early First Century AD

Among the new citizens created by Augustus was this prisoner of war who received the citizenship after a period of servitude in the imperial household. Mygdonius seems to have been captured during Augustus' Parthian campaigns on the eastern frontier in the first century BC.

I am Gaius Julius Mygdonius, a Parthian by nationality, free-born, who was captured in his youth and taken to Roman territory; when I was made a free Roman citizen, with fate as my ally, I set aside a retirement fund for when I became 50 years old. I have been heading for old age since my birth; now, oh grave, receive me. I am willing. With you, I will be free from care.

#5: Claudius Gives the Citizenship to Towns in the Italian Alps

CIL 5.5050; *ILS* 206
AD 46

The emperors accelerated the process of granting Roman citizenship to the people of the provinces. In this passage, the emperor Claudius extends the citizenship in a region that had already been partially enfranchised. This speech is preserved on a bronze table found near the town of Tridentum in the Italian Alps.

On the Ides of March in the consulship of Marcus Julius Silanus and Quintus Sulpicus Camerinus (AD 46), the following edict was published on the Ides of March (March 15th) by the emperor Tiberius Claudius Caesar Augustus Germanicus from his palace in Baiae. Tiberius Claudius Caesar Augustus Germanicus, Pontifex Maximus, holding the tribunician power for the sixth time, acclaimed *imperator* eleven times, father of his country, designated consul for the fourth time writes.

. . . [Discussion of the reports from various imperial agents in the area] . . . In the case of the Anauni, Tulliassi, and Sinduni, I have found that some, according to one of my agents, are considered under the jurisdiction of Tridentum [who already had Roman citizenship] while others are not. I realize that there is little reason for citizenship to be granted to these people. Nevertheless, they have claimed Roman citizenship for a long time because of their association with Tridentum, and I fear it would not be possible to remove it now without serious injury to this splendid municipality. I therefore permit them to remain in the status of citizens. I grant this as a special favor all the more willingly because many people from this area are already serving in my personal bodyguard (the Praetorian Guard) and some even hold the rank of junior officers. Others are enrolled in the juries in Rome and sit at public trials. Therefore, I grant them this favor that whatever they have done by virtue of their presumed citizenship within their own town or among the Tridentini or any other people shall be considered legally binding. Furthermore, the names they adopted previously by virtue of their citizenship I will now allow them to retain as citizens in fact.

#6: Legal Protection of Roman Citizens

Cicero, *Letters to His Friends* 10.32
First Century BC

One of the most important protections afforded by Roman citizenship was exemption from harsh punishments and the direct jurisdiction of governors in the provinces. In most cases, citizens always had the right of appeal to the emperor and the senate. The law dealt harshly with governors who punished citizens illegally. In this letter to his friend Gaius Asinius Pollio, Cicero recounts the story of a treasury official (quaestor) Balbus who mistreated a Roman citizen in his province of Spain.

At a gladiator show, a certain man named Fadius, a former soldier of Pompey's [whom Caesar had recently defeated in a civil war], after he had been compelled to join a gladiatorial school and fight twice in the arena without pay, now refused to take the oath to become a professional gladiator and appealed to the protection of the people. When Balbus ordered Fadius to be taken away for execution, the people threw stones at the governor. Balbus responded by ordering his cavalry from Gaul to charge the rioters. Balbus then went on with his plan to execute Fadius and had him half-buried in the ground in the gladiatorial school. Later when Balbus was taking a walk after dinner in his bare feet, in just a loose tunic and hands held behind his back, Fadius yelled out to him "I was born a Roman citizen!" To this, Balbus responded, "Then go and implore the safety of the people then." Fadius was later burned alive.

#7: Caracalla Grants Citizenship to All Freeborn Inhabitants of the Empire

The explosive growth in the number of new citizens during the first and second centuries AD slowly deteriorated the value of citizenship. New taxes on citizens removed many of their financial advantages. Many of the legal advantages were taken away from all but the wealthy. In AD 212, the emperor Caracalla passed a law granting citizenship to all freeborn persons in the empire, thus nullifying the distinction of status based on citizenship within the empire. The first passage is our most complete historical reference to Caracalla's action (in the context of a discussion on the taxes he levied against the people of the empire). The second is from a later collection of Roman legal precedent and highlights the reality of the grant.

Dio Cassius, *History* 77(78).9.4–5
Early Third Century AD

Caracalla not only created new taxes but he also replaced the five percent tax on money that changed hands when a slave was freed, gifts of money between citizens, and money inherited in wills. He also removed the exemptions from this tax enjoyed by members of the immediate family of the deceased [originally, this tax was only on money inherited from people outside the family]. Caracalla made everyone Roman citizens so that they would fall under these tax reforms. On the surface, it had the appearance of being an honor, but the real reason was to increase tax revenue as non-citizens did not have to pay this tax.

Justinian, *Digest* 1.5.17
Sixth Century AD

Everyone in the Roman world was made a Roman citizen through a decree of the emperor Caracalla.

#8: Differentiation of Punishments

Justinian, *Digest* 48.19.9.11–12 (from Ulpian)
Sixth Century AD Based on a Third Century AD Jurist

As citizenship became more common, Roman law shifted away from differentiations based on citizen status to wealth. People with more money were treated less harshly in the law than those of lower financial status. In the following passage from the late Roman law code of Justinian, the choice of criminal punishment is described as a result of status. The passage is derived from the works of the lawyer Ulpian, who wrote in the early third century and witnessed the general grant of citizenship by Caracalla in AD 212.

It must be understood that penalties are differentiated based on the class of the person to be punished. In the case of the highest classes, members of the municipal aristocracy (the *decuriones*) and higher are not able to be condemned to the mines, the fork [cross], or to be burned alive. If anyone of that class is to be sentenced to such a punishment, they are to be freed. The judge who made the original sentence is not to be the one to free the condemned in such cases. Instead, the matter must be referred to the emperor as it is by his authority that punishments are changed or remitted.

#9: Late Imperial Rights of the Equestrian Order

Theodosius, *Code* 6.37.1
October, AD 364

The following passage outlines the privileges of the equestrian order. Although it is from a much later legal code, it is interesting in that it describes how members of the equestrian order, by virtue of their class, should be treated differently from other people of lower social status. The subscript dates the enactment to October of AD 364.

> The emperors Valentinian and Valens write to Mamertinus the praetorian prefect. We wish the equestrian order to hold the second highest rank of all ranks in the city and to be chosen from freeborn Romans and citizens or from foreigners who are not bound to trade guilds. Because it is not right that men of this rank be deprived of privileges, it will be their right not to have the fear of corporal punishment and criminal prosecution. They are also to be held as immune from those taxes assessed on the senatorial order.

Defining the Aristocracy: Birth and Wealth

Distinctions based on citizenship, however, merely differentiated the Roman from the non-Roman. Within the body of Roman citizens, other methods were used to divide the social classes. An early form of social division was based on birth: a Roman citizen was born into either a patrician or plebeian family. A passage from Livy hints at the creation of the patrician families (#10). Wealth, however, became a more important method of determining social status. This section includes examples of members of the upper classes: a senator (the author Pliny the Younger, #11), equestrians (#12, #13), and a member of the municipal aristocracy (#14).

#10: Patricians and Plebeians

Livy, *Histories* 1.8
Written in the First Century BC Describing
Rome's Mythical Early History

The origin of the patrician families is uncertain and debated by scholars. In the following early passage from his history, Livy connects the creation of the patrician aristocracy to the early growth of Rome under Romulus. Unlike citizenship, patrician status could not be granted, won, or purchased. One had to be born into that status. The exception came during the imperial period when emperors assumed the power to enroll people in a different birth status.

> Romulus extended the city limits of Rome by extending the fortification wall to encompass empty space. He did this in the hope of a large population in the future rather than to accommodate any present overcrowding. Next, Romulus strove to fill that empty space with new inhabitants. Following the old practice of those who had founded cities in the past, Romulus opened Rome up to people of obscure and humble origins. He then spread the rumor that the population of Rome had sprung up from the earth itself. He opened as an asylum the place between the two groves as you go down from the Capitoline Hill. To this asylum came from neighboring cities a great multitude of people eager for a change. All were accepted, whether free or slave. This was the first

step in Rome's population expansion. When the city's strength seemed suffi-cient to him, Romulus provided for its aristocratic government. He created one hundred senators. He arrived at this number either because that number met his needs or there were only one hundred worthy men from which he could choose. In either case, these senators were called "Patres"—"Fathers"—and their offspring "Patricians" by virtue of their rank.

#11: The Senator Pliny the Younger

CIL 5.5262; *ILS* 2927; *AE* 1984, 436
Early Second Century AD

The senate was a body of aristocratic magistrates and ex-magistrates. Either as a corporate body or individually as holders of the various magistracies, the senate served as the executive, legislative, and judicial head of state. From the beginning, it seems that men of patrician and plebeian families were members of the senate. One needed to be elected to a senatorial office in order to be considered a mem-ber of the senate. By the imperial period, this almost always meant election to the quaestorship, the most junior of magistracies. The quaestors were in charge of the state finances and assisted higher level magistrates with fiscal administration. After the quaestorship, a senator was generally elected aedile (magistrates in charge of public works). Senators with plebeian background could also be tribune of the plebs (magistrates with the power of veto in the senate). The higher senatorial ranks began with the praetorship. Praetors served as judges who presided over the major courts. The two annual consuls were the chief magistrates of the senate. They had the power to convene and preside over senatorial meetings. There were other magistracies that could be held at various points in their careers. Young aristocrats of senatorial background usually held a military tribunate in a legion in their early teens. The legions themselves were under the command of ex-praetors (legionary legates). The provinces were governed by ex-praetors or ex-consuls (depending on the importance of the province). It was fairly easy for sons of senators to achieve election to the quaestorship and enter the senate, but for others it was considerably more difficult; however, under the emperors, it still did happen on a regular basis.

　Pliny the Younger is an excellent example of the type of senator one encounters in the imperial period. We know a great deal about him through not only this inscrip-tion (a statue base describing his career) but also the letters he wrote to his friends and later published. He was not born to a senatorial family, but his uncle, Pliny the Elder, had been an important courtier of the emperor Vespasian. With the help of his uncle's friends and probably the emperor himself, Pliny the Younger was elected into the sen-ate as a quaestor. He then moved up the ranks and eventually held the consulship in AD 100 under the emperor Trajan. During his career, he held multiple high-ranking administrative posts in Rome and eventually in Asia Minor. His career is given in descending order, meaning his later and more prestigious offices are listed first and his earliest offices are given last (with the exception of his consulship, which he lists first because of its importance). At the end of the text, there is a record of his bequests to his hometown of Comum, Italy (where the inscription was found).

> Gaius Plinius Caecilius Secundus, son of Lucius, of the Oufentina tribe, consul and augur. He served as imperial governor of the province of Pontus and Bithynia with consular power to which province he was sent by enactment of a senatorial decree initiated by the emperor Caesar Nerva Trajan Augustus Germanicus Dacicus, father of his country. He was also caretaker of the bed of the Tiber and of the banks and the sewers of the city, prefect of the public treasury of Saturn, prefect of the military treasury, praetor, tribune of the plebs, quaestor nominated by the emperor, one of the six men in charge of a squadron of Roman equestrians, military tribune of the third legion Gallica, and one of the ten men in charge of hearing legal cases. In his will, he requested that baths be built out of funds equal to [?] *sestertii*, with 300,000 *sestertii* added for their decoration and a further 200,000 added for their upkeep. He also granted 1,866,666 *sestertii* to the city of Comum to pay for the support of his 100 freedmen, the interest of which amount he wished in the future to be used for a banquet for the urban poor. While still alive, he gave 500,000 *sestertii* to the fund for orphaned boys and girls and 100,000 *sestertii* for a library and its upkeep.

#12: An Equestrian from Italy

AE 1996, 513
First Century AD

Rome's eastern expansion opened new markets and opportunities for overseas trade. Those with initiative and money to invest made their fortunes exploiting these new opportunities. Passed in 218 BC, the *lex Claudia* (the Claudian Law) prohibited senators from engaging in any moneymaking ventures involving foreign trade. In keeping with the memory of Rome's agricultural past, it was considered beneath the dignity of the senatorial aristocracy for their wealth to be based in anything other than the ownership of land. This law helped formalize the equestrian order, an aristocracy whose wealth was based in trade and other non-agriculturally based income. In the late Republic and especially under Augustus, Rome began to employ members of the equestrian order at first as government contractors in the provinces and then as bureaucrats and military officers. High-ranking centurions in the army and members of the municipal aristocracy who sought social advancement were the main sources of new equestrians. Under the emperors, equestrians generally progressed from service as officers in the Roman army to financial administrators of imperial property to minor provincial governors to high-ranking officials in the imperial court. The following inscription from a statue base celebrates an equestrian who had served in several tiers of the equestrian career: chief centurion in a legion, military tribune in the Praetorian Guard, and low-ranking equestrian prefectures. His service as *primus pilus* is almost certainly his earliest post. His prefecture of the military camps in Egypt is probably his highest position. The end of the text documents honors granted to him by the town of Vicus Anninus in Italy.

> To Aulus Virgius Marsus, son of Lucius. He served as the highest-ranking centurion (*primus pilus*) in the Third Legion Gallica twice, prefect of the military camps in Egypt, prefect of the engineers, and military tribune in Rome in the garrison of the divine emperor Augustus and Tiberius Caesar Augustus (first in the eleventh urban cohort and then the fourth praetorian cohort). He was named one of the four chief magistrates by the town council and people of the imperial colonis at Alexandra Troas and Marsi marruvium. In his last will and testament, he bequeathed to the townspeople of the Vicus Anninus five silver statues of the emperors along with 10,000 *sestertii*. Because of this honor bestowed upon them, the townspeople of the Vicus Anninus dedicated this statue.

#13: An Equestrian from Noricum

CIL 3.5215; *ILS* 1362b; *AE* 2002, 105
Second or Third Century AD

This is one of several statue bases celebrating the equestrian Varius Clemens. They are from his hometown of Celeia in the northern province of Noricum. The text illustrates the kind of administrative posts equestrian bureaucrats held. The offices are listed in descending order with his most senior posts listed first. A procurator was a person in charge of imperial property in a province. As shown by the number of procuratorial posts, Clemens was very well traveled.

> To Titus Varius Clemens, chief secretary of the emperor, procurator of the provinces of Belgica, both German provinces, Raetia, Mauretania Caesarensis, Lusitania, and Cilicia, military prefect of the Brittanica contingent of one thousand cavalry, military prefect of auxiliary troops (the *auxilia*) sent from Spain into Mauretania Tingitana, military prefect of the Second Pannonian cavalry contingent, military tribune of the Thirtieth Legion Ulpia Victrix, and military prefect of the second cohort Macedonica of Gauls. The citizenry of the Treveri dedicated this to him as an exemplary official.

#14: A Municipal Aristocrat from Ostia

CIL 14.375 (Portus, Italy)
First, Second, or Third Century AD

Although the senate controlled the magistracies of the central government, the local governments of the towns of Italy and the provinces were in the hands of the native aristocracy (with some oversight by the central government). Under the emperors, this body of municipal aristocrats was formalized into a class. By the second century AD, membership in the municipal aristocracy seems to have required a personal fortune equal to at least 100,000 *sestertii*. The following aristocrat from Ostia, the port city of Rome, was a member of one of the most important families of Ostia. He held the highest political and religious offices in Ostia. He spent a huge amount of his own money to benefit the people through public meals and temple construction. He even helped the town financially when the central government was demanding money from Ostia for an upcoming war.

> To Publius Lucilius Gamala, son of Publius, grandson of Publius, great-grandson of Publius, aedile of the sacred cult of Volcanus, aedile by decree of the town council (*decuriones*), member of the town council who was enrolled free of charge without payment of the usual entrance fee, priest, one of the two town mayors who held censorial powers every five years, voted caretaker of receiving and spending public funds. He gave back all money from the public treasury he received to put on games and instead spent his own money on them. With his own funds he paved the forum, from arch to arch. He gave a public banquet with 217 dining tables to the citizens of Ostia. He twice gave free lunches to the citizens of Ostia from his own funds. He restored the temple of Volcanus with his own money. He constructed temples of Venus, Fortune, and Ceres with his own money. Along with Marcus Turranius and with his own money, he made new official weights for weighing goods in the market. He built a temple to Hope at his own expense. He constructed a new marble speaker's platform in the forum. A gold-plated statue of this man was erected at public expense by decree of the town council. A bronze statue was also erected at public expense by decree of the town council next to the speaker's platform of the quaestor. These honors came especially because, at the time when the town of Ostia was being forced to sell its public land holdings to raise money for the naval war, Gamala gave 15,200 *sestertii* to the town. The town council decreed that he be granted a public funeral at the time of his death.

The Poor

The vast majority of Roman society had little personal wealth and was forced to work in order to make enough to survive. In ancient Rome, there was virtually no middle class of fairly well off individuals. Instead, a great divide separated the wealthy aristocracy from the poor. In the imperial period, the government required a minimum wealth in order to hold office or rank. For the municipal aristocracy outside of Rome, it was 100,000 *sestertii*. To be an equestrian order, one had to have 450,000 *sestertii* and 1,000,000 *sestertii* to run for office as a senator. In order to understand what these numbers mean, it is important to look at typical wages and prices. A laborer in Pompeii in AD 79 earned an estimated one to four *sestertii* per day, a decent wage; however, steady work was not always available. Most people would have lived very close to subsistence level, perhaps earning around 600–1,000 *sestertii* per year. The majority of our surviving evidence of the Romans focuses on the upper classes. Assembled here are some texts illustrating the lives of poor Romans. There is a fisherman from Plautus' play *Rudens* (#15), a market gardener from Apuleius' *Metamorphoses* (#16), a poor woman from southern Italy (#17), a man who escaped poverty by joining the army (#18), and a collection of inscriptions documenting some poor non-citizens from the province of Noricum (#19).

#15: The Plight of Poor Fishermen

Plautus, *Rudens* 290–296
Late Third Century BC

It is quite rare to hear the voice of the poor from the ancient world. Authors of literature were almost exclusively men of the aristocracy. Tombstones with details of the deceased's life were expensive and out of reach of the poorest part of society. In the prologue to Act 2 of his *Rudens*, the comic playwright Plautus has a chorus of poor fishermen describe the plight of the poor. As appears often in such texts, the poor speaker contrasts his life with that of the wealthy.

> People who are poor live miserably in every way, especially those who have no career and know no trade. Out of necessity, they must consider what they have at home to be enough. You practically know how wealthy we are from our clothing. These hooks and fishing poles are for us both our careers and our adornment. We come here from the city to the sea in an effort to make a living. This is what we have instead of exercise in the gymnasium or exercise yard.

#16: The Life of the Market Gardener

Apuleius, *Metamorphoses* 9.31-32
Second Century AD

Apuleius' second century AD novel the *Metamorphoses* (or *Golden Ass* as it is usually known today) frequently gives vignettes of life in the Roman Empire. In the novel, the curious Lucius dabbles with witchcraft and is transformed into a donkey. The majority of the novel recounts his journeys and various owners until he is rescued from his predicament with the help of the goddess Isis. In this passage, Lucius (in donkey form) has been sold to a poor market gardener. Lucius (originally an aristocrat himself) recounts the pitiful life of the kind but poor farmer.

> The certain poor market gardener purchased me for 50 *sestertii*. My new owner complained that such a sum was a lot of money to pay but hoped that I

would be worth it if I could help him with his work. It seems appropriate at this juncture to describe the daily routine of my newest servitude. Each morning, my master would load me up with produce and take me to the nearest town. There, he would sell his goods to merchants and ride home on my back. While he slaved away at digging, watering, and all his other chores, bent over from his labors, I was free to recuperate from my brief duties with pleasant relaxation... [Fall arrives]... I was shut up in a stall that was out in the open and exposed to the season's continuous rains and nighttime frost. I was in agony from the cold, but my master was no better off. Indeed, because of his extreme poverty, he was unable to buy straw or even the smallest blankets for his bed so there was little chance he could do anything to make me more comfortable. The poor man had to be content with spending his time under the thatched roof of his little hut.... My master and I ate pretty much exactly the same thing and in the same quantity (and that wasn't much to be sure): some old and rotting lettuce that had already matured to the point of producing large seeds and looking like a broom. It smelled musty and had a bitter and putrid taste.

#17: A Poor Inhabitant of Samnium in Italy

AE 2003, 567 (Interpromium, Italy)
Date Unknown; Imperial Period

This freedwoman lived a long life and is happy to have left three children behind. She describes herself as poor. Interestingly, she mentions no one else in the inscription. It is uncertain whether she commissioned the text herself when she was still alive or if the dedicator of the text was left unnamed.

I am Mevia, freedwoman who was once owned by a woman. I was born in Nicopolis in Asia, but I died here in Italy. I lived as a pauper. My 53 years seems to have been enough as I left behind three children. Goodbye.

#18: A Pauper Turned Soldier

CIL 5.938; *ILS* 2905 (Aquileia, Italy)

This soldier in the imperial fleet at Aquileia records proudly that he was born into poverty but was able to improve his status through military service. The text commemorates a father and son, one of whom, probably the father, served as a soldier in the navy.

Lucius Trebius, son of Titus, the father. Lucius Trebius Ruso, son of Lucius. Born into the deepest poverty, I [probably the father] served as a marine in the fleet

in the service of the emperor for 17 years and was honorably discharged. My
burial plot is 16 feet square.

#19: Some Non-citizen Inhabitants of Noricum

Date Unknown; Imperial Period

The following texts are some simple tomb epitaphs of inhabitants of the northern Roman province of Noricum. The lack of the three-part Roman name and
frequent non-Roman names would seem to indicate that they were not Roman
citizens. The appearance of Latin names in the case of many, especially some of the
children, would tend to signify that the local population was trying to blend in with
the Romans. The epitaphs were generally put up on the occasion of the first death
of the family although the practice in this area seems to have often been to include
still living members of the family as well in order to save money in the future.

CIL 3.5477 (Enzelsdorf, Noricum)

Quintianus son of Citto and Nigella Boudes, a freedwoman, made this while
still alive for themselves and for their son Adnamatus who died at the age of 6.

CIL 3.5496 (Colatio, Noricum)

To Urbanus, son of Ressimarus, who lived 70 years and to Resilla, daughter of
Adnamatus, his wife, who lived 70 years and to Iantumarus their son who lived
30 years and to [. . .]ia their daughter who lived 18 years. Their heir saw to the
construction of this monument.

CIL 3.5640 (Admont, Noricum)

Ittu, son of Ripanus, made this while still alive for himself and for his wife
Viatorina who died at the age of 60 and for Hilara, the daughter of Ittu, who
lived 30 years.

CIL 3.5641 (Admont, Noricum)

Secundus son of Verca and Secunda daughter of Calventus made this for themselves while still alive and for their son Firmus who died at the age of 20.

Chapter 3: Virtue and Vice

Behavior in the Roman world was governed in large part by a list of virtues prized by society. These virtues were grounded in traditional gender roles as defined by the aristocracy and as such varied widely between men and women. Because the Romans of the aristocracy valued tradition very highly, the conventional view of men and women evolved very little over the centuries even though the reality of culture did change over time.

Roman Virtue

Men's virtues fell generally in the realm of their public lives. Feminine virtue focused upon home life, devotion to the husband, and childbirth. In his *On the Happy Life*, Seneca defines virtue by contrasting it with pleasure (#20). Indeed, many of men's major virtues had to do with the man's self-control and adherence to duty (see, for example, Cincinnatus, #23). Some of the major male virtues were *virtus* (manly courage on the battlefield; described by Cicero, #21), *fortitudo* (bravery; exemplified by Horatius Cocles, #22), *pietas* (devotion to the gods, country, and family; see Livy's description of Coriolanus, #29), *moderatio* (moderation; as exemplified by Numidicus Metellus, #24, and the emperor Trajan, #25), *clementia* (the treatment of people better than they deserve; Caesar was famous for this virtue; #26), *severitas* (severity and the punishment of crime as it deserves; #27 is a legal definition of this virtue; #28 is an example of the theory in practice), *iustitia* (wisdom), and *sapientia* (wisdom).

#20: Pleasure versus Virtue

Seneca, *On the Happy Life* 7.3–4
First Century AD

In this passage, the philosopher Seneca defines virtue by contrasting it with pleasure. Through a series of metaphors, Seneca not only describes the beauty of virtue but also paints a very negative picture of pleasure. Rather than naming particular vices, Seneca describes how vice and pleasure would manifest itself in the behavior and character of a dissolute person.

> Virtue is something high up, lofty, and regal. It is indomitable and cannot be wearied. Pleasure, however, is low class, even servile. It is a fragile thing that is only momentary. Its workplace and home is in the brothel and low class restaurants around town. You can find virtue, however, in the temple, in the forum, in the senate house. You might see it standing on the walls of the city wearing

dusty and dirty clothes, its hands calloused. Pleasure is more often found lurking in the shadows around the baths, saunas, and the kinds of places that avoid the rule of law. It is effeminate and weak and stinks of wine and perfume. It is pale, or more likely has been dolled up with cosmetics. As the greatest good, virtue is immortal. It does not know how to die. It is like an extravagant dinner that does not leave you feeling full. A mind that is virtuous never varies its opinion and has no self-hatred and only changes for the better. Pleasure on the other hand disappears right when it is at its most pleasing. If it was a house, it would be very small and would fill quickly. It slumps down tired after the least exertion. You can never be certain of a thing when it is by nature always changing.

#21: The Definition of *Virtus*

Cicero, *Philippics* 4.13
First Century BC

Virtus is the Latin term for manly courage, especially as it refers to courage on the battlefield. The word is derived from the Latin word *vir* ("man") and was one of the defining virtues of masculinity. In this passage, Cicero describes how *virtus* is the reason Rome won an empire. Like Seneca, Cicero describes *virtus* as constant and unchanging, and contrasts with the lack of virtue that is soft, effeminate, and weak.

Although nature has ordained that all humans will die, *virtus* characteristically removes all of the cruelty and shame from death. This is indeed peculiar to the Romans and their descendants. I ask you, therefore, to protect this inheritance that your ancestors have bequeathed to you. Although everything else is false and uncertain, perishable and ever-changing, *virtus* alone, like a tree, is planted in the ground with extremely deep roots. The force of no wind is able to shake it down or uproot it. It was with this innate *virtus* that your ancestors conquered all of Italy, cut down Carthage, toppled Numantia, and placed very powerful kings and extremely warlike people under the dominion of this empire of ours.

#22: The *Fortitudo* of Horatius Cocles

Livy, *Histories* 2.10
Written in the First Century BC Describing
Rome's Mythical Early History

Much of Rome's earliest history highlights figures that stood as monumental examples of Roman virtue. In this passage, the historian Livy describes how Horatius Cocles saved the city from the Etruscans who were seeking to destroy the newly formed Republic and re-establish the kings.

The Bridge of Sublicius over the Tiber into Rome would have provided an inroad for the Etruscans if it had not been for one man: Horatius Cocles. On that fateful day, the city of Rome's good fortune had him as its defense. By chance, Horatius was on guard duty on the bridge when he saw that the Janiculum Hill on the other side of the bridge had been captured in a surprise Etruscan attack. Indeed, the enemy was already making a swift advance toward the bridge. He looked around and saw his fellow soldiers terrified and throwing aside their weapons and deserting their posts. Horatius criticized some of them and tried to block their escape. Calling upon the good faith of gods and humans, he shouted, "There will be no escape for any of you if you desert their posts. If you abandon the bridge, the enemy will swarm into Rome and capture its more sacred places." He shouted out these warnings and then gave the order for them to break down the bridge with tools, fire, or whatever means they could find. "I will hold back the enemy's attack for as long as I can on my own!" he shouted. He then walked alone to the far side of the bridge. He was even more visible to the advancing enemy as he stood against the backdrop of his fleeing comrades. The enemy was amazed at this vision of audacity. In the end, a sense of shame kept two men at Horatius' side: Spurius Larcius and Titus Herminius, both of whom were distinguished in family and deeds. For a short time, these three withstood the first crash of danger and chaos of battle. Soon, only a small part of the bridge remained. The soldiers who were working to bring it down called to Horatius and told him to escape while he could. Horatius told his two companions to leave but he held his ground alone. He menacingly cast savage eyes across the sea of his foes and first challenged the Etruscan chief to single combat. He then berated the whole Etruscan host saying, "You slaves of an arrogant king, ignorant of freedom, you come here to attack the freedom of others." The Etruscans hesitated for a short time. They looked at one another hoping someone else would start the charge. Eventually, shame drove them forward. They raised the battle shout and a hail of javelins flew from all directions at the lone defender. Horatius managed to block these missiles with his upraised shield and no less stubbornly held his ground. The Etruscans began to make their charge into melee range to drive Horatius from the bridge when they heard the crash of the bridge as it was broken. They could also hear the shouts of the Romans who were overjoyed at having finished their demolition of the bridge. The noise caused the Etruscans to stop their attack out of fear. Then Horatius exclaimed, "Father Tiber, I humbly pray for you to accept as an offering these weapons and even this soldier in your propitious waves!" and jumped off the bridge, in full armor, into the Tiber River. Untouched by a fresh volley of Etruscan javelins, he swam across the river to his fellow Romans. This incredible story of daring has certainly been embellished in the telling over the centuries. The state was grateful for this show of *virtus* and put up a statue of him in the public voting area. They also gave him as much land as he could drive a plow around in one day. Although it was a time of great shortages, every private person also showed his support to him by giving him whatever he could from his resources at home.

#23: Cincinnatus' Duty to the State

Livy, *Histories* 3.26
Written in the First Century BC Describing
Rome's Mythical Early History

In 458 BC, the senate decided to name a dictator to rescue a Roman army that was in serious military peril. A dictator was a temporary magistrate for emergency situations. The dictator had supreme power in the state but only held office for six months. Lucius Quinctius Cincinnatus had been consul two years earlier and had military and political experience. In this passage quoted here, the historian Livy describes how representatives from the senate arrived at Cincinnatus' farm to ask him to take up the dictatorship. The story is a good example of how a Roman aristocrat was expected to put his duty to the state before everything else. It also reflects the agrarian tradition Roman aristocrats grafted upon their memory of the past.

The only hope for the empire of the Roman people was Lucius Quinctius Cincinnatus. At that time, he had a small farm of 4 acres in a place now called the Quinctian Fields on the other side of the Tiber, opposite the place where the shipyards are now. It was here that representatives from the senate found Cincinnatus. Sources disagree whether he was working with a shovel to dig a ditch or plowing a field, but whichever is true, it is clear that he was busy with farm work. The representatives came up to him and they exchanged greetings. The representatives then asked him to put on his toga in preparation to listen to the mandate of the senate. "We hope that everything will turn out well for both the state and for you," they said. Cincinnatus was surprised at this and asked, "is everything alright?" He told his wife Racilia to go quickly and get his toga from the farmhouse. He washed the dirt from his body and put on his toga and returned to the representatives. Upon seeing him, the representatives saluted him as dictator and expressed their congratulations. They told him the extreme danger of the army and asked him to return to the city with them. A boat had been provided at public expense for Cincinnatus in which he crossed the river. When he landed on the other side of the river, he was met by his three sons as well as some other relatives, friends, and the majority of the senators. Accompanied by this crowd and following the official lictors, he made his way to his townhouse.

#24: The *Moderatio* of Numidicus Metellus

Valerius Maximus, *Memorable Deeds and Sayings* 4.1.13
Written in the Early First Century AD Describing
the Later Second Century BC

Quintus Caecilius Metellus Numidicus was a prominent conservative senatorial aristocrat of the later second century BC who vehemently opposed the popular leader

Gaius Marius. When Marius gained dominance in the state, he forced Metellus into exile. In this passage, Valerius Maximus uses Metellus as an example of *moderatio*, moderation. Metellus' straight-faced reception of good news exemplified the even temper expected of Roman aristocrats.

> After he was driven from his homeland by Marius' political party, Metellus Numidicus retired to Asia Minor. While in that province, he happened to receive a letter while visiting the town of Tralles to watch a play. This letter informed him that a vote had been taken on the issue of allowing him to return out of exile to Rome. This bill had passed with an overwhelming majority of votes from the senate and people. Despite this good news, Metellus did not leave the theater before the play had finished. He also did not reveal his happiness in any way to the people sitting near him in the theater but instead contained his joy within himself. It is reported that Metellus used the same expressions after returning to Rome as he had used while in exile. It is a testimony to his *moderatio* that Metellus employed the same strength of character in both favorable and unfavorable circumstances.

#25: The *Moderatio* of Trajan

Dio Cassius, *History* 68.7
Written in the Early Third Century AD Describing
the Emperor Trajan (AD 98–117)

The emperor Trajan's positive reputation has endured through the ages. Roman imperial historiography and biography often describe the character of emperors in light of their virtues and vices as defined by the traditional views of good behavior. In this passage, the historian Dio Cassius praises the *moderatio* of Trajan.

> Trajan is most known for his justice, bravery, and the simplicity of his way of life. Becoming emperor in his forty-second year, he was physically strong and was nearly the equal of any of his comrades when working. His mind continued to be sharp so that he had neither the impetuousness of youth nor the slowness of an old man.... I know that he has a reputation for having a passion for boys and wine, and if he had done anything shameful or bad or suffered anything in his pursuit of them, he would have earned people's criticism. As it was, however, he only drank wine until he had had his fill and remained sober. He also never hurt anyone in his relations with boys.

#26: The *Clementia* of Caesar

Valerius Maximus, *Memorable Deeds and Sayings* 5.1.10
Written in the Early First Century AD Describing
the Mid–First Century BC

Figures in Roman history often came to be remembered for virtues or vices. Horatius Cocles' name, for example, would forever be connected to his bravery on the bridge. Julius Caesar, contemplating how he would be remembered in the annals of history, cultivated a reputation for the virtue of *clementia*, the treatment of others better than they deserved. After his victory in the civil wars, Caesar forgave most of his domestic enemies and even gave some of them political posts in his post–civil war regime. It was considered a serious breach of public friendship when some of these same men took part in assassinating Caesar a few years later. In this passage, Valerius Maximus describes how Caesar's treatment of his enemy Pompey the Great fit well with the virtue of *clementia*. After losing the Battle of Pharsalus to Caesar, Pompey had fled to Egypt only to be betrayed and killed by King Ptolemy. Despite their earlier animosity, Caesar publicly wept for the death of Pompey.

> Gnaeus Pompey was a clear example of a person who received courtesy, but yet he was a terrible example of courtesy himself. A short time earlier, Pompey had placed upon the head of Tigranes the crown of the kingdom of Armenia, but now Pompey's own head had been robbed of the crowns given him in honor of his three triumphs in Rome. Indeed, Pompey's dead body was not even given a place for burial. Instead, his head, cut off from the rest of his body and kept from the funeral pyre, was carried around as an impious token of Egyptian treachery that would seem pitiful even to the victorious Caesar. When Caesar saw Pompey's severed head, he forgot their mutual feelings of hostility and looked at it rather with the eyes of a father-in-law and shed tears enough for himself as well as his daughter [who had been married to Pompey for some time]. Caesar then provided for the head to be cremated with a great quantity of the most costly perfumes. If the character of the divine leader had been shown to be not so kind, the man who a little while before had stood on the summit of Roman politics might not have even received proper burial. That is how quickly the fortune of mortals can change.

#27: The Legal Definition of *Severitas*

Justinian, *Digest* 48.19.11pr
Sixth Century AD

Severitas was a Roman virtue representing the fair treatment of others under the law especially where punishments were concerned. The Romans believed in the use of public punishment as a way of deterring others from committing future crimes. It was necessary for such punishments to be severe, but at the same time they must also not be cruel. The following passage from the late emperor Justinian's compendium of Roman law describes how a judge must be able to navigate the thin line between severity and cruelty (*crudelitas*).

A judge must take special care so as not to pass judgments that are harsher or more lenient than the particular case deserves. A judge should not strive for a reputation for *severitas* or *clementia*. Instead, he must weigh both sides of the argument carefully and make a decision that is in accordance with legal precedent for the crime committed. Clearly in cases that are more trivial, the judge should tend toward leniency. When the situation calls for more serious punishment, however, the *severitas* of the laws should be followed perhaps with a certain amount of moderation out of kindness.

#28: The Execution of a Well-Meaning Hunter

Valerius Maximus, *Memorable Deeds and Sayings* 6.3.5
Written in the Early First Century AD Describing
the Early First Century BC

It was important for a judge to avoid *crudelitas*, which could cause him to punish a criminal beyond what would seem allowed or right under the law. In this passage, Valerius Maximus tells the story of a hunter who generously brings a gift to the provincial governor only to come to an unfortunate end. Valerius Maximus describes how the story stands in the gray area between *severitas* and *crudelitas*.

The senator Lucius Domitius was resolute when it came to sticking to a decision he had made previously. While he was governor of the province of Sicily, a wild boar of amazing size was presented to him. Domitius summoned the shepherd who had killed the boar and asked him how he had killed it. When the man replied that he had used a hunting spear, Domitius ordered him to be crucified. He did this because he had earlier issued a decree that weapons such as that were to be illegal. Sicily was especially vexed by brigands, and Domitius thought this measure might help reduce the problem with them. You might say this case stands in the gray area between *severitas* and savagery (indeed you could argue for either side), but consideration for public authority does not allow his action to be considered to be excessively harsh.

#29: The *Pietas* of Coriolanus

Livy, *Histories* 2.40
Written in the First Century BC Describing the Fifth Century BC

Pietas was a person's loyalty and devotion. It was used to describe a person's relationship with the gods as well as with their family and even their country.

This passage is another story of exemplary virtue from the historical works of Livy. Gaius Marcius Coriolanus was a Roman aristocrat who had turned against his country and gone over to Rome's enemy, the Volscians. He convinced them to invade Roman territory and even personally led the attack. Only when his mother, wife, and children came to plead for him to stop the invasion did he remember the importance of *pietas* to family and country, and withdrew his army from Roman territory.

The matrons of Rome went as a group to Veturia, the mother of Coriolanus, and Volumnia, his wife. I am not certain whether the impetus for this action was a government decision or the fear of the two women. In either case, it is clear that Veturia, who was now an old woman, and Volumnia would go personally to the enemy camp. Indeed, Volumnia took with her the two small children she had had with Coriolanus. They realized that the men were no longer able to save the city with soldiers, so it was the women's duty to try using prayers and tears. When they arrived at the camp, Coriolanus was told that a large group of women had come from Rome. Previously, ambassadors from Rome had been unsuccessful in making him feel shame for the harm he was doing to Rome's glory. Priests too had failed to move him despite the religious signs they showed to him. After all of that, he thought it would be easy to stubbornly ignore the tears of women. Then one of Coriolanus' friends recognized in the crowd Veturia, who was standing between her daughter-in-law and her grandsons. "Unless my eyes deceive me," he said, "your mother, wife, and children are in the crowd of women." Coriolanus, like a crazy person, leaped from his chair so that he could go to his mother and embrace her. Veturia, however, stopped weeping and instead made her anger known and said, "Stop! Before I accept your embrace, tell me, have I come to my enemy or my son? Am I to be a captive or a mother in your camp? Has long life and unfortunate old age brought me so far that I must see my son go from citizen to exile to enemy of Rome? Are you able to ravage that country which bore and fed you? You may have come with hostile and menacing intent into Roman territory, but did not your anger leave you as you entered its borders? When you came in sight of Rome did the thought not come to you 'within the walls of this city is my home; my gods; and my mother, wife, and children?' Is it true that if I had never had a child, Rome would not have been attacked and that if I had not had a son, I would die a free woman in a free country? I can certainly neither become more miserable than I already am nor you more shameful. I could be in the depths of despair, but it would not be for long. I am an old woman. Look at these others, however. An early death or a lifetime of servitude awaits them if you continue with your hostile plan." After her speech, Coriolanus' wife and children embraced him. The whole crowd of women began weeping again and mourned for themselves and their country. Finally, Coriolanus' resolve broke down. He embraced his family and sent them away. He then moved the enemy away from the city and left the Romans in peace.

Exemplary Virtues

The previous accounts of individuals known for virtuous acts are just one part of the way in which Romans, especially of the aristocratic classes, commemorated how they and their families fit in with the traditional view of correct behavior. It was commonplace to record a person's purported virtues on their tombstones (provided their family had enough money to write a tomb epitaph that could include more than just the person's name and career). The epitaphs of members of the Scipio family from their tomb on the *Via Appia* (the "Appian Way") in Rome (#30) exemplify this practice. There are also many examples of catalogs of a person's canon of virtues (the "Shield of Virtues of Augustus," #31; Trajan as the *optimus princeps*, #32; and the emperor Maximian, #33). Such virtues demonstrated how they were worthy to hold political office or military command, and, in the case of emperors, their ability to rule the state effectively from the throne.

#30: Epitaphs from the Tomb of the Scipios

CIL 6.1284, 1287, 1288, 1289, 1290, 1293
Third to the Second Centuries BC

The Cornelius Scipio family was one of the most illustrious in the Roman Republic. Members of the family commanded armies in the Samnite Wars, the Punic Wars, and the wars with the Hellenistic kingdoms of the Greek east. The most famous Scipio of all was Scipio Africanus, who defeated the Carthaginian general Hannibal at the Battle of Zama at the end of the Second Punic War. The family mausoleum of the Scipios has been preserved on the *Via Appia* not far from the Aurelian Wall that runs around the city. Inside were discovered a number of epitaphs for members of the family. The following are translations of some of these epitaphs.

> Lucius Cornelius Scipio Barbatus, son of Gnaeus, a brave gentleman and wise, whose fine form matched his bravery (*virtus*); he was aedile, consul, and censor; he took Taurasia and Cisauna in the Samnite War; he overcame all of Lucania and brought hostages from them.
>
> Lucius Cornelius Scipio, son of Lucius, aedile, consul, censor. This man, as most agree, was the very best of all good men in Rome. A son of Barbatus, he was aedile, consul, and censor among you; he was the one who captured Corsica and the city of Aleria in the First Punic War. To the goddesses of weather he deservedly gave a temple.
>
> Dedicated to the one who wore the honored cap of Jupiter's high priest. Death caused all your virtues to be short-lived: your honor, good report, *virtus*, glory, and talents. If you had but been allowed long life in which to enjoy them, it would have been very easy for your great deeds to surpass the glory of your ancestors. Therefore, O Publius Cornelius Scipio, son of Publius, joyfully does Earth take you to her bosom.

Lucius Cornelius Scipio, son of Gnaeus, grandson of Gnaeus. Great virtues and great wisdom are implicit on this stone despite the man's short life. His life but not his honor fell short of his aspirations to a political career. He that lies here was never outdone in *virtus*. At the age of twenty, he was entrusted to his tomb. This is said, lest you ask why the man never held any public office.

Lucius Cornelius Scipio, son of Lucius, grandson of Publius, quaestor, military tribune. He died at the age of thirty-three years. His father vanquished King Antiochus in the Syrian War.

Gnaeus Cornelius Scipio Hispanus, son of Gnaeus, praetor, patrician aedile, quaestor, military tribune (twice); member of the Board of Ten for Judging Law-Suits; member of the Board of Ten for Making Sacrifices. I added my own virtues to those of my family. I had children and sought to equal the exploits of my father. I upheld the praise of my ancestors, so that they are glad that I was born of their line. My honors have improved the quality of my family.

#31: The Virtues of the Emperor Augustus

Res Gestae 34
Written in AD 14 Describing 28–27 BC

Senators were not the only ones who got involved with the competitive game of aristocratic virtues. The emperors, too, advertised their virtues. At the start of his reign, after the end of the civil wars, the senate honored the emperor Augustus with a shield inscribed with his four cardinal virtues. The original shield was put up in the senate house, but there were copies of it all over the Roman world. This passage is Augustus' own account of this shield.

During my sixth and seventh consulships, after I had ended civil wars, I was in complete control of the state by universal consensus. At that time, I transferred that control from my own power to that of the senate and people of Rome. For this act of mine, I was given the name Augustus by decree of the senate. The door of my house was decorated with laurel at public expense and a civic crown was placed over it. Also, the senate and people of Rome gave to me a golden shield that was placed in the Julian senate house bearing an inscription honoring my *virtus*, *clementia*, *iustitia*, and *pietas*.

#32: The Emperor Trajan as the *Optimus Princeps*

Pliny the Younger, *Panegyric on the Emperor Trajan* 88
Original Speech Delivered in AD 100

The emperor Trajan, as part of his program to present himself as the perfect emperor in every way, was awarded the title *optimus princeps*, "the best emperor." In this passage from Pliny the Younger's speech of praise of Trajan, he describes how the title *optimus* was connected to that emperor's superior virtues.

> Was it not with good reason that the state granted you the additional title *optimus*? It may seem cliché and commonplace, but in truth it is an innovative title. You realize that no one before you deserved the title although it was there to be applied if someone really had been worthy. Would the name of *felix* ("fortunate") have been sufficient? I would think so. *Felix* says more about a person's fortune than their way of life. What about *magnus* ("great")? That too is a more of a term that causes envy than expresses excellence. When your predecessor Nerva adopted you, he bestowed upon you his own name, but it was the senate that gave you the title of *optimus*. Indeed, I believe this title suits you better than the one you received from Nerva. To call you *optimus* is more fitting and distinctive than even your original name Trajan. Such a distinguishing name based on virtues is nothing new. The Piso family is famous for their frugality, the Laelii for their wisdom, the Metelli for their *pietas*. The difference is that the name of *optimus* embodies all virtues at once. It is not possible to consider a person as *optimus* unless he stands out as praiseworthy in every way over every other person who is good in their own single way. You deserve to have this title appear emphatically after all your other names and titles. To bear the name "emperor" and "Caesar" is less significant than to bear a title that stands for being better than all those men who have borne those names.

#33: The Virtues of the Emperor Maximian

Anonymous, Panegyric (11) 19.2
Speech Delivered in AD 291

A little less than 200 years after Pliny praised the emperor Trajan, a later, but unnamed, panegyrist wrote the following passage praising the emperor Maximian's virtues. As with the shield of Augustus and Trajan's title of *optimus*, the author stresses that the emperor exemplifies multiple virtues. At the end of the panegyric, the author takes the opportunity to differentiate types of virtue by their origin.

> Your other virtues and strengths of character evolve as you advance in age, most sacred emperor Maximian. Bravery grows as you age. Self-control develops by following the precepts of discipline. Justice is learned through the administration of the empire's laws. Finally there is wisdom, the virtue that seems to be the queen of all virtues. Wisdom comes from observing people's way of life and examining the outcome of events. *Pietas* and prosperity (*felicitas*) alone are not learned but are part of us from the moment we are born. They are prized possessions of the soul itself and the rewards of fate.

Social versus Legal Constraints

Adherence to the traditional virtues was not required by law. Law was concerned with crimes and their punishment and it did not define everyday behavior. Instead it was society that policed adherence to the traditional values implicit in the canon of virtues. If a person wanted to be remembered well by successive generations, he would be expected to follow society's behavioral rules. Vedius Pollio (#35) committed no crime, but the emperor Augustus still felt his treatment of a slave to be excessively cruel and censured his act and helped turn Pollio into an example of cruelty for the rest of time. Sometimes, however, there were attempts to legally control behavior. The Oppian Law (#34), passed after Hannibal's victory at the Battle of Cannae in 216 BC, attempted to curb extravagance.

#34: Example of Legal Constraints on Behavior: The Oppian Law

Valerius Maximus, *Memorable Deeds and Sayings* 9.1.3
Written in the First Century AD Describing 216 BC

The Romans rarely employed legal constraints on moral behavior. An interesting case of a legal constraint, however, surfaced during the panic following Hannibal's success at the Battle of Cannae in the Second Punic War. The state decided that it was necessary to reform morals in an attempt to win back the support of the gods. The law that was passed, the Oppian Law, primarily targeted women and attempted to curb their supposed extravagance by imposing *moderatio* upon them legally. See Chapter 5 for the repeal of the Oppian Law in 195 BC.

For Rome, the end of the Second Punic War and the conquest of Philip V of Macedonia gave the hope for a morally more relaxed lifestyle. At that time, the matrons of the city dared to lay siege to the house of the aristocratic family of Brutus because they were trying to block the repeal of the Oppian Law. The women wanted this law to be repealed because it prevented them from wearing multicolored clothing, own more than a *semuncia* (1/24th of a pound) of gold, or ride in a cart pulled by oxen within a mile of the city unless they were required to do so as part of a religious ritual. The women did eventually succeed in getting repealed this law which had been in effect for twenty years. The men of that era did not foresee how important the obstinate enthusiasm for the new fashions would prove or how far the audacity of the women would go once it won this first victory over the laws. If their minds could have seen beforehand the extent to which feminine adornment would carry itself as it grew daily with the addition of novel and more expensive elements, they might have put a stop to it at the start before it had turned into an example of true extravagance.

#35: The Despicable Vedius Pollio

Seneca, *On Wrath* 3.40
Written in the Mid-First Century AD Describing
the Late First Century BC

While there were occasional examples of legal constraints, social constraints were by far the most important limitation as far as behavior was concerned. Social constraints mainly came in the form of criticism of a person who was not adhering to that traditional canon of virtues. In the following example, the philosopher Seneca describes the difficulties of criticizing someone for excessive anger. His example involves a famous scene in which the emperor Augustus criticized a man for planning to kill a slave in a very unusual and cruel way.

To criticize a person who is angry will only cause him to become even angrier. Attempts to calm someone in that state will require varied approaches and generally a soft touch. If you are a very important person, then perhaps you could soothe anger in the same way that the divine Augustus did once while he was dining in the house of Vedius Pollio. A slave of Pollio had broken one of his master's crystal cups. Vedius ordered that the slave be taken and executed in a most exceptional way: to be thrown into a fishpond with some giant lampreys. Who would not think that Pollio was excessive in his punishment of the slave? The punishment was indeed excessive and therefore an example of savagery (*saevitia*). The slave escaped the grasp of his captors and fled to the feet of the emperor. He begged the emperor to let him die in some other way but not to let him be eaten. Augustus was disturbed by the novelty of the cruelty Pollio had shown. He asked that the slave be pardoned and that all of the crystal cups in the house be smashed while he watched and the fishpond containing the lampreys be filled in. This is the way a friend should be criticized by the emperor. I believe Augustus used his power correctly when he said the following to Pollio, "Do you really want to have people snatched away from the dinner party and tortured with unprecedented punishments? If your cup was broken, your response is to have the breaker's entrails pulled out? Now I have broken your cups. Do you really want to have the next person you order to be taken away to be Caesar himself?" And so, if a person's power is so great that he is able to criticize another person from such a lofty position, then let him do so more harshly, but only if it is done in the way I have described it here when the anger is of a wild, unimaginable, bloody kind which is so incurable that it will only obey something that is even harsher.

Moral Decay and Its Ramifications

Roman aristocrats took pride in their traditional system of virtues and saw virtuous living as directly connected to the prosperity and success of Roman civilization.

When the empire degraded into a state of chaos during the civil wars at the end of the Republic, it was commonplace to blame the problems on the decline of the lifestyle of the current generation who had turned their back upon the virtues of their forefathers. For Sallust, the turning point came after Rome finally defeated Hannibal (#36). Personal vice could even lead to physical deformity and disease (as Plutarch claims of the dictator Sulla, #37).

#36: Conquest Leads to Vice

Sallust, *The War against Catiline* 9–10
First Century BC

In his history of the attempted revolution of the aristocrat Catiline in 63 BC, the author Sallust describes how the Roman world had changed over the centuries, and for the worse. As was frequently the case in ancient Rome, Sallust sees political problems as connected with immoral behavior. The seeds of the civil wars of the first century BC were sown in the second century BC, and it was common to attribute that decline, as Sallust does in this passage, to the elimination of Rome's greatest enemy of the Republic: Carthage.

> In early times, the very best practices were the norm both at home and at war. Harmony among the people was at its height and greed was virtually unknown. Justice and good prevailed less through the influence of laws than natural quality. Quarrels, disagreements, and rivalry existed only with Rome's foreign enemies. Romans only competed to outdo each other with their virtues. They were generous in their worship of the gods, sparing with their household expenses, and faithful to their friends. They administered the state with two principles in mind: bravery in battle and fairness in peace. The greatest evidence of this, in my opinion, is how much more common it was to see tried in court soldiers who fought against the enemy before the order was given or who retreated from battle too slowly rather than soldiers who deserted the line during the battle or fled the field entirely after they were forced to give ground at all. In peace, too, the Romans ruled their empire more with kindness than fear and preferred to forgive wrongs than prosecute them.
>
> Things began to change, however, when the empire grew as a result of their labor and justice. The Romans overcame haughty kings in war and wild nations and strong peoples by force. After Carthage, the great rival of Rome's empire, was utterly destroyed, and the whole earth and sea were Rome's to command, only then did fortune begin to turn against them and throw everything into confusion. People who had previously had no trouble enduring hard work, dangers, uncertainty, and difficult situations now found them onerous and miserable and replaced those good pursuits with a desire for leisure and riches. At first, desire for power and then money took root as if they were the seeds of every kind of evil. Greed soon devoured honesty,

integrity, and all of the other good pursuits of life. In their place grew up arrogance, cruelty, neglect of the gods, and the spending of money. Ambition drove many people to become liars: they thought one thing hidden away in their heart but spoke something completely different with their mouths. They weighed the value of friendship and antagonism not according to their innate value but rather to what selfish benefit could be obtained from them. People also began to prefer to go around more with a pleasant appearance than a good character. At first, this situation developed slowly. Sometimes a person could be put straight again. Later, however, when the contagion had spread widely like a plague, the whole state changed. Our empire went from being an example of justice and good practices to one that was cruel and intolerable.

#37: Sulla's Vices Lead to Disease

Plutarch, *Lives*, *Sulla* 36
Written in the Late First Century AD Describing
the Early First Century BC

In this passage from the historian Plutarch's life of Sulla, the dictator consorted with a bad crowd and the vice that came from it led to a debilitating disease that manifested itself in his flesh being turned into worms. The story is a bizarre one and certainly exaggerated. What is important, however, is the fact that the Romans believed that vice could lead to physical manifestations of corruption and rot.

Although Sulla had a virtuous wife at home, he nevertheless began to associate with actresses, musicians, and other people from the theater. Throughout the whole day, he would remain in the dining room with them drinking. People like Roscius the comic actor, Sorex the head of a group of mimes, and Metrobius who played women's roles in the theater while wearing men's clothing had the greatest influence over him at this point in his life. Metrobius was already past his prime, but Sulla loved him passionately and would not deny it. This lifestyle resulted in a physical affliction. This disease began as a minor irritation of the stomach, and it was a long time before he realized that his bowels were rotting inside of him. This disease also spread to his flesh, which soon completely changed into worms. Things became very bad. He employed numerous slaves day and night to remove the worms from his body, but new worms appeared faster than the old ones could be detached. There was also a horrible discharge that fouled all of his clothing, tubs, bathwater, and food. To alleviate this problem, Sulla would often spend the whole day immersed in water in an attempt to clean and purify his body, but this did nothing to help. The change quickly took over and the multitude of worms proved too much for him to remove.

Examples of Vice

Just as there are numerous accounts of virtuous Romans who stood out as examples of acceptable behavior for to the rest of society to follow, so also were there many people who became, like Vedius Pollio, examples of vice and unacceptable behavior. Like Plutarch's account of Sulla in #37, many Roman historians seem to have developed a morbid curiosity regarding how low the depraved could sink. Valerius Maximus describes how Catiline of the late Republic was an example of lust (#38). The biographer Suetonius categorized his work on the lives of the emperors by virtue and, especially, vice (Caligula in #39 and Vitellius in #40). The later imperial author of the *Historia Augusta* followed Suetonius' methodology (Commodus in #41 and Elagabalus in #42).

#38: The Lust of Catiline

Valerius Maximus, *Memorable Deeds and Sayings* 9.1.9
Written in the Early First Century AD Describing
the First Century BC

Valerius Maximus includes in his catalog of behavior numerous examples of vice. In this passage, the revolutionary Catiline is presented as an extreme example of lust.

> The lust of Catiline was especially criminal. He was seized with an insane desire for the woman Aurelia Orestilla. He wished to marry her but saw his son as an obstacle to his plans. Aurelia had said she did not want to marry someone who already had children. His son was his only child and was already nearly at the age of puberty, but Catiline poisoned him and eagerly went from a funeral to a marriage. He offered his new-found childlessness as a wedding gift to his prospective wife.

#39: The Cruelty of Caligula

Suetonius, *Caligula* 30
Written in the Early Second Century AD Describing
the Emperor Caligula (AD 37–41)

While the emperors often promoted their virtues in order to legitimate their right to rule, it was also common for later historians to demonstrate their hypocrisy by describing their many faults and vices. In this passage, the historian Suetonius describes the cruelty of the emperor Caligula.

> Caligula did not allow anyone to be executed quickly. Instead, he had the death penalty administered through numerous small wounds. Indeed, he is

quoted as saying "The condemned should realize they are dying." This state-ment has since become a well-known maxim. Once, when a person was mis-takenly executed because of mix-up with the names, Caligula claimed that the executed person deserved his punishment as well. Caligula often was heard to quote the well-known line from tragic theater, "Let them hate me so long as they fear me."

#40: The Extravagant Gluttony of Vitellius

Suetonius, *Vitellius* 13
Written in the Early Second Century AD Describing
the Emperor Vitellius (AD 69)

The emperor Vitellius who reigned for a few months in the chaotic "Year of the Four Emperors" was famous for his gluttony. Suetonius generally begins his biog-raphies of emperors with a chronological account of their family, rise to power, and reign before moving to an account of their character categorized according to traditional virtues and vices. About some emperors, like Caligula and Vitellius, Suetonius has very little good to say. No emperor in his Twelve Caesars, however, is completely spared his criticism.

Vitellius had two major vices: extravagance and cruelty. Although the evening meal was usually the only large meal of the day, Vitellius converted lunch and dinner and even sometimes breakfast into grand feasts. He sometimes even added a fourth meal. He would vomit between meals to prepare himself for the next feast. A different person invited him to each meal of every day, and the total expenditure for the food, decoration, and entertainment was not to be less than 400,000 *sestertii*. The most notorious of all of his feasts was the dinner his brother held in his honor after he arrived in Rome after winning the civil war against Otho. Reports say that in that feast two thousand fish and seven thousand birds were served. Vitellius, however, outdid even this event with one of his own in which was served an array of delicacies on a platter that he called the Shield of Minerva, the defender of the city. On this platter could be found livers of parrotfish, brains of pheasants and peacocks, tongues of flamingos, and the intestines of the rare murena fish that naval admirals personally brought to Rome from tours of duty in the waters off Spain and the distant Parthian Empire. He was a man of not only profound appetite but was also inappropriate and indecent. He was so bad, in fact, that he did not refrain from grabbing and eating bits of sacrificial meat or cakes from the fire on the altars. While on the road, he would visit restaurants and take and eat scraps that customers had left on their plates, some of which were from the day before and even half-eaten.

#41: The Emperor Commodus' Sick Jokes

Historia Augusta, Life of Commodus 10
Written Possibly in the Fourth Century AD Describing
the Emperor Commodus (AD 180–192)

Roman history is filled with shady characters of questionable morals. The so-called *Historia Augusta*, a late Roman collection of biographies of emperors from the second to the third centuries, includes stories of some of the most colorful characters of Roman history. In the following passage, this historian describes some of the vices of the emperor Commodus. The anecdotes are almost certainly exaggerated, but they reflect the extremes of vice in the eyes of the Romans.

> Already as a child Commodus was gluttonous and sexually perverse. As a young man, he disgraced people of every class that he spent time with and was in turn disgraced by them. He would throw people to the wild beasts who laughed at him. One man who was reading the biography of Caligula in Suetonius' history he ordered also to be thrown to the wild beasts. Commodus did this because he had the same birthday as Caligula and hated people to compare the two of them. If anyone mentioned that he wanted to die, Commodus would order that he be led off to execution immediately, even if the person said he did not really mean what he said. Commodus was even dangerous when making a joke. Once he saw a man with a few dark hairs mixed in with the white ones. Commodus thought these dark hairs looked like worms, so he had a bird placed on the man's head that would go after what it thought were worms and so cause the man's head to be torn up with the bird's continuous pecking. He ordered a fat man be cut down the middle so that his intestines would suddenly spill out. He would gouge out a person's eye or cut off one of their feet and call them "One-eye" or "One-foot." He indiscriminately killed many other people, some because they were wearing barbarian clothing when they met him in the street, others because they were nobly born or good-looking.

#42: The Extravagances of the Emperor Elagabalus

Historia Augusta, Life of Elagabalus 26
Written Possibly in the Fourth Century AD Describing
the Emperor Elagabalus (AD 218–222)

The last example of vice also comes from the *Historia Augusta*, the writer of which describes the emperor Elagabalus as one of the most degenerate creatures ever to sit on the throne. He was originally a child priest of the sun god Elagabal in Syria. As with the passage describing Commodus, the *Historia Augusta* is prone to exaggeration and the following passage describing his luxurious and extravagant life is no exception.

> Elagabalus was the first Roman to wear clothing completely made of silk although there were outfits made partially of silk in use before him. He never touched linen clothing that had been washed because, he claimed, only beggars wore clothing more than once.... He summoned to a public temple all of the prostitutes from the circus, theater, the baths, and all other similar places. He then addressed them like a general addresses his soldiers before battle. He called them his "fellow soldiers" and taught them various positions and techniques. He later summoned to a similar assembly the pimps and all of the dissolute and sexually immoral young boys and youths he could find. When he had addressed the prostitutes, he had done so in women's dress with his breast exposed. In his speech to the second group, however, he wore an outfit similar to a boy prostitute. After the speech, Elagabalus announced that he would give them a cash bonus of three gold pieces each, as if they were soldiers in the army, and asked them to pray to the gods that they find new recruits to recommend to him.

Chapter 4: The Family

The family was the most important institution within Roman culture. Being a patriarchal society, the Romans placed the power within the family in the hands of its oldest living male ancestor on the father's side (the *paterfamilias*). This head of the household had complete control over the people and property within his family. Marriage practices emphasized the production of legitimate children who could inherit the family's property and control after the death of the *paterfamilias*.

The *Familia* and the *Paterfamilias*

The Roman concept of the *familia* included all persons and property that fell under the power (*potestas*) of a single man (the *paterfamilias*, "father of the family"). This included the *paterfamilias*, children, sometimes the wife (although she often remained in the *familia* of her father rather than her husband), grandchildren, slaves, freedmen and other free client dependents, as well as all of the family's property and wealth. This first section of this chapter focuses on the power of the *paterfamilias*. Selections #43 and #44 from the surviving law codes of late antiquity give legal definitions of *familia*, *paterfamilias*, and *potestas*. A passage from Dionysius of Halicarnassus describes the absolute power of the *paterfamilias* to a Greek audience (#45). Selections from Valerius Maximus (#46) and Seneca (#47) illustrate how that power could extend even to the execution of a son. Although there were few legal constraints on the power of the *paterfamilias*, there were, nevertheless, social limitations. In a letter to a friend, Pliny criticizes a father for scolding his son (#48). The final selection (#49) is an excerpt from Gaius' *Institutes* explaining how a person could become legally independent (*sui iuris*).

#43: Legal Definition of the *Familia*

Justinian, *Digest* 50.16.195
Sixth Century AD

At the end of his *Digest*, Justinian compiles a list of important terms and ideas and gives their legal definition. Included among these definitions is *familia*. His explanation of *familia* reveals a complex word that delineated ownership and control under the head of the Roman household: the *paterfamilias*.

> Let us now turn our attention to how the term *familia* is to be understood. Indeed, the term is defined in various ways as it can refer to both things and persons. When the Twelve Tables, for example, says "let the oldest male relative be in control of the *familia*," it is clearly referring to things. When later law,

however, speaks of patrons and freedmen with phrases such as "from the *familia*" and "into the *familia*," it is agreed that it is describing individual persons.

The term *familia* also refers to any kind of group that is defined as having a status specific to the people in the group or a status shared by similar people. In the case of a specific status, we call a *familia* those several persons who, by virtue of nature or legal enactment, are under the power (*potestas*) of one person: i.e., the *paterfamilias*. This would include his wife, sons, daughters, and so on as well as to those that follow them namely the grandsons and granddaughters.

The person who has control over the household is called the *paterfamilias*. He has this name even if he does not have a child. This is because the term refers not only to personal relationships but also to his legal rights and powers over people as well as property. Indeed, it is even possible to call an infant a *paterfamilias* provided he has the legal powers implicit in the term. When the *paterfamilias* dies, every male person who was subject to his power will then begin to have his own *familia* as each of them will enter the status of being *paterfamilias*. The same is true in the case of people who have been emancipated as they obtain their own *familia* by virtue of becoming legally independent (*sui iuris*).

#44: The Power Structures within the Family

Gaius, *Institutes* 1.48–52, 55–57, 97, 108–110, 116–118
Mid-Second Century AD

Individuals were considered to be either legally independent (*sui iuris*) or under the power of someone else (*alieni iuris*). The *paterfamilias* was *sui iuris* and those under his authority were *alieni iuris* by being either in his *potestas* ("power"), *manus*, ("hand"), or *mancipium*, ("possession").

The next section of this legal work covers the rights of persons. Some people are legally independent (*sui iuris*), others are subject to the power another person (*alieni iuris*). Of those who are *alieni iuris*, some are in his *potestas*, others in his *manus*, and others in his *mancipium*. Let us look more closely at those who are *alieni iuris*. It will be easier if we begin with those people who are *alieni iuris*, as we will better understand what is meant by the term *sui iuris* by knowing who is under the power of someone who is *sui iuris*. In this way, if we should understand who those persons are, we might understand at the same time those who are *sui iuris*. Slaves are in the *potestas* of their masters...

Likewise our children whom we have begotten in a legal marriage are also in our *potestas*. This right is unique to Roman citizens (there are few other peoples who keep their children in their *potestas* in the same way that we do). This fact is made clear in the edict of the divine emperor Hadrian in which he made a declaration about those who were petitioning him for Roman citizenship both for themselves and their children. I am not forgetting however the case of the Galatian people who also consider the children to be in the *potestas* of their parents.

Roman citizens are understood to have the right of entering a marriage and begetting children who will be in their *potestas*. This is true whether the marriage is with a woman with Roman citizenship, Latin rights, or even a foreign woman provided they have the right of marriage (*coniubium*). A component of a citizen's right to legal marriage is that the children of the union take the status of their father and are in his *potestas*. It is for this reason that imperial legal enactments granted some retired soldiers the right to legal marriage with women with Latin rights as well as foreigners as long as the marriage took place after their discharge and that any children resulting from these marriages would become Roman citizens and would be under the *potestas* of their father...

Not only are our natural children in our *potestas* according to the above discussion but also those whom we adopt...

Now let us turn to those persons who are in our *manus*. This also is a right unique to Roman citizenship. Although both males and females can be in someone's *potestas*, only women can be under our *manus*. In antiquity, women could pass into the *manus* of a man by three methods: cohabitation without marriage, through an antiquated marriage ceremony involving a sacrifice to Jupiter Farreus, or through a ceremony in which the bride is fictitiously "sold" into her husband's family...

#45: The Powers of the *Paterfamilias*

Dionysius of Halicarnassus, *Roman Antiquities* 2.26
Written in the First Century AD Probably Describing 485 BC

The power structures within the Roman family subordinated the people and property within the *familia* to the *potestas* of the *paterfamilias*. Few legal enactments limited this power. As the following passage by the first century BC Greek historian Dionysius of Halicarnassus explains, the lifelong power of the *paterfamilias* over those under his authority was unique to Roman society. According to Dionysius, the powers the state granted to the *paterfamilias* were designed to inspire in children a greater loyalty and devotion to their parents (most notably the father).

Romulus, the lawgiver of the Romans, granted the father what could be considered absolute power over the life of his child. The *paterfamilias* has the power to imprison, beat, chain, compel to forced labor in the fields, and even put to death his son, even if his son is already of advanced age and engaged in political life and has reached the highest magisterial offices and is winning glory for his actions on behalf of the state. We have record of a certain famous man who was delivering a speech from the speaker's platform in the forum against the senate and in support of the common people. Indeed this man was winning a great deal of approval with his words when his senatorial father came and pulled him down from the tribunal and dragged him away to punish him in whatever way his father saw fit by virtue of this law. As his father dragged his son through the forum, not one of the onlookers was able to come to his aid: not the consul, or the tribune, or any one of the common people. Just recently, the son had been flattering all of these people in order to gain power over them, but now none of them could help him.

#46: Cassius Executes His Son

Valerius Maximus, *Memorable Deeds and Sayings* 5.8.2
Written in the First Century AD Describing 485 BC

Dionysius' account of the unnamed father who dragged his son from the speaker's platform in the forum and executed him is almost certainly an allusion to the story of Cassius who, in 485, punished his son for proposing an agrarian law that would benefit the poor at the expense of the rich. The author Valerius Maximus, in his collection of trivia, tells the same story (translated here).

Cassius executed his son Spurius Cassius. The son, while tribune of the plebs, had been the first to propose an agrarian law along with other popular measures and had thereby won over a great deal of public favor. After the son left office, the father convened a council of relatives and friends and accused his son of trying to become king. The father condemned the son in his house, beat him with whips, and then ordered his execution. The father then consecrated to Ceres the property he had given his son as an allowance.

#47: Public Reactions to Two Fathers' Condemnations of Their Sons

Seneca, *On Clemency* 14.3–15.2
First Century AD

To the modern reader, the *paterfamilias'* power to punish or execute his own children seems quite harsh. Roman tradition and social reality, however, often diverged. Although there were few legal restrictions upon the *potestas* of the *paterfamilias*, there were social constraints. Society looked down upon the harsh treatment of wives, children, or slaves. The following passage by the philosopher Seneca on how an emperor, like a father, should be slow to punish children harshly, illustrates how the public will express their opinion on a father's exercise of his right to condemn his children.

A father should be slow to kill his own family members. Indeed, after killing a family member, he should desire to restore them and, in the act of execution, after long hesitation, should feel sorry for considering the act. I believe that a father who condemns too quickly should be censured more than a father who condemns too harshly. Within our own memory, a mob tried to stab with their writing utensils a Roman of equestrian status named Tricho because he had beaten his son to death. It was only when Augustus Caesar intervened that Tricho was rescued from the hostile hands of these fathers and sons. In another example, a certain man named Tarius arrested his son on the charge of parricide. After hearing his case in a private trial, the father found his son guilty. No one looked down on the father because he was content to send his son into a comfortable exile in Massilia and provided him an annual allowance equal to what he had received before his condemnation. This condemnation had the effect that, in a society in which a patron is never lacking for criminals, no one doubted that the condemned son was guilty because his father did not hate him but yet fulfilled his duty and condemned him.

#48: Pliny Criticizes a Father for Scolding His Son

Pliny the Younger, *Letters* 9.12
Early Second Century AD

In a similar passage, Pliny the Younger castigates a severe father. Pliny encourages this *paterfamilias* to use tolerance when dealing with youthful misbehavior. Implicit in the letter is the social unacceptably of a *paterfamilias* immoderately punishing someone under his control.

A certain man I know was chastising his son because the boy was in the habit of spending too much on horses and dogs. After sending the boy away, I said to the father, "Look here. Did you never do something your father could have condemned? You certainly did. From time to time you still do things that your son could criticize with equal gravity if your places were unexpectedly reversed and he was the father and you the son. Are not all people (including yourself) guilty of one fault or another? Should you not indulge your son in this wrongdoing as someone else would overlook your faults? I have spoken to you this admonition out of our mutual respect so as to allow you to avoid immoderate severity. I do not want you to ever treat your son too harshly or severely. Remember that he is a boy just as you yourself once were. Therefore, bear in mind that you are the father so that you remember that you are a human being and so is your son."

#49: Becoming *Sui Iuris*

Gaius, *Institutes* 1.127
Mid-Second Century AD

Before the father's death, a child could be released from the *potestas* of his father by several means. A daughter could be transferred through a *manus* marriage to the power of her husband's family (leaving her still *alieni iuris*). Children and slaves could also be manumitted, i.e., freed, from the power of their father/master. The act rendered the son or freedman *sui iuris* and free to set up his own family as *paterfamilias*. Most people, however, generally only became *sui iuris* after the death of the *paterfamilias*. After a man's death, his sons became *sui iuris* and *patresfamilias* of their own families. His daughters who were unmarried or married in a *sine manu* marriage (in which she was not transferred to the *potestas* of her husband's family) also became *sui iuris*. The following passage from the legal compendium of the writer Gaius illustrates how the power is passed from father to son. Gaius makes no reference to women who would not become *sui iuris* after the death of their father because *manus* marriage were virtually unheard of at the time he was writing.

> Indeed, a person who is in the *potestas* of his or her father becomes *sui iuris* after his death. A distinction must be made however. It is not always the case that sons and daughters become *sui iuris* after their father dies. Grandsons and granddaughters will only become *sui iuris* after their grandfather dies if they are not under the *potestas* of their own father. Thus, if the son's grandfather dies but his father is still alive and was previously in the *potestas* of the deceased man, then the grandson will come under the *potestas* of his father after the death of his grandfather. If, however, the son's father was already dead at the time of the death of his grandfather, or the father had for some other reason left the *potestas* of his father, then the son will be *sui iuris* because he is not able to fall under the *potestas* of his father.

Marriage

The central concern for the Romans when it came to marriage was the production of legitimate heirs who would one day be able to inherit the property of their fathers. A boy, it was hoped, would someday replace his father as *paterfamilias* of his own family while the girl would marry and produce new children for another family. Roman law, therefore, focuses on defining marriage and the production of legitimate children. In selection #50, Justinian summarizes rulings on marriage. Aristocrats often helped one another find suitable spouses for their children. In one of his letters, Pliny the Younger recommends a young acquaintance for his friend's daughter (#51). With the need to produce as many children as possible, it was typical for women to marry at a young age. It was also common for the wife to be significantly younger than her husband. This collection includes a number of funerary inscriptions documenting the age difference between husband and wife (#52). Two other inscriptions were dedicated to young girls who died shortly before their wedding days (#53). As shown in a letter of Pliny the Younger, it was also not uncommon for wives to die in childbirth or from complications related to giving birth (#54). This section ends with a set of inscriptions describing happy marriages (#55).

#50: Laws Governing Marriage

Justinian, *Institutes* 1.10
Sixth Century AD

The following text outlines what unions were considered to be legal in the eyes of
Roman law and thus were able to produce legitimate children.

> Roman citizens who are united according to the precepts of the laws form
> between one another what is considered to be legal marriages. The men must
> have reached the age of puberty and women must be of marriageable age.
> This is the case of all citizens whether they are *sui* or *alieni iuris*. In the case
> of those who are *alieni iuris*, however, they must receive the consent of the
> father in whose power they are. That the consent of the parent precedes the
> marriage is a necessity both of civil law and the natural order of things. From
> this statement, however, arises the question of whether or not the daughter or
> son of an insane person is able to marry. Although there still remains doubt in
> the case of the son, we previously made a legal decision in which the daughter
> of an insane father was without the formal consent of the father able to marry
> according to the method prescribed in our constitution.
>
> Although the right of marriage is a prerogative of Roman citizens, neverthe-
> less, a man is not able to marry any woman he chooses. There are some mar-
> riages that are forbidden. For example, people may not marry a direct family
> ascendant or descendant: father and daughter, grandfather and granddaughter,
> mother and son, grandmother and grandson, and so on. Marriages between such
> people are to be considered criminal and incestuous. The same is true in the case
> of persons adopted: people in the place of parents or children too are unable
> to marry one another. So strong is this law that even if the adoption should be
> dissolved, the precept remains in effect. Thus you may not marry a woman who
> is your adopted daughter or granddaughter, even if you should emancipate her.
>
> Similar prohibitions (but to a lesser extent) are in effect for people who are
> parallel relations. Of course, a brother and sister are not allowed to marry, even in
> cases in which they have only one parent in common (step-children). In the case
> of an adopted sister, intermarriage is not allowed as long as the woman's adoptive
> status continues. If, however, the adoption should be dissolved through emanci-
> pation, then there is no restriction to a brother marrying his former adoptive sister.

#51: Looking for a Suitable Husband

Pliny the Younger, *Letters* 1.14
Early Second Century AD

A formal marriage ceremony was not required for a marriage to be considered
legal. The government did not keep records of marriages or divorces. The Romans

did, however, consider marriage to be an important milestone in a person's life, especially for girls, as it signaled a new stage of life. In the lower classes where family connections and political alliances meant little or nothing, marriages were usually not arranged. Brides and grooms had the freedom to choose their prospective spouse. In the aristocracy, however, arranged marriages were much more common. In such cases, the groom or his *paterfamilias* would consult with the bride's parents. Only then would the girl be consulted. In the following letter, Pliny the Younger responds to a request from a family friend to find a husband for his daughter. Pliny describes the attributes that make his friend a worthy candidate to marry the girl. The letter is a fine example of what aristocrats would look for in an arranged marriage.

Gaius Plinius to his friend Junius Mauricus. You have asked that I find a prospective husband for your daughter. I feel honored that you have given me this most important duty. For you know in what great esteem I held her father and what great advice he gave to me when I was still a young man. He also taught me how to deserve the praise he gave me. There is no greater or more agreeable task you could have set me and no more honorable duty that I could have accepted than that of choosing a young man who will be the future father of the grandchildren of Arulenus Rusticus. Finding such a young man would have been a long and difficult process if I were not acquainted with Minicius Acilianus. We are the greatest of friends, like two chums in the prime of life (although I am a few years older than he is) but yet he respects me as though I were an old man. He has wished to emulate me just as I once wanted to emulate you and your brother (Rusticus). He is from the town of Brixia in our own region of northern Italy. Brixia still retains its simple frugality and ancient rustic charm. Acilianus' father was Minicius Macrinus, a leader of the equestrian order, a social position with which he was satisfied although he could have risen to greater heights. Indeed, he had been given the opportunity by the divine emperor Vespasian to enter the senatorial order with the rank of ex-praetor but he resolutely preferred his honorable retirement to this [senatorial] life of ours (should I call it an ambitious lifestyle or distinguished?). His grandmother on his mother's side is Serrana Procula from the town of Patavium. You know the reputation of that place, but Serrana is a singular example of severity. His uncle Publius Acilius is also a model of gravity, prudence, and loyalty. In short, there is nothing in his family heritage that you would not be happy to have in your own family. Acilianus himself lives a life of great vigor and industry although also the greatest modesty. He is a member of the senatorial order and has already served as quaestor, tribune, and praetor and so it will not be necessary for you to canvass on his behalf for those offices. He has a handsome face with a nice, healthy, red complexion. His whole body is naturally good-looking with a senatorial charm. I do not think you should consider these things as trivial but rather as a worthy gift for the chastity of your daughter. I am not sure whether I should add that his father is very rich. I realize that the sort of person who asks me to find a husband really needs no mention of the young man's wealth, but we both know the way of the world as well as the laws of the state in which a person is classified most importantly by his financial means. Therefore, as I consider the union's posterity as well as these many other concerns, it is only right that some calculation of his wealth come into play. Perhaps also you may suspect that I exaggerate the man's qualities because the friendship I have with him, but I solemnly promise that you will find that all his qualities surpass my description. Indeed I ardently cherish the young man (as he deserves), and for that very reason I would not overload him with too much praise. Good-bye.

#52: Age Difference between Husband and Wife

First to Third Centuries AD

One surprising aspect of Roman marriage is the age difference between bride and groom. Both needed to have reached puberty (generally considered to be fourteen for boys and twelve for girls). Girls usually married shortly after puberty. Many boys, however, waited until their mid-twenties to marry. Some aristocratic girls entered their arranged marriages between ten and thirteen in order to cement the political bonds created through the marriage more quickly. It was extremely common, therefore to have age differences of five to ten years between and husband and wife. The following funerary inscriptions give both the age of the deceased at the time of death and the length of time the deceased was married, allowing us to reconstruct the age at the time of marriage. Unfortunately, very few texts record so much detailed data for both husband and wife on the same stone.

CIL 6.3604 (Rome)

To the deceased Ragonia Cyriaces, sweetest and most incomparable wife, married to just one man in her life, chaste and good, who lived twenty-one years, nine months, and two days; I, Quintus Julius Donatianus, staff officer of the military century in the third cohort, dedicated this to the well-deserving woman with whom I lived well for eight years, nine months, and twenty-four days. She was twelve years, eleven months, and fourteen days when I married her. She sleeps here.

CIL 13.2189 (Lugdunum, Gallia Lugdunensis)

To the Spirits of the Dead and the eternal rest of Juventia Felicissima, a most faithful woman. She lived thirty years. Marcus Aurelius Agathopus, freedman of the emperor, took care of constructing this to his wife and lady of the house with whom he lived from her childhood for twenty-three years without any harming of the spirit. He dedicated this monument while it was still under construction.

AE 1920, 90 (Jewish Cemetery, Rome)

To Aelius Primitivus, archon-elect, an incomparable husband who lived thirty-eight years and with whom I, his wife Flavia Maria, lived for sixteen years without any quarrel. Flavia made this for her sweetest, well-deserving husband.

CIL 6.9072 (Rome)

To the Spirits of the Dead; to Lucida, born a slave of the emperors, an incomparable wife, who lived thirty-three years, two months, and twenty-five days; Catervarius, freedman of the emperor working in the records office put this up to his sweetest wife with whom he lived without any discord for fifteen years, eleven months, and twenty days.

CIL 6.37317 (Rome)

To the Spirits of the Dead; to Caesia Daphnes; Tiberius Caesius Advena dedicated this to his most chaste and faithful wife, with whom he lived in incomparable sweetness for twenty-seven years without any offense of spirit. She lived forty-two years, four months, one day, and three hours. Caesia, in the seventh day of her illness, after taking her husband's hands (who was weeping at her bedside) and holding them over her eyes, repaid her debt to nature.

IPOstia-A 261 (Ostia, Italy)

To the Spirits of the Dead; Olympus, slave of Matidia, daughter of the empress, made this for his wife Urbica, with whom he lived one year, eight months, twenty-two days, and three hours. She died at the age of fourteen years and eleven months.

#53: Two Unfortunate Brides-to-Be

First to Third Centuries AD

The entrance into married life was one of the most important transitional points in a young girl's life. The following two texts poignantly memorialize two girls who died just before their wedding days.

CIL 3.2875 (Nedinum, Dalmatia)

To Opinia Neptilla, daughter of Marcus, thirteen years old, an unfortunate maiden, who died just before her wedding day. Marcus Opinius Rufus and Gellia Neptilla her parents dedicated this tombstone.

AE 1905, 107 (Koudiat Aty, Numidia)

To the Spirits of the Dead and to Memory. Julia Sidonia Felix, *felix* (lucky) in name only, whose life the Fates cruelly snatched away before her time. Alas, her fiancé never was able to take part in her marriage ceremony. All of the Dryads [wood nymphs] and girls of the world mourn her. The goddess Diana herself, now that the light of this girl's wedding torch has been put out, weeps because she was a virgin and the sole delight of her parents. She had been a priestess of the goddess of the tambourine of Memphis (in Egypt). In this place [her tomb], the buried girl will remain silent in the eternal bonds of sleep. She lived nineteen years, four months, fourteen days. She is buried here.

#54: A Happy Marriage

Pliny the Younger, *Letters* 8.5
Early Second Century AD

With life expectancy as low as it was in the ancient world, the premature death of either the husband or the wife frequently broke up families. Even though Romans frequently married very young, wives often succumbed to an early death due to difficulties during childbirth. In the following letter, Pliny the Younger tells his friend of the death of the wife of another friend.

Gaius Plinius to his friend Geminus. Our friend Macrinus has suffered a heavy blow. He has lost his wife, a woman of exemplary character (one comparable even with those great women of the past). He was married to this woman for thirty-nine years without quarrel and offense. This woman treated her husband with the greatest respect and indeed deserved the same in return. So many and so great were the virtues that she exemplified in every stage of her life! Indeed, Macrinus has one great solace in that he had such a good thing for so long. However, I am sure for the same reason he hurts even more because of the knowledge of what he has lost. This example clearly illustrates how the pain of loss grows proportionally with our enjoyment of a pleasure. Therefore I will be anxious for this great friend of mine until such time as he is able to give himself over to diversion and allow his wounds to heal. His grief will not subside except with equal portions of necessary acceptance of his loss, time, and the end of grief. Good-bye.

#55: Inscriptions Recording Happy Couples

First to Third Centuries AD

Almost all of our descriptions of marital bliss come from the funerary epitaphs of husbands and wives. Like the letter of Pliny quoted above, these inscriptions emphasize mostly the virtues of the deceased and the length of marriage. These texts, designed to preserve the memory of the deceased for eternity, tend to be formulaic as the families sought to incorporate themselves and their loved ones into the traditional view of good men or women.

CIL 9.2603 (Terventum, Samnium, Italy)

Sacred to the Spirits of the Dead; to Suitia Secundina, daughter of Sextus; Gaius Munatius Marcellus, son of Gaius, of the Voltinia tribe, aedile, *duovir* with the right of conducting the census, quaestor, and caretaker of the grain supply, made this for himself and for his best and most honest wife with whom he lived for [. . .? thirty-one or forty-one . . .] years in continuous, incomparable harmony.

CIL 2.3596 (Dianium, Hispania Citerior)

Sacred to the Spirits of the Dead of Titus Junius Achilleius, scribe and clerk of the three decuries in the records office of the quaestors [possibly in Rome]. Pacideia Hedone, his wife, made this shared monument for her loyal and incomparable husband so that she might never be separated even in death from the man with whom she lived a pleasant life for thirty-five years in equal harmony.

CIL 6.26467a (Rome)

Lucius Sestius Sotericus made this for himself and for Sestia Prisca, another freed slave and his well-deserving wife, with whom he lived thirty years and who never grieved him in any way except with her death. It is also dedicated to Titus Titius Bassus, their friend and the best of men and of exemplary character as well as to their freedmen, freedwomen, and their posterity. The burial plot is twelve feet in front and twelve feet deep.

AE 1987, 179 (Ostia, Latium, Italy)

To the Spirits of the Dead; to [. . .]nia Sebotis, daughter of Publius; Quintus Minucius Marcellus, son of Quintus, of the Palatina tribe, made this for his dearest, most faithful, most chaste, conjugal wife who never wished to go anywhere without me: not out in public, not to the baths, not anywhere. I married her when she was fourteen years old and still a virgin. With her I have one daughter. I have spent the best years of my life with my wife and she has made me a fortunate man. I would have preferred it, however, if you, my wife, my felicity, were still alive and I had been the one to die and leave you alive. She lived twenty-one years, two months, and twenty-one days.

AE 1973, 231 (Castrum Novum, Etruria, Italy)

To the Spirits of the Dead; stop, traveler, and read this inscription. I was unworthily snatched by death as a young man of twenty-eight years old. I was lacking neither virtues nor good looks. Flavia Ianuaria made this for Olympus, her well-deserving husband with whom she lived from her earliest childhood without injury. We were born with unequal fates and were so quickly separated. May the earth rest lightly upon you.

Divorce, Adultery, and Marital Problems

Despite the many accounts of happy homes that adhered to the traditional system of virtues, Roman brides and grooms did not always live happily ever after. Many wives outlived their older husbands. Also, due to the dangers of childbirth and low life expectancy in general, it was not uncommon for husbands to lose their wives. Marriages could also end in divorce. Like marriage itself, divorce required no legal act. Divorce required that the husband repay the wife's full dowry (a concern primarily for the richer members of the upper classes). He was only allowed to keep portions of it if there were children from the marriage (one-fifth per child), or if the wife had been convicted of adultery. Valerius Maximus claims that the first cases of divorce were a result of the wife's inability to bear children (#56). By the first century BC, however, divorce (and remarriage) had become quite common, especially among the upper classes (as exemplified by the emperor Augustus, #57 and the unusual inscription of a man named Mindius Dius, #58). The emperor Augustus chose to pass a law condemning adultery as a factor that was detrimental to his focus on family values (#59). Our surviving evidence, with its emphasis on describing marriage and family life in traditional terms only, gives few examples of adultery. One interesting inscription includes a curse upon an adulterous wife (#60). Valerius Maximus describes a temple to the goddess Viriplaca ("Man-Placater," who protected wives from angry or abusive husbands) (#61). The section ends with three examples of men who killed their wives (#62, #63).

#56: The Origins of Divorce in Rome

Valerius Maximus, *Memorable Deeds and Sayings* 2.1.4
Written in the Early First Century AD Describing
Events of the Middle of the Third Century BC

As marriage's primary goal was the production of children, the failure of a woman to produce children was considered a legitimate reason for divorce. In the following passage, Valerius Maximus cites barrenness as the reason for the first recorded example of divorce, from the middle of the third century BC. It is interesting to note, however, that Valerius Maximus contrasts the legality of the action with its acceptance by society.

> From the foundation of the city [in 753 BC] until its 523rd year [231 BC], no husband and wife had ever asked for a divorce. Spurius Caruilius was the first to divorce his wife because of her inability to produce children. Although he seemed to have made the decision for an acceptable reason, nevertheless he did not escape criticism. There were those who believed that not even the desire for children should be put before conjugal fidelity.

#57: The Wives of the Emperor Augustus

Suetonius, *Augustus* 62
Written in the Early Second Century AD Describing
the Emperor Augustus (27 BC–AD 14)

By the first century BC, members of the aristocracy often married and divorced multiple times. In the following passage from Suetonius, the biographer lists the wives of the emperor Augustus and the (sometimes trivial) reasons for his divorces.

As a young man, Augustus was betrothed to the daughter of Publius Servilius Isauricus. After his reconciliation with Mark Antony after their first public political break, the soldiers of both statesmen asked that the two be joined by some kind of family relationship. Therefore, Augustus married Antony's step-daughter Claudia, the daughter of Fulvia (Antony's wife) with her earlier husband Publius Clodius. Augustus married her even though she was barely of marriageable age. Later, after a disagreement arose between Augustus and his mother-in-law Fulvia, he divorced Claudia, who was still a virgin. Next he married the woman Scribonia who had been married twice before to ex-consuls (she had produced a child with one of them). He later divorced her as well and wrote that he had become tired of the perversity of her habits. Immediately after his divorce from Scribonia, he married Livia Drusilla whom he snatched from a marriage to Tiberius Nero (indeed she was pregnant by Tiberius at the time of her marriage to Augustus). Nevertheless, Augustus loved Livia and cherished her solely for the rest of his life.

#58: Multiple Wives

CIL 14.5026; *AE* 1981, 160
Second or Third Century AD

It is from the pages of the ancient historians and biographers that we read of divorce and remarriage. The epigraphic record on funerary monuments is almost completely lacking in evidence for divorce (and even remarriage). The following text is odd in that it mentions three women in connection with the man who dedicated the stone. The inscription attributes to each of the three women a different word that can mean "wife": *coniunx*, *marita*, and *contubernalis*. The first woman to appear on the stone receives the most attention. The name of the third woman appears to have been written over the erasure of some earlier text (perhaps a fuller description of the second woman). The stone gives no details on the status of the three women (although it is likely that all three were Roman citizens). It is possible that the dedicator is commemorating his three successive marriages.

Lucius Mindius Dius made this for himself and for Genucia Tryphaena, his incomparable wife (*coniunx*) with whom he lived twenty-four years and three months, and for Lucceia Ianuaria, his wife (*marita*) and for Annia Laveria, his most chaste wife (*contubernalis*) as well as for his freedmen, freedwomen, and their posterity. Let it be known that this monument is not to pass to his heir. The burial plot is thirty feet wide and thirty-one feet deep.

#59: The Legal Definition of Adultery
in the *Julian Law on Adultery*

Paulus, *Sententiae* 2.26.1–2, 4–8, 11, 14, 16
Third Century AD

Although considered to be a serious offense because it introduced the possibility of illegitimate heirs to a *paterfamilias'* estate, formal legal procedure against adultery did not exist until Augustus. As part of his program of moral restoration after his victory in the civil wars, Augustus enacted several laws intended to reinstitute the integrity of the Roman *familia*. The most significant of these laws was that aimed at adultery and passed in 18 BC. This law made adultery a criminal offense and created a new court to decide cases involving adultery. The law defined adultery as a woman having sexual relations with a man other than her husband. The following passage from the legal text of Paulus describes actions that could be taken against adulterous wives and their lovers. Much of the concerns expressed relate to the rights of the father and husband of the woman. As shown in the last translated section, men having sexual relations with a slave was not considered adultery. In all of the examples given, *sine manu* marriages are assumed and so the daughter was still *alieni iuris* on the *paterfamilias* from her own family.

In the second chapter of the Julian Law on Adultery, it is permitted to the father (natural or adoptive) to kill his daughter's adulterous lover (whatever class he may be) as well as his daughter when he catches them in the act either in his own house or in the house of his son-in-law...

If a man who is still under the *potestas* of his father should catch his daughter in the act of adultery, although the law would seem to state that he does not have to the right to kill her as she is not in his *potestas*, nevertheless he should still be permitted to kill her...

Only the following types of persons are legal for the husband to kill provided he catches them in the act of adultery: persons of bad reputation, those who sell their bodies for a profit, slaves, and freedmen (both his own as well as those belonging to his wife, his parents, or children). He does not have the right to kill his wife, however [as she is under the *potestas* of her father's family]...

It has been decided that a husband who kills his wife when he catches her with an adulterous lover should be punished more leniently because he was driven to it by the rashness caused by his justified grief...

After the husband has killed his wife's adulterous lover, he should immediately divorce her and declare within a three-day period with whom she had committed adultery and in what place she was caught...

When a husband catches his wife in the act of adultery, he can only kill his wife's lover and not his wife if he catches them in the act of adultery in his own house...

It has been decided that if a husband catches his wife in the act of adultery and does not divorce her that he can be accused of being a pimp...

It has been decided that a person cannot be accused of adultery if the act was done with a woman who works as a merchant or runs a shop...

Women who are convicted of adultery are to be punished with the loss of half of their dowry and a third of their estate and are to be exiled to an island. The man with whom she committed adultery should be punished with the loss of half of his property and be exiled to an island. Of course, it is understood that the woman and her lover will be exiled to different islands...

In the case of men, sexual intercourse with a female slave should not be considered adultery unless the act decreases the monetary value of a slave belonging to another person or the act should be done to gain access to the slave's mistress...

#60: Curse upon an Adulterous Wife

CIL 6.20905 (Rome)

Many of the stories from the ancient world involving adultery involve members of the aristocracy. The following tomb inscription, however, records the story of one unfortunate man of the lower classes. The inscription includes two texts written at different times. In the first text, a despondent mother and father commemorate their dead eight-year-old daughter. The text informs the reader that it is hoped that the ashes of the mother and father would someday be interred in the same tomb. Sometime after this text was carved, however, things had changed. The mother's name—Acte—was scratched out of the earlier text and a second inscription was carved beneath the original inscription to put a curse upon the adulterous woman. The following is a translation of this second text.

> Here has been written the curse upon the freedwoman Acte, a poisoner and grievous liar with a hard heart: may she hang by the neck in a noose of harsh Spanish broom! May she burn alive in white-hot pitch! As thanks for her manumission, she pursued an adulterous lover, defrauded her patron [her husband], and stole away from him as he slept two of his slaves: a slave girl and boy. Now her husband remains in despair, alone, abandoned, an old man robbed of his marriage! May the same curse follow her lover Zosimus!

#61: The Goddess Viriplaca and Marital Problems

Valerius Maximus, *Memorable Deeds and Sayings* 2.1.6
Early First Century AD

Although often kept out of sight, marital problems and disputes did occur. In fact, there was a deity dedicated to ending marital strife. In this passage, Valerius Maximus mentions a temple to the goddess Viriplaca ("Man-Placater"). Valerius Maximus ends the passage with yet another reiteration of the male-dominated ideology that permeated Roman views on men, women, and marriage.

> Whenever some kind of argument arose between a husband and wife, the custom was to come to the shrine of the goddess Viriplaca on the Palatine hill. While there, each would have a turn to speak his or her mind. Once their argument was settled, they would return home in harmony. It is said that the goddess received this name from her function of placating husbands. In view of her as the guardian of daily peace in the home, I believe this goddess deserves special worship with unique and exquisite sacrifices as her very name emphasizes the honor owed to the majesty of the husband by the wife in the equal yoke of love.

#62: Two Murderous Husbands

First to Third Centuries AD

The following two tomb inscriptions record unfortunate wives who were murdered at the hands of their husbands. As seen in the first text, the term "deceived" was a common euphemism for "killed." Unfortunately, neither text records what happened to the murdering husband.

IPOstie-A 210 (Ostia, Italy)

> Restutus Piscinesis and Prima Restuta made this for their dearest daughter Prima Florentia who was deceived by her husband Orfeus in the Tiber River. Her relative December erected this monument. She was fifteen years old.

CIL 13.2182 (Lugdunum, Gallia Lugdunensis)

> To the Spirits of the Dead and to the eternal rest of Julia Maiana, a most chaste woman, who was killed most cruelly by the hand of her husband. She died before her fated time. She lived with her husband for twenty-eight years and with him bore two children, one of whom is nineteen years old, the other eighteen. O Faith! O Loyalty! Julius Maior her brother took care of erecting this monument along with her sons Ingenuinius and Ianuarius. The monument was dedicated while still under construction.

#63: A Husband Throws His Wife out
of Their Bedroom Window

Tacitus, *Annals* 4.22
Written in the Early Second Century AD Describing Events of AD 24

In earliest Roman history, the husband had absolute authority (including the power of life and death) over his wife. That power had eroded over time, however. By the first century BC, the majority of women legally remained in the family of their father's family (in a *sine manu* marriage), protecting them from arbitrary action against them on the part of their husband or his family. Tacitus tells the following story of an unfortunate incident from AD 24. This story of aristocratic marital intrigue, murder, and mystery is one of our first examples of crime scene investigation. It is important to note that it is not the state that initiates action but rather the woman's father (in whose power she had remained after her marriage).

For unknown reasons, the praetor Plautius Silvanus threw his wife Apronia out of the window of their house and killed her. His father-in-law Lucius Apronius immediately had him arrested and taken before the emperor Tiberius. Answering the emperor's questions as if still half asleep, Plautius claimed to be ignorant of what happened. "She must have jumped out on her own!" he exclaimed. Tiberius immediately went to the house and investigated the bedroom. There he found signs of a struggle and forceful ejection out the window. Tiberius therefore referred the case to the senate. By the time the judges had been appointed, however, Plautius was already dead. Urgulania, Plautius' grandmother, had sent him a dagger. Because Urgulania was good friends with the emperor's mother Livia, Plautius had taken this as a warning from the emperor himself. Although still not pronounced guilty, he tried to commit suicide by opening his veins. When he was unable to do so, he had someone else do it for him. A short time later, his first wife, Numantia, was accused of having caused her husband's insanity through spells and potions. She was, however, acquitted.

Chapter 5: Women

As exemplified by the power of the *paterfamilias*, Rome was a patriarchal society. Virtually every extant written source from the Roman world was authored by a man. We have almost no literary source that reveals a woman's perspective on her own life or the role of women in general. Therefore, when approaching Roman sources that discuss women, it is important to keep in mind that they were written from a male perspective. The extant sources are informative, however, as long as that inherent masculine bias is kept in mind. It is important, therefore, always to consider not only the audience for which each text was written, but also the extent to which the role of women has been filtered, distorted, or even misunderstood by its male author.

The Traditional View of Roman Women

Unlike men's virtues, women were praised for their home and married life. Their virtues included sexual fidelity (*castitas*), a sense of decency (*pudicitia*), love for her husband (*caritas*), marital concord (*concordia*), devotion to family (*pietas*), fertility (*fecunditas*), beauty (*pulchritudo*), cheerfulness (*hilaritas*), and happiness (*laetitia*). This section includes a number of examples of virtuous women: the second century BC woman Claudia (#64), Livy's account of the virtuous Lucretia (#65), the funeral eulogy to Murdia (#66), Pliny the Younger's letter about his new wife Calpurnia (#67; also included are Pliny's letters to his wife, #69), the orator Quintilian's wife (#68), and a selection of funerary inscriptions of other women (#70).

#64: The Wife and Mother Claudia

CIL 6.15346 (Rome)
Second Century BC

This tombstone from the second century BC recounts one woman's domestic virtues. The text, written in verse, includes a play on words. The term lovely (*pulchra*) is similar to the word for tomb (*sepulchrum*).

> Stranger, my message is short. Stop and read it through. This is the unlovely tomb of a lovely woman. Her parents named her Claudia. She loved her husband with her whole heart. She bore two sons; of these she leaves one on earth; she has placed the other under the earth. She was charming in her mannerisms, yet proper in bearing. She kept house. She made wool. Good-bye.

#65: The Virtue of Lucretia

Livy, *Histories* 1.57
Written in the First Century BC Describing
Rome's Mythical Early History

The historian Livy's account of the early history of Rome is filled with moral tales intended to indoctrinate the youths of Roman culture in the traditional view of acceptable behavior for men and women. In this story, the virtues of the Roman woman Lucretia contrast sharply with the Etruscan women whose morals were considerably more lax. The story comes from the period when the Etruscans ruled Rome.

Occasionally, the royal Etruscan youths would spend their free time with one another in dinners and drinking parties. By chance, at one of these drinking parties given by Sextus Tarquinius, when Collatinus (the son of Egerius) and Tarquinius were present, the conversation turned to their wives. Each man present praised his wife in exaggerated terms. When the competition heated up, Collatinus exclaimed that it was not possible to settle the matter with words and that with only a few short hours, they could see for themselves how his own wife Lucretia clearly stood out above the rest. He said, "We are young and vigorous. Why shouldn't we mount our horses and see first-hand the virtues of our wives? The best test of their character will be seeing what each of them is doing when they are not expecting their husbands to come home." The group was already pretty well drunk, so they agreed and exclaimed, "let's go!" And so, spurring on their horses, they sped to Rome. They arrived as the first shadows of night were beginning to set in. They went to Collatia where they found Lucretia in very different pursuits from the wives of the Etruscan princes. For they saw the Etruscan women were spending their time eating and in idleness with their friends. They found Lucretia, on the other hand, even though it was late at night by that time, sitting in the middle of the house busy with her wool working with her servant girls working beside her. The victory in the contest of women clearly belonged to Lucretia. She kindly greeted her husband and the Etruscan princes when she saw that they had come. Her victorious husband kindly invited the royal youths to remain as his guest.

#66: The Eulogy of Murdia

CIL 6.10230 (Rome)
First Century BC

This inscription from the first century BC records the funeral eulogy delivered by a son for his mother. The preserved portion of the text comes from the middle of the speech. The first part of the surviving text describes provisions from the woman's will. The speaker is Murdia's son by her first husband. After the death of her first husband, Murdia re-married. After discussion of the will, the speaker turns to the woman's virtues. At the end of the text as it has been preserved, the speaker mentions the similarity of virtues among good women, a fact made very clear by the uniformity of praises given to the women in Roman literature.

[. . . the first part of the text is lost . . .] in order that she might make their lives easier with her fortune and make them stronger and more pleasant, she made all of her sons equal heirs in her will after making a bequest to her daughter. Her maternal love was proven by her love for her children and the equality of their share of the property in her will. She bequeathed to her husband a fixed amount so that the money that he was required to pay as a dowry would be increased because of his choice to marry her. Keeping in mind the memory of my father and calculating its value and the trust between them, she left to me a certain sum in her will. She did not do this to show preference to me and create feelings of enmity but out of remembrance of my father's generosity and was merely repaying what was owed to me. For after his death, my father had decided to bequeath to my mother what should have been my inheritance. And so she was restoring to me what my father had originally left for me.

In her will my mother decided to revere with obedience and proper behavior the marriages to worthy husbands that her parents had arranged and as a married woman to become more acceptable through her merits, to be considered more dear for her faithfulness, to be left more honorable through her decisions regarding her will, and so be praised after her death in the agreement of all of the people. This was accomplished because the division of her estate would make clear her grateful and faithful feelings toward both of her husbands, her fairness toward all her children, and the justice in her truthfulness.

For these reasons, funeral eulogies of all good women tend to be simple and similar because their natural and individual good qualities and continued trustworthiness do not require overly long speeches. It should be enough that all virtuous women have done the same good deeds that make them worthy of a good reputation. Indeed, it is difficult for a woman to win new types of praise since they live lives with fewer variations. So by necessity we praise them for their common qualities so that nothing lost from the usual canon of virtues should spoil all of their other praiseworthy attributes.

Even so, my dearest mother deserves even greater praise than all the others because in modesty (*modestia*), goodness (*probitas*), chastity (*castitas*), obedience, wool-working industry, and faithfulness she was equal and similar to all other good women, nor did she ever come second to any other woman in virtue, labor, or wisdom in danger. [. . . the rest of the text is lost . . .]

#67: Pliny's Wife Calpurnia

Pliny the Younger, *Letters* 4.19
Early Second Century AD

This text is an excerpt from a letter of the early second century AD written by
the senator Pliny the Younger to his wife Calpurnia's aunt, Calpurnia Hispulla.
At the time he wrote this letter, Pliny had recently married Calpurnia (his third
wife).

> Calpurnia is very bright, and very frugal; she loves me, and so I am certain
> that she is sexually faithful. She has also undertaken the study of literature,
> an idea she got from her love for me. She carries with her my literary works,
> reads them repeatedly, and even memorizes them. She is anxious when I am
> working as a lawyer in court, and she is happy when I am finished. She sends
> slaves who will tell her what applause I won and what the verdict was. When I
> give a public reading, she sits behind a nearby curtain, and listens to my praise
> with eager ears. She even sets my poetry to music and plays the songs on her
> cithara. In this, talent is not her instructor, but love, the best teacher. For these
> things, I am led to the most certain hope that our love and marital harmony
> will increase from day to day. Indeed, it is not my body that she loves (for that
> will gradually grow old) but my glory.

#68: Quintilian's Wife

Quintilian, *On Oratory* 6, Preface 4–6
Late First Century AD

Quintilian was the head of a prestigious school of oratory in Rome in the first century AD and the author of the influential book *On Oratory*. The following passage
describes the death of his wife and his remorse at her loss. Although Quintilian does
not give the details of her death, a reference to her escape from a more serious fate
may indicate that she suffered from a serious illness or that something had driven
her to commit suicide.

> The mother of my children was taken from me. She had not yet completed
> her nineteenth year and had given birth to two sons. Although she was taken
> in the harshest of fates, nevertheless her death was a blessing. Even so, I was
> so afflicted by this one bad event that no good fortune was ever to make me
> happy after it. Endowed as she was with every virtue which is possible for a
> woman to have, her death caused an inconsolable grief to me her husband.
> Also, she was of such a young age at the time of her death that, especially
> when her age is compared to my own, it would be possible to count my loss
> of her as equal to losing one's only child. Nevertheless, the children we had

together were still alive at the time of her death. I too am still alive, a fact that seemed to me to be a crime of nature but yet she herself had said that my survival was her desire. Her swift departure from life, however, saved her from the worst of tortures. My youngest son had just turned five when he was the first of my two children to die. The loss of this son was like losing one of my eyes.

#69: Letters from Pliny to His Wife Calpurnia

Early Second Century AD

These three letters are the only correspondence to be preserved in Pliny's extensive published letters that are addressed to his wife. Like the preface of Quintilian quoted above, these letters reveal a great deal more emotion than much of the rest of his letters. It must be kept in mind, however, that like the rest of his surviving letters (other than the contents of Book 10, which were published posthumously), Pliny edited and deliberately published these in order to show how he was an exemplary Roman aristocrat. Although Roman aristocrats of the imperial period were expected to be stern and self-controlled, genuine emotion was allowed when it was motivated by love for one's wife. All of these letters seem to have been written at a time when Calpurnia was away from Pliny because of some illness, perhaps the miscarriage Pliny reported to his father-in-law a couple of years after the marriage.

Pliny the Younger, *Letters* 6.4

Gaius Plinius to his wife Calpurnia. Never have I complained more about my duties in Rome, which have not allowed me to come with you as you left Rome to go to Campania for the sake of your health or to follow in your footsteps soon after. Now I especially want to be with you so that I can see with my own eyes how you are getting strong and healthy again. I would also very much like to see how, untroubled, you have been spending your time in the pleasures of the country and the richness of that part of Italy. Even if you were healthy, I still would have a hard time being apart from you. I am apprehensive and anxious because I know nothing, but that is natural when we worry about someone we love so ardently. Now concern for your absence and sickness worries me as my mind considers the possibilities. I fear everything. I imagine all of the horrible things that could go wrong. Indeed, this is natural for people who are worried. I invent in my mind the things I fear the most. I ask you all the more sincerely therefore that you take thought of my fear and write me a letter every day or even twice a day. As I read your letters, I will be more relaxed. As soon as I have finished reading your letters, however, I will immediately begin to worry again. Good-bye.

Pliny the Younger, *Letters* 6.7

Gaius Plinius to his wife Calpurnia. You wrote to me and said that you are severely affected by my absence but that you have this one consolation: namely that you read my notebooks to think of me and spend considerable time in doing so. It is nice to hear that you miss me. I am glad too that you are able to find some rest in these comforts. For my part, I pick up and read your letters over and over again as if I had only just received them for the first time. But this just drives me to miss you all the more. Your letters contains such charm, but even as I read them, I think to myself how actual conversation would be so much sweeter. So, write as often as you can even though in doing so you cause me as much pain as pleasure.

Pliny the Younger, *Letters* 7.5

Gaius Plinius to his wife Calpurnia. It is amazing how much I am missing you. The primary reason for this is my love for you, but there is also the fact that we have not really spent much time apart. As it is, I lie in bed most of the night thinking of you. When day finally comes, at the normal hour that I would go to visit you, my feet spontaneously take me to your bedroom. That is the absolute truth. Then, finding your room empty, I go away again sick, gloomy, as if I were one of those lovers you read about in love poems who are not allowed to visit their girlfriends. The one time that I am free of these torments is when I am kept busy in the forum and in my legal cases involving my political associates. In your opinion, what kind of a life am I leading when I find respite in my work and solace in misery and cares? Good-bye.

#70: Funerary Inscriptions of Virtuous Women

First to Third Centuries AD

The epigraphic evidence for women's virtues demonstrates the same formulaic nature as the literary evidence. The following tomb epitaphs of women exemplify the range of virtues attributed to women. The variation in location shows that the traditional view of women upheld in literary texts permeated the whole empire.

CIL 6.9275 (Rome)

To the Spirits of the Dead; Gaius Vergilius Martanus, farmer on the estate of Caelius Aeneus put this up to Anulena Certa, farmer on the same estate, his wife who lived twenty-two years. She was loving, chaste, dear, good, loyal, faithful, sweet, most loving, most desired, the sharer of all my good intentions, and well-deserving.

CIL 6.20908 (Rome)

To the Spirits of the Dead; Junia Sabina, an incomparable wife and most loyal mother rests here. To this well-deserving woman, from his own funds, her husband Junius Callistratus along with his sons Maratho and Callistratus dedicated this monument and put up this inscription as a memorial of her loyalty (*pietas*) and so fulfilled their duty to a wife and mother.

CIL 6.13300 (Rome)

To the Spirits of the Dead; to Aurelia Cleopatra who surpassed the examples of all chaste women of ancient time and excelled in every pursuit and activity to which she applied herself. She lived thirty-two years and was married to me in total harmony for eighteen years. I, her husband Aurelius Eutyches, dedicated this to her who was without equal and obedient.

InscrIt 10.10.82 (Pola, Italy)

To the Spirits of the Dead; to Claudia Eugenia, daughter of Quintus, who made life pleasant for her husband with her chastity and obedience and at the same time thwarted those attempting to tarnish the reputation of her husband. Quintus Mursius Celer, public *haruspex* [interpreter of religious signs through the entrails of sacrificed animals] in the town of Pola made this while still alive for his wife and for himself and their posterity.

CIL 5.4029 (Sirmio, Italy)

To the Spirits of the Dead and the memory of Quintia Horestilla, a woman of surpassing loyalty and unique chastity; Cornelius Iustus made this for his most virtuous wife. So too her children put this up for their most loyal mother.

CIL 8.24986 (Carthage, Africa Proconsularis)

Sacred to the Spirits of the Dead; buried here is Tannonia Annibonia, the sweetest wife and dearest, incomparable woman, an example of chastity, frugality, decency, industry, and all the other good virtues. She lived thirty-two years. She rests here with her father-in-law since both were both killed in the same misfortune. [. . .]us Victoricus put this up from his own funds.

Male Control of Women

Roman aristocratic (and therefore male) literature emphasizes the dominance of the men over the women in their society. Surviving literature defines women as an inferior gender that is in need of male control (for example, the legal requirement for women without husbands to have a guardian, #71). The structure of the Roman family, centered on the *paterfamilias* and his power, served to reinforce this belief. The speech the historian Livy attributes to Cato the Elder on the repeal of the Oppian Law in the early second century BC is an excellent expression of this traditional, conservative viewpoint (#72). Also interesting is Valerius Maximus' description of a husband who punished his wife for being drunk (#73).

#71: The Legal Requirement for Women to Have a Guardian

One aspect of Roman daily life in which women's perceived inferiority was recognized in law was in the case of guardianship. The law required women to have a guardian oversee their public financial transactions. The following two texts help us understand the law and the rationale behind it. Both Cicero and Ulpian assert that women are unable to understand the complexity of business transactions and so need to have a (male) guardian to help them.

Cicero, *Defense of Murena* 12.27
Speech Originally Delivered in 63 BC

Although very many laws have been passed for our benefit, nevertheless most of these have been corrupted and perverted by the cunning of lawyers. For example, our forefathers wished that all women should be under the power of guardians due to the lack of mental capacity. These lawyers, however, have found ways to create guardians who would in reality be under the power of the women they have been hired to help.

Ulpian, *Rules* 11.1, 25, 27
Early Third Century AD

Guardians are required for both men and women, but for men only until the age of puberty because of the weakness of their age. Women must have guardians, however, both before and after puberty due to the weakness of their sex and their lack of understanding of public affairs.

The guardians of young boys and girls before the age of reasoning take care of their business transactions and approve of their affairs. The guardians of women beyond the age of puberty only approve their transactions.

Indeed, the authority of the guardians of women is necessary in business transactions. These transactions include legal affairs, making contracts, the conduct of private business, permitting a freedwoman to cohabit with the slave of another master, and the sale of property to an outside buyer.

#72: Cato's Speech against the Repeal of the Oppian Law

Livy, *Histories* 34.2–4
Written in the First Century BC Describing 195 BC

In his account of the early second century BC, Livy records a speech he attributes to the great conservative senator Marcus Porcius Cato, in which he warns Rome of the danger of granting privileges to women. The context is a debate over the repeal of the Oppian Law (see Chapter 3 for a text describing its creation), which prohibited women from wearing more than an ounce of gold, wearing multicolored clothing, or riding in a carriage in Rome. The Romans had passed the law during the difficult Second Punic War when Hannibal was ravaging Italy. It was believed that a return to a stricter morality was necessary to avoid disaster. Now that the danger had passed, the women of Rome had risen up and demanded the law's repeal. In this speech, Cato expounds on the need to keep women under control of the traditional value system. The voters did not follow Cato's advice, however, and the law was repealed, which indicates that even in the early second century BC, the majority of Romans no longer shared Cato's views.

If every one of us as Roman citizen males had determined to protect the rights and power of a husband in the case of our own wives, we would have to spend less time debating on women as a whole. Now we have lost our freedom even at home to the "powerless" woman. This has happened not only in private but also even in our public places of business. Now, because we were unable to restrain them individually, we fear them as a group... [Discussion of how public demonstrations by the women of Rome have upset Cato because they are interfering with public business] ... Our ancestors passed laws requiring women transact all business (even private business) through a guardian. Women remained in the power (*manus*) of the parents, brothers, and husbands. We, on the other hand, allow them to take control of the state and to mix freely with the men in the forum, assemblies, and elections. Now we can see them filling the streets and intersections. They can be seen pressuring the tribunes of the people to make a motion and demanding the repeal of the law. If you give free rein to their unrestrained nature and uncontrollable spirit, there will be no reason to hope that they will ever set limits upon their licentious behavior. Look at how women are acting with such hostility over a law that is really one of the more insignificant that our ancestors created to limit feminine excess. What these women really desire is the freedom (of, if we should speak truthfully, the license) to do whatever they want. If they should win in this case, what will they not have the courage to attempt? Think back to all of the laws regarding women through which our ancestors tried to control women's license and subjugate them to the powers of their husbands. Even with all of these limitations, you are now scarcely able to control them. If you continue to allow these measures to fall away and perish one after another and in the end make women men's equals, do you believe that the world will be tolerable? The very moment they are given equality, they will become your superiors... [Cato makes the argument that by repealing the law, the state would weaken all of the laws. He also claims that greed and the competition that it creates are the root of all of the state's ills] . . . Do you want your wives to be involved in this kind of competition in which the rich want to have what no one else can afford and the poor spend more than they have so that they might not seem so poor? As soon as women begin to be ashamed of what they should not be, they will not be ashamed of what they should be. She will get what she can with her own means, but if she can't afford it with her own money, then she will ask her husband for the money. I pity the poor fellow. If he gives in to his wife's demands, the wife has won. If he does not give in, then he will have to watch her get the money from someone else.

#73: Egnatius Mecenius' Drunken Wife

Valerius Maximus, *Memorable Deeds and Sayings* 6.3.9
Written in the Early First Century AD

Roman society expected the law, husbands, fathers, and guardians to control women's behavior as it was believed women were unable to control themselves. In the following passage, a husband kills his wife because he finds her drinking. Valerius Maximus explains how society excused him because it was his duty to control his wife's behavior. It is impossible to know whether the anecdote reflects a real event, but in any case the story became a part of Roman folklore (the story is preserved in several sources).

Egnatius Mecenius killed his wife by beating her with a club because she had been drinking wine. Not a single person came forward to accuse him of murder. It was impossible, in fact, to find someone who felt that he had done anything wrong. Everyone believed that her punishment for her lack of sobriety was exemplary. Indeed any woman who immoderately thirsts after wine shuts the door on all virtues and opens herself to vice.

Negative Depictions of Women

Roman men tended to describe their wives in the glowing terms that reflected the traditional expectations of feminine behavior that had gone unchanged over the centuries. Roman literature, however, also contains examples of very negative depictions of women. These depictions generally follow the ancient belief that women lacked self-control and so were slaves to their baser desires. In all of the following accounts, the women described do not have a strong male figure who can control them. Either the male figure is not present at all or else the woman has cowed the man to make him subservient to her. Sempronia sided with Catiline in his attempt at revolution (#74). The miller's wife is just one (although extreme) example of an evil woman in Apuleius' novel *Metamorphoses* (#75). The final text is a selection of excerpts from Juvenal's scathing satire about women (#76). All of these texts exaggerate the evils of women, sometimes to a ridiculous degree, and leave as much of a distorted view of women as the overly positive descriptions of wives and daughters that appeared in the previous sections.

#74: The Evil Sempronia

Sallust, *The War against Catiline* 25
First Century BC

Sempronia was the sister of the Gracchi brothers, who had risen to political greatness with popular support only to be killed by the aristocracy for their revolutionary actions. There were also accusations that Sempronia sided with Catiline in his bid to overthrow the government. In this passage, the historian Sallust recounts the evils of the woman.

Among these women was Sempronia, who had often committed many crimes of masculine daring. This woman was very fortunate due to her birth; beauty; and, notably, her husband and children. She was trained in Greek and Latin literature. She could play the cithara and dance better than was becoming in a virtuous woman. She was also skilled in many other things that were more in the realm of luxury. All of these qualities were dearer to her than honor and chastity. It is by no means easy to determine whether she was more frugal with her money or her reputation. Her sexual desire was so keen that she was more often the one to pursue lovers than the one who was pursued. Often before her involvement in the present conspiracy she broke her word, defaulted on loans, and was an accomplice to murder. She often moved between the extremes of luxury and poverty. She did have a few somewhat praiseworthy talents. She could compose poetry; make jokes; and hold a conversation that was modest, tender, or shameful as needed. In short, she had in her much that was witty and charming.

#75: The Miller's Wife

Apuleius, *Metamorphoses* 9.14
Second Century AD

The negative depiction of women in Roman Literature sometimes goes as far as to describe them as evil, sexually voracious monsters. The second century AD author Apuleius' novel *The Metamorphoses* is filled with women characterized by their sexual insatiability. The witches Meroë (in book 1) and Pamphile (in book 2) use their magical arts to ensnare men. One aristocratic woman lusts for Lucius (the hero of the story, then in the form of a donkey) and pays to enjoy his sexual favors. Stories of wives engaging in adultery fill the novel. Apuleius' description of the adulterous miller's wife is especially enlightening regarding the stereotype of the lustful woman.

> Fortune had made a joke of this poor miller by giving him the most terrible wife possible, the worst of all women, who inflicted on him what seemed like a death penalty at home and in bed. It was so bad that I frequently groaned for him in silence. There was not a single vice that the absolutely worthless woman was lacking. Like some kind of filthy toilet, every kind of crime flowed straight into her. She was savage, perverse, man-hungry, drunken, stubborn, nagging, greedy in base forms of gain, and lavish in spending money in her lustful purposes. She was a liar and an enemy of marital fidelity. To top it off, she had rejected and spurned the gods and had latched onto the lies of another religion and worshiped a god called "the One and Only." She used a whole series of invented religious rituals to deceive everyone, including her miserable husband, so that she could be left alone to enjoy days full of drinking and prostitution.

#76: Juvenal's Satire against Women (*Satire* 6)

Late First/Early Second Centuries AD

Juvenal's sixth satire is certainly the most extreme case of the negative depiction of women in Roman literature. Throughout his satires, Juvenal pokes fun at society with his exaggerated view of the squalor of the city of Rome. The following passages come from a 660-line satire that accuses women of the foulest of crimes. The extreme negativity of these passages can be hard to read and should not be taken literally.

Lines 19–49: Juvenal Warns His Friend against Marriage

Step by step, Justice returned to the heavens and Chastity was her companion. These two sisters equally fled the earth. To ruffle another man's bed and to spoil the sanctity of the marriage bed, my friend, is an ancient and long-standing tradition. The first adulterers appeared during the Silver Age. Later, in the Iron Age, all of the other crimes came into existence. Even so, my friend, even though you know all about the problems of this degenerate age, you are engaged and plan to get married. Is it too late? Have you already had your hair cut for the ceremony by a master barber and put the ring on her finger? You used to be sane. Are you *really* getting married? Has some madness taken hold of you? Did a snake bite you? How could you prefer to trap yourself in a marriage when there are so many escape routes you could use to save yourself from this disaster? If escape is not possible, then there are many open windows in the tops of tall buildings out of which you could jump, not to mention the bridge downtown with the low side rails? These methods of suicide are easy and there are many more that I could mention as well. Do none of them appeal to you? Then would it not be better for you to just sleep with a pretty boy? A boy at least would not squabble with you at night or demand from you little gifts. You future wife will lie there on the bed and complain that you don't satisfy her sexually or moan as much as she demands.

The Julian Law rewarding large families fired up the notorious adulterer Ursidius. He got it in his head that he wanted a sweet little heir even though it would mean doing without the delicacies he was used to: fat pigeons, the beards of mullets, and the inheritances he conned out of lonely old ladies by sleeping with them. If Ursidius could find someone to marry, then why should you have any trouble? I suppose you are following the example of that notorious adulterer who used to be known for hiding in the closets of the pretty wives of old Roman husbands but now sticks his stupid neck out for the marital noose. And what is it that you are looking for? A wife with old-fashioned values! Doctors, come and suck out the poison that has made this man delusional! I vow that on my hands and knees I would worship Jupiter before his altar on the Capitoline Hill and slaughter a decorated bull to Juno if you actually find a wife of verified chastity!

Lines 82–112: A Senator's Wife Runs off to Egypt with Her Lover

Did you hear about Eppia? She was the wife of a senator but she ran off with a gladiator to Egyptian Pharos, the Nile, and the monstrous buildings of the Hellenistic kings. Such an act was enough to even make degenerate Egypt blush. This woman forgot all about her home, her husband, her sister, and not to mention her country. The fact that this shameless woman abandoned her weeping children is not as surprising as her willingness to leave the theatrical plays of Rome and her favorite actor Paris. As a child, she was brought up with every comfort; she slept on feather beds and segmented couches. She hated the sea. Now, she no longer cares about her reputation (a common occurrence among the aristocratic ladies of the present time). Now, with unswerving courage, she faces the waters of the Tyrrhenian Sea and the crashing waves of the ever-tumultuous Ionian Sea. When the purpose for enduring hardships is just and honest, then women become frightened and they freeze up with a terrified heart and can no longer stand on their trembling legs. When they turn to evil intentions, however, suddenly they develop a courageous spirit. If it had been her husband who had ordered it, she would have had a very hard time boarding the ship. The bilges make her sick and the sky above reels in her eyes. The same woman now follows after her low-class lover with an iron stomach. The woman who had vomited on her husband with seasickness now has dinner with the sailors and wanders along the deck and takes pleasure in helping with the rigging. What good-looking gallant set Eppia on fire? What youth captured her heart? What did she see in her lover to make her willing to be called a gladiator groupie? Here he is, her darling Sergius. He is the one with the raspy voice and a body that screams out for early retirement. His face is particularly deformed. His head shows multiple scars from his helmet, a huge lump sits on his nose, and his eyes constantly drip. But he is a GLADIATOR. That fact makes them all equal to the gorgeous Hyacinthus. This is what she preferred to her children, her country, her sister, and even her husband. It is the sword that they love. As soon as her Sergius gets his freedom and retires from the arena, she will lose interest and see him as nothing better than her former husband.

Lines 161–171: Virtuous Women are Usually Arrogant

Do you really think you will be able to find a worthy wife among the girls of today? Maybe you actually believe that you could find a woman who is beautiful, decent, rich, and fertile; who fills her house with portraits of her illustrious ancestors; or has her virginity more intact than all the Sabine women who, with disheveled hair, wept over their abduction by the Romans and whose fathers went to war to protect their virtue. I wish you the best of luck. That kind of woman is a rare bird indeed: like a black swan or something. But then who could stand a wife who was so virtuous? I would prefer, yes, I said prefer, a whore like Venustina than a virtuous Cornelia, the mother of the famous Gracchi. I just do not think that the virtuous Cornelia would be an acceptable trade for her family's reputation and noble ancestry. I realize that your family can boast about defeating Hannibal and conquering Africa and Carthage, but I would rather you just move along.

Lines 208–219: Women Who Torment Their Husbands

These days, women delight in torture. One may be on fire with lust but takes joy in tormenting her lover by making him wait and squirm. The conclusion is that the better and more desirable you are as a husband, the less virtuous your wife will be to you. You will never be able to give anything to anyone if your wife is unwilling; you will not be able to sell anything if she begs you not to; it is the same thing with making purchases if she says no. She will even involve herself in your personal life. One friend, now an old man, will be kept out of the house even though he has visited many times in the past. Pimps, gladiatorial agents, and even the gladiators themselves have freedom when it comes time to write out a will, but you will have to include more than one of your rivals for her love in your last will and testament.

Lines 268–278: Women Who Torment Their Husbands

The bed in which your wife sleeps is always filled with quarrels and complaints. Sleep is the most difficult thing to find there. In bed, a wife is a heavy burden to her husband, worse than a tigress that has lost her young. She feigns some unhappy groaning although she herself is guilty of all kinds of secret sins. Either she hates the slave boys or cries over some imagined mistress. She always is full of tears and has them waiting in reserve, ready to be called in at a moment's notice. You convince yourself that her tears are a sign of her love. You, you poor worm, try to please her and kiss away her tears. How many notes and messages from adulterous lovers would you find if you went through your wife's desk?

Lines 286–300: The Source of the Problem

You may ask where these monsters come from and what the source of their evil is. Once upon a time, humble fortunes kept Latin women chaste. Labor and short nights kept vice from entering their little huts. Their hands were worn and calloused from working at their knitting. They were also worried about their husbands who stood ready at the gates of the city awaiting the imminent arrival of the invading Hannibal. Now, however, we suffer the evils of a long peace. Luxury, more savage than war, has settled over our civilization and is taking vengeance on the world. From the time that Roman poverty perished, there has been no lack of crime and lustful deeds. The vices of Sybaris; Rhodes; Miletus; and even garlanded, drunken, and horny Tarentum all came to our fair city and its hills. It was dirty wealth that first brought foreign morals to Rome. Abundant riches have broken our generation with shameful self-indulgence.

Lines 434–456: Arrogant Women with Too Much Education

Worse still is the woman who sits down to dinner and praises Vergil and makes excuses for the suicidal Dido. She moves the conversation to the poets and compares them: on one side of the scale she places Vergil and in the other Homer. Grammatical experts yield to her. The orators give up. Everyone at the dinner is silent: even the lawyer is too afraid to speak. The other women are quiet too. So forceful is her shower of words that you would think that someone was clanging together some metal bowls and bells. No one needs to feel the need to get people's attention with a horn or trumpet when she is around. She alone could convince the moon to finish its course in the heavens. Wisdom sets limits even on honorable endeavors. If this woman really wanted to be considered eloquent, then she ought to tie her tunic up to the level of the middle of her legs and sacrifice a pig to the country deity Silvanus and pay the penny to bathe humbly in the public baths. A married woman ought to sit next to her husband at dinner and not speak in some elevated way or beat out a twisted argument with circular reasoning. She should not know all the details of history. There should be some details in the books she reads that she does not understand. I hate the woman who reads and re-reads the grammatical dictionary until she has it memorized. Such a woman's speech observes every rule of syntax and is so antiquated that there are parts of it that I can't even understand. Such a woman does not endear herself to her husband. She even criticizes the words of her uneducated lady friends and even corrects her husband's grammatical mistakes.

Lines 592–605: Poor Women Have Children; Rich Women Get Abortions

Poor women at least endure the difficulty of childbirth and tolerate all the hardships of motherhood that poverty thrusts upon them. The types of women who sleep in gilded beds hardly ever have children. So good are the skills of such a woman; so good are the drugs she can take to keep herself from getting pregnant or to kill the fetus in the womb. Cheer up, you luckless fellow, and give her the drug yourself, whatever it may be. If she had preferred to stay pregnant and let the babies kicking inside her damage her belly, then you might have become the father of an Ethiopian baby that soon would be the heir of your property even though you would be ashamed for it to be seen in public. I say nothing about the abandoned children, the pride and joy of some new family although they had originally been dumped off next to some filthy sewer grate. These children born in your household that you believe are your own, co-opted into your family, will someday run for the highest priesthoods although they look nothing like their father or the other aristocrats.

Empowered Women

Women of the first century BC enjoyed freedom unparalleled in earlier Roman history. They could inherit property, which they alone would possess and control, even without the need for a guardian. *Sine manu* marriages, in which the girl remained a dependent of her father, rather than be transferred to the family of her husband, were also becoming the norm. Among the lower classes, the traditional view of women meant little as it was often necessary for all members of a family to work in order to make a living (#77). I have also included the poems attributed to Sulpicia, the only female poet whose works have survived (#78).

#77: Working Women

First to Third Centuries AD

The financial realities of the lower classes also led to an increasing number of independent women who were forced to enter the workforce in order to earn enough money for their families to survive. The stay-at-home aristocratic wife, kept out of the political life of her husband, may have envied the poor woman for her freedom of movement outside her home and closer relationship with her husband. The following tombstone inscriptions illustrate the working women of the lower classes.

CIL 5.2542 (Ateste, Italy)

Sacred to the Spirits of the Dead; to Lucretia Placidia, freedwoman of Marcus, mender of clothes.

CIL 6.9214 (Rome)

Sellia Ephyre, maker and seller of gold-embroidered clothing on the *Via Sacra*.

CIL 6.9683 (Rome)

To the Spirits of the Dead; to Abudia Megiste, freedwoman of Marcus, most loyal; Marcus Abudius Luminaris, her patron and husband, put this up to her, a well-deserving woman. She was a seller of fruit and legumes at the central steps. Luminaris also dedicated this monument to himself, his freedmen, freedwomen, his posterity, and to Marcus Abudius Saturninus, his son, in the lesser Esquiline tribe of elders; he lived eight years.

CIL 6.9720 (Rome)

To Claudia Trophime, midwife; Titus Cassius Trophimus, her son, put this up to his most loyal mother; Tiberius Cassius Tropimianus also participated in memory of his grandmother as well as to her posterity; she lived seventy-five years, five months.

CIL 6.9801 (Rome)

To Aurelia Nais, freedwoman of Gaius, seller of fish in the Warehouse of Galba; Gaius Aurelius Phileros, freedman of Gaius and her patron and Lucius Valerius Secundus, freedman of Lucius, dedicated this monument.

CIL 6.10128 (Rome)

Sophe Theorobathylliana, lead dancer of a pantomime troupe.

CIL 6.37802 (Rome)

Vergilia Euphrosyne, freedwoman of Gaius, scribe.

AE 1973, 71 (Rome)

To [...?... (name lost)], olive oil and wine dealer in the province of Baetica, of incomparable chastity, and to Gnaeus Coelius Masculus, most pious father; Coelia Mascellina put this up to her parents.

CIL 8.24679 (Carthage, Africa Proconsularis)

Asyllia Polla, daughter of Lucius, medical doctor, is buried here. She lived sixty-five years; Euscius, her freedman, put this up at his own expense.

#78: The Poems of Sulpicia
First Century BC

From the first century BC come the writings of the only female poet to have survived intact from the classical period of Rome. Her name was Sulpicia, a young, unmarried woman of the upper class who moved in the literary circles of her day. In her poems, she describes her love of a young aristocratic boy she calls Cerinthus. The first poem is especially important because she directly addresses the question of traditional values for girls. The following is the complete corpus (six poems) of Sulpicia's poetry.

Poem 1

I have finally fallen in love. This is the kind of love that, if kept hidden, will benefit my reputation more but revealing it to someone else is likely to damage it. I prayed for love to Venus with my poetic talent and she brought it and dropped it in my bosom. Venus fulfilled her side of the bargain; now let me tell my story so that everyone can know. I did not want to put any of it down in sealed documents just for my beloved to read. It is nice to go against the grain, as it is tiresome for a woman to constantly force her appearance to fit her reputation. I only want to be thought worthy of my worthy love.

Poem 2

My birthday is here, and I hate it. I will have to spend it sadly on my family's wretched country estate, far away from my Cerinthus. What is sweeter than Rome? Could a country villa and the cold stream in Arrentine territory really be more suitable for a girl? Hey Messalla! You are keeping me on too short of a leash! Give me a break! There are good times and bad times for trips, cruel uncle. You take me away and I leave behind here my heart and soul and do not allow me to live at my own discretion.

Poem 3

Do you know that dreary trip your girlfriend was to suffer? It has been called off. Now I can spend my birthday in Rome! We can celebrate my birthday together! Even so, I am a bit suspicious. Is my staying in Rome what you really wanted?

Poem 4

Thanks a lot! You are so secure in our relationship that you feel you can take liberties at my expense and in the process have made me painfully aware of what a fool I was to fall for a guy like you. You seemed to be more concerned for that low-class whore in her slutty outfit than for Sulpicia, the daughter of Servius! Perhaps it is for the best. There are others who care for me, and while you were my boyfriend, Cerinthus, they have been worried that I might end up in the bed of some nobody.

Poem 5

Are you wracked with dutiful concern for your girlfriend, Cerinthus, now that a fever has gripped my tired body? I would never hope to get better from this sad disease unless I could believe that you would want me to recover. But what is the use of recovering if you really don't care that I am suffering.

Poem 6

I realize that I have been the object of your hot passion the past few days. I really do not deserve to be so loved, however, after I left you alone the other night. What a fool I was! I only left to hide my own passion for you.

Chapter 6: Children

The stereotype of a Roman woman as dutiful and chaste yet fertile stemmed from societal expectations for Romans to reproduce within the context of marriage. Ideally, Roman wives were expected to become pregnant as frequently as possible until infertility, death, or divorce made it impossible. The significance placed upon large families was in part attributable to the generally short life expectancy of adults as well as a high mortality rate of infants and children.

Constraints on Population Growth

Problems such as infertility, miscarriage, and stillbirth worked against Roman couples as they strove to produce children (Pliny the Younger's account of his wife's miscarriage, #79). There were also forms of contraception (such as that posited by Pliny the Elder, #80). Without the help of modern technology, Roman children often faced congenital health problems, undernourishment, and a legion of childhood diseases. As a result, as many as thirty percent of children born died before the age of one. Cornelius Fronto lost numerous children (#81). A soldier's wife from Pannonia had six children, but only one was still alive at the time of her death (#82). Pliny the Younger mourned the daughter of one his friends (#83). The high mortality rate continued during childhood (#84). Also covered in this section is the startling practice of child abandonment. Although there is insufficient evidence to know how widespread it was, abandonment of newborn infants on local garbage dumps or doorsteps seems to have been somewhat prevalent among members of the lower classes who may have not had the financial means to provide for a newborn (#85 and #86).

#79: Calpurnia's Miscarriage

Pliny the Younger, *Letters* 8.10.1–2
Early Second Century AD

Pliny the Younger was married three times, but none of his wives carried a baby to full term. Apparently, the closest Pliny ever came to fatherhood was with his third wife, Calpurnia, but she miscarried her first pregnancy before she even knew she was pregnant. Calpurnia was evidently very young at the time of her miscarriage. We do not know if Calpurnia was subsequently able to conceive or sustain a pregnancy, but Pliny's silence on the matter in his last letters might indicate that she never did. The following is the heartfelt letter Pliny wrote to his grandfather-in-law Calpurnius Fabatus after Calpurnia's miscarriage.

I know how much you want us to provide you with great-grandchildren, so you will be very sorry to hear that your granddaughter has had a miscarriage. Childishly, she did not realize she was pregnant and failed to take proper care of herself and did things she should not have done. She has paid for her mistake and seriously endangered her life. Therefore, as hard as it is to accept your old age, robbed of a descendent already conceived, you should thank the gods that, although they have denied you great-grandchildren for now, nevertheless they have spared your granddaughter's life. They have also shown that the hope for future children is certain, although the proof of her fertility has been unfortunate.

#80: Spiders Used as a Contraceptive

Pliny the Elder, *Natural History* 29.27 (85)
First Century AD

Despite the desire for pregnancy, the Romans also knew methods for artificially limiting childbirth. Frequent references by medical writers indicate that contraception was widely practiced. In the following passage, Pliny the Elder (Pliny the Younger's uncle and adoptive father) claims that a treatment involving worms taken from the head of a certain type of spider could prevent conception. Roman authors, however, sometimes disparage both forms of birth control because they undermined the traditional goal of the family to procreate. It is important to note also that Pliny mentions forms of contraception only for cases in which women were so fertile and had so many children that contraception was one method of allowing time to pass between pregnancies.

There is a certain type of spider the Greeks call the "Phalangion" although they sometimes refer to it as the "wolf spider." It is hairy with a very large head. When that head is cut open, it is said that inside there are two small worms. If these worms are put into a piece of deerskin and attached to a woman's body before sunrise, then she will not conceive. This is what Caecilius claims in his commentaries. This treatment lasts for a full year. I am obliged to say that this is only one of all of the methods of contraception because the fertility of some women is so rich with children that some rest needs to be given.

#81: Fronto's Lost Children

Cornelius Fronto, *On the Loss of His Grandson* 2
Middle of the Second Century AD

In the following letter addressed to his friend the future emperor Marcus Aurelius, Marcus Cornelius Fronto describes his own sad luck with children.

Fortune has plagued me with many sorrows of this kind throughout my entire life. I will pass over my other misfortunes to mention that I have lost five children, a fact that has made my time on Earth most wretched. I lost them one after another. I passed alternatively from having a single child to being childless, as I would only have another child once the previous one had died. As a result, I always lost my children without any remaining consolation and would father another child with my grief still fresh from the death of the last one.

#82: A Woman from Aquincum

CIL 3.3572 (Aquincum, Pannonia)
Second or Third Century AD

The effects of the high infant mortality rate can be seen frequently in the epigraphic record. The following inscription from the Danube commemorates the death of a twenty-seven-year-old woman. During her eighteen years of marriage, she produced six children, but only one survived her.

Here is buried a matron whose name, Veturia, matched her family. She was the wife of Fortunatus. Her father was Veturius. The poor woman was twenty-seven years old at the time of her death and she had been married for sixteen years. She slept with one man during her life and was married only once. She gave birth to six children, but only one was still alive at the time of her death. Titus Julius Fortunatus, centurion of the Second Legion *Adiutrix* Loyal and Faithful put this up to his incomparable and virtuous wife out of his own loyalty.

#83: The Death of a Young Girl

Pliny the Younger, *Letters* 5.16.1–6
Early Second Century AD

In this letter, Pliny the Younger tells his friend that the daughter of a mutual friend has died. He recounts the virtues of the young girl and demonstrates how she was in many ways wise beyond her years. As so often, we see in this letter a reflection of the traditional view of virtues Roman society imposed upon its members. Also interesting is the note that the girl, only thirteen at the time of her death, was betrothed and about to be married.

Most sadly I write to tell you that the younger daughter of our friend Fundanus has died. I have never before known a young girl to be more playful and loveable. She seemed worthy not only of a longer life but almost an everlasting one. She had not yet reached her fourteenth birthday but already she was in possession of wisdom of someone much older. She combined the seriousness of a matron with the sweetness of a young girl and a maiden's modesty. She lovingly would cling to her father's neck and with friendliness and modesty she embraced her father's friends. She showed respect to her nurses, tutors (*paedagogi*), and teachers, each according to their duties. She read with eagerness and intelligence. She indulged in her playing only sparingly and cautiously. She endured her final illness with self-control, patience, and bravery and followed all of her doctor's orders. She spoke words of encouragement to her sister and father, and when her body had lost all strength she sustained herself with the vigor of her mind. Thus she endured right up until the very end. Neither the long illness nor the fear of death broke her. It was this final show of strength that has left us more frequent and heavier reasons for missing her and grief at her loss. Oh wholly sad and harsh death! The timing of her death was more unfortunate than the death itself! She had been betrothed to an excellent young man. The day of their wedding was set. We had received our invitations. How sad that our joy for her coming marriage should be changed to grief over her funeral.

#84: Inscriptions of Children Who Died Young

First to Third Centuries AD

The following are inscriptions of children who died at a young age. As in Pliny the Younger's letter, these texts exemplify the kinds of virtues attributed to young children and the mourning of the parents.

CIL 6.28044 (Rome)

Sacred to the Spirits of the Dead; to Lucius Valerius, an infant, who was taken away unexpectedly. He was born during the sixth hour of the night, a sign of a fate not yet clear. He lived seventy-one days. He died at the sixth hour of the night. I hope that your family, oh reader, may be happy. The burial plot is 2.3 feet wide and 2.3 feet deep.

CIL 6.17313 (Rome)

To the Spirits of the Dead of Eucopio, who lived six months, three days, the sweetest, most delightful, most pleasant infant, who had not yet learned to talk; Terminalis, born a slave, and Sosipatra his parents, made this for their most delightful boy Lucius Curius.

AE 1988, 306 (Ephesus, Asia Minor)

To the Spirits of the Dead of Publius Clodius Celsianus, a handsome and attractive infant, who lived fifteen months; his grandmother Clodia Ephesia and his most unlucky parents Macedo and Celsa dedicated this.

CIL 6.21113 (Rome)

To the Spirits of the Dead of Larcia Aprylla, who lived five years, ten months, eighteen days; Aulus Larcius Aprio and Philumene made this for their sweetest, most delightful daughter as well as to themselves and their posterity.

AE 1984, 347 (Pagus Interpromium, Samnium, Italy)

Sacred to the Spirits of the Dead. Antinoe and Phoebe were two sisters and fellow slaves of the Marcus Volusius and Aemilianus Volusius. They are now buried here. Phoebe lived six years, ten months, and fifteen days. Antinoe lived one year and twenty days. Phoebus and Rhodope (along with Tertius) put this up to their most dutiful daughters.

CIL 5.1808 (Maniago, Italy)

To Gaius Virginius Pulcher, son of Gaius, who lived ten years, two months, six days; Gaius Virginius Marcellinus, son of Gaius, and Lollia Prisca, daughter of Lucius, most unlucky parents, dedicated this to their sweetest and incomparable little son.

CIL 6.28695 (Rome)

To Vettia Chryses, daughter of Gaius; I ask you passerby to not walk over the remains of the miserable infant buried here in the ground. She will be mourned whenever people remember how her youth was taken from her. The parents who gave birth to her mourn for her. She was born for no better reason other than that she now undeservedly lies here. Her bones have become ashes, and the daughter can no longer talk to her parents.

#85: The Practice of Child Abandonment

Oxyrhynchus Papyrus 744
Written in 1 BC

The following papyrus fragment from Egypt documents a letter containing instructions from a man named Hilario to his sister Alis to abandon her unborn child if it is a girl. Hilario (perhaps in his role as *paterfamilias*) gives no reason for his wishes. Cases in which children were abandoned because the father believed the child to be illegitimate are known. Cases such as the one here, however, involving members of the lower classes may point to financial restraints. Although it is not certain, Hilario may have preferred to abandon a girl because of the added expense of the wedding dowry for daughters. Abandonment was not necessarily a death sentence, however. There is evidence that slave traders or even other couples may have frequented common locations of child abandonment.

> Hilario sends to his sister Alis many greetings, also to Berous his wife and Apollonarion. Know that I am still in Alexandria. Please do not be overly concerned for me. If the rest of my unit leaves, I will remain in Alexandria. I ask and implore you to take care of the infant. As soon as I receive my pay, I will send it up to you. If you give birth, I wish you the best of luck. If the child is a boy, keep it. If it is a girl, abandon it. You said to Aphrodisias, "Don't forget me." How could I forget you? I ask you therefore not to worry. Sent in the twenty-ninth year of Caesar on the twenty-third of Payni.

#86: Orders to Expose a Girl

Apuleius, *Metamorphoses* 10.23
Second Century AD

Apuleius, borrowing themes from Greek and Roman comedy, describes how a father, before going on a journey, instructed his wife to expose their unborn child if it should be a girl. When a girl was born, the mother, unwilling to abandon her, gave the child to neighbors to rear.

> When the father was preparing to go out of town, he instructed his wife (who was pregnant at the time) to kill the child immediately after birth if she should give birth to a girl. While her husband was away, the woman did give birth to a girl. But the woman, overcome by her instinctive love for her child, decided to disobey her husband and gave the daughter to neighbors to rear as their own. When her husband returned home, the woman claimed that she had given birth to a daughter and killed the baby.

Birth and Infancy

This section contains a number of sources related to birth and infancy. When a mother was ready to give birth, a professional midwife was called in to the home to deliver the child. Childbirth was medically risky, and many women (and many infants) died during or after labor (#87 and #88). While the parents were often the primary caregivers of young children, many families, especially those of the upper classes, entrusted at least some of the responsibilities to others. While many authors praise a woman for breastfeeding her own child (#89, #90, and #91), it was very common for families to employ a wet nurse (#92 and #93).

#87: Aeturnia Zotica Dies in Childbirth

CIL 3.6759 (Ancyra, Galatia)
Second or Third Century AD

The following inscription memorializes a woman named Aeturnia Zotica who died from complications resulting from childbirth at the young age of fifteen years.

> Sacred to the Spirits of the Dead of Aeturnia Zotica; Annius Flavianus, decurial attendant and lector of Fufidius Pollio, governor of Galatia, made this for his well-deserving wife who lived fifteen years, five months, thirteen days. She died sixteen days after her first childbirth. Her son survived.

#88: The Death of Two Women in Childbirth

Pliny the Younger, *Letters* 4.21.1–2
Early Second Century AD

In this letter, Pliny mourns the death of two daughters of one of his friends. The girls seem to have been young and probably had only recently married.

> Sad and harsh is the calamity that befell the sisters of Helvidius! Both died in childbirth. Both died delivering daughters. I am afflicted with grief, but yet I do not mourn too much. Their deaths are, nevertheless, upsetting for me, seeing as how they died in their prime and in their most productive childbearing years. I am especially upset for the lot of the infants who were immediately, as soon as they were born, bereft of their mothers. I also feel sorry for their husbands who have lost their wives.

#89: Breastfeeding Children

Aulus Gellius, *Attic Nights* 12.1.4–6, 22–23
Second Century AD

In the following passage from Aulus Gellius' *Attic Nights*, the Philosopher Favorinus goes to the house of an aristocratic family to congratulate the father on the occasion of the birth of a son. During his visit, he asks about the status of the mother and whether she plans to personally breastfeed her son. When he hears that the mother prefers not to breastfeed her baby, Favorinus expresses his concern.

Favorinus asked how long the birth had taken and how difficult the labor pains had been. He learned that the girl, exhausted from the delivery and being awake from so long, was now sleeping. Favorinus then began to speak more at length and said "I have no doubt that your wife will breastfeed the child with her own milk." The mother of the girl, however, explained that they had decided to spare the girl and provide wet nurses so that the girl, already worn out by the difficult birth, would not have to add the heavy and difficult burden of nursing the baby to her labors. Favorinus replied, "I beg you, woman, let the girl take on the whole and entire role of mother for her new son. For it would be an imperfect and reduced motherhood and contrary to nature to allow a girl to give birth but then take a major part of that motherhood away from her.... When a child is given over to someone else and removed from the mother's sight, the mother begins to gradually lose some of the strength of her maternal instinct. Every sound of her impatient anxiety for her baby is silenced. If a mother hands over her child to some other woman to nurse, soon she begins to experience a loss of feeling for the child. There is little difference between a woman who uses a wet nurse and a mother whose child has died. In addition, the feelings of love and companionship of the infant itself rest wholly in the one by whom it is nursed. Soon the child, just as happens in the case of children that are exposed at birth, loses any feeling for his birth mother. For that reason, once the elements of natural motherly love are lost and destroyed, to whatever extent the child is brought up to love its father and mother, that love is more likely than not a natural form of love but one that is polite and obligatory.

#90: Cato's Wife

Plutarch, *Lives*, *Cato the Elder* 20
Written in the Late First Century AD Describing
the Third/Second Centuries BC

Plutarch's account of Cato's wife reflects Favorinus' opinion that breastfeeding helped to form the bond between mother and child. Roman history forever remembers Cato as a bastion of old Roman conservatism. It is likely, therefore, that

Cato's wife's feelings regarding breastfeeding her own children reflect the traditional Roman view.

> After his son was born, there was no duty so necessary (unless it was some kind of state business) that it prevented him from being present when his wife bathed or dressed his infant son. His wife always breast fed her son with her own milk. Indeed, she would often nurse the children of her slaves in order to produce in them a natural love for her son since they had in infancy shared the same milk.

#91: A Praise-Worthy Mother

CIL 6.19128 (Rome)
Second or Third Century AD

In this funerary inscription, a woman breastfeeding her own child is numbered amongst her virtues.

> To Graxia Alexandria, a woman of exemplary virtue and chastity, who nursed her children with her own milk; Pudens, a freedman of the emperor, her husband, dedicated this to her. She lived twenty-four years, three months, sixteen days.

#92: Roman *Nutrices*

First to Third Centuries AD

Despite the traditional view that Roman mothers should breastfeed their own children, the frequent appearances of wet nurses (*nutrices*) in literature and inscriptions indicates that families frequently employed or owned wet nurses. The following texts preserve the memory of several such *nutrices*. The first text mentions a wet nurse from a prestigious aristocratic family. The second seems to commemorate two (most likely successive) wives of the same man, the second of whom began as the *nutrix* of his children. The final text demonstrates how in larger households (in this case that of the emperor himself), the child could be exposed to a wide array of specialized caregivers.

CIL 6.16450 (Rome)

> To the Spirits of the Dead; To Sergia Cornelia Sabina, freedwoman of Sergius; Sergius Cornelius Dolabella Metillianus made this for his well-deserving nurse and "mamma."

AE 1960, 190 (Valhelas, Lusitania)

Sacred to the Spirits of the Dead; Proculinus, the slave of Proculus, dedicated this to himself and his most devoted wives Valeria and Amabilis who was the *nutrix* of my sons.

CIL 6.37752 (Rome)

To Tiberius Claudius Eunus, freedman of the emperor and cradle-rocker of the emperor Nero; to Tiberius Julius Secundus, freedman of the emperor, ear doctor; to Claudia Cedne, freedwoman of the emperor and wet nurse; to Claudia Hermione, born a slave; Tiberius Julius Eunus and Tiberius Claudius Duter made this for their parents, for their *verna* [a slave born into slavery] Tiberius Claudius Felix, and their freedmen, freedwomen, and their posterity.

#93: A Proper *Nutrix*

Quintilian, *On Oratory* 1.1.4–5
Late First Century AD

In many wealthier houses, the wet nurse also served as a nanny after the child had been weaned. As a result, the nurse was one of the most important influences on the young child. In this text, the teacher Quintilian recommends that wet nurses be able to speak clearly so that the child would learn to talk correctly.

When considering the character of prospective *nutrices*, nothing should be given a higher priority than that she should speak correctly. Her words are the first thing the child will hear. Her words are also what the child will try to speak by imitation. We by nature hold on most tightly to those things which we learn with our infant minds. Just like a taste that is absorbed by a new vessel tends to stay with it forever and the natural whiteness of wool is impossible to completely remove when it is dyed. Also, the worse tends to stick more stubbornly and the good more easily turns to the worse. When were you ever really able to change mistakes into something good? Therefore, do not allow your child to make a habit of something inferior, even if he is just an infant. It will be very difficult to correct him when he is older.

Childhood

Roman children kept themselves entertained by playing games with their siblings or friends. Seneca describes some of the games children played (#94).

As young children, boys would typically wear the *toga praetexta*, a toga with a purple stripe. When the boy's family decided to celebrate his coming of age (usually in their mid-teens), they would hold a ceremony in which the boy replaced his boyhood toga with a fully white adult toga, the *toga virilis* (#95).

#94: Childhood Games

Seneca, *On the Constancy of the Wise Man* 12.2
First Century AD

In this passage, Seneca lists a number of childhood activities to draw a comparison between adults and children.

> There is no one who can truly say that there is a major difference between adults and children. Children are greedy for knucklebones, nuts, and penny coins. Adults on the other hand lust after gold, silver, and land. Children play amongst themselves at being magistrates. They wear the senatorial toga and make imitation *fasces* and give speeches. Adults play the same things for real in the election places, forum, and senate house. Children build castles on the beach from mounds of sand. Adults work at their great projects and pile up stones to build walls and ceilings and in so doing convert what should be a simple protection for the body into a danger.

#95: A Dedication in Honor of a Child's Assumption of the *Toga Virilis*

CIL 6.41182 (Rome)
First to Third Centuries AD

This inscription is a dedication in honor of one boy's assumption of the *toga virilis*.

> In honor of the *toga virilis* of Lucius Clodius Tineius Pupienus Bassus, a senatorial young man; Tineius Eubulus, freedman of his mother, dedicated this along with the rest of his family.

Education

A child's formal education generally began at the age of seven. Although the conservative Cato the Elder preferred to teach his son himself (#96), those with the means would enter a school run by an elementary teacher (the *litterator* or *magister*). Although rare in Rome's early history, elementary schools were quite common by the late Republic. The term "school," however, is used loosely, as there were probably no buildings dedicated to elementary education. Instead, the teacher and his pupils would conduct their lessons in a public portico or corner of the forum (#100). Classes began very early in the morning. The curriculum included reading, basic writing, math, and history (used to illustrate basic morality). The rich often had slave teachers living in their homes (#102; see also #99 for the slave *paedagogus*). The orator Quintilian includes a section in his book *On Oratory* describing his theories of early childhood education (#97; see also #101 for his discouragement of the use of corporal punishment). One young aristocratic boy demonstrated poetic talent before his untimely death at the age of eleven (#98). Around the age of fourteen or fifteen, boys (but girls very rarely) left the elementary school of the *litterator* and began their rhetorical training under a *grammaticus* (#103). Under this person's tutelage, students improved their reading, writing, and speaking skills. They read and memorized great works of literature and philosophy, especially those works with moral lessons. After the *grammaticus*, families hoping their child would embark upon a public career often sent their child to a professional teacher of oratory, a *rhetor*. Schools of oratory, such as that of Quintilian, were often in major urban centers (#104 and #105).

#96: Cato Educates his Son

Plutarch, *Lives, Cato the Elder* 20
Written in the Late First Century AD Describing
the Third/Second Centuries BC

Cato the Elder took a very conservative view of his son's education and preferred to teach him himself. The subjects Cato chose for his son also reflect a desire to bring up his son in a traditional Roman way.

> When his son came of age, Cato took charge and educated his child himself. He did this despite the fact that he had a trained slave teacher named Chilo who had the job of teaching many other children. Cato did not think it appropriate, as he says in his own writings, for his son to be told he is wrong or have his ears pulled by a slave when the slave thinks the child is learning his lessons too slowly. He also did not think it right that he be in a debt of thanks to a slave for something as valuable as the education of his son. Cato therefore taught his son grammar, law, and athletics. As far as athletics were concerned, he not only taught his son how to throw a javelin, to fight in armor, and ride a horse, but also how to box, to endure heat and cold, and swim through the eddies and rough waters of the swift Tiber River. He himself claims how he wrote his histories in his own hand with large letters so that his son might have at home the resources necessary to learn about Rome's ancient traditions and heroes. Cato avoided using foul language in the presence of his son as much as he would when with the Vestal Virgins. He would also never bathe while his son was in the room. This indeed seems to have been the custom with the Romans

of the time. In those days, sons-in-law took care not to bathe in the presence of their fathers-in-law so as not to see each other naked. Later, however, when they learned how the Greeks exercised naked, they began to do the same in imitation of the Greeks, even if women were present.

#97: Theories on Early Childhood Education

Quintilian, *On Oratory* 1.1.12–14, 20, 24–26
Late First Century AD

These passages from Quintilian's lengthy work on education illustrate some of his theories regarding the education of young children.

I prefer a child be instructed in the Greek language right from the beginning because he will learn Latin, which is the language of everyday life, whether we want him to or not. It also seems right that the child work on Greek subjects first since subjects based in Latin are derived from the Greek. I would not, however, recommend the child should speak and read Greek exclusively (a practice that is relatively common these days). Doing so can lead to many errors in speech in Latin. They are more liable to speak with a foreign accent and their speech can become flooded with Greek idioms. These problems can be difficult to remove when speaking in a different language. Therefore, the study of Latin should follow closely the study of Greek. As a result, with equal attention to both languages, the child will learn both and neither will cause problems for the other...

I am keenly aware of how receptive children of different ages are to learning. I firmly believe that the young should not be given work that was too difficult too early. The most important thing is to take care that young children learn to love their schoolwork, or at least not to hate it. In doing so, they will less likely in their later years feel bitterness regarding what he experienced as a young child. Education should be fun. Children should be questioned and praised and learn how to be happy when they have done well. At times when a child is less willing to learn, the teacher should turn his attention to another student so that the unwilling child should become envious. Sometimes the child should have to compete so that he can feel that he has won more often than he has lost. The child should be encouraged with the kinds of rewards that would appeal to a child of his age...

Although it is in general use today, I am not at all happy with the practice of teaching children the names of the letters and their order in the alphabet before their forms. This method hinders the child's ability to recognize letters later since they do not focus on the shapes as long as they allow themselves to rely on their earlier memorization of the alphabet. It is for this reason that teachers, after they believe their students have correctly memorized the alphabet, instruct their students to then write out the alphabet backwards and in

various other arrangements until they can recognize the letters from appearance rather than from their order in the alphabet. Therefore, I recommend that
children be taught the shapes and names of the letters at the same time, just as
they learn to recognize people. My objection to this method of teaching the
alphabet does not carry over to teaching children the sounds of the letters. I do
indeed approve of giving children ivory pieces in the shape of letters to play
with as a method of teaching them letter sounds. This follows my usual preference for making education a delight to children of a very young age. Touching,
looking at, and naming the letters become games for the child.

#98: A Young Poetic Talent

CIL 6.33976 (Rome)
Late First Century AD

The following inscription celebrates a young boy who achieved great poetic
achievements before his untimely death. The stone includes a transcript of the boy's
extemporaneous verses.

> Sacred to the Spirits of the Dead; to Quintus Sulpicius Maximus, son of Quin-
> tus, of the Claudian tribe. He was born in Rome and lived eleven years, five
> months, and twelve days. At the third holding of the Capitoline Games [AD
> 94] in a competition of fifty-two Greek poets, he won favor on account of his
> young age. He inspired everyone with admiration for his poetic talent and
> left the competition with honor. The verses he composed extemporaneously
> have been inscribed on this stone so that his parents' feelings can be seen as
> genuine. Quintus Sulpicius Eugramus and Licinia Ianuaria, his most unlucky
> parents, put this up to their most dutiful son as well as for themselves and their
> descendants.

#99: The *Paedagogus*

Quintilian, *On Oratory* 1.1.8–9
Late First Century AD

In many wealthy Roman households, a slave called a *paedagogus* accompanied the
child to school and kept him focused on his studies. This slave could also help
with the child's education. In this passage, the educator Quintilian gives advice on
choosing a suitable *paedagogus* for a child.

> As far as *paedagogi* are concerned, I would recommend that they be well edu-
> cated. If they are not, then it is very important that they should know they are

not educated. The worst *paedagogi* are ones who have received an education barely beyond learning the alphabet but believe incorrectly that they have a more profound knowledge. These often think it below their dignity to play the part of teaching and instead, believing they are now in a position of authority over the child (an idea *paedagogi* often arrogantly take on), assume a domineering and sometimes cruel attitude as they pass on their stupid notions to the child. The same can happen in the area of moral upbringing. For example, it is said that Alexander the Great learned some bad habits from his *paedagogus*, a Babylonian named Diogenes. Because Alexander learned these habits at a young age, he stubbornly clung to them for the rest of life, even when he was the most powerful king in the world.

#100: A Difficult Classroom

Martial, *Epigrams* 9.68
Late First Century AD

The poet Martial wrote the following epigram about a nearby school. Teachers often resorted to corporal punishment of their students. These beatings seem to have left a lasting impression, figuratively as well as literally, on many youths.

What have I ever done to you, cursed elementary school teacher? You have a face that every young boy and girl hates. Not yet have the crested roosters broken the silence when you are already thundering with your savage yelling and beatings as loudly as the bronze echoes with hammering strokes when the artist attaches the bronze image of a lawyer to the statue of his horse. The shouting in the Colosseum is quieter when a victorious gladiator's fans cheer him on. Your neighbors ask you to let them get some sleep. Maybe I do not need to sleep the whole night; a little insomnia is not too much to worry about, but to spend the whole night awake is terrible! Send your students home! Would you be willing, you chattering fool, to keep your mouth shut for the same price as you receive for shouting?

#101: Quintilian's Discouragement of Beating Students

Quintilian, *On Oratory* 2.4.10–12
Late First Century AD

Certainly not every teacher treated his students as harshly as Martial's shouting schoolmaster, but there seems to have been enough of them to warrant Quintilian's advice to avoid fear and corporal punishment in favor of inducements and persuasion.

It would not seem out of place for me to advise you not to use harsh punishment to correct students' mistakes. Such punishment can cause the student to despair of ever getting the right answer. It may even drive them to feel negatively toward their school lessons and finally to hate them altogether. The worst thing about this is that the student will accomplish nothing as long he is afraid of everything. . . . The teacher therefore should be kind in the case of young students especially. Correction, which is by nature sometimes harsh, should be applied with a gentle hand. Praise the student sometimes. Endure some mistakes but correct others. In the case of correction, however, be sure to explain the reason a change needs to be made. It is even useful sometimes to illustrate to the student the reasons for the change by bringing in some experience from the teacher's own past. Sometimes it will be useful for the teacher himself to dictate all of the material so that the child can imitate the dictation and perhaps in the end grow to love the material and take ownership of it.

#102: Some Teachers

First to Third Centuries AD

Teachers themselves were generally of low social status and relied upon the fees they charged their pupils in order to survive. The following are some examples of teachers known only from their tombstones.

CIL 2.2236 (Corduba, Baetica)

Sacred to the Spirits of the Dead; Domitius Isquilinus, Greek grammar teacher who lived 101 years is buried here. May the earth rest lightly over him.

CIL 2.3872 (Saguntum, Spain)

To the Spirits of the Dead of Lucius Aelius Caerialis, teacher of the literary arts; Lucius Aelius Aelianus, his freedman, put this up to his well-deserving patron. He lived eighty-five years.

CIL 13.1393 (Augustoritum, Aquitania)

Here lies Blaesianus Biturix, trainer of the literary arts and teacher of morals as well a lover of the Muses. His body is now wrapped in eternal sleep.

#103: Pliny Finds a Rhetorical Trainer for a Friend's Son

Pliny the Younger, *Letters* 3.3
Early Second Century AD

In this letter, a family friend asks Pliny to find a teacher for her son. Pliny moved in the literary circles of Rome and seems to have an acquaintance with some of the best teachers.

Your son will grow up to be great like all the other members of your family if he should be given a proper education by someone who is a skilled teacher. Until now, his youth has kept your son at home where he had private tutors. There, he had little or even no opportunity for straying. Now, however, his studies can only be advanced by leaving home. And so we must look around for a Latin rhetorical trainer whose school should be a model of severity, modesty, and especially moral correctness. It is a fact that this boy has grown up to be very good-looking with the clear benefits of nature and fortune. Therefore, it is important that we not only find a teacher for someone at this precarious time of life but also a guardian and moral trainer. I would therefore recommend for your consideration Julius Genitor. I have great affection for this man. My decision does not come from my affection but rather my affection comes from my decision. He is a man free of faults. Indeed he may be a little too bristly and serious for the license of our times. As far as his eloquence is concerned, you can trust the many people who have witnessed it firsthand because his ability to speak is public knowledge and always on display. The private lives of people, however, are usually buried deep and have many hiding places, but I can vouch for Genitor's character. You son will hear nothing from this man except for things by which he will profit. He will learn nothing that he would be better off not learning. He will hear from Genitor no less than he would from you or me of how he must live up to his ancestors and family's legacy. With the gods willing, then, entrust your son over to a teacher from whom he will first learn morals and then eloquence. It is difficult to learn eloquence without an understanding of morals.

#104: Sending Students to the Schools of Oratory

Quintilian, *On Oratory* 2.1
Late First Century AD

In the following passage, Quintilian explains the differences between the *grammaticus* and the *rhetor* and complains that there is a trend in which parents wait to send their child to the *rhetor* until the child is older than the normal age.

There is a practice going around of sending students to the teachers of oratory later than is reasonable. This practice has become more common as time
goes on. It is now always the case with students of Latin oratory and is sometimes also with Greek as well. There seems to be two reasons for this. First,
the *rhetores*, especially the ones in Latin, have started abandoning some of
their original subjects and the *grammatici* have taken on subjects that were
not always theirs. On the one hand, as far as the delivery of speeches goes,
rhetores accept as part of their job description teaching students both the
theory and practice of public speaking. They do, however, limit the scope of
their training to matters of deliberation and judicial matters and look down
on other topics as beneath their professional ability. *Grammatici* on the other
hand are not satisfied with the disciplines that originally the *rhetores* left to
them (something we should perhaps be thankful for) and have begun teaching public speaking in the areas of character description and persuasion,
areas in which the greatest burden is placed upon the speaker. Thus, it has
happened that the subjects that originally came earlier in a youth's education have been most recently moved to the later stages. As a result, students
who are old enough for more advanced studies have been kept back in their
education and have begun to learn the art of oratory from the *grammaticus*.
Thus, the big joke now is that a student will not be sent to a teacher of public
speaking until he knows how to speak in public.

#105: A Student in the School of the Emperor

CIL 6.8991 (Rome)
Mid-Second Century AD

The schools in Rome and especially Athens attracted the best students and teachers. The emperors, eager to train new generations of senatorial and equestrian
bureaucrats with knowledge of jurisprudence, financially assisted many schools.
The following inscription illustrates the strong desire of some people for a good
education, as well as how the emperor often acted as a patron of education. The
emperor Hadrian traveled throughout the empire and spent a considerable amount
of time in Athens. The student commemorated here, perhaps the son of a freedwoman, joined what was probably a school of oratory whose members traveled
with the emperor.

Lucius Marius Vitalis, son of Lucius; lived seventeen years, fifty-five days; having gone through my elementary education, I persuaded my parents to let me
learn the art of oratory. I therefore left Rome in the entourage of the emperor
Hadrian. While I was studying, the fates envied me, snatched me away from
my studies, and dropped me in this place (death). My mother Maria Malchis,
most unlucky, made this for her most virtuous son.

Roman Pets

Ancient texts and funerary art suggest that the Romans kept animals for personal enjoyment (#106). Texts suggest that Romans kept a wide range of pets, from monkeys, horses, and foxes, to cats, fish, and a wide variety of birds (both songbirds, such as nightingales and sparrows, and birds which could be taught to speak, such as crows and magpies). The wealthy were known to have constructed aviaries and fishponds for holding and displaying their pets, which were often not only regarded as sources of personal pleasure, but also as status symbols. Pet dogs were sometimes depicted on funerary monuments, usually in conjunction with children (#107 and #108).

#106: A Dog Fight

Petronius, *Satyricon* 64
First Century AD

One of the most favored species of pet was the dog. The ancient authors classified dogs into three general categories: hunting dogs, watchdogs, and pet dogs. Some of the more well-known breeds were imported from the East, including the Laconian and Cretan hounds (good hunting dogs), and the Molossian hound (a large watchdog, similar to the modern mastiff breed). Ancient authors often describe pet dogs as small, white in color, with long, silky hair and a curled tail. Not every pet dog was white in color, however. In Petronius' *Satyricon*, Trimalchio's pet slave boy Croesus owns a pet dog of his own, described as a fat, black puppy named, rather ironically, Margarita ("Pearl"). In this passage from the novel, the slave boy Croesus unwisely attempts to incite his puppy against Scylax, Trimalchio's ferocious watchdog (probably a Molossian).

Trimalchio imitated a trumpeter and turned to his pet slave boy named Croesus, a bleary-eyed boy with rotten teeth. Croesus was playing with a small, black, disgustingly fat puppy. He wrapped the puppy up in a green scarf and put half of a piece of bread in front of it on the couch. When the puppy refused to eat the bread (he was already sick from overfeeding), the boy force-fed it. Trimalchio, watching Croesus, was reminded of his own duty and ordered that Scylax, the "guardian of house and family," be brought in. Without delay, a huge dog was led in on a chain. The porter kicked Scylax to get it to lie down and it stretched out in front of the table. Trimalchio threw it a piece of white bread and said, "No one in my household loves me more." Croesus, upset because his master had praised Scylax so much, put his puppy on the ground and encouraged it to attack Scylax. Scylax fell back on his canine nature and filled the dining room with loud barking and nearly tore apart Croesus' puppy (named Margarita). Nor was the ruckus confined to the fight. In the commotion, a candelabrum fell over onto the table and broke all of the crystal cups and spewed hot wax on several dinner guests. Trimalchio, in order not to seem upset by the situation, kissed the boy and ordered him to climb onto his back. The boy did not delay but used Trimalchio like a horse and slapped his master's shoulders with his palm to get him moving.

Figure 6.1 Tombstone Depicting a Pet Dog
(Getty Museum).

#107: Image of a Puppy on a Girl's Tombstone

Second or Third Century AD

Figure 6.1 is a relief from a tomb preserved in the Getty Museum. It shows an image of what probably was a pet dog. It is interesting to note that the dog appears alone on the stone, with no people or other images, suggesting the high regard the owner or dedicator had for the animal. The relief commemorates Helena, an *alumna*. If we assume that this dog was her pet, it is significant, because it demonstrates that although pets were more frequently recorded in an upper-class context, even those of low social status could enjoy them.

#108: A Tombstone to a Dog

Anthologia Latina 1512
Date Unknown

A few epitaphs are recorded which were apparently dedicated to deceased pet dogs. This text records the kind of affection people could have for their dogs.

> How sweet she was, how kind, who while she was living, was lying on my chest always a partner in my dreams and in my bed. The day that you died was indeed a terrible day, Myia! Sometimes you would bark unrestrained, if some rival was near your mistress. The day that you died was indeed a terrible day, Myia! Now a deep tomb holds you. You are not able either to bark or to jump up. You can no longer show your affection for me with your gentle bites.

Chapter 7: Slaves

Slaves were a common sight in the cities of the empire as they fulfilled a variety of duties in the home and the government. Slaves came from a variety of sources. Prisoners of war were enslaved and sold at auction. Exposed children were often picked up by slave traders, trained, and then sold. Even citizens could become a slave due to the inability to repay debts, or as a criminal punishment. Yet, in ancient Rome, it was possible to achieve freedom after being enslaved. Indeed, it was quite common for masters to manumit some or even all of their slaves. Yet, the life of a Roman slave was often difficult and unpleasant. Slaves were viewed legally as property in the power of the *paterfamilias*. Masters had the right to beat, torture, abuse, and even kill the slaves in their power, although the society developed an ever-growing number of social and legal constraints upon mistreatment.

The Institution of Slavery

In Roman law, a slave was the possession of another person and so was without the human rights given to freeborn (or freed) people (#109). People bought and sold slaves in markets (#110), sometimes for very high prices, especially in the case of distinctive or well-trained slaves (#111).

#109: Legal Rights

Justinian, *Institutes* 1.5.3–5
Sixth Century AD

In his mammoth compendium of Roman law, the eastern emperor Justinian collected viewpoints on human status in regards to freedom. In his law code, he sees the distinction between human and slave as being one of the most basic when determining social status. Indeed, differentiation based on birth, wealth, and citizenship were only open to those who were free. As property, slaves had little to no status under Roman law.

> Certainly the most important distinction as far as human status goes is the division of people as being either free or slave. (Based on Gaius, *Institutes*.)
> Freedom is the natural capacity to do what one wishes as long as he is not restrained by compulsion or law. Servitude is an institution of universal law

in which, against nature, a person is subjected to the ownership of another person. The name "servus" (slave) is derived from the practice of triumphant generals to sell at auction prisoners of war. To do this, they would preserve (*servare*) rather than kill them. The term used of slave possession (*mancipium*) comes from the fact that slaves are captured by the hand (*manus*) of their enemies. (Based on Florentinus, *Institutes*.)

There is only one status of slaves, but for free people there are two: to be freeborn or freed. Slaves are made the possession of a person either by the process of civil law or the law involving foreign peoples. In the case of civil law, servitude begins in the case of someone who is older than 20 and agrees to be sold into slavery by sharing in the price. By the law involving foreign peoples, slaves in our society are those who are taken by us as the slave's original enemy or children who are born to slave women in our household. (Based on Marcian, *Institutes*.)

#110: Record of a Slave Sale

CIL 3, p. 936 (p. 2215) (Rosia Montana, Dacia)
AD 139

Slaves were considered property, and as such, could be bought, sold, and traded. There was a thriving slave trade. The following text was discovered in the province of Dacia on a wax tablet. It records the sale of a slave girl named Passia to a man named Maximus. The girl is described as a foundling, so it is very likely that she was exposed as a child and picked up by the slave trader Dasius and sold as a slave.

Maximus, son of Bato, purchased and acquired by the right of ownership (*mancipium*) the slave girl Passia (or whatever other name she may call herself), being in age around six years old. Maximus purchased the slave at the cost of 205 *denarii* from Dasius Pirusta, son of Verzo, from Kavieretium. The girl originated as a foundling. The seller guarantees that the girl is healthy, that was not obtained through theft of forcible abduction, and that she is neither a vagrant nor a vagabond. If anyone should demonstrate that this girl or any part of her is less than was advertised, whether the person demonstrating the problem should be Maximus, son of Bato, or the person to whom he might later legally sell the girl, the seller will return twice the sale price to the buyer. Maximus, son of Bato, requested this guarantee and Dasius Pirusta, son of Verzo, from Kavieretium, made the guarantee in regards to the slave girl described above. Dasius, son of Verzo, affirms that he has received the agreed upon price of 205 *denarii* from Maximus, son of Bato. The sale was made on the sixteenth day before the Kalends of April (March 17th) when Titus Aelius Caesar Antoninus Pius for the second time and Bruttius Praesens for the second time were consuls (AD 139).

#111: Antony Buys Two Expensive Slaves

Pliny the Elder, *Natural History* 7.56
First Century AD Describing Events of the First Century BC

Slaves were a luxury item in the Roman Empire. Some slaves who were better looking or had special skills could bring very high prices on the slave market. It was not unheard of for slave marketers to try to get higher prices from their buyers by unsavory means. In the following passage, the triumvir Antony is made to pay a high price for what he thought were a good-looking pair of twin boys.

Toranius sold to the great Antony (then a member of the second triumvirate) two exceptionally handsome slave boys. One of these boys was from Asia, the other from the Alps. Toranius sold them as twins because the two were so alike in appearance. Later, however, the deception was revealed when the boys spoke with different accents. A furious Antony brought his complaint to Toranius. Among his other grievances, Antony argued that he had paid too much for boys who were not twins (the price tag had been 200,000 *sestertii*). The clever slave merchant, however, replied that he had charged such a high price precisely because they were *not* twins. He argued that such wondrous similarity was nothing special in identical twins but finding two boys who looked so similar from different parts of the world was in reality priceless. With this timely argument based on flattery, Toranius won his case. Antony, fresh from the slaughter of the proscriptions and still raging with abuse, came to believe that there was nothing else in all of his possessions that better matched his lofty political position.

Rural Slaves

There were several types of slaves in Roman society. Urban slaves commonly worked in the city houses of the financially well-off. Rural slaves worked primarily on farms in the country. Others (usually state-owned slaves) worked in the mines or other government facilities. In the pre-industrial world of ancient Rome, humans and animals rather than machines provided labor. On some farms, slaves were the primary source of harvesting, processing, and herding manpower. Agricultural authors like Varro (#112) and Cato (#113), included discussions of slave labor in their farming manuals. Some epigraphic examples of slaves on rural estates have also been included (#114).

#112: Varro's Recommendations for Farm Workers

Varro, *On Agriculture* 17
First Century BC

Work on a farm could be difficult. Varro describes how some farmers used a combination of hired hands and slaves but advocates the use of hired hands rather than slaves. Slaves, he argues, were less likely to do a good job.

All fields are farmed through the work of free men, slaves, or both. Many free men either do the farm work themselves or, as is the case with many poor farmers, with the help of their children. Some farmers pay wages to workers to do the work for them or to help with that work. This is especially the case in some of the more labor-intensive activities such as grape or crop harvesting when farmers will hire workers (our ancestors called these *obaerarii*). These men work on farms to get out of debt. Even today, many of this kind of worker can be found in Asia, Egypt, and Illyricum. In all cases, I would say that it is better to cultivate more difficult land with hired hands than with slaves. The same can probably be said as well of good land and the more difficult farm tasks like planting fruit trees, picking grapes, and harvesting wheat. The writer Cassius has the following to say about good agricultural workers: "You should choose as farm laborers those who are able to do hard work. They should not be younger than twenty-two years old and should have an understanding of agriculture. You can find out how much they know by having them do other chores and then watch to determine their skill and knowledge. You can also ask their former employer what they are able to do. When you do use slaves, they should be neither timid nor arrogant."

#113: What to Do with Old and Sick Agricultural Slaves

Cato, *On Agriculture* 2
Mid-Second Century BC

In this text from his manual on agriculture, Cato describes the tasks of the owner when he visits an agricultural estate. These visits could be infrequent, so it was important for the owner to pay close attention to the state of his land and investment.

Inspect the sheep and decide which ones you should send to auction. Sell the olive oil if you can get a good price. Sell any extra wine and grain. Also get rid of any older cattle, worn-out plow oxen, sheep with spots, the wool, hides, old carts, worn tools, old slaves, sick slaves, and anything else that has outlived its usefulness. A *paterfamilias* should be a seller rather than a buyer.

#114: Some Slaves from Rural Estates

First to Third Centuries AD

There are vastly fewer preserved funerary monuments in honor of rural slaves than their urban counterparts. The following are two examples of specialized slaves that could be found on a country estate owned by an aristocrat or even the emperor.

AE 1995, 248 (Near Malafede, Italy)

To Mars of Ficana; Agathon, slave of the emperor and steward (*vilicus*) of the estate employees dedicated this as a gift in fulfillment of a vow. His family also participated in the dedication.

AE 1972, 102 (Tarentum, Italy)

Camulus, slave of Crispinilla, shepherd, who lived thirty-five years, is buried here.

Urban Slaves

The lives of urban slaves were generally much easier than their rustic counterparts. They often received better care and were granted freedom more regularly. They were also very numerous, especially in the city of Rome, where the concentration of wealth was greater than anywhere else in the Roman world. Many of these slaves were part of huge slave families belonging to members of the central or local aristocracies (#115 and #117). In such large households, slaves often filled very specialized roles (#116 has a number of examples from the tomb of the slaves of the empress Livia). Less wealthy families owned slaves in smaller numbers. Businessmen also employed slaves as cheap labor or to work in shops, docks, or warehouses. The emperor himself was the owner of the largest number of slaves. The emperor used these slaves to staff his imperial residences and serve in low-level bureaucratic positions such as the state grain supply (#118 has a number of examples). Other slaves worked as entertainers, athletes, and prostitutes. Slaves were expected to be faithful to their master and even protect him from danger. In the story of Urbinius Panapio, one slave willingly sacrificed his life on behalf of his master (#119).

#115: A Busy Scene at Home
Juvenal, *Satires* 14.59–63
Late First/Early Second Centuries AD

This passage from Juvenal illustrates the chaotic scene when an anxious homeowner hurriedly prepares for visitors. While exaggerated, the scene was probably not atypical for an aristocratic household in which scores or even hundreds of slaves lived and worked.

When a guest is about to arrive, not one of your slaves can take a break, "Sweep the floor! Make those columns shine! Clean up the dust and cobwebs! You, polish the silver! You, wash the fine china!" The voice of the master rages as he stands over them and brandishes his whip.

#116: Urban Slave Specialization

CIL 6.3926–3929, 4000, 4008, 4010, 4014, 4016, 4021, 4025, 4027, 4028, 4032, 4036, 4039, 4042, 4045, 4046, 4226a, 4231, 4240, 4242 (Rome)
First Century BC/First Century AD

One of the most interesting aspects of the urban slave household was the high degree of specialization of its slaves. Only in the smallest households were slaves expected to perform every domestic task. In very large households, tasks were so specialized that it is hard to imagine the slave having enough to do to occupy his or her day. A large tomb on the *Via Appia* in Rome contained the remains of household staff of the empress Livia (the wife of Augustus). This group of slaves, certainly one of the largest of its day, demonstrates a great deal of specialization, a sign of the owner's tremendous wealth.

3926: Euphro, slave of Tertius, temple attendant; Atimetus, comic actor.

3927: Zeuxis, freedman of Livia, goldsmith; Rufa, freedwoman of Tertius.

3928: Philomusus, freedman of Tertius, gilder in gold.

3929: Philomusus, freedman of Tertius, steward.

4000: Gaius Julius, maker of cloaks.

4008: Heracla, freedman of the emperor, painter.

4010: Cnismus, baker.

4014: Felix, slave of Tiberius Caesar, property accountant.

4016: Cissus, slave of the emperor, originally in the estate of Maecenas; Parmeno, slave of the Empress Livia, originally from the estate of Maecenas, in charge of the wardrobe of purple clothing.

4021: Tiberius Claudius Castor, freedman of the emperor, slave in the office of the city regions.

4025: Eros, freedman of the emperor, social secretary.

4027: Marcus Livius Aphrodisius, freedman of the emperor, in charge of religious items.

4028: Ampelius, freedman of Livia, clothes mender.

4032: Agrypnus, slave of Caesar Augustus, originally from the estate of Maecenas, slave in charge of statues.

4036: Venustus, slave of Tiberius Caesar, originally in the possession of his mother, slave in charge of the furniture.

4039: [. . .] Aman [. . .], freedman of the emperor, slave in charge of the incense.

4042: Marcus Livius Phryx, freedman of the emperor, slave in charge of the wardrobe.

4045: Galene, masseuse of Livia.

4046: Helico, slave in charge of the making of ointments.

4226a: Calamus Pamphilianus, slave of Tiberius Claudius Caesar, caretaker of the Lollian Gardens.

4231: Apollonius, slave in charge of the silver, dedicated this to Antigonus, the chamberlain of Livia.

4240: Stephanus, storehouse caretaker of the emperor.

4242: Epander, secretary of Livia, dedicated this funerary urn to Tatio his mother.

#117: The Difficulty of a Large Household

Seneca, *On the Tranquility of the Mind* 8.8
First Century AD

Here, Seneca describes how it is best to avoid the jealous eye of Fortune by not being too wrapped up in worldly possessions. As an example, he cites a man who lost his one slave but realized that the loss was not too major. At the end of the quoted passage, Seneca describes how the large slave household is difficult and costly to maintain. Indeed, slaves required the master to make a substantial investment, not only for their original purchase, but also their daily care. The otherwise sober Seneca also betrays his belief in the common perception that slaves had innately bad natures or criminal tendencies.

> Manes, the only slave of Diogenes ran away once. Later, while Diogenes was walking about town, a friend pointed out his runaway slave to him, but Diogenes did not try to get him back but said, "It would be a shame if I cannot live without my slave Manes if my slave Manes can live without me." In saying this, it would seem that what Diogenes was saying is, "Fortune, mind your own business. I am of no interest to you. Yes, my slave has run away, but I firmly believe that I am really that one who has been freed." You see, a slave household requires clothing and food; we must always be tending to the bellies of these exceptionally greedy animals. We must buy clothing and at the same time guard their extremely rapacious hands. We must use those slaves who constantly cry and curse. Diogenes seems to be the more fortunate because the only slave that Fortune could have taken away was one that he was able to give up extremely easily. The majority of us, however, simply do not have the same strength of character as Diogenes, so we should reduce our possessions so that we will be exposed less to the vicissitudes of Fortune.

#118: Some Imperial Slaves

First to Third Centuries AD

Like the large slave households of the aristocracy, the slaves of the emperor also had very specialized tasks. In addition, however, to the normal household or business duties assigned to slaves, imperial slaves also served functions in the imperial bureaucracy. The following texts exemplify the types of jobs imperial slaves held.

CIL 6.5188 (Rome)

Alexander Pylaemenianus, slave of Gaius Caesar Augustus Germanicus [Cal-igula], in charge of the Greek library in the Temple of Apollo on the Palatine, lived thirty years.

CIL 6.8423 (Rome)

To the Spirits of the Dead; to Abascantus, freedman of the emperor, assistant in the Temple of Neptune, which is in the Circus Flaminius and Flavius Ascanius and Pallans, slave of our emperor, assistant in the accounts office made this for their most loyal father.

CIL 6.8527 (Rome)

To the Spirits of the Dead; Eutychus, slave of our emperor, born a slave, atten-dant in charge of wine; Callistus, slave of our emperor, born a slave, working in the administrative offices of the imperial palace, put this inscription up to his most loyal and well-deserving brother.

CIL 6.8669 (Rome)

To the Spirits of the Dead; to Felix, slave of the emperor, steward of the Gardens of the Maiani; Julia Melitene put this up to her well-deserving husband.

CIL 6.8909 (Rome)

Tiberius Lyrius Celadianus, slave of the emperor Tiberius Caesar Augustus, eye doctor, who lived thirty years, is buried here in perpetuity.

CIL 3.349 (Nacolia, Asia)

For the health of the emperor Caesar Marcus Aurelius Commodus Antoninus Augustus and to the city of Nacolia; Craterus, slave of our emperor, born a slave, tax collector in the region of Nacolia, gave this as a gift.

#119: A Faithful Slave

Valerius Maximus, *Memorable Deeds and Sayings* 6.8.6
Written in the Early First Century AD Describing
Events of the First Century BC

In a section containing stories of faithful slaves, Valerius Maximus records how one slave was willing to die for his master. Slaves were indeed expected to put the lives of their masters before their own, but that expectation was not often put to the test. The master, Urbinius Panapio, had been made an outlaw in the proscriptions enacted at the creation of the Second Triumvirate. The rest of Panapio's household had informed some soldiers of his whereabouts in the hopes of freedom and monetary enrichment. A proscribed person's life was forfeited, allowing him to be killed on sight. One slave, however, stood up for his master in the face of death.

I should also mention the admirable faithfulness of the slave of Urbinius Panapio. His master had been listed in the proscriptions. When he learned that the other household slaves had turned Panapio in and soldiers were coming to his country estate villa in Reate, the slave changed clothes with him. He even put on his master's signet ring and sent him out the back door so that he could escape. The slave then went into a bedroom and climbed into bed and allowed himself to be killed as Panapio. The story is brief, but there is no small amount of praiseworthy material. Imagine what it would have been like to see the soldiers suddenly arrive outside the house and break the door down, to hear them yell and threaten, to behold their angry faces and shining weapons. If you put yourself in the slave's shoes you can get a good idea of how much courage it took for him to perform that act.

The Treatment of Slaves

Slaves were considered property, under the ownership of their master (#120). As such, the master could do whatever he wanted to his slaves. If we are to believe the author Plutarch, Cato the Elder treated his slaves callously (#121). We have many examples of tags that attached to iron collars hung around the necks of some slaves (#122). Harsh treatment was sometimes seen as the best way of avoiding slave revolt (#123). When they testified in court, the law required that they be tortured in order to obtain truthful testimony (#124 and #125). As with the story of the inhumane slave owner Vedius Pollio related earlier, there are many accounts of cruel masters (#126).

As time went on, however, as a result of the ease with which free persons could become slaves as well as how often slaves were freed, people increasingly looked at slaves as human beings (although of much lower social status). In one of his letters, the philosopher Seneca advocated for fair treatment of slaves (#127). Constraints, social at first and later legal, began to protect slaves from the whims of violent masters. Numerous examples of legal constraints on masters are included (#128 and #129). Among these is the decree on public burial attendants and torturers, a copy of which was discovered in Puteoli, Italy (#130).

#120: Slaves Defined as Property

Justinian, *Digest* 33.7.8pr
Sixth Century AD

This section from Justinian's *Digest* quotes a passage from the early third century AD lawyer Ulpian. The passage describes what farming implements could be passed down via testamentary legacy. It lists not only the inanimate tools and livestock, but also the slave workforce.

> Sabinus in his books to Vitellius clearly defines farming implements as those items that are used for producing, harvesting, and protecting crops. This would therefore include any people who cultivate the land as well as slaves who oversee or have other positions of authority. This latter category would include the *vilicus* (steward) and *monitor* (overseer). By this definition, then, domesticated cattle and sheep would also be included as their manure is used for fertilizing the fields. The tools of agriculture would also be in this category, including plows, hoes, mattocks, pruning shears, and any similar instruments. Items used for harvesting would also be included: presses, baskets, sickles, scythes, and the vineyard baskets in which grapes are transported. In the category of preservation, we should include storage jars, including those that are not set in the ground, and barrels. In some regions, we should also add specialized slaves. If there is a more upscale house, then include the majordomo and house cleaners. If the estate has gardens, then include the gardeners. If the land includes forests and pastures, then include the flocks of sheep, shepherds, and groundskeepers.

#121: Cato the Elder's Attitude toward His Slaves

Plutarch, *Lives, Cato the Elder* 21
Written in the Late First Century AD Describing
the Late Third/Early Second Century BC

Cato the Elder, the great conservative Roman of the second century BC, was an owner of both rural and urban slaves. In this passage, Cato's biographer demonstrates how Cato maintained discipline among his slaves.

> Cato owned many slaves and usually bought those prisoners of war who were young and still capable of being reared and trained like calves or colts. None of his slaves ever entered the house of another man unless Cato or his wife had

expressly sent him there. If the slave was asked what Cato was doing, he was always ordered to respond, "I don't know." Cato expected his slaves either to be at work or asleep. Indeed, he preferred the sleepy ones as he considered them more docile than the wakeful ones. Also, those who were able to sleep were generally better off for their work than those who did not sleep enough. Believing that a slave's sexual passions were one of the main reasons he might get into trouble, Cato allowed the males to have sexual relations with the females for a fixed price, but he never allowed them to approach any other woman.

#122: Slave Tags

Unknown Date

Several iron slave necklaces or, more truthfully, name collars, have been found from across the empire. The inscriptions on these objects record the name of the slave and inform the reader to whom the slave belongs in case the slave is a runaway. Slaves may have worn these as a form of punishment for bad behavior or attempting to escape.

CIL 15.7176 (Rome)

I am Petronia. Apprehend me because I have fled. Return me to the house of Teodotens to my master Vitalio.

CIL 6.41335 (Rome)

Apprehend me because I have fled. Return me to my master Cethegus, a man of senatorial status. He is near the marketplace of Livia in the third region of the city.

CIL 15.7178 (Rome)

I am the slave of the administrative clerk Leontius. Apprehend me so that I not escape and return me to Triarius Street.

CIL 15.7187 (Rome)

Apprehend me because I have fled and return me to the Via Lata to Gemellinus the physician.

AE 1996, 1732 (Bulla Regia, Africa Proconsularis)

I am the prostitute Adulteria. Apprehend me because I have fled from the city of Bulla Regia.

#123: The Base Nature of Slaves

Pliny the Younger, *Letters* 3.14
Early Second Century AD

In his published letters, Pliny the Younger often touted his own virtues. This included fair and kind treatment of his slaves. In one letter, he boasts how he allowed his slaves to write wills as if they were "real" people who could possess and bequeath property to heirs. In this letter, Pliny records how some slaves murdered their master. In the letter, Pliny says that the master in some way deserved what he got because he had been excessively cruel to his slaves. He also, however, adds some comments about what he describes as a base and criminal slave nature.

I must relate to you a terrible deed and one worthy of a letter. Larcius Macedo, a man of senatorial status who had held the office of praetor, was killed by his slaves. Going against him was the fact that he was an arrogant and cruel master and one who did not remember well enough (or perhaps it was that he remembered too well) that his father has been a slave. Macedo was bathing in his villa in Formiae when suddenly his slaves surrounded him. One punched him in the jaw; another struck him in the mouth; others in his chest and stomach; one, and this is shameful to mention, struck him in the genitals. After this beating, when they saw that he was unconscious, they threw him down on the hot pavement to test whether he was still alive. Macedo, either because he really was knocked senseless or merely wanted to seem that way, did not move and remained sprawled out on the hot floor. This was enough for his attackers to believe that he was dead. The murderous slaves, claiming Macedo had been overcome with the heat, carried him out and put him in bed. His more faithful slaves found him and realized what had happened. His concubines ran about the house wailing and shouting. The slaves became alarmed when, stirred by the noise and the coolness of the place, Macedo opened his eyes and moved his body. The slaves fled. The majority of them, however, have been apprehended. The authorities are still searching for the rest. Macedo lived a few days longer but only barely recovered consciousness. He did die, however, with the consolation that his slaves would be punished for his murder, something that usually would only happen after the master's death.

You see how many dangers, threats, and mockeries surround us! It is also not the case that a master can protect himself by being lax in his discipline or kind. The slaves' opinion of their masters is not what kills but rather their criminal nature.

#124: The Torture of Slaves in Court

Justinian, *Digest* 48.18.1.1
Sixth Century AD

Because slaves legally were mere property and had no official status, Roman law sanctioned the use of torture against slaves who were to be questioned during a court case. In fact, Roman law believed that slaves could only give truthful testimony under torture. In the Republic and early Empire, Roman citizens were exempt from torture in legal cases. By the late Empire, however, torture was used on even poor free persons. The following legal text documents an attempt to limit the use of torture of slaves in court.

The words of the rescript of Hadrian say as follows: "The courts should only resort to the torture of slaves when the accused is already suspected of being guilty and a guilty verdict is so close by other arguments that only the confession of the accused's slaves would seem to be lacking."

#125: A Loyal Slave

Valerius Maximus, *Memorable Deeds and Sayings* 6.8.1
Written in the Early First Century AD Describing
Events of the First Century BC or Earlier

In this story recorded by Valerius Maximus in a section on faithful slaves, a slave remains faithful to his master while being interrogated through torture in court. By the late Empire, however, as recorded in the law codes, slaves were not allowed to give testimony against their master, under torture or otherwise.

Once, Marcus Antonius, a very famous orator from the time of our grandfathers, was accused of incest. During the trial of this man, the prosecution adamantly demanded that one of his slaves be brought in to give testimony. The prosecution claimed that this slave had carried a lantern when his master had gone to commit the crime. This slave, still a beardless youth, present and standing in the crowd of onlookers, realized that this demand in fact meant that he would be tortured. Even so, the slave did not flee. When they arrived back home during a court recess, Antonius was very troubled and worried for his slave's safety, but nevertheless the slave encouraged him to turn him over to the court for "questioning." The slave assured him, "No word will pass my lips that could hurt your defense." Indeed, the slave kept his word with miraculous endurance. Although he was beaten many times with whips, was placed upon the rack, and was burned with hot plates, he overturned the prosecution's whole case and protected the interests of the accused. Fortune can deservedly be accused of having placed within the body of a slave a spirit so loyal and brave.

#126: A Cruel Mistress

Juvenal, *Satires* 6.475–485
Late First/Early Second Centuries AD

The physical abuse of slaves did not stop in the courtroom. Beating was one form of punishment open to masters. The physically abusive master or mistress was a common literary motif. In this passage, the satirist Juvenal condemns a mistress for her cruel treatment of her slaves. Not every master and mistress treated their slaves in this way, but passages like this suggest that abuse was not unheard of.

If during the night her husband sleeps with his back to her, his female secretary suffers; the wardrobe girls pull down their tunics to receive their lashings. She accuses her litter bearer of being late and punishes him for oversleeping. One woman prefers rods cracked over her slaves' back, another whips, and a third straps. Some women even pay their professional slave torturers an annual salary. While the slave is beaten, one woman calmly applies her makeup, listens to her girlfriend's chatter, or inspects the golden hem of her embroidered dress. Crack goes the whip but she is reading through the articles in the newspaper. Crack goes the whip but she pays no attention until the torturers have become weary and then only shrilly shouts "Get out!" as the signal that the questioning is at an end.

#127: Seneca Advocates the Fair Treatment of Slaves

Seneca, *Letters* 47.1–17
First Century AD

The social constraints on a master's treatment of his slaves came from the upper crust's belief that an aristocrat should be an example of self-control (*moderatio*) as well as an increasingly humanized view of slaves. Following Stoic philosophy, in this passage Seneca advocates for treating slaves more like people than "talking tools." Central to his argument is his belief that Roman slavery was based upon bad fortune rather than any innate factor, such as race or base nature. This passage also includes a glimpse of the kind of specialization one would find in the slaves of a large aristocratic household.

I was glad to hear from your letters that you live on friendly terms with your slaves. That fact fits with your overall sensibility and education. "They are slaves!" someone may exclaim. My response is "Yes, they are slaves, but they are also human beings." "They are slaves!" "Yes, but they are also our companions," is my response. "They are slaves!" To this I must remind them that they are also our friends, although of lowly status. "They are slaves!" It would be more correct to call them fellow-slaves if you only understand how Fortune has the same power over both slaves and aristocrats...

There is a proverb going around that addresses the kind of arrogant treatment slaves have to put up with: "You have as many enemies as you have slaves." I, however, say that we do not buy these slaves as enemies, but we make them so with our actions. I will omit the other aspects of the cruel and inhuman treatment they receive. Indeed, we do not treat our slaves as human beings but rather more like farm animals. For example, when we recline at dinner, we compel our slaves to perform a variety of demeaning tasks. One slave cleans the vomit from the floor; another hides under the table and picks up any food that falls. One slave carves expensive avian delicacies. With skilled strokes the slave's artful hand cuts pieces of meat from the breast and rump. Unhappy is the man whose life revolves around a single, specialized job such as this...

I do not want to embroil myself in too large a question and dispute the treatment of slaves in general, to whom we are extremely arrogant, cruel, and abusive. Nevertheless, this is the sum of my advice: treat your inferior in the same way you would wish your superior to treat you. Whenever you reflect on how much power you have over your slave, bear in mind that your master has just as much power over you. "But I do not have a master," you may say. You are still young. Perhaps you will have one someday...

#128: Growing Legal Constraints on Masters

Gaius, *Institutes* 1.52–53
Mid-Second Century AD

Social pressures, however, were not the only constraint upon masters' treatment of their slaves. Roman law increasingly limited the power of the *paterfamilias'* ability to punish and kill the slaves in his *potestas*. The following passage from Gaius' legal compendium shows how Roman law placed slaves completely under the power of their masters as property but that there were laws in place to keep masters from being excessively cruel.

Therefore, slaves are in our *potestas*. This power of life and death over our slaves is part of universal law as it appears in the law codes of all peoples. Therefore, whatever the slave acquires is done so on behalf of the master. Although that is true, however, it is allowed neither to Roman citizens nor to anyone under Roman rule the right to treat slaves excessively cruelly and without cause. According to a declaration by the most sacred emperor Antoninus Pius, anyone who kills one of his own slaves without just cause will be punished with no more leniency than someone who kills a slave belonging to someone else. Another declaration by the same emperor also restricts excessive harshness. This edict came about after several provincial governors consulted Pius concerning what should be done with slaves who fled to holy ground or to the statues of the emperors for asylum. In response, Pius declared that if the savagery seems to be beyond reason, then the master is to be compelled to sell

the slaves involved in the incident. It seems to me that Pius was correct in his
pronouncement. This is because we ought not to abuse our power.

#129: Examples of Legal Constraints

The legal constraints that the emperor Antoninus Pius imposed were the culmina-
tion of a series of laws passed by emperors in the first and second centuries AD. The
following passages exemplify earlier attempts emperors had made to enforce the
more humane treatment of slaves.

Suetonius, *Claudius* 25
Written in the Early Second Century AD Describing
the Emperor Claudius (AD 41–54)

When some masters were abandoning their weak and sick slaves on the Island of
Aesculapius to avoid the expense of treating them, the emperor Claudius commanded that all of the slaves who had been exposed were to be free and would
never return to the possession of their former masters, even if they should recover
from their illness. Claudius went further, however, and also made it known that if
any of these masters should prefer to kill their sick slaves now rather than expose
them, that he would prosecute them on the charge of murder.

Justinian, *Digest* 48.8.11.1
Sixth Century AD Describing a Legal Act of the
Emperor Nero (AD 54–68)

If a slave is exposed in the amphitheater to the beasts without judicial sentence, the court is to punish not only the man who sold the slave but also the
one who bought him for display in the games. This mandate appears in the *lex
Petronia* of Nero's reign. A senatorial decree was added to this law that states
that masters will no longer have the power to arbitrarily expose their own
slaves to the beasts in games they themselves are holding. Now if the slave is
turned in to authorities and the charge made by the master is to be just, then
the slave will be handed back over for punishment.

Historia Augusta, Life of Hadrian 18.7–11
Written Possibly in the Fourth Century AD Describing
the Emperor Hadrian (AD 117–138)

The emperor Hadrian enacted a law requiring a master to hire a third party to
execute slaves and required that slaves be condemned in courts of law if they

could be justly accused of a crime. He also prohibited the sale of slave men or women to pimps and gladiatorial agents.

Justinian, *Digest* 1.6.2
Sixth Century AD Describing a Legal Act of the
Emperor Hadrian (AD 117–138)

The divine emperor Hadrian once exiled for five years a matron named Umbricia because she had treated most atrociously some slave girls for very trivial reasons.

Justinian, *Digest* 50.17.32
Sixth Century AD

In civil law, slaves are considered to be nothing (i.e., not human). In the law of nature, however, because it applies to the natural order of things, consider humans of all statuses to be equal.

#130: Public Burial Attendants and Torturers

AE 1971, 88 (Puteoli, Italy)
First Century AD

One of the most interesting legal texts to survive from antiquity is a fragmentary stone inscription of the first century AD from the Campanian town of Puteoli quoting a law regulating professional undertakers. In addition to the collection of bodies, the undertakers could also be hired as professional torturers/executioners. This law takes the job of torture and execution from the hands of the master and gives it to public contractors. This text outlines the procedure the masters and the contractors were to follow when a slave was to be tortured. As physical abuse of slaves often came in the heat of the moment (as with Juvenal's cruel mistress) while the master was most angry, such drawn-out preparations might cause a master whose temper had cooled to stop a severe punishment before it was carried out.

[. . . the early part of the text is lost . . .] If someone throws a dead body into the street and is caught, that person is to pay the contractor or his associate a fine of 60 *sestertii* per body. To assess the fine, the city magistrate is to hold a hearing to determine the amount the offender is to pay according to the constitution of the town. Workers who are trained in this profession are not to live any closer to the city than the tower where the grove of Libitina

now stands (the goddess of funerals). They must also not go to the baths
before the first hour of the night. They may also not enter the town unless
they do so to transport a body, bury one, or inflict punishment. Whenever
they do enter town on official business, they must do so while wearing a
special colored cap on their heads to indicate who they are. The workers
must be between the ages of twenty and fifty. People who are bow-legged,
have only one eye, are crippled, limp, are blind, or have tattoos may not
serve as workers. The contractor must also have no fewer than twenty-three
workers.

In the case of those who wish to inflict punishment on a male or female
slave privately [i.e., in the household] the law prescribes the following for
the one who wishes to inflict the punishment. In the case of crucifixion, the
contractor will provide the beams, chains, and ropes for the punishment as
well as the punishers themselves. The person wishing to have the punishment inflicted is to pay four *sestertii* for each worker: the people carrying
the beams, the floggers, and the executioner. Whenever a magistrate will
administer a public execution, he must first give the order. After he has given
the order, the contractor must be prepared to administer the punishment. He
will ensure that the crosses are erected and that there are nails, pitch, wax,
candles, and whatever else will be needed for the event, all free of charge.
If the orders of execution include that the corpse of the executed is to be
dragged away with a hook, the contractor must provide workers, dressed in
red and carrying a bell, who will drag away the body or bodies (if there are
several).

Whenever someone wishes any of the actions outlined in this law to
be done, he must fill out the appropriate forms or send someone to do so
before the contractor of this public duty, one of his associates, or the person responsible for the work if none of these people will be present at the
location where the contractor either does his job of grave digging or in the
place he has established to do so. On the paperwork, the person wishing
to hire the contractor must give the day, place, and the job he wants done.
Once this paperwork has been filed, the contractor, one of his associates, or
the person responsible for the work will take care of the job in the order in
which requests are made. If, however, the request involves the funeral of a
town magistrate or a mass burial then the contractor is to give them prece-
dence. All other funerals will be handled in the order in which the requests
were received. It is the contractor's responsibility to make sure he either
sends or brings himself all of the items required in this law. If the request is
to remove a hanged man, the contractor is to be sure that the job is finished
within an hour. If the request is to remove a dead male or female slave and
the request was made before the tenth hour of the day, the contractor is to
remove the body before the end of the day on which the request was made.
If the request was made after the tenth hour, then the body must be removed
before the second hour of the next day.

Freedmen

It was common for Roman slaves to receive their freedom (manumission). All that was required for a slave to be freed was a formal declaration before a magistrate; specific instructions in the deceased master's will; or, in a later development, the master's expression of his wish to free his slave (#131 is a legal text describing limits on manumission). A freed slave received Roman citizenship at the time of manumission. The slave became free but not independent. The freedman or freed-woman (*libertus/liberta*) took the first and second names of his former master (the praenomen and nomen) and remained a technical member of his former *familia*. He or she was expected to be obedient and often continued to work in the former master's shops, businesses, or farms (#133 cites a case in which a former slave did not give his patron the required respect). Because they had once been in the possession of another person and therefore had the stigma of former slave status, however, freedmen were excluded from full participation in civic life. As such, they were also not allowed to enter the ranks of the senatorial, equestrian, or municipal aristocratic orders and could not run for public office. Despite these limitations, some especially wealthy freedmen participated indirectly in the life of their towns by acting as a public benefactor (#134). There are also some epigraphic examples of freedmen (#132) including the wealthy freedman Trimalchio from Petronius' novel *Satyricon* (#135).

#131: Limitations on Manumission

Gaius, *Institutes* 1.42–44
Mid-Second Century AD Discussing a Law Passed in 2 BC

Not only did Roman law attempt to limit the master's ability to treat his slave harshly, but it also restricted the master's ability to free slaves in his will. It seems that masters were freeing large numbers of slaves in their will in an attempt to win the gratitude and love of their former slaves after their deaths. This action, however, also diminished the value of their heirs' inheritance and, especially in the case of large slave households in Rome, flooded the citizenry with new freedmen. This text from Gaius' *Institutes* comments on the *Lex Fufia Caninia*, a law passed in 2 BC to limit testamentary manumission. As evidence for the number of slaves a master could own, the original law made arrangements for households of as many as five hundred slaves although Gaius explains that households larger than five hundred slaves were possible.

> The *Lex Fufia Caninia* set limits on the number of slaves a master could manumit in his will. A master who has between three and ten slaves may manumit half of the total number of slaves. A master who has between eleven and thirty slaves may manumit a third. A master who has between thirty-one and one hundred slaves may manumit a fourth. Finally, a master who has between one hundred and one and five hundred slaves may only manumit a fifth. The law

makes no specific statement about households larger than five hundred slaves, but we must follow the idea of the law and allow no more than one hundred slaves to be freed in a master's will. Also, the law does not apply to a master who has only one or two slaves. He has complete freedom as far as testamentary manumission goes. The law also has nothing to say in the case of masters who free slaves in situations other than their will. Therefore, it seems that when it comes to the granting of freedom by public declaration, written record, or before witnesses, the master will have complete freedom, even to the point of manumitting his whole household, provided that there is no other legal restriction to granting the slaves their freedom.

#132: Two Freedman Friends

CIL 6.22355a (Rome)
Second or Third Century AD

The following funerary text was dedicated by one freedman to his friend, another freedman. Although they have different *cognomina*, both have the same praenomen and nomen because they had a former master in common.

To Aulus Memmius Clarus; Aulus Memmius Urbanus dedicated this to his fellow freedman and dearest friend. Between you and me, my fellow freedman, there was never any quarrel that I was aware of. I call to witness the gods above and below with this tombstone that you and I were brought together into the same household when our master purchased us. We were also likewise made freedmen together. No day ever saw us separated until the day you died.

#133: Bad Relations with a Freedman

CIL 6.11027 (Rome)
Second or Third Century AD

Not all freedmen had a good relationship with their former master. The following text has a typical allowance for the burial of other members of the family (as well as freedmen and freedwoman) in the tomb monument. The inscription, however, has an added clause that prohibited a specific freedman from having any access to the family tomb.

Marcus Aemilius Artema made this for Marcus Licinius Successus, his well-deserving brother and for Caecilia Modesta, his wife, as well as for himself, and all of his freedmen and freedwomen and their descendants with the exception of the freedman Hermes whom, because of his crimes, I prohibit from entering, walking near, or having any access at all to this tomb monument.

#134: A Wealthy Freedman Benefactor

CIL 11.5400 (Assisi, Umbria, Italy)
Second or Third Century AD

Freedmen were sometimes in a decent economic position after their manumission. The following text from Assisi records a former slave who was a specialized physician. The text tells us that he paid fifty thousand *sestertii* for his freedom, a price possibly equivalent to his original slave purchase price (a large amount of money but not atypical of specialized slaves). He was also wealthy enough (from money made through his profession before and after his manumission) to enrich his hometown with generous bequests. The value of his estate at the time of his death was only just less than the property qualification for entrance into the senatorial order. Because he had been a slave, however, the man could never hold public office or serve the city government in any official capacity.

> Publius Decimius Eros Merula, freedman of Publius, a clinical and surgical eye doctor, a member of the board of six men. Merula paid fifty thousand *sestertii* for his freedom. For his membership on the board of six men, he paid two thousand *sestertii* to the city government. He also gave thirty thousand *sestertii* to pay for new statues in the temple of Hercules. He donated thirty-seven thousand *sestertii* to the town so that the roads in town could be re-paved. On the day before he died, his estate was valued at eight hundred thousand [the number is corrupt and not certain] *sestertii*.

#135: Trimalchio's Servile Origins

Petronius, *Satyricon* 75–76
First Century AD

One example of a wealthy freedman is the fictional character Trimalchio. This Trimalchio was a fabulously wealthy, overbearing, arrogant, and silly freedman in Petronius' novel *Satyricon*. In the following text from the description of a dinner party given by Trimalchio, the author has the host tell of his background to his guests.

> My frugality is what got me to my present fortune. When I arrived as a slave from Asia, I was no taller than this candlestick right here. Indeed, every day I would use it to measure myself and see if I had gotten any taller. Afterward, I would smear wax from it on my upper lip in the hopes that I would grow a moustache more quickly. For fourteen years, I was the plaything of my master. Don't look down on me for that. There is no disgrace in doing what your master tells you to do. Indeed, I also kept my mistress satisfied (you know what I mean). I won't talk about all of that though. I am not like the rest of

you braggarts. At last, as far as the gods would allow it, I became the master of the house. Yes, my master was still alive, but I was the brains of the operation. What more can I say? When he did finally die, my master made me his heir (along with the emperor). I received from his will an inheritance equal to what it takes to become a senator. Still, no one is ever completely satisfied. I decided I wanted to get into the mercantile business. So as not to bore you I will get straight to the point. I built five ships and loaded them with wine (at that time, wine was as valuable as gold) and sent them off to Rome. On the way, however, every one of the ships sank. You would have thought that I had done it purposefully to collect the insurance, but I didn't. That is what really happened. I am not making it up. In a single day, Neptune drank thirty million *sestertii* worth of wine. Do you think I gave up after this setback? By heavens, No! This only made me hungry to try again as if I had never tried in the first place. I built more ships, this time larger, better, and luckier so that no one could say that I was not a brave man, and, as you know, a large, expensive ship requires a great deal of bravery. I loaded these ships with wine, bacon, beans, perfumes, and slaves. At that time in my life, my wife Fortunata did an extremely loyal thing. She sold all of her gold and fancy clothes and gave to me one hundred gold coins for my new investment. This was the fertilizer that my little nest egg required. When the gods wish for something to happen, it happens quickly. With this one voyage I made a profit of ten million *sestertii*.

Chapter 8: Three Cities in Italy

An ancient Roman city served a number of important functions. In addition to be the residence of many people, cities were the political, judicial, religious, and cultural centers of the Roman world. This aristocracy organized as a town council (generally called the *decuriones* in Romanized cities) met for official business in a public building known as a *curia* (town hall). Legal trials presided over by aristocrats, sometimes with a jury of citizens, were held in a basilica (law court). Throughout the cities were numerous temples to various gods where priests, mostly from the aristocratic classes, conducted public forms of ritual worship. The most important temple in a Roman city was the *capitolium,* which was dedicated to the so-called Capitoline Triad (Jupiter, Juno, and Minerva), Rome's three chief deities. These three deities had their main temple on the Capitoline Hill in Rome, which hill was the source of the name of the municipal *capitolia.* The *curia,* basilica*, and capitolium* were generally located in the central marketplace, the forum. The forum was located at the convergence of the two major roads in a Roman city, the north–south-running *cardo* and the east–west-running *decumanus.*

Cities were also hubs in a vast trade network running from one end of the Roman Empire to the other. Within the city itself, marketplaces (*macellum*) and shops for the buying and selling of merchandise were common features. Warehouses (*horrea*) held goods imported or waiting for exportation. Cities also were the homes of numerous, small-scale industries. Because of the many mercantile and industrial opportunities, many people of the lower classes migrated to the cities from the country in the hopes of achieving riches and social advancement.

The high population of an ancient city also spurred a demand for certain amenities that generally served to improve the quality of life or entertained the inhabitants. Aqueducts brought fresh water from nearby mountains to the city. Fountains distributed the water. Many houses even had indoor plumbing. Sewers took refuse out of the city. Entertainment became a major industry in a typical Roman city. Shows involving various types of professional entertainments were often held in specialized structures known as theaters, amphitheaters, and circuses, all of which were designed to hold large numbers of spectators. People could bathe, exercise, and meet socially in public bath complexes.

Rome

In many ways, it is inconsistent to consider Rome in a study of life in a typical Roman city; Rome was anything but typical. Of all of the cities of the ancient Roman Empire, Rome stands out not only as the largest but also the grandest and most luxurious city. More than a million people packed its houses and streets by the first century AD. In addition to numerous houses of the rich, and tenement apartment buildings of the poor, numerous public buildings of lavish size and grandeur crowded the city. This section includes a map of Rome (#136) and a detailed map of the forum (#141). A passage from Cicero describes the natural advantages of the site (#137). Pliny the Elder mentions the size of the city and its ancient walls (#138). Two late imperial descriptions of Rome (after it had ceased to be the central authority of the empire) are especially interesting (#139 and #140). Dionysius of Halicarnassus and Livy describe how the forum came to be built (#142).

#136: Map of the City of Rome

The most dominant natural feature of Rome is the Tiber River, which runs from north to south on its way to the Mediterranean Sea about fifteen miles southwest of the city (see Figure 8.1). West of the river and Tiber Island is a low-lying area created by the bend of the Tiber called Transtiberim, "Across the Tiber" (modern Trastevere). In Roman times, this district was filled with low-income housing. On the hills overlooking the western bank of the Tiber and Transtiberim were many gardens and grand villas of the senatorial aristocracy. The center of Rome was located among the hills to the east of the Tiber. The Palatine Hill was the location of the earliest settlement of the city. In imperial times, it was where the palaces of the emperors were situated. The Esquiline Hill, northeast of the Palatine, was also a major residential area. The tall hill west of the Palatine, the Capitoline Hill, was considered sacred to the gods and was the location of the great Temple of Jupiter, Juno and Minerva.

On the outskirts of the city to the north and east, the wealthy built huge suburban villas with spacious gardens on the Pincian, Quirinal, and eastern Esquiline hills. More aristocratic villas stood on the Caelian Hill to the east of the forum and on the Aventine, south of the Palatine. The poor tended to dwell in densely populated apartment buildings lining the streets at the lower elevations closer to the center of town.

Huge warehouses for storing imported food and other goods which were ferried up the Tiber from Ostia stood along both sides of the Tiber to the south of the Aventine and the Janiculum hills. The impressive ruins of one of these, the *Porticus Aemilia*, has been revealed as a structure almost seven hundred yards long.

In the middle of the city, the river bends sharply westward then southeastward, creating an elbow of low-lying land. The Romans called this district on the east side of the Tiber the Campus Martius ("the Field of Mars"). During the Republic, soldiers trained and citizens voted on this flat, open plain. Later, triumphant generals wishing to commemorate their victories began to fill the field with temples, theaters, and decorative porticos. Augustus and his general Marcus Agrippa, too, spent massive amounts of money to develop the site into a grand celebration of the glory of Rome and the new monarchy of Augustus. Among the new constructions were a giant sundial (the *Horologium*); the Altar of Peace (the *Ara Pacis*); baths; the first manifestation of the Pantheon; and Augustus' own funerary monument, the Mausoleum of Augustus. Rome of the emperors was also not lacking in buildings for entertainment. The two most important of these are the Circus Maximus, a chariot

Figure 8.1 The Topography of Rome.

racetrack between the Palatine and Aventine hills, and the Colosseum, an arena for beast hunts and gladiatorial combat, in the basin where the Palatine, Esquiline, and Caelian hills meet.

The emperors also constructed great public baths such as the Baths of Agrippa and Nero in the Campus Martius, the Baths of Titus and Trajan on the slope of the Esquiline near the Colosseum, the Bath of Caracalla south of the Caelian Hill between the *Via Appia* and the *Via Ardeatina*, and the Baths of Diocletian on the Esquiline.

#137: The Natural Advantages of the Site of Rome

Cicero, *On the Republic* 2.10–11
First Century BC

Rome's location in a hilly part of the flat plain of Latium near the Tiber River was often the topic of praise by authors who sought to ascribe some of the Romans' success to Rome's natural geography. In this passage, Cicero explains how Romulus ingeniously used the river and hills to give his new city of Rome every topographical advantage.

How could Romulus have more divinely given his Rome the advantages of being a maritime city and avoid the problems of being on the sea than to place it on the bank of a calm river that flows all year and on a wide course to the sea? This situation allows the city to import by sea the things that it lacks and to export what it has in abundance. The same river allows Rome not only to bring in by sea but also transport over land the items necessary to feed its population and allow a higher quality of life. Even that long ago at the time of foundation, Romulus was able to foresee that someday Rome would be the center of a great empire. A city placed in any other location in Italy would never have more easily been suited to the great heights of power which Rome has achieved.

Indeed, the natural defenses of the city are such that a person who has looked at them would be hard-pressed to ever forget their impressiveness. In their wisdom, Romulus and the other kings built a wall whose course and construction was well suited to its purpose. The whole wall is protected by rough and steep hills, and the one section that is accessible between the Esquiline and Quirinal Hills is protected by a deep ditch and tall rampart. The citadel on the Capitoline Hill is well fortified by its steep precipice and rocks piled together so well that it seems as though they had been cut and placed together by hand. So well fortified is the citadel that during the terrible invasion of the Gauls in the fourth century BC it remained safe and intact. Romulus also chose a site for his city that has abundant access to fresh water even though much of the surrounding territory has disease-ridden swamps. Even the hills are an advantage. They allow the wind to blow through and provide shade to the valleys between them.

#138: The Walls and Early Layout of Rome

Pliny the Elder, *Natural History* 3.5.66–67
First Century AD

In this passage, Pliny the Elder describes the enormity of the city walls of Rome. These walls, however, were already ancient by the time of Pliny in the second century AD. The city had long since outgrown its walls and spilled out into the neighboring territory. It was not until the dangerous times of the later third century AD when the emperor Aurelian built a new wall to protect this much larger city from the threat of foreign invasion.

Romulus left a city with three gates or perhaps four, if we believe some authors. In the year AD 73, when Vespasian and Titus were emperors and censors, the walls encompassed an area of thirteen miles and two hundred yards. This area included the seven famous hills of Rome. The city itself is divided into fourteen regions and 265 neighborhoods defined by the shrines to the guardian deities of crossroads (*lares compitales*). If one were to draw a line from the Golden Milestone placed in the center of the Roman Forum to each of the thirty-seven gates (counting each of the major double gates as only one and omitting the seven ancient gates which no longer exist), the total distance would be twenty miles and 765 yards. If we measure instead from the Milestone to the most distant houses that are considered part of the city (counting also the barracks in the camp of the Praetorian Guard on the far reaches of the Esquiline), and let the measuring line pass through the neighborhoods along the streets, then the measurement would be longer than seventy miles. If to this figure one were to take into consideration the height of the buildings in the city, it would be easier to form a more realistic idea of the tremendous size of Rome. Certainly no other city in the whole world is able to compare in size to Rome. On the east side, the city is walled in by the rampart of Tarquin the Proud. This rampart is a tremendous sight and is just as high as the walls on the other sides of the city most vulnerable to attack. These other parts of the city are fortified either with lofty walls or steep cliffs. Nowadays, however, the city has grown so much that it extends beyond the walls and has swallowed up some of the neighboring towns.

#139: The Beauty of Rome

Claudian, *On the Consulship of Stilicho* 3.66–71, 130–137
Early Fifth Century AD

Claudian was a poet of the later fourth and early fifth century AD. He came to the western imperial court from Egypt and was one of the court poets of the western emperor Honorius, the son of Theodosius. His works are primarily speeches in praise of the current regime. The following passage praising the wonder of Rome was written in honor of the consulship of Stilicho, the son of a Vandal chieftain who had been adviser of Theodosius and was, at the time of the writing of this poem, regent for the young Honorius.

Behold the seven hills! The glint of gold from these hills is like the rays of the sun. Behold the triumphal arches decorated with the spoils of war. Behold the temples that rise to the clouds. Behold all of the other constructions that celebrate so important a triumph. Look about with amazed eyes at all of the benefits and city services.

It is you, Stilicho, consul most like the gods, who protects this great city, a city greater than any on the earth. No eye can grasp the size of Rome, no heart can imagine its beauty, and no voice can sing its praise. The shine from Rome's tall, gilded buildings makes them rivals to the nearby stars. Its seven hills imitate the seven zones of heaven. Rome is the founder of the military might and civil law that serve as the foundation of the empire that now covers the globe. Here was the cradle of justice. Once a tiny hamlet of no importance, Rome's power now stretches to both extremes of the world. From humble beginnings, Rome's warmth spreads as far as the sun shines.

#140: Constantius II Visits Rome

Ammianus Marcellinus, *History* 16.10.13–15
Later Fourth Century AD

Another fourth century AD writer, the historian Ammianus Marcellinus, presents another image of Rome through the eyes of the amazed tourist. Originally from Antioch, Ammianus did not spend any significant time in Rome until late in life. It was in Rome, however, that he completed his great historical work. During his discussion of the emperor Constantius II's visit to Rome in AD 357, Ammianus indulges in the kind of hyperbole that we saw in the description of Rome in Claudian. Ammianus mentions many of Rome's most important ancient buildings. Some of these, such as the forum, the Colosseum, the Pantheon, and the Forum of Trajan still amaze tourists today.

Constantius entered Rome, the birthplace of empire and all virtue. When he had come to the Rostra (the speaker's platform in the forum), he gazed upon the forum, the seat of ancient power. The emperor was amazed at the number of amazing sights that met him in whatever way he turned his eye. He addressed the aristocracy in the senate house and the people from the tribunal. Having won approval on both fronts, he retired to the palace and enjoyed the happiness that he had been hoping for. Several times, while giving some equestrian games, he was delighted in the talkativeness of the crowd. This talkativeness was neither arrogant nor rebellious after the long period of freedom they had enjoyed in Rome. Constantius himself also reverently observed a proper degree of moderation and did not, as took place in other cities, allow the games to go on as long as he wished but only until the prescribed ending event, as was the usual custom. He then traveled around the summits of the seven hills and the luxurious suburban villas to see the famous sites on the slopes and plains. In each district, whatever he saw first he declared to be the most impressive thing he had ever seen. There was the Temple of Jupiter on the Capitoline, as superior to everything else as heaven is to earth. He saw baths the size of provinces and the enormous edifice of the Colosseum, constructed out of stone from Tibur, the top of which was barely visible to the human eye. He visited the Pantheon, enclosed with a high dome that makes the interior look like world in miniature, complete with vaulted heaven. The wonder of this building was increased all the more with the lofty platforms bearing the statues of consuls and past emperors and reached only by staircases. He saw the Temple of Venus and Rome, the Forum of Peace, the Theater of Pompey, the Stadium, and all of the other wonders of the eternal city.

He also visited the Forum of Trajan, a building whose equal cannot be found on earth. Indeed, I believe that even the gods themselves are amazed when they look upon it. Constantius stood dumbfounded as he looked around the huge building. It would be impossible for a person to either express its grandeur in words or ever again build that could match it. The emperor right then gave up all hope of ever beginning a construction project that could even come close to the Forum of Trajan. He did say, however, that he would try (and in fact would be able) to imitate the statue of the horse of Trajan, which carried the statue of the emperor that stood in the middle of the front courtyard of the forum.

#141: The Roman Forum

The heart of Rome was the forum (see Figure 8.2). Numerous public buildings stood on either side of the main road running through the forum, the *Via Sacra* ("the Sacred Way"), including two basilicas for the administration of justice (the Basilica Aemilia and the Basilica Julia); the Curia (senate house); and numerous temples such as those dedicated to Vesta, Concord, and Saturn. The prison (the *Carcer Tullianum*) stood at the eastern foot of the Capitoline Hill, close to the Curia. At the western end of the forum is the Capitoline Hill, which was crowned in antiquity by the imposing temple dedicated to the Capitoline Triad. To the south of the forum rose the Palatine Hill. Rome, however, quickly outgrew its forum. Julius Caesar, Augustus, Vespasian, Nerva, and Trajan dedicated new imperial forums to the north of the original forum. All were monumental achievements of architecture that served to glorify certain emperors, as well as create more space for mercantile activity within the central part of Rome.

Figure 8.2 The *Forum Romanum* from the Southwest (Photograph by B. Harvey).

#142: The Creation of the Forum

Early Roman history attributes the draining of the marshy valley between the Capitoline, Palatine, and Esquiline Hills to the kings. This work made the area inhabitable (the earliest evidence of human activity in the forum is a series of Iron Age burials). Soon after they drained the forum, the kings paved it and began constructing public buildings. The first passage is a quote from the Greek historian Dionysius of Halicarnassus. He describes the enlargement of the city under the early kings. The second passage, written by the historian Livy, describes the draining of the forum and the beginning of the construction of the temple of Jupiter on the Capitoline Hill.

Dionysius of Halicarnassus, *Roman Antiquities* 2.50
Written in the First Century BC Describing
Rome's Mythical Early History

The followers of Romulus and Tatius next enlarged the city of Rome by adding two hills: the so-called Quirinal Hill and the Caelian Hill. Each of the leaders established a residence separate from each other. For his group's residence, Romulus took the Palatine and Caelian (which is next to the Palatine). Tatius took the Capitoline (which he had taken control of at the beginning) and the Quirinal. They cleared the low-lying area beneath the Capitoline Hill by cutting down the trees and filling in the marsh with dirt. This marsh first appeared because runoff from the hills collected in the lower ground in this area. The filling of the marsh was the major step in the creation of the forum, which even today is the center of public life in Rome. The forum is where the Romans conduct assemblies. They conduct their business transactions in the Temple of Vulcan that stands a short distance up the road from the forum. In the forum both leaders constructed temples and dedicated altars to the gods to whom they made vows in the heat of battle. Romulus built one to Jupiter Stator near the Mugonian Gate, which stands over the road that runs from the Sacred Way in the center of the forum up to the Palatine. In a recent battle, Romulus had prayed to this god and his army had stopped its retreat, reformed, and began to fight again. Tatius built temples to the Sun, the Moon, Saturn, Rhea, as well as Vesta, Vulcan, Diana, Enyalius, and other gods whose names are difficult to say in Greek.

Livy, *Histories* 1.38
Written in the First Century BC Describing
Rome's Mythical Early History

The parts of the city at a lower elevation around the forum and in the other valleys between the hills were quite marshy because the terrain used to trap water from the hills. Romulus drained these by running a drain from them to the Tiber. He also built a large podium on one side of the Capitoline Hill, which would one day serve as the foundation for the temple of Jupiter. Romulus had vowed to build this temple during his war against the Sabines. From the enormous size of this project Romulus saw clearly Rome's future greatness.

Ostia

Although not as grand or well documented in history as Rome, the extensively excavated and well-preserved ruins of Ostia give us a privileged glimpse of ancient urban life. In Rome, the majority of preserved ruins come from magnificent public buildings. Little remains archaeologically to give a sense of the life of the common person or merchant in the less grand parts of Rome, such as the densely populated Subura. Ostia, a city filled with ruins of brick apartment buildings, shops, and warehouses provides more information about everyday life in a busy commercial town (as Rome itself was) than any other preserved ancient site. Originally founded to guard the mouth of the Tiber and the nearby salt mines (#143), Ostia grew to prominence in the early Empire when emperors built harbors to make transportation of goods to Rome easier (#144). Ostia was abandoned during the Middle Ages and the site saw little new construction. As a result, its ancient buildings fell into ruin, but were not torn down to make room for new construction. Eventually the city disappeared beneath layers of dirt accumulation. Excavations in the early twentieth century included the restoration and reconstruction of damaged walls and ceilings. Although much of the marble facades and decorative elements are missing (burnt in the late Classical period for lime) today, the ancient streets are lined with houses and shops made of brick-faced concrete (see #145 for a map of Ostia). Some of these buildings reach a height of three stories. The modern visitor can wander endlessly through the immense excavations (about half of the city's original area has been excavated) and perceive approximately what a city like Ostia (and thereby Rome) would have looked like in the second century AD.

#143: The Origins of Ostia

Ostia was originally founded to mine the salt beds along the Tiber. In the mid-fourth century, as Rome began to unite Italy under its rule, a military colony was established on the site to protect the river access to Rome against invasion by sea. A fort was constructed some distance south of the river. A civilian settlement of ambitious merchants seeking to take advantage of foreign trade grew up to the west of the fort. Ostia's trade activity enjoyed increased dramatically in the third and second centuries BC as Rome both began to annex provinces across the Mediterranean and began to demand more imported goods. The following two texts are our primary evidence for the origins of Ostia during the regal period. Standing at the point where the Tiber reached the sea, Ostia had a considerable strategic advantage. The low-lying, marshy area nearby was also a major source of salt.

Livy, *Histories* 1.33
Written in the First Century BC Describing
Rome's Mythical Early History

Ancus Marcius did not confine his work to Rome only. He extended Roman dominion to the sea and founded the city of Ostia at the mouth of the Tiber River. On both sides of the river salt works were constructed.

Florus, *Epitome of Roman History* 1.1
Written in the Second Century AD Describing
Rome's Mythical Early History

Ancus Marcius built the colony of Ostia at the place where the sea and Tiber River meet. Even at that early period, Ancus clearly foresaw how that city would become the maritime emporium to which the wealth and commerce of the whole world would come.

#144: The Imperial Harbors at Ostia

When Italy, where cash crops like grapes and olives were increasingly farmed, could no longer provide the grain Rome needed to feed its population, the city turned to foreign markets to provide the majority of its food supply. Much of this imported grain passed first through the harbors at Ostia. The Roman central government took an active role in Ostia's well-being as it strove to ensure the smooth operation of the grain supply to Rome. In the middle of the first century AD, Claudius constructed a major harbor across the Tiber to the north. In the early second century AD, Trajan added a second, more protected harbor to the east of Claudius' harbor. By this time, Ostia had become a large, thriving town. As demand increased, real estate prices soared. As happened in Rome in the first to second centuries AD, Ostia stretched less outward and more upward. Tall apartment buildings began to replace the independent atrium-style houses of the Republic and early Empire. New construction and renovation continued into the third century, when the empire's economic problems began to hurt Ostia's growth and prosperity.

The following passages document the development of Ostia's harbors. The first written by Strabo in the reign of Augustus describes the city before the harbors. The second and third passages mention Claudius' harbor and the large ship that was used to construct the mole in the harbor. The fourth is an inscription mentioning the canal constructed by Trajan as part of his new harbor.

Strabo, *Geography* 231–232
First Century BC/First Century AD

Ostia itself does not have a harbor because the Tiber deposits a great deal of silt at its mouth due to the many small streams that feed the river. It is more dangerous for the transport ships to anchor farther out in the open water, but Rome's need for grain overrides that danger. Ostia, however, has such a large number of small transport boats that it is possible for the large ships to unload their cargo and reload with other goods for export very quickly and sail away again without even coming close to the mouth of the river. In some cases, once the boats have been emptied of some of their cargo, it is possible for them to sail into the river and unload the rest of their cargo in town or even in Rome itself.

Suetonius, *Claudius* 20
Written in the Early Second Century AD Describing
the Emperor Claudius (AD 41–54)

Claudius completed some major public works that were more useful than numerous. He completed a harbor at Ostia even though he knew that the task had been considered on several occasions by the divine Julius Caesar but never begun because of the difficulty of the task. He constructed this port by drawing out piers on the left and right. In front of the entrance between these piers he constructed a large mole to protect the harbor by keeping waves from entering it. As a foundation for this mole, Claudius sunk a huge ship that had been used to transport an obelisk from Egypt. He constructed pillars and placed upon them a very high lighthouse like the one at Alexandria. At night, ships could direct their course toward the light in this lighthouse to find the entrance to the harbor.

Pliny the Elder, *Natural History* 36.14 (70)
First Century AD

For a number of years, the divine Claudius kept the ship that Gaius Caesar (Caligula) had used to import an obelisk. This ship was one of the most amazing sights ever to be seen on the water. Pillars of cement were constructed in the ship at the harbor of Puteoli before it was sailed north to Ostia where Claudius had it sunk for the construction of his harbor.

CIL 14.88 (Ostia, Italy)
Reign of Trajan (AD 98–117)

The emperor Caesar Nerva Trajan Augustus Germanicus Dacicus, holding the tribunician power for the [?] time, acclaimed *imperator* [?] times, consul [?] times, father of his country, son of the divine Nerva, ordered the renovation of the ditch which is designed to prevent the flooding that plagues the city of Ostia all year round.

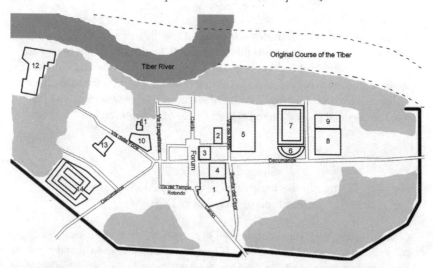

Figure 8.3 The Topography of Ostia (1: Forum Baths; 2: House of Diana; 3: House of the Thermopo-
lium; 4: Forum of the Heroic Statue; 5: Grand Warehouse; 6: Theater; 7: Plaza of the Corporations; 8:
Baths of Neptune; 9: Barracks of the Fire Brigade; 10: Republican Temples; 11: House of Cupid and
Psyche; 12: Palace; 13: Baths of the Seven Sages; 14: Garden Apartments).

#145: Map of Ostia

The reconstructed Ostia that is visible today essentially preserves the city in its hey-
day in the second century AD (see Figure 8.3). Like other Roman towns, Ostia's
two major roads were the east–west *decumanus* and the north–south *cardo*. These
two roads meet at the forum. Ostia's forum is a long rectangle stretching north
and south of the *decumanus* in the center of town. The large *capitolium* on its high
podium dominates the northern end. On the southern end stands the Temple of
Rome and Augustus. On the west side, on either side of the *cardo* are the *curia*
and basilica. The large Forum Baths, constructed by Antoninus Pius in the middle
of the second century AD, are situated just south of the forum. Warehouses and
dock offices dominate the *cardo* north of the forum. East of the forum are numerous apartment-style buildings, including the well preserved and restored House
of Diana (see Figure 8.4) and House of the Thermopolium. A large open market
(the Forum of the Heroic Statue) lies south of the *decumanus*. Farther east and
north of the *decumanus* is the area that had been appropriated as state property in
the late Republic. Notable structures include the "Grand Warehouse" built in the
Julio–Claudian period. The Augustan theater stands nearby. North of the theater is
the "Plaza of the Corporations," an open park surrounded by a portico containing offices of the major importers operating in Ostia. Farther east are the Baths of
Neptune and barracks of the fire brigade (the *vigiles*). South of the *decumanus* and
east of the Forum Baths is a maze of residential structures and warehouses. Much of
this area, especially southeast of the theater, has not been excavated.

Figure 8.4 The House of Diana in Ostia (Photograph by B. Harvey).

West of the forum stand four temples preserved from Ostia's early history. Beyond them are a series of warehouses mixed in with the remains of some impressive late imperial houses such as the House of Cupid and Psyche. A very large house, perhaps an imperial palace, has been uncovered in the largely unexcavated section close to the Tiber, in the extreme northwest corner of the city. Farther south are more houses, shops, and baths, including the grand Baths of the Seven Sages. In the southwest corner of town is the ritzy apartment complex called the "Garden Apartments." Built in the reign of Hadrian, this structure consists of two long buildings containing upscale apartments that stand in the middle of a large, open lawn.

Pompeii

Unlike Ostia, which grew, then shrank, and eventually died a slow death, the city of Pompeii on the Bay of Naples was destroyed suddenly in AD 79 as a result of a volcanic eruption (see #148 for a map of Pompeii). While it, too, had enjoyed a long history stretching back centuries, the city's quick and agonizing death and burial preserved a rare snapshot of life in a Roman city during the first century AD.

A people called the Oscans founded Pompeii probably in the eighth century BC as a seaside trading center in Campania. The Sarno River enters the Bay of Naples very close to Pompeii, and the river valley, fertile with volcanic soil, made the town an ideal agricultural center. Its location along several major roads and on the Bay of Naples also made it an important commercial town.

The Samnites arrived in the late fourth century BC and settled in the city. After the Romans defeated the Samnites in three wars during the third century BC, Pompeii allied with Rome. For two centuries, Pompeii curried the attention and favor of Rome but was not granted Roman citizenship because of Rome's conservative attitude toward extending citizenship to towns like Pompeii after the Second Punic War (218–201 BC). In 90 BC, many of the allied cities of Italy rebelled against Rome in a war known as the Social War. During this war, Rome besieged Pompeii in 89. Despite Rome's victory over the revolting cities, the Roman Senate decided to grant citizenship to all of Italy, including Pompeii, shortly after the end of the war. Pompeii was granted the status of colony, but was also compelled to accept a contingent of at least two thousand retired Roman soldiers. Many of the locals were driven off their land so that it could be given to these ex-Roman soldiers.

In AD 62, a severe earthquake hit the then prosperous Pompeii. A great deal of the city was severely damaged. Reconstruction was slow due to a lack of state aid from Rome. Seventeen years later, when the eruption of Vesuvius destroyed the city, many buildings were still in ruins or in some state of disrepair due to the earlier earthquake. A relief sculpture from the House of Caecilius Iucundus shows buildings and temples in the forum with extensive earthquake damage.

The volcano Vesuvius erupted late one morning in August of AD 79. The eruption lasted a little more than twenty-four hours, but during that time the city was buried beneath volcanic debris (#146 and #147). Pompeii remained buried until the eighteenth century when the Italian military rediscovered it while digging a canal. The site became a haven for treasure hunters seeking to sell its treasures to the nobility. Excavations began in the 1860s and have continued to the present day and have succeeded in uncovering about three-quarters of the city.

#146: The Eruption of Vesuvius: The Investigation of Pliny the Elder

Pliny the Younger, *Letters* 6.16
Early Second Century AD

In two letters written to the historian Tacitus, the writer Pliny the Younger, an eyewitness of the volcanic eruption that destroyed Pompeii, describes the event. The eruption began around noon on August 24th. For the rest of that day and through the night, the volcano spewed a huge cone of ash into the air. Occcasionally, the cone collapsed sending clouds of super-heated poison gas at tremendous speed down the side of the volcano. The ash rained down upon Pompeii, burying it under yards of debris. Early the morning of the 25th, the final and largest surge reached Pompeii, killing all who had remained in the city as the poison gasses asphyxiated them. By the time the eruption was over, the city was gone, buried beneath ash, rock, and lava. The ash layer preserved not only buildings, but also materials and organic matter, which, under normal conditions, would have decomposed or been reused in antiquity. In this first letter, Pliny describes the first day of the eruption and how his uncle, Pliny the Elder, went to investigate the event and rescue people from imminent danger. Unfortunately, Pliny the Elder lost his life the following morning in Stabiae while waiting for the winds to change so that he could sail back across the bay.

You have asked that I write to you about the death of my uncle so that you can use my account to describe the events more accurately in the history you are writing. I thank you for the opportunity because I know that if his death is commemorated by you that his glory will be everlasting. Although he died in a disaster that devastated a very beautiful part of Italy, killed many people, and destroyed cities, it will be as if my uncle will live forever in the pages of your history. My uncle himself wrote many classic books himself, but the enduring fame of your own writings will only add to the survival of my uncle's name. Indeed, I believe that those people are happy to whom the gods have given the ability of either doing things worthy of being recorded in books or writing books that are worth reading. Most happy, however, are those who can do both. My uncle is certainly in this latter category as he will be remembered both for his own literary works and for his actions as they will be recorded in yours. I take up this request you have made of me, therefore, all the more willingly.

At the time of the eruption, my uncle was commander of the fleet at Misenum. On August 24th, a little after noon, my mother pointed out to him a cloud of unusual size and appearance. My uncle had finished his morning routine of going for a walk, taking a cold bath, and having a small lunch and was then reclining on a couch and reading. When my mother showed him the cloud, he asked for his sandals and climbed up a nearby hill from which he could see the phenomenon more clearly. It was indeed a cloud but one rising from the earth. As we looked at it from such a distance, we could not determine from which mountain it was coming (it was later learned that it was Vesuvius). In shape, it resembled an umbrella pine tree because it seemed to grow from the ground on a very long trunk but then high up in the air it spread out in all directions as if on branches. I believe it had been driven out of the ground by a strong force but then, when that force weakened as the column reached a higher altitude, the cloud spread out wider into the sky. In places, the cloud was white, but in others it was dark and splotchy, I suppose, in accordance with how much earth and ash was in the cloud. My uncle, a very learned man, believed that this was a very important event and one that needed to be investigated from a closer vantage point. He ordered a light, swift ship to be prepared. He asked me if I wanted to come along, but I responded that I preferred to stay behind to work on my studies (as it happened, I had some homework that he himself had given me). As he was leaving the house, he received a letter from a woman named Rectina, the wife of Tascus. She was frightened by the danger that hung over her. Indeed her villa was directly beneath the cloud and it seemed to her that there would be no hope of escape except by ship. Therefore, she had written to ask my uncle to come and rescue her from danger. He immediately changed his plan and what he had originally undertaken for intellectual reasons he now did for the most noble. He had some larger warships prepared and boarded them with the intention of not only rescuing Rectina but also many others (the pleasantness of the shore had attracted a great number of inhabitants). And so my uncle hastened to the place from which others were fleeing and made his course straight into danger. Nevertheless, he maintained a remarkable calm so that he could take very careful notes of all of the movements and appearances of the eruption.

Soon, ash from the mountain began to fall onto the deck of the ship. The closer they got to the event, the hotter and denser the ash became. Then pumice stone and rocks that were black, charred, and broken by the fire also began to fall. As they approached their destination, they were met with new obstacles. The water was unexpectedly shallow and large chunks of rock had fallen into the water and were blocking their approach to the shore. The helmsman told my uncle that they should turn back. My uncle hesitated and considered following his advice but then yelled back to the helmsman, "Fortune comes to the aid of the brave! Make your course for the estate of Pomponianus." Now Pomponianus lived in the town of Stabiae, which was withdrawn from the main part of the bay by a modest inlet created by the gradual curving of the shore away from the main part of the bay. Indeed, being farther south and somewhat sheltered from the devastation, Stabiae was still safe although the danger was clearly visible and very close and getting closer. My uncle landed near the house of Pomponianus and loaded his friend's belongings onto the ships. They were not able to leave again immediately as the wind was blowing against them and made sailing impossible. This wind, which had been behind them as they crossed the bay, had carried my uncle to Stabiae with remarkable speed. Nevertheless, my uncle was certain they would be able to set sail and get away as soon as the winds died down. He embraced Pomponianus who was terrified and could think of nothing but escape. My uncle consoled him and told him there was nothing to fear in the hopes that he could calm his friend by appearing unconcerned himself. He then asked that they be directed to the bath complex in the house. After a time, they returned. Having washed, the group reclined in the dining room and had some dinner. My uncle was cheerful in all of this, or at least gave the appearance of being cheerful, something that is just as noteworthy.

During this time, large patches of fire could be seen on the slopes of Mount Vesuvius. The darkness of night made these shine all the more clearly. My uncle, however, in order to calm the nerves of his friend, claimed that what they saw were fires the local farmers had left behind when they had fled the disaster and that those fires had been allowed to burn out of control now that the estates on the slopes of the mountain had been deserted. After this attempt to calm Pomponianus, my uncle decided to get some rest. Indeed, he was so calm that he slept very deeply. His snoring, which was always heavier and louder than normal because of the heaviness of his body, was able to be heard by people who were in the next room. A short time later, however, the courtyard off of which my uncle's room opened began to fill with a mixture of ash and pumice. Indeed, if my uncle had stayed in the room longer, the debris would have risen so that that he would not have been able to get out again. As it was, however, the slaves woke him up and he returned to Pomponianus and the others who had been unable to sleep at all. The group debated what their course of action would be. Should they remain indoors or take their chances out in the open? Both options seemed dangerous. The buildings were being shaken from frequent and powerful earth tremors. Indeed, in many cases, the buildings seemed to have been ripped from their foundations and were moving here and there with nothing to hold them down. Out in the open, however, the falling of the charred pumice was feared. Although each stone was relatively light, it was falling very thickly. At last they decided to take their chances out in the open. In the case of my uncle, one idea seemed better than the other. With the others, however, one terror seemed less horrible than the other. They tied pillows to their heads to protect themselves from the falling debris.

It was daytime everywhere else but under Vesuvius it was blacker and thicker than any night that had ever been. Nevertheless the lanterns and other lights of my uncle's group pierced the gloom. They started by going back to the shore to check the situation and see if the sea had calmed down. The waves, however, were still large and the wind was still blowing inland. There my uncle laid himself down upon a sail cloth they spread out for him. He asked once and then again for cold water, which he drank. Then the flash of flames and the strong smell of sulfur made the others flee and woke up my uncle. Leaning on two slaves, he stood up but immediately fell dead. From what I have been able to gather, his breathing was obstructed by some thick fumes, which shut off his windpipe, which had always been weaker and narrower by nature and so was often inflamed. When the sun finally returned to that area (and that was the third day after the eruption had begun), his body was discovered. It was still intact and without a mark of violence upon it and still clothed in the way I had seen him when he left. Indeed, when I saw it, it looked more like my uncle was asleep than dead.

During all of this, I was in Misenum with my mother. Our story, however, does not have anything to do with your history. You asked to hear about nothing other than the death of my uncle. I will, however, add that all of these events that I have described I either took part in personally or heard at the time from those who were present during them. I leave it up to you to take the facts that you need for your history. I completely understand that what is good in a letter may not be in a published history because one is written to a friend while the other is for public consumption. Good-bye.

#147: The Eruption of Vesuvius: Adventure in Misenum

Pliny the Younger, *Letters* 6.20
Early Second Century AD

In his second letter on the eruption of Vesuvius, Pliny the Younger describes the worry he and his mother experienced after his uncle had departed across the bay.

He also describes the terror in Misenum when the final surge from Vesuvius hit the town.

> You say that the letter I wrote to you about the death of my uncle has made you wish to learn what fears and dangers I faced while remaining in Misenum when my uncle departed to investigate the eruption. I realize that my account broke off at that point. "Although my entire being shudders to remember, I will begin..."

After my uncle left, I worked to finish my allotted time for my studies. It was, after all, the reason I had stayed behind in Misenum. After I finished my studies, I bathed, had dinner, and went to bed. My slumbers, however, were restless and I did not sleep much. There had been earthquakes for many days before the eruption, but that was not that surprising as Campania tends to be plagued by such events. That night of the eruption, however, the earthquakes became so strong that it seemed like the earth was not just moving but turning inside-out. My mother rushed into my bedroom to awaken me, but I was already up and on my way out to awaken her. We went outside into a courtyard that is between the sea and the rest of the house. I hesitate now whether to call my actions at that time bravery or foolishness (I was only eighteen years old at the time), but I asked a slave to bring me a copy of the histories of Livy. When I received the book I began reading it and taking notes, as if there was nothing unusual happening. While I was doing that, a friend of my uncle who had recently arrived from Spain came out of the house and joined us. When he saw us sitting calmly and me reading a book, he scolded my mother for her serenity and me for my lack of concern for my own safety. His reproof, however, had no effect, and I went on reading as intently as before.

Morning arrived but the sun was not very bright as if there was a haze blocking its light. The buildings around us were shaking. Although we were out in the open, the way was narrow and there was ever the fear that the buildings around us would topple. For that reason, we decided to leave town. We soon found a group of terrified people following us. Indeed, when a person is afraid, everyone else's plan appears better than one's own. And so this throng pressed us and drove us on as we tried to make our escape. After we had left town behind us, we stopped and looked around us. Many amazing and dreadful things came to our eyes. The carts that we had been using began to roll or be pulled in odd directions even though the ground there was very flat. We tried to use stones to brace the wheels, but they did not stop the movement. Also, we could see the sea being pulled back onto itself, presumably from the force of the earthquakes. Certainly the water had retreated farther from the shore. Now on the much larger beach, we could see many sea creatures stranded on the dry sand. Across the bay toward Vesuvius we could see the dark and frightful cloud. The force of the eruption had ripped this cloud apart into twisted and shaking tendrils and in the cracks we could see long flashes of fiery light that looked like bolts of lightning only larger. Upon seeing this phenomenon, my uncle's friend from Spain exclaimed to us quite sharply and insistently, "if your brother, your uncle, is still alive, he would want the two of you to be safe. If he is dead, then he would want you to survive this. Knowing that, why do you stop here and not make your escape?" We replied that we could not think of our own safety when we were uncertain of his. Hearing that, my uncle's friend did not delay but hurried off and escaped from the danger as quickly as possible. Not long after that, the cloud descended to the earth. It obscured the sea. It went out to sea and covered Capri and hid it from view. It then spread to Misenum, which juts out into the sea, and soon it was gone as well. Then my mother at first asked and then urged and finally ordered me to flee as best as I could. "You are a young man," she said, "but I am elderly and overweight and so would only slow you down. I will die happily, though, if I know that I am not the reason for your death." I replied that I could not be safe unless she was as well and so refused to leave her. Taking her by the hand, I compelled her to continue on. She reluctantly obeyed and criticized herself for slowing me down.

Now ash began to fall on us, although in only limited quantity. I looked back and saw the dense cloud spreading out over the land behind us. It was catching up to us. I said to my mother, "Let us turn off the road while we can still see where we are going. I am afraid that the crowd behind us will trample us in the darkness if we stay on the road." We got off the road and sat down. We had scarcely done so when dark night overtook us. This was not the dark of a moonless or cloudy night but was dark like a closed room is dark when the light is turned off. In the darkness, we could hear the cries of women, the shrieking of infants, and the shouts of men. Some were calling out to their parents, others their children, still others their spouses in the hopes that the one they were looking for would recognize their voice. Some were feeling sorry for their own fate, others the fate of their families and loved ones. There were a few even who prayed for death out of fear of dying. Many lifted their hands in supplication to the gods, but many believed that there were no gods anywhere and that this darkness was the final, everlasting night of the world. There were also some who intensified the real dangers by making up or lying about new ones. There were people who had come with us from Misenum who were shouting that Misenum had fallen into the sea or that it was on fire. Certainly these claims were false, but there were people who believed them. The light came back gradually. Our first thought was that this was a warning of a rush of fire coming toward us rather than the return of daylight. In truth, the final surge of fire stopped some distance from us but it was still close enough to shroud us in darkness again. Ash began to fall in large quantities. Quite often we had to stand up and shake the ash off lest we eventually be covered and crushed by its weight. I suppose I could boast that in such a dangerous situation not a groan or a frightened cry escaped my lips, but in truth I had taken great solace in believing that my life was going to end along with everyone else with me. Indeed, it seemed like the whole world was going to perish.

At last, however, the darkness faded much as smoke or a cloud dissipates after a while. Soon, it was daytime again, and the sun shone brightly, although the sun's light was pale as it is when it sets. As we gazed across the landscape, everything seemed changed to our still-trembling eyes. A thick layer of ash like snow lay upon everything. We returned home to Misenum. We were still very nervous but we tried to sleep. All that first night after the eruption our minds switched back and forth from hope to fear and back again. Fear, however, was the more common emotion we experienced. The earthquakes continued. There were also quite a few lunatics who ran around making terrifying predictions and claimed that the terrible events they had already experienced were nothing in comparison to the calamities that were still to come. Even in the face of all that we had experienced and still expected to happen, however, my mother and I took no thought of leaving Misenum until we could receive news of my uncle.

That is the story of my adventures during the eruption of Vesuvius. You will read it although I am sure you will not consider it worth including the details in your history. Indeed, if you think them worthy of such a long letter, you have only yourself to blame as you asked me to write to tell you about it. Good-bye.

#148: Map of Pompeii

The city walls of Pompeii, beginning with courses that run north and east from the port, extend around the city in a narrow rectangle (see Figure 8.5). Unlike Ostia, Pompeii, with its roots in the pre–Roman past, has no defined *decumanus* and *cardo*. The western, oldest part of town is a labyrinth of winding streets. In the east, however, the traditional grid pattern of streets is visible in the part of town that

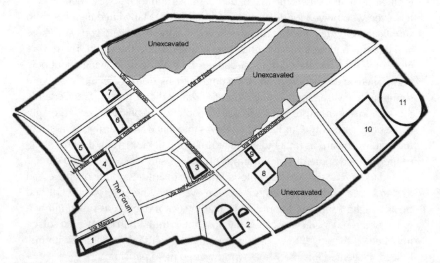

Figure 8.5 The Topography of Pompeii (1: Temple of Venus; 2: Theater District; 3: Stabian Baths; 4: Forum Baths; 5: House of Pansa; 6: House of the Faun; 7: House of the Vettii; 8: House of Menander; 9: *Fullonica* of Stephanus; 10: Gladiator Barracks; 11: Amphitheater).

Figure 8.6 Looking East Down the *Via della Fortuna*, Pompeii (Photograph by B. Harvey).

was constructed later. The town's most prominent street is the *Via dell'Abbondanza* ("Street of Abundance"), which runs across the southern side of the town from the forum to the extreme eastern gate by the amphitheater.

The forum in Pompeii is situated in the center of the oldest part of town (see Figure 8.6). As it is preserved today, Pompeii's forum is dominated by the large *capitolium* at the northern end. The eastern side of the forum has two markets, a sanctuary of the public *lares* (the protecting spirits of the city), and a temple of Vespasian (the ruling emperor at the time of the eruption). A public granary and the temple of Apollo stand on the western side. The offices of the public magistrates were built at the southern end. South of the forum and close to the sea is the large temple of Venus constructed when Sulla converted Pompeii into a Roman colony in the early first century BC. Several of the major entertainment buildings also are in this region. The theater complex lies in the south. The Stabian baths stand along the *Via dell'Abbondanza* a short distance west of the forum. The Forum Baths are immediately north of the forum. The northwestern region of the city was primarily a residential district with many houses, including the House of Pansa, the House of the Faun, and the House of the Vettii. A sizable portion of northeastern Pompeii has not yet been excavated. This area, included in the earliest walls, incorporated an agricultural population who worked on small grape and olive plantations within the city limits or larger farms just outside the city. The part of town south of the *Via dell'Abbondanza* was also primarily residential. The House of Menander is one of the finest so far excavated in Pompeii. Also nearby is the laundry (*fullonica*) of Stephanus, an excellent example of an industrial facility in Pompeii. In the eastern corner of town are the gladiatorial barracks and the amphitheater.

Chapter 9: The Urban Experience

With a population of around one million people in the first century AD, Rome was a huge city by ancient standards. Pompeii and Ostia were much smaller but still major cities in their own right. In this chapter, you will see some evidence for the hustle and bustle of a Roman city. In the first section, you will read passages about the busy streets of Rome and the generally hectic urban lifestyle in general. In the second section are numerous examples of graffiti from the Roman period.

Literary Scenes of Busy Streets

It was only natural that a city as large as Rome would be a busy place. Roman satire frequently alluded to the crowds and noise of the streets of Rome. These passages provide great vignettes of the urban experience. In his *On Clemency*, Seneca mentions Rome's ever-growing population (#149). Juvenal's third satire describes the busy street running through Rome's Subura (#150). Martial, too, describes the sights and sounds of the diverse population of the city (#151).

#149: The Large Population of the City of Rome

Seneca, *On Clemency* 1.6.1
First Century AD

In this passage, the first century AD philosopher Seneca aptly describes the ever-expanding and extremely busy city of Rome.

> Think about this city of ours. Here, the crowd, flowing like a rushing river without stop along its wide streets, is crushed together whenever something blocks the path. In this city, three theaters are needed to contain its population. Indeed, here the population is so large that it consumes whatever food is harvested in every part of the world.

#150: Rome's Busy Streets

Juvenal, *Satires* 3.234–248
Late First/Early Second Centuries AD

The early second century AD satirist Juvenal echoes Seneca's somewhat alarming statements about Rome's busy streets. Litters were covered couches with poles for handles carried by slaves that allowed a wealthy person to get from one place to another without having to walk in the street like the poorer members of society. Higher magistrates in Rome and the municipalities, in fact, had officials called *lictors* who walked in front of them through the streets. The *lictors* carried the *fasces*, an axe bound up in a bundle of rods. The *fasces* symbolized the magistrate's ability to punish citizens; they also came in handy to clear crowded streets to allow the magistrate to pass without being tousled by the crowd. Nighttime was no better. Because they were prevented from doing so by day, carts filled the streets at night and created a whole new kind of noise.

What rental property in the city will allow a poor person to get some shut-eye? Only the very rich can sleep in this city. That is the very root of the problem I have been talking about. The comings and goings of the carts in the narrow streets of the city and the heckling of the cart driver who is stopped in a traffic jam would tear even that log-headed emperor Claudius from his slumbers, and usually nothing would wake him up. When morning comes and the day's business calls, the rich man passes through the yielding crowd in his litter. He sails across the sea of faces as if in a great ocean liner. Inside as he passes along, he reads or writes or even takes a nap since the litter's closed curtains make it easy to sleep. Of course, he reaches his destination before we do. The wave of people in front of us blocks us as we try to hurry along. Meanwhile, the mass of humanity behind us gives our groin a jab to get us moving. One guy strikes me with his elbow; another pokes me with the hard pole of the litter he is carrying. Someone else brings his two-by-four down on my head while another whacks me with the ten-gallon jug he is carrying. My legs are crusted with mud. Soon, other people's giant feet are trampling on mine. Finally, some soldier plants his hobnail through my toe.

#151: A Busy Street Scene

Martial, *Epigrams* 12.57.3–15
Late First Century AD

The poet Martial, whose satirical epigrams are reminiscent of his contemporary Juvenal, describes how the busy streets of Rome are the main reason he sometimes leaves the city to visit his country villa even though he loves the cosmopolitan nature of Rome.

My friend, the city gives the poor man no chance to think or nap. The schoolteacher denies you your salutary nap by day, as do the bakers by night. Those little hammers of the metalworkers go all day long. On one side of the street, a moneychanger sits at his dirty table and lovingly fondles his bag of higher quality coins that come from old Nero's reign. On the other side of the street, a worker in Spanish gold dust constantly strikes his worn-down stone with his shining mallet. The frenzied worshippers of Bellona never take a break from the wild dances in honor of their goddess. That shipwreck victim, his body bandaged, never stops complaining about his misfortune. Always begging is that child from the eastern deserts of the empire. His craft is nothing new however; his mother originally taught him how to beg. Then there is that half-blind huckster who is always hawking firewood that reeks of the sulfur he dunked it in to make it burn more easily.

Graffiti from Pompeii

Preserved literary sources reveal much about the day-to-day experience of life in the busy streets of Rome. Also important is the chance preservation of ancient graffiti on buildings and city walls. While generally considered to be a nuisance in modern times, graffiti provides valuable insights into the everyday lives of even the most obscure inhabitants of an ancient city. Sealed in the volcanic deposit of Vesuvius, graffiti survived in Pompeii better than most ancient sites. This section merely gives a representative sample of the more than twelve thousand graffiti that were found by excavators while unearthing Pompeii. These examples provide a unique glimpse into the everyday lives of ordinary people. Many examples of painted election campaign posters have been preserved (#152 and #153). One of the oldest examples from Pompeii is an advertisement for the return of a missing pot from a shop (#154). The plaster walls of Pompeii served as a form of ancient social media for myriad individuals who scratched personal statements onto them (#155, #156, #157, #158, #159, #160, and #161).

#152: Election Campaign Posters from Pompeii

CIL 4.113, 202, 275, 425, 429, 576, 581, 710, 768, 787, 1146, 1147, 2887, 3235, 3702, 3775, 6626, 7065
First Century BC to AD 79

Much of the graffiti from Pompeii is in the form of advertisements of candidates who were running for political office. These election notices were painted in bright, red letters on the exterior walls of the buildings lining the streets. Requests for electoral support for various candidates running for the position of town mayor (*duovir*) and aedile (a financial officer) appear throughout the ancient city. The following exemplify the typical formula found in these election posters.

113: The muleteers ask that you elect Gaius Julius Polybius *duovir*.
202: The fruit vendors and Helvius Vestalis unanimously promote Marcus Holconius Priscus for *duovir* with judicial power.
275: Saturninus and his students support Gaius Cuspius Pansa for aedile.

425: Claudius' sweetheart is voting for him for *duovir*.

429: Gaius Julius Polybius for aedile. He will get you good bread.

576: The petty thieves support Vatia for aedile.

581: The late-night drinkers unanimously support Marcus Cerrinius Vatia for aedile. Florus and Fructus wrote this.

710: The goldsmiths unanimously support Gaius Cuspius Pansa for aedile.

768: Vote for Marcus Epidius Sabinus for *duovir* with judicial powers. He is a worthy defender of the colony. In the opinion of the solemn judge Suedius Clemens, with the agreement of the whole council, Sabinus' merits and honesty make him worthy of service to his town. Sabinus, master of ceremonies, put up this notice and applauds the candidate.

787: The worshippers of Isis unanimously promote Gnaeus Helvius Sabinus for aedile.

1146: The worshippers of Venus ask that you make Paquius *duovir* with judicial powers.

1147: The ball players unanimously support Aulus Vettius Firmus for aedile.

2887: May all who refuse to vote for Quintius be turned into a donkey!

3235: I ask that you elect Marcus Cerrinius Vatia aedile. Faventinus and his friends ask that you do so.

3702: Elect Bruttius Balbus *duovir*. He will protect the town treasury.

3775: Your neighbors urge you to elect Lucius Statius Receptus *duovir* with judicial powers. He is a worthy candidate. Aemilius Celer wrote this and may you rot if you maliciously erase it! Celer wrote this alone by moonlight.

6626: If modesty in life should be considered worth anything at all, then Lucretius Fronto is worthy of the office.

7065: Absolutely everyone approves of Proculus for aedile. His natural modesty and loyalty demand it.

#153: Unwanted Endorsements from Barmaids

CIL 4.7841, 7862, 7863, 7864, 7866, 7873
First Century AD

People of lower reputation also voiced their opinion on the local elections. Felicio, the owner or manager of a brothel (*lupinarius*) appears on two posters (*CIL* 4.3423 and .3483). Even the local barmaids voiced their opinion of the candidates as is the case with the following graffiti. One candidate, Gaius Julius Polybius, however, does not seem to have wanted their support. The two election posters promoting him were not removed, but the names of the girls, Zmyrina and Cuculla, were erased.

7841: [[Cuculla]] asks that you elect Gaius Julius Polybius *duovir*.

7862: Aegle asks that you elect Gnaeus Helvius Sabinus aedile. He is worth of holding office in the town.

7863: Asellina and Zmyrina urge you to vote for Gaius Lollius Fuscus for town mayor in charge of the drainage system and the upkeep of civil and religious public buildings.

7864: [[Zmyrina]] asks that you elect Gaius Julius Polybius *duovir* with judicial powers.

7866: Maria asks that you elect Gnaeus Helvius Sabinus aedile. He is worth of holding office in the town.

7873: Asselina asks that you elect Ceius Secundus *duovir* with judicial powers.

#154: Reward for the Return of a Missing Pot

CIL 4.64
First Century BC

Graffiti was also used to post notices as in this example of a pot that has gone missing.

A copper pot went missing from my shop. Anyone who returns it to me will be given sixty-five bronze coins (*sestertii*). Twenty more will be given for information leading to the capture of the thief.

#155: Random Notes Scratched on the Walls of Pompeii

CIL 4.1321, 1512, 1842, 1852, 2060, 2071, 2163, 4066, 4087, 4838, 6702,
8162, 8304, 8792b, 8903, 10619
First Century BC to AD 79

Just as with modern graffiti, some ancient Pompeians liked to leave evidence of their visit for persons walking nearby. Some were written by lovers. Others greet the reader with a friendly hello. One even includes recommendations for the best local food and drink.

1321: Publius Comicius Restitutus stood right here with his brother.

1512: Hello, people of Nola!

1842: Gaius Pumidius Dipilus was here on October 3rd, 78 BC.

1852: Pyrrhus says hello to his friend Chius. I have a heavy heart because I have heard that you died. And so, my friend, I bid you good-bye.

2060: Romula hung out here with Staphylus.

2071: Hello, friends!

2163: The warmest hello to Saenecio Fortunatus, wherever he may be.

4066: Daphnus was here with his girlfriend Felicia.

4087: Staphylus was here with Quieta.

4838: Secundus says hello to his friends.

6702: Aufidius was here. Good-bye.

8162: We two dear men, friends forever, were here. If you want to know our names, they are Gaius and Aulus.

8304: Satura was here on September 3rd.

8792b: Antiochus hung out here with his girlfriend Cithera.

8903: Gaius Sabinus says a fond hello to Statius. Traveler, eat bread in Pompeii but go to Nuceria to drink. At Nuceria, the drinking is better.

10619: Apollinaris, the physician of the emperor Titus, defecated well here.

#156: Criticism and Invective in Graffiti

CIL 4.1816, 1820, 1826, 1864, 1880, 1881, 1926, 2048, 2375, 2409a,
4993, 5251
First Century BC to AD 79

Graffiti sometimes recorded personal antipathy and loathing or sought to curse someone else. The walls of Pompeii proved to be a convenient location to advertise one's anger.

1816: Epaphra, you are bald.

1820: Chie, I hope your hemorrhoids hurt so much that they burn worse than they ever have before.

1826: Phileros is a eunuch.

1864: Samius to Cornelius: go hang yourself.

1880: Hey, Lucius Istacidius, I consider a man a barbarian who does not invite me to dinner at his house.

1881: Virgula to her friend Tertius: you are disgusting.

1926: Epaphra is not good at ball games.

2048: Secundus is a pederast.

2375: Amplicatus, I know that Icarus is buggering you. Salvius wrote this.

2409a: Stronius Stronnius knows nothing.

4993: Ampliatus Pedania is a thief.

5251: Restitutus has deceived so many of his girlfriends.

#157: Advertisement for a Rental Property

CIL 4.138
First Century AD

In this text, a wealthy local aristocrat named Gnaeus Alleius Nigidius Maius, who is known from a variety of election posters and advertisements for amphitheatrical games, advertises a house for rent.

The city block of the Arrii Pollii in the possession of Gnaeus Alleius Nigidius Maius is available to rent from July 1st. There are shops on the first floor, upper stories, high-class rooms, and a private residence. A person interested in renting this property should contact Primus, the slave of Gnaeus Alleius Nigidius Maius.

#158: Graffiti from Lovers

CIL 4.1797, 1808, 1824, 1928, 1951, 2146, 3042, 3117, 3131, 3932, 4485, 4637, 6842, 7086, 8364, 8408a, 10231
First Century BC to AD 79

Just as in modern times, love is one of the most frequent topics of the wall-writers of Pompeii. The following are some examples of people in love, notes to lovers, and people disappointed with love.

1797: No young buck is complete until he has fallen in love.
1808: Auge loves Allotenus.
1824: Let everyone in love come and see. I want to break Venus' ribs with a club and cripple the goddess' loins. If she can strike through my soft heart, then why can't I smash her head in with a club?
1928: Love dictates to me as I write and Cupid shows me the way, but may I die if I should prefer to be a god without you.
1951: Sarra, you are not being very nice, leaving me all alone like this.
2146: Vibius Restitutus slept here alone and missed his darling Urbana.
3042: Cruel Lalagus, why do you not love me?
3117: Serena hates Isidorus.
3131: Figulus loves Idaia.
3932: Weep, you girls. My penis has given up on you. Now it penetrates men's behinds. Good-bye, wondrous femininity!
4485: Hectice, baby, Mercator says hello to you.
4637: Rufus loves Cornelia Hele.
6842: If anyone does not believe in Venus, they should gaze at my girlfriend.
7086: Marcus loves Spendusa.
8364: Secundus says hello to his Prima, wherever she is. I ask, my mistress, that you love me.
8408a: Lovers are like bees in that they live a honeyed life.
10231: Adimetus got me pregnant.

#159: The Rivalry of Severus and Successus

CIL 4.8258–8259
First Century AD

The following graffiti recount the story of the rivalry between Successus and Severus. Both men were in love with the same girl, an innkeeper's slave girl named Iris.

[Severus]: Successus, a weaver, loves the innkeeper's slave girl named Iris. She, however, does not love him. Still, he begs her to have pity on him. His rival wrote this. Good-bye.

[Answer by Successus]: Envious one, why do you blurt out such rubbish? Don't even think to speak badly of a man more handsome than you especially one who is both most vicious when crossed and yet also good.

[Answer by Severus]: I have spoken. I have written all there is to say. You love Iris, but she does not love you. I Severus have written this to you, Successus.

#160: Warnings on Tombs

CIL 4.6641, 7716, 10488
First Century BC to AD 79

Pompeii's dark streets and tombs afforded the needy traveler a place to relieve him or herself when a public latrine was not readily available. In a variation of the common "X slept here" graffito type, there are numerous cases of people scrawling on the wall while doing their business. One man writes, "Secundus defecated here" three times in succession (*CIL* 4.3146). Another simply writes "*memor*" ("Here's a souvenir!" *CIL* 4.1339). The first graffito comes from the side of a tomb outside of the northern gate of Pompeii. The last two examples here warn people who might potentially foul the location.

6641: Defecator, may everything turn out okay so that you can leave this place.

7716: To the one defecating here. Beware of the curse. If you look down on this curse, may you have an angry Jupiter for an enemy.

10488: Anyone who wants to defecate in this place is advised to move along. If you act contrary to this warning, you will have to pay a penalty. Children must pay [?] silver coins. Slaves will be beaten on their behinds.

#161: Miscellaneous and Random Examples of Graffiti

CIL 4.1393, 1714, 1811, 1904, 1937, 4235, 5279, 8972
First Century BC to AD 79

With paper so expensive in the ancient world, the Pompeians were happy to scrawl just about anything on their walls. In this final set of examples, you can see some random statements, nonsensical rhyme, a laundry list, some maxims, and even the musings of a person who is amazed there is so much graffiti around town.

1393: On April 20th, I gave a cloak to be washed. On May 7th, a headband. On May 8th, two tunics.

1714: It took 640 paces to walk back and forth between here and there ten times.

1811: A small problem gets larger if you ignore it.

1904: Oh walls, you have held up so much tedious graffiti that I am amazed that you have not already collapsed in ruin.

1937: Would someone like to invite me to dinner?

4235: Barbara barbaribus barbarant barbara barbis.

5279: Once you are dead, you are nothing.

8972: On April 19th, I made bread.

Chapter 10: Housing

Housing in the Roman world was as varied as it is today. In the cities, dwellings ranged from the large urban mansions of the senatorial aristocracy to the tiny and dark apartments of the poor. In the country, sprawling villas at the center of the aristocratic agricultural centers (the *latifundia*) coexisted with the poor farm houses and hovels of the tenant farmers who worked the land.

While archaeology has uncovered Roman houses from throughout the empire, some of our best evidence for urban housing comes from the Italian towns of Pompeii and Ostia. Within the walls of these cities many examples of Roman housing have been well preserved. The seaside town of Pompeii, with its many neighborhoods of larger homes, exemplifies a thriving but not overpopulated town of the first century AD. Ostia, too, had numerous independent houses but more importantly it had many multi-story apartment buildings, which were constructed in response to the explosion in population that accompanied an economic boom in Ostia during the second century AD. Although sparse, the remains of housing in Rome itself indicate that it resembled those found in Pompeii and Ostia. Also, the third century AD marble plan of Rome, fragments of which are still preserved, depicts not only the large aristocratic houses similar (but on a much larger scale, generally) to the houses seen in Pompeii, but also the taller, multi-storied structures encountered in Ostia.

The Parts of a Roman Aristocratic House

In a modern house, a room's shape and furnishings in context with its location within the house provide information by which we can interpret the plausible function of the room. One of the most important factors affecting the layout of the rooms within the house is the proximity of various rooms to the door that serves as the primary entrance into the house. For example, in most multi-room homes of any substance, it is extremely rare to have the home's main entryway open into the master bedroom. Rooms in which the owner entertains guests tend to be closer to the front door, while more private rooms such as bedrooms and family rooms are generally in more remote areas. When one examines the layout of Roman houses, a similar pattern emerges. "Public" rooms for meetings and entertainment were closer to the entrance, while "private" areas for family and close friends were positioned farther away.

Although multi-purpose rooms were common, certain rooms served specific purposes, especially those used by visitors and guests. Specific names for these rooms are mentioned by the first century AD Roman architect Vitruvius, whose

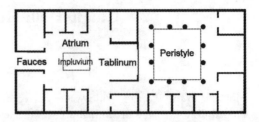

Figure 10.1 Typical Floor Plan of an Atrium-
Style House in Pompeii (1: Fauces; 2: Atrium; 3: Tablinum; 4: Peristyle).

book *On Architecture* describes some of the key rooms (see Figure 10.1 for a typical
floor plan of an atrium-style house; #161). The main door of the house generally
opened onto a corridor, called the *fauces* ("jaws"). This was because many houses
were recessed ten to twenty feet from the street to allow for shops on either side
of the front door. The first room encountered was the atrium, a large rectangular
entrance hall with an opening in the roof (*compluvium*) over a shallow pool, which
caught rainwater (*impluvium*). The shrine to the household gods (the *lares* and
penates) stood on one side of the atrium. Various rooms opened off the atrium,
including the *tablinum*, which generally stood on the opposite end of the atrium
from the *fauces*. The owner of the house would sit in the *tablinum* and meet his
clients during the morning greeting ritual (*salutatio*). An open courtyard or garden called the peristyle was usually behind the *tablinum*. A colonnaded walkway
generally surrounded the peristyle, with a series of rooms opening off the walkway,
the largest of which were the reception room and dining rooms (*triclinia*). Other
smaller rooms, called *cubicula*, were general-purpose rooms, which could serve as
bedrooms or more intimate meeting rooms. In some cases, such as the House of
the Faun (#163), private baths were added to give the house an even greater sense
of luxury. The House of the Vettii, also in Pompeii, is much smaller but significantly
more elaborately decorated (#164).

#162: Construction and Room Functions
in the Roman House

Vitruvius, *On Architecture* 6.3–5
First Century BC

In this passage, the architectural writer Vitruvius describes the different forms of
atriums and the rooms that are associated with them. At the end, he discusses how
the other rooms should be placed in order to most benefit from the light at different times of the year.

There are five types of atria classed according to their appearance: the Tuscan, Corinthian, *tetrastylum* (with four columns), *displuviatum* (with an opening
in the top), and *testudinatum* (closed at the top). The Tuscan atrium has beams
and crossbeams stretched across the length of the open space and gutters from
the corners of the walls to the corners formed by the joining of the beams and
crossbeams. In this way, rain falls through the *compluvium* (the hole in the roof

of the atrium) from rafters that slope down into it. In the Corinthian atrium, the rafters and *compluvium* are placed in the same way as the Tuscan style, but the beams are separated from the walls and supported by columns. In *tetrastyla* atria, columns are placed beneath the angles of the beams and give strength and support to the beams. In this way, they neither sag from their own weight nor are they burdened by the size of the crossbeams. The *displuviatum* style of atrium has a roof in which rainwater runs down the outward slope of the roof and away from the house instead of into it. This style is especially useful for winter houses since the rafters slope away from the *compluvium* rather than into it and so do not obstruct light from the dining room as much. This kind of roof, however, is more trouble because it requires repair more often because more water flows down toward the outer walls of the building. Although there are pipes to carry away the water, they cannot keep up with heavy rains and so water can back up and surge out of the pipes causing damage to the interior and the walls. The *testudinatum* atrium is used when the size of the enclosed room is not that large. This roof also allows for spacious rooms to be built over the atrium.

The length and width of atria are determined in three ways. In the first method, the ratio of length to width should be five to three. In the second, the ratio should be three to two. In the third, the builder should begin with a square in which all sides are equal. The length of a diagonal line across the square is then equal to the length of the atrium. The height of the atrium (measured to the underside of the beams), should be one-fourth of the length. That remaining one-fourth is assigned for the panels and ceiling beneath the crossbeams. The *alae* (wings) to the right and left of the atrium, when the atrium is between thirty and forty feet long, should be one-third its length. If the atrium is between forty and fifty feet, the *alae* should be one-fourth its length. If the atrium is between sixty and eighty feet, the length of the *alae* should be two-ninths. If the atrium is between eighty and one hundred feet, the length of the *alae* should be one-fifth that of the atrium. The lintel beams of the *alae* should be placed high enough so that the width and the height are the same.

The *tablinum* should be two-thirds the width of the atrium if the atrium is twenty feet wide. If the atrium is between thirty and forty feet, the *tablinum* should be half the width of the atrium. If the atrium is between forty and sixty feet, the *tablinum* should be two-fifths the width of the atrium. This arrangement is because smaller atriums cannot have *tablina* with the same relative proportions as the larger ones. If we used the larger proportions with smaller atria, the *tablinum* (and *alae* as well) would not be as useful, and if we applied the smaller proportions to the larger atria we would be left with rooms that were too large and empty. For this reason, I thought it best to describe exactly the relative dimensions so that they would be good both in their usefulness and appearance. The height of the doorway into the *tablinum* (to the lintel beam) should be one-eighth more than the width. The space between the beam and the roof should be raised a further third.

The entrance passageway (*fauces*) into the atria should be one-third of the width of the *tablinum* in smaller atriums and half the width of the *tablinum* in larger atriums. The images of the ancestors kept in the atrium and all of their decoration should be placed at a height equal to the width of the *alae*. As for the height and width of the exterior doors, in the case of atria having Doric entrances, use the Doric style. If the entranceway is in the Ionic style, use the Ionic as described in the fourth book of the volume on doorways where it describes their dimensions. The *compluvium* in the ceiling should be no less than one-fourth the width of the atrium and no more than one-third. The length should be in proportion to the rest of the atrium.

The peristyle should be one-third longer than the atrium. The columns of the peristyle should be the same height as the width of the portico running around the peristyle. The space between the columns should be no less than the total of the diameters of four columns. An exception should be made in the case of Doric-style columns, as I have described in the fourth book on Doric columns. In this case, modules should be measured out and the spacing of the triglyphs above the columns should be done according to those modules.

The dining room (*triclinium*) should be twice as deep as it is wide. The heights of the oblong interior rooms of the house should be determined in the following way. The height of the room should be half of the total achieved by adding the depth and width of the room. If the smaller *exedrae* and *oeci* (the room that stood at the far end of the peristyle) used for entertaining guests in a smaller environment should be square (with an equal width and depth), then make their height equal to one and a half times their width. Picture galleries (*pinacothecae*) and *exedrae* should be built large.

The *oeci* in the Corinthian, tetrastyle, and Egyptian styles should have similar proportions to what was described above in reference to the *triclinium*. Because the *oeci* have columns, however, they should be built on a larger scale than *triclinia*. The difference between Corinthian and Egyptian *oeci* is that the Corinthian has columns of a single order with architraves and cornices (made out of wood or plaster) placed above and with a semicircular ceiling above the cornice. Egyptian *oeci* have an architrave over shorter columns with an upstairs wooden floor stretching from them to the walls. This floor should be paved over the wooden boards allowing for an open-air walkway all around the *oecus*. Perpendicularly over the architrave of the lower columns should be placed columns a fourth smaller than the columns below. Over these the architraves and cornices should be decorated with ceilings. Windows should be placed between the upper columns. In this way, they should have an appearance similar to a basilica rather than a Corinthian *triclinium*.

Italian *oeci* are of a different form from other *oeci*. The Greek version of the *oeci*, called *cyzicenoi*, face north usually looking out over a garden and have doors in the middle. These are so long and wide that they can hold two dining tables facing one another and with room to walk around them. They have windows on the right and left that can be opened like doors so that the gardens can be seen through them from the dining room. Their height is equal to one and a half their width.

In all these rooms, the proportions must be made to best accommodate the situation and without causing difficulties for other rooms. For example, if windows would not be blocked by the height of walls they look out upon, then the construction is easy. If, however, the construction of windows should be blocked by proximity to adjoining walls or other difficulties, there must be made provision with the dimensions through skill and care so that the pleasing effect will not be much different from following the prescribed dimensions.

Now I will explain how the different types of rooms should be situated for the best use and to account for time of the year. Winter *triclinia* and bath complexes should face the west so that they can get more of the evening light and warmth since the setting sun will shine into them better. Bedchambers (*cubicula*) and libraries should face the east so that they can get more of the morning light and so that the books in the library not rot. Rooms facing south and west suffer from worms and moisture because the moist winds entering the room from that direction feed vermin and spread moisture and destroy the books with mold.

Spring and autumn *triclinia* should face the east so that even though exposed to the sunlight in the morning, the room will be cool when the sun has moved to the west and so be an appropriate temperature when the room is used in the evening for dinner. Summer *triclinia* should face north. Other rooms will be too hot because of the summer heat, but if the *triclinium* faces north, it will not be exposed to the sun's course and so always be cool, healthy, and pleasurable when it is used. Picture galleries (*pinacothecae*), and rooms used for weaving and painting should have the same north facing so that the colors used by paintings and spinners should remain constant with the unchanged lighting.

Now that the arrangement of the *triclinia* has been assigned according to the seasons, attention must be given to the situation of the different kinds of rooms in the house: private rooms are those reserved for the *paterfamilias* and public rooms are open to guests. Not everyone may enter the private rooms, unless they are invited. These include the *cubicula, triclinia*, private baths, and other rooms with similar functions. Public rooms, however, are those that anyone may enter, even if they have not been invited. These include the vestibule [the atrium], interior courtyards, the peristyle, and other similar areas. Therefore, people of lower social status have no need of vestibules, *tablina,* or atriums because those kinds of people visit patrons of higher status and are not themselves visited by clients of their own.

Those people who store goods from the country in their house need to have in their houses booths, shops, vaults, granaries, storerooms, and other such things that are more suited to storing produce than providing charm and elegance. In the same way, houses of bankers and tax collectors should be more comfortable and attractive while still safe from thieves. Lawyers and the well educated should have more elegant and spacious homes in order to receive guests. Aristocrats, however, because they offer their services as part of their political position and magistracies, must have regal vestibules, tall atria, very large peristyles, gardens, and wider walkways to match the dignity of their social status. There could also be picture galleries, meeting halls not unlike those found in the magnificence of public buildings. This is because quite frequently in their house, decisions affecting both public and private life are decided.

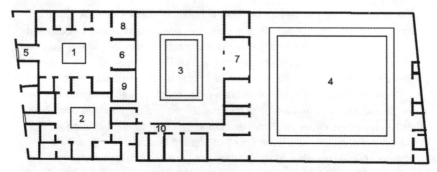

Figure 10.2 Plan of the House of the Faun, Pompeii (1: Atrium, 2: Atrium; 3: Peristyle; 4: Peristyle; 5: *Fauces*; 6: *Tablinum*; 7: Alexander *Exedra*; 8: Possible *Triclinium*; 9: Possible *Triclinium*; 10: Bath Complex).

#163: The House of the Faun, Pompeii

The House of the Faun occupied an entire city block, and, at thirty-one thousand square feet, was one of the largest houses in Pompeii (see Figure 10.2). This opulent house was originally constructed during Pompeii's pre-Roman (Samnite) period. In the second century BC, the wealthy owners of the house renovated, expanded, and redecorated the house on the model of the Hellenistic palaces in the eastern Mediterranean. The house featured two atria, side-by-side, at the front of the house, and two peristyles, one smaller in the middle of the house and one larger in the rear. The wall paintings throughout the house are characterized by relatively simple painted panels in imitation of the marble architecture of the great public buildings such as temples and basilicas.

#164: The House of the Vettii, Pompeii

The much smaller House of the Vettii (Figure 10.3) was constructed during the second century BC. However, after two freedmen of the prominent Vettius family purchased it in the decade before the eruption of Vesuvius, it underwent substantial renovation and redecoration. The new owners replaced the older decoration in their house with paintings of three-dimensional architectural designs, mythological scenes, and still lifes reminiscent of public galleries.

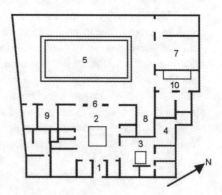

Figure 10.3 Plan of the House of the Vettii, Pompeii (1: *Fauces*, 2: Atrium; 3: Service Atrium; 4: Service Kitchen; 5: Peristyle; 6: Columned Portal; 7: *Triclinium*; 8: *Exedra*; 9: *Exedra*; 10: Courtyard).

Figure 10.4 House of the Vettii, Pompeii; Looking from the *Fauces* into the Peristyle (Photograph by B. Harvey).

Much of the decoration in the front part of the house alluded to the commercial lives of the owners. On several paintings, cherubic "cupids" are depicted engaged in various types of trades. On the northeastern side of the atrium was a doorway to the slaves' quarters. This area of the house included a small courtyard and kitchen in which were discovered bronze cooking vessels. Unlike the House of the Faun, this house had no *tablinum*, which enabled visitors to have a very clear view, beyond the atrium, into the peristyle garden with its numerous statues and fountains. A columned portal between the atrium and peristyle clearly divided the "public" and "private" sections of the house.

Three major rooms open off the peristyle (see Figure 10.4). The largest (the northern room) was probably the main *triclinium*. Its deep red and black decoration includes a delicately painted depiction of Apollo's defeat of Python. The reception or dining room in the northeastern corner contains primarily red architectural designs as well as large paintings of the punishment of Ixion, and also a portrayal of the craftsman Daedalus presenting the wooden bull to Pasiphae. Another similar room in the southeastern corner is filled with motifs painted in gold, including depictions of the stories of the infant Hercules killing two snakes, the punishment of Dirce, and the Maenads' slaughter of Pentheus. In an annex to the east, adjacent to the peristyle's *triclinium*, a miniature courtyard opens onto two more richly decorated rooms.

Apartments

Not everyone could afford to live in spacious and luxurious homes. Affordable housing was even more of a challenge in crowded or desirable cities where real estate prices were highest. At Pompeii, there is evidence of smaller houses and also the rental of a room or rooms to individuals of lesser means. Many lived in rooms above their shops. Indeed, frequently the Roman solution to inadequate space for new building in the face of ever-growing demand was to build up rather than out (although apartments on the upper floors were not the more valuable, as shown by Juvenal, #165). While Rome certainly experienced this type of construction trend, the paucity of archaeological evidence often prevents us from visualizing it. The better-preserved town of Ostia, however, exemplifies a prosperous city in which population growth stimulated vertical construction. Ostia, indeed, can help us envision how the crowded residential areas within Rome would have appeared. While Pompeii's houses often showed evidence for at least a partial second story, Ostia's apartment buildings routinely reached heights of three and even four stories. In this section, the Casette-Tipo apartments in Ostia (#166) and the Ara Coeli apartment building in Rome (#167) will be presented as examples.

#165: A Dangerous Apartment Building

Juvenal, *Satires* 3.190–202
Late First/Early Second Centuries AD

The satirist Juvenal paints a rather bleak picture of the apartment building and the life of the person living there. Fire was a constant danger in Rome, where people generally cooked over cooking braziers and illuminated the darkness with oil lamps. Wood, being lighter than brick or stone, was often used to construct the upper floors of apartment buildings. Undoubtedly, many apartment buildings throughout the Roman Empire were flimsy, dangerous, and badly maintained.

> We live in a city propped up on thin pillars for the most part. That is how the apartment manager keeps them from falling over. While he hides old cracks in the foundation, he tells his tenants to sleep secure of impending doom. We should be living in a place where there is no danger or fear of fire in the night. Your heroic downstairs neighbor is already asking for water and moving his possessions out while your third floor apartment is only just starting to fill with smoke. You don't know what is going on. If the terror begins on the bottom floors, the last one to burn will be the one who lives so high up that only the roof tiles protect him from the rain and where the doves lay their eggs.

#166: The Casette-Tipo Apartments, Ostia

The Casette-Tipo apartment buildings are located just south of the *Via della Foce* on the far western side of the excavated part of Ostia. They are composed of two long, narrow, rectangular blocks facing one another (see Figure 10.5). Staircases opening onto the street leading to a second and perhaps third story divide each block into two halves. Each half was then divided horizontally into two independent apartments.

The ruins of the ground floor are all that is visible today (see Figure 10.6). The main entrance to each of the four apartments on the ground floor opened from

Figure 10.5 Street between the Two Blocks of the Casette-Tipo Apartments, Ostia (Photograph by B. Harvey).

the street between the two blocks onto a wide central hall (the *medianum*), which ran lengthwise down the front of the street side of the block. The *medianum* functioned much like an atrium in the houses of Pompeii, with the other, more interior rooms opening off of it. In each apartment, there were two smaller *cubicula* (possibly, sleeping quarters) in the center; a large room and passageway frame the *cubicula*. The largest rooms were located at either end of each apartment and probably had windows on three sides, therefore possibly functioning as *triclinia*. The other rooms included the rooms adjacent to the more interior side of the *cubicula*, which had small latrines next to them. Simple mosaic floors and painted walls indicate that even in these more humble homes, decoration was important.

The building was certainly multiple stories tall as extant external staircases provide access to at least a second story. The weight-bearing walls of the Casette-Tipo,

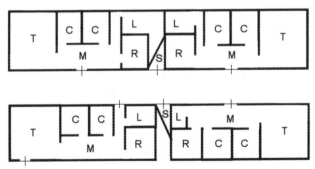

Figure 10.6 Plan of the Ground Floor of the Casette-Tipo Apartment Building, Ostia (S: External Staircases; M: Hallway (*Medianum*); T: Large Room (Possible *Triclinium*); C: *Cubicula*; R: Room on the Opposite End of the *Medianum* from the Large Room; L: Latrine).

however, were thinner than many of the other apartment buildings in Ostia (about one and a half feet in thickness), and so a third floor might not have been possible. The floor plan of the second story is no longer able to be determined. It is likely that it duplicated that on the ground floor, but it is also possible that it contained smaller apartments accessed by a balconied walkway that ran along the side of the structure.

Although relatively spacious (the Casette-Tipo apartments were about eleven hundred square feet each), apartments from Ostia lacked basic features one would expect in modern dwellings. There were no kitchens. Tenants either bought prepared food or cooked over portable braziers. As was typical, these apartments did not have running water, indicating that the residents had to carry their own water from an external supply (most likely, a public fountain). This building, like so many others, would have suffered from a lack of heat in winter (except perhaps the meager warmth of a small stove). These apartments were unusual, however, in having the luxury of their own latrines for each unit.

#167: The Ara Coeli Apartment Building, Rome

Literary references like Juvenal's satire on the rickety apartment building indicate that this style of housing, so common in Ostia, was also the norm in Rome itself. Although the modern city has obscured most of the remnants of Rome's ancient housing, one example has survived in the side of the Capitoline Hill, beneath the stairs leading to Santa Maria in Ara Coeli on the *Via Giulio Romano*. The floor plan is similar to the apartment buildings in Ostia. Unlike the Ostian evidence, however, the Ara Coeli apartment building preserves parts of four stories. The building was originally square in shape with an open-air courtyard in the center, but all that remains today is the section of apartments that stood north of the courtyard. The apartments on each side of the preserved section opened both onto the streets surrounding the building as well as the courtyard. The same plan was also common in Ostia (e.g., the House of Diana, northeast of the Capitolium).

As was undoubtedly common in most apartment buildings of this sort, the varied floor plans of each story catered to different types of tenants. On the first floor were rows of shops of the type commonly seen in the streets of Ostia. The second floor is a mezzanine level of small rooms in which the shopkeepers lived. Wooden staircases led from the shops on the first floor to these rooms above. The third floor was probably a *medianum*-style apartment like the Casette-Tipo in Ostia. The apartment was probably accessed from a wooden balcony on the courtyard side of the building. The fourth floor has a central corridor running along the length of the building (see Figure 10.7). Along the central corridor are openings leading to three separate corridors, which run perpendicular to the central corridor. These three perpendicular corridors run alongside what once were probably three independent, small apartments. Like the *medianum* of the Casette-Tipo, each apartment's corridor functioned as an entranceway to the interior rooms, which consisted of at least two smaller *cubicula* and a larger room at the end of the corridor. This larger room might have served as a dining area/*triclinium*. It had access to natural light via a window. The hall of the apartment at the far eastern end of

Figure 10.7 Plan of the Fourth Floor of the Ara Coeli Apartment Building, Rome.

the row also opens onto a large corner room lit by three windows. This corner room might have been a common room for the floor, but more likely it was an additional room in the last apartment, giving this more spacious corner unit a potentially higher rental value than the other two.

Country Villas

#168: Pliny the Younger's Villa at Laurentum

Pliny the Younger, *Letters* 2.17
Early Second Century AD

The richest members of society had both urban houses and country estates with large residential villas surrounded by often vast tracts of land for agriculture or hunting. In this passage, Pliny the Younger describes his country estate in Laurentum, not far from Rome and Ostia. Pliny describes the layout of the house and the advantages of the arrangement of its rooms. Members of the senatorial aristocracy, like Pliny, would have had numerous country estates.

In your last letter, you said that you were surprised that I was so fond of my villa at Laurentum (or, if you prefer, the villa that I call "my Laurens"). You would cease to be surprised, however, if you were to experience firsthand its beauty, convenience of location, and access to the sea. It is seventeen miles from Rome, meaning it is possible that I can spend the night at the villa after spending the day in the city finishing my daily chores. The villa can be reached not by a single road but by two. If you are coming by the road to Laurentum, turn off at the fourteenth milestone, and if you are coming by the road to Ostia, turn off at the eleventh milestone. The road both ways is a bit sandy in spots, and so the journey takes a bit longer and is more difficult by carriage, but it is short and easy on horseback. The countryside that you will pass through has plenty of variety. In some places, the woods come right up to the road; in other places, the land opens up and extends over large pastures. In the latter, there are many flocks of sheep and herds of cattle and horses. When the winter is over, these animals come down from their mountain pastures to enjoy the spring foliage and warmth.

The villa itself is large enough for my purposes, and is not too expensive to maintain. Inside the entrance, there is a modest but well-kept atrium. After this you enter a small, cheerful courtyard that is enclosed within two colonnades each shaped like the letter "D" facing outwards. These colonnades are a terrific refuge against bad weather since they are protected with windows and the projection of the roof. As you pass between the colonnades and go farther into the house you come into a pleasant courtyard and then a dining room that is satisfactorily beautiful. This dining room extends outward from the house to the seashore. In fact, when there is a southwest wind, the waves come in and lightly break upon the base of the room's outer walls. All around this dining room there are folding doors or windows the size of the doors. When all of these are open, you can look out from the sides or the back and gaze upon the sea in all three directions. If you look back toward the entrance of the room, you can see the inner courtyard and the porticos beyond. Even farther, you can see the atrium at the entrance, and even the woods and distant mountains. On the left side of this dining room (as you face the sea) and a little drawn back from the sea is a large *cubiculum*. Beyond that is another, smaller *cubiculum* that has two windows: one facing the east and the other the west. This room also looks out over the sea but from a little farther away and with less of the noise. The angle formed by the connection of the dining room and the *cubicula* captures and intensifies the heat of the sun. As a result, I use this suite as my winter quarters and exercise area. That suite is shielded from all of the winds except those that bring clouds. As a result, the sun comes back out before we lose the use of the room to the cold. This suite has another *cubiculum* that is circular in shape. This room has windows on all of its exterior walls so that the sun can come in throughout the whole day. On the interior wall is a bookcase that contains my favorite books: the type that demands re-reading often. A passage connects this room with a bedroom. This passage is raised slightly to allow pipes through which flows warm air to this room. The rest of this part of the house is designated for the use of my slaves and freedmen. Even so, the majority of the rooms in this part of the house are elegant enough that my houseguests could stay in them. On the other side of the dining room is a very elegant *cubiculum*. Beyond that is what you could call either a large *cubiculum* or a small dining room. This room is very bright both from its exposure to the sun and the reflection of the sun from the sea. After this comes a *cubiculum* with an antechamber. This is a nice room in the summer because of its height and in the winter for the thickness of the walls, for it is shielded from the wind in every direction…

[Description of the bath complex in the house]

…At the far end of the large colonnaded garden is a covered walkway that passes from the garden to a spacious *cubiculum* that is very much my favorite part of the house. I feel I am qualified to say they are my favorite as I had them built to my specifications. In this suite there is a sunroom, one side of which faces the garden and the other side the sea. Both sides, however, get plenty of sun. Folding doors separate this *cubiculum* from the covered walkway and windows look out over the sea. Against the center wall a little room recedes back from the rest of the room toward the sea. This room can be made part of the main room or be separated from it with the use of windows and curtains that can be opened or closed. This recess has a couch and two chairs. When reclining on the couch, you can see the sea in front of you, neighboring villas behind you, and forests to the side. The arrangement of the many windows allows you to take in these sights either individually or as a single vista. Joined to this is a *cubiculum* for nighttime and sleeping. Here, nothing disturbs me unless I open the windows: not the voices of the slaves, the murmur of the sea, the clash of thunder, the flash of lightning, or even daylight. The deep seclusion of this hideaway was by design as I had the *cubiculum* and the garden separated by a corridor. The intervening space blocks out every sound...

[Descriptions of the delights of the secluded suite of rooms, the general convenience of the location of the villa, and how Pliny acquires provisions.]

... Now that you have heard about my villa, do you think I am justified in keeping, living in, and loving such a country retreat? If it does not sound like something you would like then you are just too attached to the city. I only wish you liked it well enough to come and visit! I am sure your time here as my guest would prove that my praise of this little villa's many and great charms are justified. Good-bye.

Chapter 11: Neighborhoods, Water, Sanitation, and the Grain Supply

The Romans spent a great deal of time and money on providing for their cities all of the amenities needed to maintain a large population. Few houses had running water, but there were ample sources of water in the local neighborhoods. Aqueducts brought water from springs and rivers often located a great distance from the cities. Despite Rome's huge population, the water system brought in not only enough water for people to drink but also for recreation and decoration. The sewer system directed used water and refuse out of the cities. While all cities required means for bringing food to the city dwellers from the surrounding countryside, Rome's one million inhabitants required an especially elaborate transportation system for importing food from all over the Roman world.

Neighborhoods

The Romans spent a great deal of time in their neighborhoods—at their jobs, fetching water from fountains, bathing in the baths, eating in the restaurants, relieving themselves at the latrine, and dumping garbage in the sewer. Although the wealthy might be able to afford their own bath complex, indoor plumbing, and kitchen staff, the poor had to look outside of their homes for many of the amenities that we in the modern world take for granted. As a result, the ancient Roman spent a great deal of his or her day engaged in social activities in the neighborhood. Even the houses of the wealthy were open for social experiences with clients visiting during the morning *salutatio* and dinner parties that usually involved guests (see below Chapters 12 and 18). This section will examine the structure of neighborhoods in a Roman city. Augustus divided Rome into regions (*regiones*) and neighborhoods (*vici*) (#169; see also #170 for a religious shrine dedicated to the guardian spirits of the crossroads of a neighborhood). Offices within Rome kept records of the neighborhoods, their magistrates (*vicomagistri*), and buildings (#171 and #172). Selection #173 looks in detail at one city block in Pompeii in order to exemplify the mixture of buildings one would encounter in a neighborhood.

#169: Augustus Organizes Rome into Regions and Neighborhoods

Suetonius, *Augustus* 30
Written in the Early Second Century AD Describing
the Emperor Augustus (27 BC–AD 14)

In 7 BC, Augustus divided the city of Rome into regions and neighborhoods. To keep track of this system, Augustus also created an official register listing all of

Rome's buildings by *vicus* and region. In order to better oversee city administration on a local level, Augustus placed a local magistrate, the *vicomagister*, over each *vicus*. The *vicomagister*, normally a freedman, administered any public funds or property owned by the neighborhood as a whole. The *vicomagister* was almost certainly partially responsible for keeping the city's real estate records up to date.

> The urban space within the city of Rome Augustus divided into regions (*regiones*) and neighborhoods (*vici*). He also arranged for there to be annual magistrates elected by lot to administer these districts. In the case of the *vici*, the magistrates, called *vicomagistri*, were elected out of the inhabitants of each of those neighborhoods. Against the threat of fire, he also set up nocturnal guard posts and a fire brigade.

#170: A Neighborhood Shrine from Pompeii

Cities like Pompeii and Ostia followed Rome's lead in establishing local administrative divisions by *vici*. Inscriptions from Pompeii refer to *vici* and *vicomagistri*. The *lares compitales* were the guardian spirits (*lares*) of the crossroads (*compitia*) that stood at the center of the neighborhood. Shrines to the *lares compitales* are still visible at several of Pompeii's major road junctures. In Figure 11.1 you can see a photo of one of the shrines from Pompeii. It is preserved in the second region in the far eastern part of the city near the amphitheater.

Figure 11.1 Shrine to the *Lares Compitales* in Pompeii (Region II.4.7a) (Photograph by B. Harvey).

#171: The *Regionaries* Entry for Region I of Rome

Date Unknown

We have preserved a group of medieval manuscripts called the *Regionaries*. Although scholars debate their authenticity, these documents seem to be derived from an ancient catalog of the regions, buildings landmarks, and houses of Rome. The following passage is a translation of the entry for *Regio I*, the area just outside the old *Porta Capena* in the Servian wall in the southeastern corner of Rome, near the Baths of Caracalla and along the first stretch of the *Via Appia*. The locations of many of the landmarks mentioned as belonging to the first region are unknown. The names, however, combined with the enumeration of private and service buildings give us a glimpse of the character of that region.

> Temple of Honor and Virtue; Grove of Camena; Reservoir of Prometheus; Bathhouse of Torquatus; Public Baths of Severus and Commodus; Courtyard of Apollo and Splenis, and Calles; Glassmaker's Quarters; Courtyard of the Bread Makers; Trading Post of the Emperor; Bathhouses of Bolanus and Mamertinus; Courtyard of Carriages; Bathhouses of Abascantus and Antiochianus; Temples of Mars, Minerva, and the Seasons; Stream of the Almo; Arches of the Divine Lucius Verus Parthicus, the Divine Trajan, and Drusus.
> Totals: 10 *Vici*, 10 Shrines of the *Vici*, 48 *Vicomagistri*, 2 Head *Vicomagistri*, 3,250 *Insulae*, 120 *Domus*, 16 Warehouses, 86 Bathhouses, 81 Reservoirs, 20 Bakeries.
> 12,219 Square Feet.

#172: Register of *Vicomagistri* from Region I

CIL 6.975 (Rome)
AD 136

This passage comes from an inscription dated to AD 136 from Rome. It catalogs the urban *vici* complete with the names of the *vicomagistri*. This inscription lists nine *vici* in the first region. Some names were derived from landmarks listed in the *Regionaries*, others from streets. The *Vicus* of Camena was close to the Grove of Camena. The *Vicus* of Drusus must have been close to the Arch of Drusus. The two streets of Sulpicius (nearer and farther) ran perpendicular to each other, starting at the beginning of the *Via Appia* near the Baths of Caracalla. This document and the *Regionaries* have similarities and differences. As with the previous passage, this inscription gives us an idea of the character of *Regio I*. Most of the people mentioned are freedmen, but a few are freeborn (as shown by the filiation in their name).

> In honor of the emperor Caesar Trajan Hadrian Augustus, Pontifex Maximus, holding the tribunician power for the twentieth time, acclaimed *imperator* twice, consul three times, father of his country, son of the divine Trajan

Parthicus, grandson of the divine Nerva; the following were the *vicomagistri* of the fourteen regions of the city while Lucius Ceionius Commodus and Sextus Vetulenus Civica Pompeianus were consuls [AD 136]. In the first region of the city the following were the magistrates:

The caretaker of the whole region: Curtius Iucundus, freedman of a woman. Herald: Publius Helvidius Hermes, freedman of Publius.

Vicus of Camena: Gaius Publilius Chrestus, freedman of a woman; Marcus Ulpius Pyrallus, freedman of Marcus; Tiberius Julius Atimetus, freedman of Tiberius; Marcus Servilius Celer, freedman of Lucius.

Vicus of Drusus: Gaius Julius Verus, son of Gaius; Quintus Trebonius Primigenius, freedman of a woman; Decimus Lucilius Thallus, freedman of Decimus; Quintus Caecilius Thallus, freedman of Quintus.

Outer *vicus* of Sulpicius: Gaius Julius Theodorus, freedman of Gaius; Publius Publilius Seleucus, freedman of Publius; Tiberius Claudius Bathyllus, freedman of Tiberius; Gaius Valerius Athenaeus, freedman of Gaius.

Inner *vicus* of Sulpicius: Lucius Valerius Diodorus, freedman of Lucius; Titus Volusius Maximus, son of Titus; Gaius Vivatius Severus, freedman of Gaius; Gaius Julius Gryphius, freedman of Gaius.

Vicus of Fortuna the Obedient: Publius Motilius Hermes, freedman of Publius; Tiberius Claudius Placidus, freedman of Tiberius; Marcus Mucius Faustus, freedman of Marcus; Marcus Popilius Victor, freedman of Marcus.

Vicus of Pulverarius: Gaius Atilius Silvester, freedman of Gaius; Lucius Otacilius Trophimus, freedman of Lucius; Marcus Julius Stephanus, freedman of Marcus; Lucius Domitius Sosibius, freedman of Lucius.

Vicus of Honor and Virtue: Malanius Salutaris, freedman of a woman; Lucius Baebius Hilarius, freedman of Lucius; Quintus Umbricus Moderatus, freedman of Quintus; Lucius Pontius Dicaeus, freedman of Lucius.

Vicus of the three triumphal arches: Lucius Valerius Euhodus, freedman of Lucius; Gaius Pontulenus Plutio, freedman of a woman; Titus Helvidius Eutyches, son of Titus; Gaius Julius Ephesius (who was also called Masculius), freedman of Gaius.

Vicus of the artisans: Titus Furius Nerva, freedman of Titus; Tiberius Claudius Epictetus, freedman of a woman; Tiberius Claudius Epictetus, freedman of a woman; Lucius Turranius Primus, freedman of Lucius; Anicius Demetrius, freedman of a woman.

#173: A City Block in Pompeii

City block 6 in Pompeii's first region is a good example of the kind of mixture of building function and occupant wealth levels that typified the urban experience in an ancient Roman city (Figure 11.2). The block is just east of the *Via di Stabia*, the major north–south road through Pompeii. The doors on the block's northern side gave four adjacent houses access to the grand *Via dell'Abbondanza*, Pompeii's major east–west road. Manufacturing facilities such as the ironworker's shop, a restaurant,

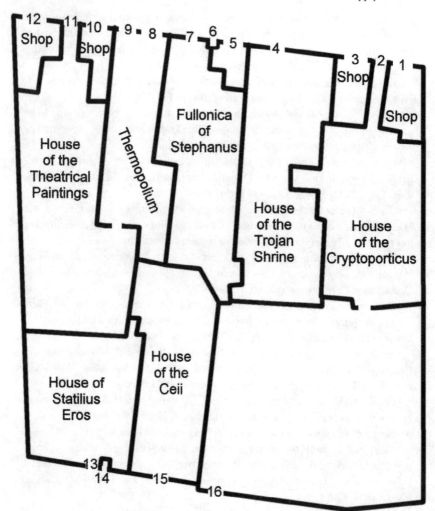

Figure 11.2 Plan of Block I.6, Pompeii with Door Numbers.

a fuller's shop, and small rental apartments all co-existed in this block with large aristocratic houses. Numerous other doors opened from the block's southern side onto the smaller *Vicolo del Menandro*. No doors opened onto the small alleys to the east and west of the block (nor do block 6's neighbors appear to have had street-level access to the alley from the sides of their buildings).

The largest and farthest east of the four houses is the House of the Cryptoporticus (doors 2 and 16). It extended all the way to the southern side of the block where a small door opened onto the street to the south. Small rooms opening onto the street (doors 1 and 3), which probably functioned as shops, flanked its entrance-way (*fauces*). Numerous metal tools, including a surveyor's tool (*groma*), were found in one of these shops. The house itself had an atrium, a large peristyle, and its own small bath complex.

West of this house was the significantly smaller House of the Trojan Shrine (door 4), and farther west was a small shop with a back room (doors 5 and 6). A staircase opening onto the *Via dell'Abbondanza* at one time led to a small living unit on the second floor.

West of this shop was the fuller's shop (*fullonica*) of Stephanus (door 7). The establishment had the floor plan of a typical house, but basins and vats for cleaning the clothes were added to the house's small atrium and peristyle, indicating that it was converted from a house into a fullery.

West of this *fullonica* was a *thermopolium* (doors 8 and 9), a snack bar that sold hot and cold drinks and soups to customers passing by on the adjacent street. The floor plan of the building suggests its use as a sit-down restaurant as well. A door in the back of the *thermopolium* opened into the spacious House of the Theatrical Paintings (door 11), probably an indication that the owner of the house also owned the *thermopolium*. The house was filled with especially rich finds, including bronze statuary, silver cups, gold jewelry, and wall paintings of theatrical scenes in the atrium. On either side of the entrance way to this house were shops (doors 10 and 12). Numerous ironworking tools and keys found in one of these shops (door 12) may indicate that this was a shop of a craftsman. Both shops had living quarters in the back for the owner/renter of the shop. Door 10 has stairs leading to a second floor.

On the southern side of the block were two other houses: the House of Statilius Eros (doors 13 and 14) and the House of the Ceii (door 15). Both houses were relatively small. The former had a staircase leading from the street to a second floor apartment.

Aqueducts and the Water Supply

In an ancient Roman city, running water in a private house was a rare luxury that only the most privileged members of society could afford. The household atrium, with its hole in the roof (*compluvium*) and basin in the floor (*impluvium*) was originally designed to catch rainwater, which could then be used by the inhabitants. The majority of a city's inhabitants, however, obtained the water they needed from wells, cisterns, or public fountains supplied by an aqueduct (#174). Aqueducts utilized gravity to lead fresh water from springs and streams at higher elevations into the city. The aqueducts were one of Rome's most significant engineering achievements. Between the late fourth century BC and the third century AD, Republican aristocrats and Roman emperors constructed a system of eleven aqueducts, which brought more fresh water into Rome than any city since until very recent times (see #175 for Rome's first aqueduct, the *Aqua Appia*). Aqueducts diverted fresh water from higher elevation to the city through a cut stone channel or pipes of terracotta or lead. Water flowed through the channels by natural gravity, rather than pumps. Over the entire course of the aqueduct, therefore, it was vital to keep the water running downstream via a continuously downward-sloping channel.

Figure 11.3 Fountain South of Region VII.14.13, Pompeii (Photograph by B. Harvey).

After its trip through the aqueduct, the water emptied into a distribution tower (*castellum*), usually in a high part of the city. The water was then carried through a pipe system to the various buildings and fountains that the aqueduct served.

The government exercised a high degree of control over the water distributed by the aqueducts. While most was distributed publicly, some was leased out to wealthy private citizens who paid a tax for use of the water. It is likely that income from leasing water helped pay for the upkeep of the aqueducts and water distribution system within the city (#176).

#174: Fountain on the *Via della'Abbondanza* in Pompeii

Collecting water in clay pots was a daily task generally performed by the women or female slaves of the household. The photo in Figure 11.3 shows a fountain that was discovered on the side of the busy *Via della'Abbondanza* in Pompeii. Water was pumped through a spout into a basin from which the water could be drawn.

#175: The Construction of the *Aqua Appia* in Rome

Frontinus, *On the Aqueduct System of the City of Rome* 1.5
Written at the End of the First Century AD Describing 312 BC

A high-ranking senatorial magistrate called the *praefectus aquarum* oversaw Rome's water system. One of these prefects, Sextus Julius Frontinus, wrote a treatise describing the entire system during the late first century AD. His work *On the Aqueduct System of the City of Rome* gives us invaluable insight into how the system worked. The following passage from this book describes the history and course of Rome's first aqueduct, the *Aqua Appia*, which spanned a distance of ten miles. Its source was a mere eighty feet above sea level while the aqueduct's eventual destination was fifty feet above sea level, a change in elevation of only thirty feet, an average grade of not more than half a percent. Roman engineers, whenever possible, preferred to cut channels or lay pipes at ground level. When there was a rise in ground level, however, they would often tunnel the channel into the ground, sometimes even through mountains. When the terrain dropped too steeply, the engineers could place the channel on top of a raised structure, which was sometimes supported by arches. The long lines of tall, arched bridges still visible outside of Rome (such as those of the *Aqua Claudia*) still evoke wonder as impressive feats of engineering skill.

While Marcus Valerius Maximus and Publius Decius Mus were consuls [312 BC], in the thirtieth year after the beginning of the war against the Samnites, work on the *Aqua Appia* was completed. It is named after the censor Appius Claudius Crassus who was later known as "the Blind." This is the same man who constructed the Appian Way, which runs from the Porta Capena in Rome all the way to the city of Capua in the south. Appius' colleague in the censorship was Gaius Plautius, who was later given the extra name of "the hunter" because he is the one that found the source of the water for the Aqua Appia. Unfortunately, Plautius was tricked by Appius to resign his office early after only eighteen months and so, when the aqueduct was completed, it got its name from Appius alone. Appius had told Plautius that he was going to resign his office early as well, but he then continued to delay his resignation. In the end, Appius extended his tenure as censor until the time when both the road and this aqueduct were completed. The source of the water for the *Aqua Appia* is on the estate of Lucullus on the road to Praeneste, between the seventh and eighth milestone, near a crossroad but 780 feet to the left. From its source to the salt flats, which are located near the Porta Trigemina, the aqueduct has a course of 11,190 feet; 11,130 feet of this stretch is in the form of an underground channel. The other sixty feet of its span is above ground; partially on platforms; and, near the Porta Capena, on arches. Near the monument of Spes Vetus, on the edge of the suburban estates of Torquatus and Epaphroditus, it is met by a branch of the *Aqua Augusta*, which was built by the emperor Augustus to supplement the supply to the *Aqua Appia*.

#176: Distribution of Water in the City

Vitruvius, *On Architecture* 8.6.1–2
First Century BC

In this passage, the architectural writer Vitruvius describes some of the details of the system of water distribution.

Water is conducted in three ways: in streams through specially built channels, lead pipes, or tubes made of clay. The following is the rationale for choosing one method or another. If channels are to be used, the structure must be as solidly built as possible. The bottom of the channel should slope no more than a half foot for every one hundred feet of channel. The channels should also have an arched roof covering to shield the water from sunlight as much as possible. At the point where the aqueduct reaches the city walls, a reservoir should be built. Within this reservoir are three tanks for collecting the water. Within the reservoir are placed three pipes, one for each tank. When the first tank fills to capacity, the runoff flows into the second tank. The pipes in the first tank supply the basins and fountains. The other tank supplies the private bathhouses. The water tax imposed upon these establishments therefore provides a steady income to the public treasury. The water from the final basin supplies private households. Because the incoming water fills the first tank first, there should not be a lack of water for public use. Water for private use should not deplete the public water if the pipe system is correctly constructed. I have noted how the system works so that the administrators who oversee the collection of taxes for water used privately can understand it.

Sewers and Latrines

The ancient Romans devised not only a system to bring water into the city, but also extensive networks of sewers to drain away used water, sewage, and excess groundwater from the low-lying parts of the city. Rome's first sewer was called the *Cloaca Maxima* ("Biggest Sewer"; #177). It drained the previously marshy area between the Esquiline and the Tiber, including the forum, and emptied the excess water into the Tiber near Tiber Island. Most of the later sewers drained into the *Cloaca Maxima*.

One significant function of the sewers was the removal of human excrement from the city. Roman toilets did not "flush." Unlike modern outhouses, however, which open onto sewage pits or store the refuse in receptacles until it can be removed, Roman toilets opened directly onto the sewer below them. The sewage fell into the sewer, and the flow of water through the system flushed the sewage away to the river. Limited access to sewers meant that most people used toilets in communal latrines. The rare latrines in private houses and apartment buildings (like those in the Casette-Tipo Apartments in Ostia) were generally small affairs with two or three seats tucked away in the wasted space beneath a staircase. Larger, public latrines, some with seating for twenty to forty people, could be found near major gathering areas, such as the forum, or in baths (#178). For more details on the use of public latrines, see #179 for the "sponge on a stick."

#177: Praise for Rome's Sewer System

Pliny the Elder, *Natural History* 36.104–106
First Century AD

Pliny the Elder ranks the sewage system as one of the Romans' most noteworthy accomplishments. In this passage, he describes the wonders of the *Cloaca Maxima*.

At that time, the old men could look with amazement at the large size of Rome's old wall, the subterranean structures cut into the Capitoline Hill, and especially the sewer system, certainly the greatest work of them all. As I noted earlier, our ancestors dug beneath the hills of Rome so that today's city is suspended over an underground, watery city through which a boat could sail, as Marcus Agrippa once did while he was aedile after he had been consul. Seven channels, like rivers, pass beneath the city. In them, the water rushes along in its course like a torrent and gathers and carries off all of the refuse in its path. The force of the rushing water in the rainy season slams into the bottom and sides of the sewers with great force. Sometimes, when the Tiber is overflowing, the excess water flows into the sewers rather than out and the waters flowing in opposite directions does battle in the sewer, but still the strength of the system perseveres.

#178: The Public Latrine near the Forum Baths, Ostia

The well-preserved, twenty-seat latrine near the Forum Baths in Ostia is a great example of a public latrine (Figure 11.4).

Roman toilets were stone or wooden slabs raised on brick piers about two feet off the ground to form a kind of long bench (Figure 11.5). The long benches extended along the interior walls of the latrine and stood over a sewer channel. At intervals along each bench were small holes over which people would sit. These holes extended to the front edge of the bench to allow for easier "wiping." In most of the larger latrines, toilets lined the three walls opposite the entrance. Bathroom privacy would not have been possible in these public latrines, as the holes in the benches were located quite close together with no dividing walls to enclose a single toilet. Also, nothing indicates

Figure 11.4 Public Latrine Near the Forum Baths, Ostia (Photograph by B. Harvey).

Figure 11.5 Seating in the Latrine Near the Forum Baths, Ostia (Photograph by B. Harvey).

that the genders were separated. The long drapery of typical Roman clothing, however, meant that people remained relatively well covered while relieving themselves.

#179: The Sponge on a Stick

Seneca, *Letters* 70.20–21
First Century AD

In this passage, the philosopher Seneca gives an example to prove his point that people will, when faced with a death that is not of their choosing, use whatever they can find to end their lives. The man in this passage uses an instrument that the Romans used to wipe themselves: a sponge attached to a wooden handle.

> Recently, there was a German man in the training school for the beast hunts. One day, when he was being prepared for an appearance during the morning show in the amphitheater, he entered the latrine to relieve himself (this is the only place he could go without a guard and so have some privacy). While there, he found the wooden handle to which the sponge is attached. This instrument is used to clean a person's unmentionables. The man took the handle and crammed the whole thing down his throat and so died of suffocation. This certainly ranks up there among the foulest ways to die. How silly it is, in truth, to be finicky when it comes to choosing a manner of death. This German was certainly a brave man and one who deserved the chance to choose how he would die.

The Grain Supply

Rome was dependent on a steady supply of grain. As a result, grain production and importation for a city the size of ancient Rome became an enormous industry. While gardens could provide some of the food the urban population required, as the city grew in population, it became necessary to supplement the food supply by importing grain into the city. This population increase, coupled with the extent to which Italian agriculture had come to favor cash crops over grain production, made it ever more difficult for the city to receive adequate food supplies. As a result, Rome was forced to import grains from distant overseas provinces.

The sources included here focus on the infrastructure of the grain supply. The emperor took personal responsibility for importing the grain (#181), a duty that, while popular, could also earn him the anger of the people if things did not go well (#180). A papyrus from Egypt details taxes that were levied on grain producers (#182). Another papyrus describes the transport of the grain by ship to Rome (#183). The ship owners (the *naviculari Ostienses*) were one of the largest and most important guilds in Ostia (#184). A unique mosaic from Ostia shows the grain being measured and loaded off of the ship at the port (#185). Once it was off the boat, it was delivered and stored in one of the Ostia's warehouses (#186). Once the grain reached its destination, it was milled and baked into bread (#187).

#180: Importing Grain to Rome

Tacitus, *Annals* 12.43
Written in the Early Second Century AD Describing Events of AD 51

As Rome expanded during the late Republic, Sicily, Sardinia, North Africa, and Egypt became Rome's primary suppliers of grain. Rome, however, being fifteen miles inland, had no harbor itself for importing goods by sea. For a long time, goods were imported into Puteoli, which lay south of Rome on the bay of Naples, and then were transported by oxcarts north to Rome or by smaller ships to Ostia. Later, however, after Claudius constructed the first major harbor in Ostia, ships sailed up the coast and unloaded their cargo at Ostia. It was then transported to Rome via the Tiber River. In this passage, the historian Tacitus comments on how Rome's reliance upon foreign grain could lead to serious problems in Rome.

At one time, there was a bad harvest and a famine followed. The people of Rome took this as a sign of the gods' unhappiness. The people did not only grumble in private. Indeed, Claudius was holding a trial in the law court when an unruly crowd surrounded him with shouting. This mob drove him by force into a corner of the forum. He was only able to escape the angry people with the help of an armed escort. The people had learned that Rome only had enough food supplies to last another fifteen days. Indeed, it was only by the great kindness of the gods and a mild winter that Rome was saved from this dire plight. There was a time when grain from Italy fed the legions in distant provinces. Even now, however, Italy is not ravaged by infertility. Instead, we would rather farm Africa and Egypt and entrust the life of the Roman people to ships and the possibility of disaster.

#181: Claudius' Attention to the Grain Supply

Suetonius, *Claudius* 18–19
Written in the Early Second Century AD Describing
the Emperor Claudius (AD 41–54)

As shown in the previous passage, reliance upon imported grain had several drawbacks. Prices were naturally higher because of the greater cost of shipping grain over long distances. Drought, severe weather, and political problems could destroy crops and limit farming activity, leading to famine in the worst cases. Storms could delay ships from reaching Ostia. In fact, ships usually did not sail at all in the winter. This passage is Suetonius' version of the incident that Tacitus reported in the previous text. In addition to providing more details, Suetonius also takes the opportunity to mention what else Claudius did to help the people and the shipping companies involved in the grain supply. When a serious fire threatened the *Porticus Aemilia*, a massive warehouse facility built in the second century BC, Claudius oversaw the efforts to put out the fire. This warehouse was located along the Tiber at the foot of the Aventine Hill and was the major storage facility for grain shipments that came up the river from Ostia.

Claudius was always very careful in his management of the grain supply. When the fire brigade was having trouble putting out a fire that had broken out in the *Porticus Aemilia*, he spent two nights in the giant building where elections were held in the Campus Martius. When the urban military garrison and his own palace slaves were not enough to put the fire out, he sent the *vicomagistri* out to their districts to summon the commoners. When the people had assembled, he asked for volunteers to help with the firefighting effort and offered them bags of money for their services so that they would have adequate compensation for the risks they would be taking.

There once was a serious shortage of grain because of a long drought. A mob detained Claudius in the forum and yelled criticisms and threw pieces of bread at him. The situation got so bad, in fact, that he barely managed to escape into the palace through a back door. Afterward, he did everything in his power to make sure grain was imported as soon as it became available. He even encouraged the grain ships to transport their cargos in the dangerous winter months by offering to the shipping agents free insurance if they should lose ships or cargo due to the harsh weather. He also established special privileges to people who built merchant ships. These privileges were determined based on the status of the builder. Citizens were given exemption from the law that imposed penalties upon people without children. People with the limited version of citizenship called Latin rights were given the rights of full citizens. Women were given the privileged status usually granted only to women who had borne four children. All of these privileges are still in use in my time [the second century AD].

#182: Production of Grain at the Source

Oxyrhynchus Papyrus 3.518
AD 179/180

Grain was grown on farms owned by private individuals and worked by tenant farmers. On the farms, the grain was kept in barns until it could be transported to the provincial harbor, such as Alexandria in Egypt, where it would be loaded onto a ship and sent to Rome. This text records the payment of a tax on grain production in Egypt. It records how much grain was deposited and provides a receipt that proved the person did pay their tax.

> This certifies that the produce of grain was deposited into the public granary for the nineteenth year of our lords and Caesars Aurelius Antoninus and Commodus. Record was made by the overseers of the public granary of the western district of Epi[. . . ?...]. A payment of four measures (that is, four measures of wheat) was made by Sarapion, son of Charisius. [Second hand]. I, Diogenes the overseer of the public granary, certify that the granary has received the four measures of wheat.

#183: The Shipment of Grain to Rome

Berlin Papyrus 1.27
Second Century AD

Most of the ships used to bring the grain from overseas were not owned directly by the emperor, but rather belonged to private shipping companies, which acquired contracts from the central government to transport the grain. The trip could take a considerable amount of time. In the passage here, a man writes home and tells of his trip. After arriving, he and all of the other crews involved in the grain transport were delayed in what is probably the port of Ostia.

> Irenaeus to my dearest brother Apollinarius, many greetings. Every day I pray that you are well. I am fine. I wanted to write and tell you that I reached port on June 30th. We finished unloading our ship on July 12th. I went up to Rome on July 19th. The place treated us as the gods wished. Now, every day we are waiting for permission to return home. In fact, until the present time, no one in the grain fleet has been allowed to leave. Say hello to your wife and Serenus as well as all your other friends that I know as well. Sent on August 2nd.

#184: The Ship Builders Guild Honors a Patron

CIL 14.168
April 11th, AD 195

In Ostia, the ship owners (the *naviculari Ostienses*) organized their own guild. This guild was quite large and prosperous, as demonstrated by their large guild hall, the so-called Schola of Trajan (building IV.5.15). In this inscription, the guild honors a benefactor from the equestrian class. Wealthy members of the community either of Ostia or even Rome would support local trade guilds as an outlet for their benefaction as well as to improve their business dealings. The occasion of the dedication of this statue base was April 11th, AD 195, the birthday of the then-current emperor, Septimius Severus.

> To Gaius Julius Philippus, a Roman *eques*; the guild of the ship builders of Ostia, to whom was given the right to meet by decree of the senate of Rome, put this up at their own expense. This statue was dedicated on the third day before the Ides of April [April 11th] while Tertullus and Clemens were consuls [AD 195]. In charge of its dedication were the leaders (*quinquennales*) for life Gaius Vettius Optatus and Marcus Clodius Minervalis as well as the freedman Calocaerus.

#185: Mosaic from the House of the Grain Measurers, Ostia

Third Century AD

After a one- or two-month journey from Egypt or Africa, the grain arrived in Ostia. When the ship arrived in the harbor, a boat met it and a grain measurer (*mensor*) boarded the ship to check the shipment. Grain was usually shipped loose, so, upon its arrival, it would have been measured and put into sacks. The mosaic shown here comes from the so-called House of the Grain Measurers (Figure 11.6). The building was probably a guild hall for the grain measurers of Ostia. It shows grain being poured into a measuring device called a *modius* while the *mensor* watches.

#186: The Warehouse of Hortensius in Ostia

After the grain was unloaded from the ship, it was delivered to a warehouse (*horrea*). Many warehouses have been preserved in Ostia, especially in the northern part of the city, along the ancient course of the Tiber. They were usually large buildings with central courtyards with small storage rooms opening off the courtyard. Some were two-storied with ramps and staircases for easy access to the second floor. In the case of grain warehouses, the floors were often raised to allow better air circulation beneath the floor and help keep vermin out of the grain. Figure 11.7 shows a plan of the Warehouse of Hortensius in Region V of the city. It is south of the eastern *decumanus* not far from the eastern gate of the city.

Figure 11.6 Mosaic from the House of the Grain Measurers Showing *Mensores* (Grain Measurers) (Photograph by B. Harvey).

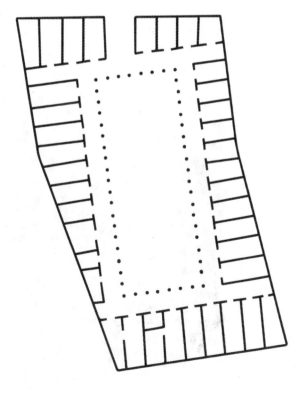

Figure 11.7 Plan of the Warehouse of Hortensius, Ostia (V.12.1).

#187: The Tomb of Eurysaces, Rome

CIL 6.1958a, b
First Century BC

Transport between Ostia and Rome was done by ferries. Small boats were loaded and then pulled by men or animals walking along towpaths on the banks. In Rome, the grain would once again be stored in a warehouse (such as the *Porticus Aemilia* mentioned above). People could either buy raw grain from the warehouses, or they could purchase baked bread from one of the professional bakeries. Very few houses had the means to grind their own grain or bake their own bread. As a result, bakeries were a common feature in the urban landscape. The flour ground in the mills was made into dough and kneaded in special machines with large blades turned in a manner similar to the mills. The dough was then shaped into loaves and baked in large ovens.

One baker of the first century BC from Rome, Eurysaces, made for himself a unique tomb monument in the shape of a *panarium*, a storage cabinet for finished loaves of bread (see Figure 11.8). The monument has rows of openings on each side. The inscription runs along all four sides of the monument. It would seem that Eurysaces was a contractor who supplied bread to the state and became extremely wealthy by doing so. His wife was buried in the monument as well. A frieze running around the top of the monument detailed the process of making bread from the measuring of the grain until the baking of the bread.

> This is the monument of Marcus Vergilius Eurysaces, baker and state contractor. This was Antistia, my wife, who lived as the best woman. The remains of her body, whatever there was left, are buried here in this bread cabinet.

Figure 11.8 The Tomb of Eurysaces, Rome (Photograph by B. Harvey).

Chapter 12: The Daily Routine

This chapter investigates how the Romans spent their day. The Roman workday was considerably shorter in Roman times, but it also began earlier. Without the benefit of electric lights, the Romans tended to confine their activities to the daylight hours. The day began at dawn and ended at sunset. The Romans divided the day into twelve hours of equal length. The first hour began at sunrise, the seventh hour began at noon when the sun was at its highest point in the sky, and the twelfth hour ended at sunset. Because the number of Roman hours never changed but the amount of daylight did, Roman hours lengthened or shortened, depending on the time of year. In the summer, when days were longer, the Roman hour lasted about seventy-five minutes. In the winter, however, when the days were shorter, the hour was only about forty-five minutes.

Descriptions of the Day's Routine

The day began with everyone going about jobs and official business. Clients visited their patrons. Government officials held meetings and performed their civic duties. The law courts were in session. The workday, however, ended before midday and the rest of the day was free time for relaxing or visiting the baths until the evening meal.

Descriptions of how people (at least of the upper classes) spent their day make frequent appearances in literature. The following are some examples that are especially helpful in understanding how the Romans spent their days. An epigram by Martial mentions activities and the hours of the day in which a person typically did them (#188). A letter of Pliny the Younger describes his uncle Pliny the Elder's typical daily routine (#189). Pliny the Elder also mentions how he tended to work on his literary pursuits late into the night (#190). In another letter, Pliny the Younger describes the activities that fill up a person's day (#191).

#188: Martial's Day

Martial, *Epigrams* 4.8
Late First Century AD

In this passage, the satirist Martial describes the typical activities of the day hour by hour. It is one of our best sources for the breakdown of a Roman day.

The first and second hours wear out the people as they go about greeting their patrons. The third puts the hoarse lawyers to work. Rome stretches out its various labors until the end of the fifth hour. The sixth brings rest to the weary

Romans, but the seventh ends their siesta. The people, shining with oil, find the eighth to the ninth hours to be the best time for exercising in the athletic field. The ninth hour bids all to come to find their way to the couches of the dining table. The tenth hour is the time for my little books, Euphemus, when it is your duty to govern the heavenly feast of the emperor. That is when our good Caesar is soothed by the celestial nectar contained in the tiny cup he holds in his giant hand. Then let fly the jokes. Our Thalia, muse of comic verse, is afraid to take a step, even when she is prompted toward Jupiter of the Morning.

#189: The Routine of Pliny the Elder

Pliny the Younger, *Letters* 3.5.7–13
Early Second Century AD

The life of an aristocrat was not just parties and relaxation. Official duties could take up a considerable amount of the day. In this passage, Pliny the Younger describes his uncle's daily routine. Pliny the Elder was a high-ranking member of the equestrian order and was involved in imperial service under the Flavian Emperors. He was also an accomplished author. Pliny the Younger's purpose with this description was to explain how his uncle was able to accomplish so much in his lifetime.

Perhaps you are surprised that a man so busy could find time to write so many learned works of literature. You will be even more amazed when you find out that he worked as a lawyer for a considerable number of years. He died when he was sixty-six years old and spent much of his life engaged in the most important public duties, including friendship with emperors. He did have, however, a sharp intellect, incredible enthusiasm, and an astounding wakefulness. From late summer, he would begin to wake up about midnight. He did this not so much to improve his prosperity but rather to begin his literary studies. In the winter, he would get up in the seventh or (rarely) eighth hour of the night, and often at the sixth. He was very prone to sleepiness. Sometimes, even in the midst of his studies, he would doze off and then wake up again. Before dawn, he was in the habit of going to pay his respects to the emperor Vespasian (who was another person who made use of the night hours) and then go from there to perform the duties the emperor gave to him. He would then return home and devote what time there was left of the morning to his studies. At midday, he would eat a small and easily prepared lunch reminiscent of the light meals eaten by our ancestors. After that, in the summer, if he was free of other official duties, he would relax in the sunshine. A book would be read to him, and he would take notes and copy down quotes for later use. He would, indeed, take notes on everything he read. He used to say that there was no book so bad that there would not be something useful to be gotten from it. After his time in the sun, he would take a cold bath, eat a snack, and then sleep for a very short time. He would soon wake up again and begin to work as if it was a new day.

He did this until it was time for dinner. Even during dinner he was in the habit of having a book to read. He would again take notes as the book was read. I remember a time once when one of his friends asked the reader to go back and repeat a word that he had mispronounced. My uncle said to the friend, "You understood what the reader said, didn't you?" "Yes I did," his friend replied. "Then why do you make him go back and repeat it? We could have heard ten more lines if not for this interruption," my uncle said to him. That is how frugal he was with his time. He was also not one to linger at the dinner table. In summer, he would leave dinner when the sun went down. In the winter, he would remain until the first hour of the night. He was so strict with this practice that it seemed like he was compelled to do so by law.

#190: Pliny the Elder's Use of the Night

Pliny the Elder, *Natural History* Introduction 18
First Century AD

Pliny the Younger may have had this passage in mind when he described the amazing volume of Pliny the Elder's published literary works. The passage comes from the introduction to his *Natural History*, a massive work that filled thirty-seven volumes. In it, Pliny the Elder describes how he had to make liberal use of his nights in order to get the book written.

I do not doubt that there are things that I have failed to mention in this work. I am a human being, and one who is very busy with official duties. I have been forced, therefore, to compose much of this at odd hours, especially at night. Therefore, I hope that none of you think that I even took off the nighttime hours. I have devoted the daytime hours to you. I get as much sleep as I need to stay healthy. Indeed, I am content with the one reward, that while we ponder these things, we live longer lives. In truth, as Marcus Varro said, to live is to be awake.

#191: The Hustle and Bustle of Life in the City

Pliny the Younger, *Letters* 1.9.1–4
Early Second Century AD

Aristocrats tended to equate their life in the city of Rome with their official lives. Most, however, had the means to escape the city and visit country villas they themselves or their friends owned for a holiday away from Rome. In this letter written to a friend named Minicius Fundanus, Pliny contrasts the busy life of Rome with the simplicity of country life. Because he speaks from the perspective of a

wealthy landowner, his lifestyle would not have been the same as the vast majority
of Romans who as urban or rural poor had to, in the former case, live in the city
close to their jobs or, in the latter case, work constantly on their own farms or those
owned by aristocrats like Pliny and his uncle.

> It is amazing how you can know or at least seem to know the plan for an indi-
> vidual day, but it is not possible when you try to do the same thing for a series
> of successive days. If you were to ask someone, "What did you do today?"
> he would respond about how he went to a boy's coming of age ceremony, or
> attended a betrothal ceremony or wedding or witnessed the signing of a will or
> spoke in court on someone's behalf, or sat on a jury. On the day you did those
> things, everything seemed to be necessary, but when you think about how you
> did those same things every day, they suddenly seem trivial. This triviality of
> life in Rome has become even clearer to me now while I am on holiday in the
> country. "I have wasted so many days on useless activities," is the thought that
> keeps coming into my head.

Waking Up

Romans used the small *cubicula* in their houses as bedrooms. These small chambers
had space for little more than a bed, a chest, and a chamber pot. Beds themselves
were little more than couches. Without electricity, the Roman day essentially began
and ended with the rising and setting of the sun. The Roman was generally awake
by dawn or even earlier (even if they did not want to; #192). Breakfast was a simple
and quick affair. Bread and water seem to have been the norm (#193).

The dress of a Roman male included a loincloth (*subligaculum*), a tunic (*tunica*),
and some kind of outer garment (the *amictus*). The tunic was the most basic form of
attire. It resembled a long shirt made up of two pieces sewn together. It had short
sleeves and was fastened around the waist with a belt. The most common *amictus*
was a second tunic (#194 describes Augustus' habit of wearing multiple tunics;
Aulus Gellius discusses long-sleeved tunics in #195). Sandals (*soleae*) were the basic
footwear. The upper classes might wear leather slippers (*crepidae*). Over everything,
a man might wear a toga, the formalwear of the Roman world (#196). Men were
expected to not spend much time worrying about their physical appearance (#197).

The fashion for a long time for men was to be clean-shaven. The barber (*tonsor*
in Latin) would cut a man's hair and trim his beard (#198 and #199).

#192: The Impossibility of Sleeping Late in Rome

Martial, *Epigrams* 12.57
Late First Century AD

Earlier, Pliny the Younger described how his uncle, even in retirement, would awake
before dawn to visit the emperor Vespasian (who also was an early riser). Indeed, the

hustle and bustle of the city began shortly after daybreak and it could be very difficult for someone to sleep past the first hour even if he wanted to. In this passage, Martial complains how the noise in the streets was enough to keep him from sleeping late while living in his house in the poor, crowded Subura district in Rome.

You were asking me the other day why I like to run off to my tiny country estate in dry Nomentum and the squalid hearth of my villa there. My friend, there is no place in Rome for a poor man to either think or rest. There are too many things that keep me from living a decent life. The street is filled with noise. In the morning, it is the school teachers, at night the bakers, and all day long the hammers of the blacksmiths. On the one hand the idle money exchanger shakes his dirty table with coins from back in the day when they still had some weight to them. On the other hand, the metalworker of Spanish gold makes his worn-out stone reverberate with his shining hammer. The crowd of crazed worshippers of Bellona never cease from their noisy adulation of the goddess. Then there is the man who survived a shipwreck. He is always chattering while he gets around on a bandaged leg. The Jewish boy who was trained by his mother never stops begging. That watery-eyed merchant of sulfur products never stops shouting. With all of this going on, who can tally up the hours of lost sleep? Perhaps they could also count up how many hands bang on bronze pots in Rome when the moon goes into eclipse as a result of a witch's spell. I would venture to guess that you know nothing of these things. You are in the lap of luxury in your suburban villa. Even the ground floor of your house looks down on the tops of the other hills of Rome. It is as if you have a country estate right in the city. In the autumn, you have a grape harvest right in Rome that rivals anything we would see in wine country. You have a wide road for your carriage even inside your estate's walls. There, you enjoy the most profound sleep, and the talking of people in the street does not disturb your rest. Indeed, you are able to shut the day out completely until you are willing to let it in. The noise of the throng passing by in the street wakes me up. It is as if my bed was right out in the street. And so, when I want to get some sleep, I go to my country villa.

#193: Children Buy Breakfast on Their Way to School

Martial, *Epigrams* 14.223
Late First Century AD

In this passage, Martial describes children buying something called *adipata* for breakfast on their way to school. It seems to have been some kind of rich pastry either filled with or coated in fat.

Wake up! It is time for the baker to sell breakfast (*adipata*) to the children on their way to school. All around the crested birds of the morning sing their songs.

#194: Augustus' Habit of Wearing Multiple Tunics

Suetonius, *Augustus* 82
Written in the Early Second Century AD Describing
the Emperor Augustus (27 BC–AD 14)

Getting dressed was more time consuming on days when the Roman male was required to wear his toga. The upper classes, whose public duties required men to regularly wear a toga, had the advantage of owning slaves who could help drape the toga's voluminous folds over the man's body.

> In winter Augustus protected himself with four tunics and a heavy toga, as well as an undershirt, a woolen chest-protector, and long pants and heavy socks. In the summer, however, he slept with the doors of his bedroom open, and sometimes even in the peristyle of the house near a fountain. He would also sometimes have a slave fan him all night. Yet he could not endure the sun even in winter, and never walked about in the open air without wearing a broad-brimmed hat, even at home.

#195: Disapproval of Long-Sleeved Tunics

Aulus Gellius, *Attic Nights* 6.12
Second Century AD

Out of a sense of modesty, women's clothing covered more of the body than men's did. It was believed that men's tunics should be short-sleeved and not extend very far down the thigh. In this passage, Aulus Gellius describes how long-sleeved tunics were considered unbecoming for a man.

> At Rome and in Latium it was considered to be improper for a man to wear a tunic long enough to reach below the elbow, the hand, or the fingers. Romans usually call tunics of that type by their Greek name "Chirodytae" (long-sleeved), but they think that is a type of longer-fitting clothing only appropriate for women so that they can hide their arms and legs from sight. Roman men originally wore the toga alone without a tunic beneath it. The tunic was added only later and then only as a more form-fitting and shorter garment that extended only below the shoulder. The Greeks call this kind of garment "exomidae" (sleeveless).

#196: Attempts to Require People to Wear a Toga

Suetonius, *Augustus* 40.5
Written in the Early Second Century AD Describing
the Emperor Augustus (27 BC–AD 14)

For a man of the lower classes, who did not have the help of a slave, donning a toga was a tedious process. Despite attempts by emperors (such as Augustus in this passage from Suetonius' biography of that emperor) to get members of the lower classes to wear togas, most people shunned them.

> Augustus was keen to bring back old-fashioned forms of clothing. Once, at a voting assembly, he saw a crowd of people wearing dark cloaks. He became furious at this and shouted, "Behold the Romans, masters of the world, a nation who can always be found in their toga!" He went further and assigned to an aedile the task of making sure that after this no one should be allowed into the forum unless they were wearing their toga and not a cloak.

#197: Men Who Put Too Much Effort into Their Appearance

Ovid, *The Art of Love* 3.433–448
End of the First Century BC

Roman men were generally expected to be relatively unconcerned with their physical appearance. Men who worried about fashion and made themselves up were often looked upon as effeminate. It seems, however, that some men became slaves of fashion. In this passage, Ovid advises women to avoid such men.

> Women, avoid men who pay too much attention to their clothing and bodies, and those who style their hair. What they told you they have told a thousand other girls: "I am a swinger. There is no single home for my love." What should a woman do when her boyfriend is more frivolous than she is (and may have more boyfriends on the side as well)? You may have a hard time believing me, but believe me anyway. Troy would still be standing if the Trojans had followed the advice of Cassandra. There are some men who will deceitfully claim that they love you just to win you over, but all you are to them is another notch on the bedpost. Don't fall for their slicked-back hair, their fancy shoes, high thread count togas, or that fancy ring (or rings) on their finger. The best looking of this whole group may just perhaps be a thief who is more in love with your outfit than you.

#198: Inscriptions of Barbers

CIL 6.5865, 6366, 9940, 37822 (Rome)
First to Third Centuries AD

The following are several funerary inscriptions commemorating *tonsores*, including a female (*tonstrix*).

> 5865: Diogenes Pompeianus, litter bearer; Iole Pompeiana, female barber (*tonstrix*).

6366: The mother of the barber Cadmus made this for her son as well as for Popularis.

9940: Publius Petronius Philomusus, freedman of Publius, barber on the Vicus Scaurus; his burial plot is twelve feet wide and sixteen feet deep.

37822: To the Spirits of the Dead; Julius Festus Gemmula made this for himself, his daughters, his wife, his freedmen and freedwomen, and their descendants; Gemmula the barber is buried here.

#199: A Shady Female Barber

Martial, *Epigrams* 2.17
Late First Century AD

Here, Martial describes a female barber who has a shop in the Subura, not far from the forum. In the epigram, Martial alludes to the fact that she does not actually cut hair but is engaged in some other occupation, perhaps prostitution.

A girl calling herself a "female barber" can be found hanging out on the street in the Argiletum, the place where the road running through the Subura meets the forum. This is where the whips of the torturers hang and many shoemakers sit in their shops. My friend Ammianus, it is surprising, but this female barber does not cut hair. Does NOT, I say. What does she do then? She fleeces her customers, of their money that is.

The *Ornatrix*

Shortly after she awoke, the first order of the day for an aristocratic lady was to have her slave hairdresser/cosmetician (*ornatrix*) apply her makeup and arrange her hair. Ovid devotes a portion of his book, *The Art of Love* to the art of the *ornatrix* (#200). The aristocratic lady at her toilette was one of the most common motifs involving women depicted in Roman art. A wall painting from the Villa Farnesina in Rome (now in the Palazzo Massimo) depicts an *ornatrix* doing Venus' hair while being observed by her son Cupid. Another wall painting from Pompeii shows a lady surrounded by several female attendants. In the famous painting from the Villa of the Mysteries in Pompeii, an *ornatrix* combs a woman's hair while a cupid holds a mirror so that she can see her reflection. On a relief sculpture from Trier in Gaul, an older woman sits on a chair while one slave works on her hair and another slave girl holds a mirror. Two other slaves hold pitchers of cosmetics, perfume, or water.

Combing and styling the hair was a major task of the *ornatrix* (#201 tells how one woman managed to ruin her hair by dying it). Surviving statues of women show a vast array of ornate hairstyles, perhaps none more so than the statue of the so-called "Flavian Lady" in 'Rome's Capitoline Museums and mentioned also by

Juvenal (#202). This section ends with a number of epigraphic examples of *ornatri-ces* from Rome and Ostia (#203, #204, and #205).

#200: The Art of the *Ornatrix*

Ovid, *The Art of Love* 3.133–152
End of the First Century BC

Ovid, the Augustan poet famous for his love poetry, addressed his third book of the *Ars Amatoria* ("The Art of Love") to his female readers. A major part of the book was dedicated to what women should do to improve their appearance. In the following passage, Ovid encourages women to pay special attention to their hairdo.

> It is elegance of appearance that attracts us men, so do not neglect your hair. A skillful hand can make or break a good hairdo. That does not mean that there is a single way for a woman to arrange her hair. A girl should choose a style that suits her, so be sure to look in your mirror before deciding. A long face goes best with a simple parting of the hair. That is how the virtuous Laodamia did her hair. A girl with a round face should tie her hair up in a bun on the top of her head so that her ears are exposed. Another should choose to let her hair down so that it hangs on both of her shoulders in the way that Apollo appears when he is prepared to play his lyre. Another puts her hair in braids like Diana does when, with skirt hitched up, she chases fleeing animals while hunting in the woods. One woman lets the wind blow through her loose hair. Another prefers it to be out of the way and so pins it back. Some like to comb their hair straight with tortoiseshell combs while others prefer to curl it. You would laugh if someone were to ask you to count the number of acorns on an oak tree or bees in a meadow in Sicily. That is how I feel when asked to list all of the ways a woman can adorn her hair. Every day brings some new hairdo.

#201: A Woman Ruins Her Hair

Ovid, *The Loves* 1.14
Late First Century BC

Occasionally, a woman would decide to dye her hair or style it with curls. Either of those activities could damage the woman's hair. In this passage, also by Ovid, a woman has ruined her hair and is forced to wear a wig until her hair grows back.

> Didn't I tell you to stop treating your hair? You wouldn't stop dying your hair and now you have ruined it. No one's hair grew better than yours, but you could not leave it alone. It had grown long right down your side. It was very fine, too, so fine, in fact, that you were afraid to style it. Your hair was like the silk of one of those screens the Chinese make or the filament a spider weaves when it weaves

its delicate web under some deserted beam. Your hair was neither dark nor blonde, but a mixture of the two, like the color of a lofty cedar when the bark has been peeled away in some dewy valley beneath tall Mount Ida. Don't forget either that your hair was so pliant that it could be put into a hundred styles and still not cause you any pain. You never needed a pin or a comb to separate it. Your *ornatrix* was safe. Often I have personally watched her work on your hair and never once did I see you grab a hairpin and stab her in the arm with it in retaliation for painful combing. Often in the early morning I have seen you reclining on a purple cushion before you had done anything with your hair, but even in this "messy" state it was still fetching. It reminded me of a Maenad of Thrace who, after running wild around the countryside, collapses exhausted and stretches out in the green grass without a care in the world. Your tender hair used to be the image of youthfulness, but, alas, how much it has suffered from your recent attempts to dye it. Earlier, you decided to go with those tight curls that are in fashion now, so you brought out the hot curling irons. Your hair put up with that though. It told you that it was a crime, a travesty to singe your hair. "Leave it alone," I said, but you wouldn't listen. "Out with this savage violence! Your hair is not the kind of thing that should be burned." I firmly believe that your former simple hairstyle could teach all of the fancy hairstyles in vogue these days a thing or two. Now your beautiful hair is gone. Yours was hair that an Apollo or Bacchus would have been proud to have on their own heads. Your hair was easily comparable to the hair in that famous painting of Venus where she is holding it in her wet hands as she comes out of the sea. Why do you now complain about your ruined hair? Why do you, silly girl, only now sadly look at yourself in the mirror? You are looking at yourself with eyes that are not accustomed to the sight. If you want to like what you see, then you need to forget what you used to be. It is not the enchanted herbs of some jealous rival in love that has cursed you. No witch has washed your hair with poisoned water. It was not even some disease that has done this to you (and may you never suffer such a calamity). No woman envious of your hair whispered an incantation to make it fall out. No. It was none of these things. You did it all to yourself, and your loss is completely your own fault. You mixed the evil concoction and put it on your own head. Now some captive girl in Germany has to send you her hair for a wig. It seems a bit ironic that your head will be topped with an offering from a conquered people. You used to be embarrassed by the people who constantly would come up to you to complement your hair. Now you have to live with the realization that people are looking at you because of something you bought and that they praise some woman of the Sugambri instead of you. "I remember when my reputation was based on something of my own!" you may lament. Poor girl, you try to hold back the tears. I have seen you try to hide with your hand your cheeks, red now with embarrassment. You kept your old, ruined hair and it now sits in your lap and you look at it in despair. Alas. I can think of far more worthy things you should be holding in your lap than some discarded hair. Put your mind at ease and smile. The damage can be repaired. After a while, it will grow back and you will be known for your own hair again.

#202: The Flavian Lady

Juvenal, *Satires* 6.501–504
Late First/Early Second Centuries AD

For many women of the aristocracy, keeping up with the most up-to-date hairstyles was of the highest importance. Surviving portrait busts of women from the Roman world exhibit a wide range of hairstyles. Some sculptures, in fact, have removable hair so that, when the style changed, the woman's sculpted depiction could change to follow the fashion trends. In the late first/early second centuries AD, the style in vogue was a complex pile of curls mounted on the top of the front of the head. A statue head of an empress or aristocratic lady with just such an elaborate and piled-up hairstyle has been preserved and is on display in the Capitoline Museums (see Figure 12.1). In his sixth satire on women, Juvenal describes the same style.

Figure 12.1 Front of the So-Called "Flavian Lady" in the Capitoline Museum, Rome (Capitoline Museum; Photograph by B. Harvey).

So serious is the attention paid to beautification; so many are the tiers and layers piled up on a woman's head! From the front, you would think you were looking at the especially tall Andromache; she is not as tall from behind. In fact, you would think she was a different woman.

#203: Epigraphic Examples of *Ornatrices* from Rome

CIL 6.3994, 5539, 7297, 8880, 8958, 9731, 33099, 37811
First to Third Centuries AD

Because of the personal time they spent together every morning, the *ornatrix* enjoyed a closer relationship with her mistress than did other slaves. This relationship is reflected in the fact that *ornatrices* are one of the best documented servile roles in the epigraphic record. Their proximity to the mistress gave these slaves prestige, made them valuable allies amongst their fellow slaves and freedmen, and sometimes enriched them through cash gifts and bequests from their mistress.

3994: Gemina, freedwoman of the empress, *ornatrix*, dedicated this funerary urn to her freedwoman Irene.

5539: To Paezusa, *ornatrix* of Octavia, the daughter of the emperor Claudius; she lived eighteen years; Philetus, slave in charge of the silver jewelry of Octavia, the daughter of the emperor Claudius, dedicated this to his dearest slave wife as well as to himself.

7297: Sacred to the Spirits of the Dead; to Panope, *ornatrix* of Torquata, the wife of Quintus Volusius, and Phoebe, girl in charge of the mirror; Panope lived twenty-two years and Phoebe thirty-seven years; Spendo made this for his well-deserving good friends as well as for himself; the place of burial was granted by permission of their domestic burial society.

8880: To Dionysia, *ornatrix* of the mother of the emperor Tiberius Caesar Augustus; their fellow slaves the scribe Tertius and Anta put this up.

8958: Sacred to Juno; Dorcas, freedwoman of the empress Livia, *ornatrix*, she was born a slave on the island of Capri; Lycastus, her fellow freedman, man in charge of clothing, made this for his dearest wife as well as for himself.

9731: Pieris, *ornatrix*, who lived nine years; her mother Hilara dedicated this to her.

33099: Chloe, *ornatrix* of the slaves of the emperor Tiberius; she lived twenty years; her sister dedicated this.

37811: There are buried here two funerary urns: Pollia Urbana, freedwoman of a woman, *ornatrix* on the Via Aemilia; Marcus Calidius Apollonius, freedman of Marcus, barber on the Via Aemilia.

Figure 12.2 Tomb Epitaph of the *Ornatrix* Psamate (Capitoline Museum; Photograph by B. Harvey).

#204: Tomb Epitaph of the *Ornatrix* Psamate

CIL 6.9732 (Rome)
Second or Third Century AD

Psamate was the *ornatrix* of a woman named Furia. She died at the age of eighteen and was buried by a baker named Mithrodates. Mithrodates was the slave of a man named Flaccus Thorius. *Ornatrices* were generally described as being the slave of a woman rather than a man, so it is feasible that Furia was the wife of Flaccus Thorius and so Psamate and Mithrodates were members of the same household. The tomb itself has long been lost, but the inscription was recovered in the Middle Ages and is currently on display in the Capitoline Museum (Figure 12.2).

Psamate, *ornatrix* of Furia, lived eighteen years; Mithrodates, baker of Flaccus Thorius, made this.

#205: A Group of *Ornatrices* from Ostia

CIL 4.5306
Second or Third Century AD

This bronze tablet from Ostia records a group of *ornatrices*. All of them come from different families, so all of them may have belonged to the same burial society. Those women who are not described as belonging to a particular person may have been freelance *ornatrices* or may have just chosen not to list the name of their master.

The purpose of the list is not known, but the fact that it is written on a bronze tablet may mean that it is a *tabula defixionis*, a curse tablet.

> Agathemeris, slave of Manlia; Achulea, *ornatrix*, slave of Fabia; Caletuche, *ornatrix*, slave of Vergilia; Hilara, *ornatrix*, slave of Licinia; Chreste, *ornatrix*, slave of Cornelia; Hilara; *ornatrix*, slave of Seia; Moscis, *ornatrix*, Rufa, *ornatrix*, slave of Apeilia; Chilia, *ornatrix*.

The Morning *Salutatio*

After his quick preparations for the day, a man would leave the house and set about his daily chores. For many, including the aristocracy, the day's first major task was the *salutatio*, the period when clients ceremonially greeted their patrons. By the bonds of official friendship (*amicitia*), upper-class citizens extended their protection and assistance to the lower classes, while those lower on the social scale promised to show political support to their patrons. This mutual exchange of acts of kindness (*beneficia*) between social allies (*amici*) was a time-honored tradition that characterized relationships between the classes. While in one sense it brought the upper and lower classes together, it also helped to more sharply delineate between the wealthy with the resources to help others and those who depended upon others for their social survival. In the Republican period, senators sought the support of the masses in order to win enough votes for election to senatorial office. After receiving the vote of clients, the senator reciprocated this *beneficium* by offering to his clients the opportunity to ask advice and, in some cases, to receive financial assistance (#206). Aristocrats of the Imperial period, although they no longer needed popular support in order to be elected to senatorial office, still sought to have a multitude of clients (many of whom were their own freedmen, obliged to them for life by the bond of *amicitia*). Just as a larger, more elegant house was a means by which aristocrats demonstrated their prestige, so also a larger corps of clients was a symbolic show of influence (#207).

Although it lost much of its intrinsic political significance, the morning *salutatio* became a social chore for both the patron and the client (#208 and #209). The client was obligated to personally greet his patron. In exchange for his support and appearance, the patron rewarded his clients with a gift of money or food. While these handouts were not enough for a poor family to live on, they could help enormously, especially at times when seasonal work was not available.

#206: Clients Lend Voting Support to the Aristocracy

Cicero, *Defense of Murena* 70–71
Speech Originally Delivered in 63 BC

In the following passage, the orator Cicero speaks on behalf of Lucius Murena, who had been accused of bribery when running for election to the consulship. One point of attack was that he had bribed members of the lower classes to attend him on his official business and vote for him. Cicero maintains that all of the senators do the same thing and that the poor are happy to oblige because the electoral support of their higher class patrons is what they are able to offer in the way of *beneficia*.

Many people did indeed follow Murena, but I ask you to prove to me how this could be considered bribery. If you can, then I will admit that what he did was a crime. If you cannot, then what is there in his actions that you find blameworthy? "Why does he need a crowd of people to follow him?" the prosecution asks. Are you really asking me to explain to you the need for a tactic that every one of us has used? Following us around when we are running for election is the one and only chance the poor have for asking or deserving *beneficia* of people of senatorial status. It is not possible or even right for us who are members of the senatorial order or those who are *equites* to ask these poor people to follow around the candidates to which they have been bound for whole days at a time. If these people sometimes visit our house, escort us when we are spending time in the forum, or appear with us while we are working in the courts, we prefer to say that we are being treated and honored with the respect that we deserve. Activities such as these are, in fact, the occupation of poorer people who are unemployed. There is certainly no lack of people like that for men of good character and who are willing to engage in the exchange of *beneficia*. Would the prosecution really take from these men of humble means the ability to earn what they can from their chosen business? Please, allow these people to participate in the exchange of *beneficia*: they rely on us for everything, so do not take from them the ability to give something back in return for our support. They indeed are so poor that they have little of value to contribute to the exchange of *beneficia* except their vote. They themselves are in the habit of reminding us that they cannot speak on our behalf in court, back us financially, or invite us to their house. All of these things, however, they ask of us. They also have acknowledged that they have no way of compensating us for these *beneficia* than to back us with their support and votes. It is for this reason that the poor themselves protested the Fabian law, which sought to limit the number of people who could attend a candidate for office. They did the same thing against the senatorial decree forwarded by the consul Lucius Caesar. No punishment exists that could keep members of the poorer classes from demonstrating their thanks for the kind of support we give them.

#207: An Aristocrat's Crowd of Clients

Seneca, *On the Shortness of Life* 14.4
First Century AD

In the following passage, Seneca, in his book *On the Shortness of Life*, bemoans the lot of the unappreciated client whose patron seems to prefer not to be bothered by his clients.

How many are the clients who, after being tortured with a long wait, are just rushed through in haste? How many patrons avoid going through an atrium filled with clients altogether and prefer to flee through some hidden back door of their house as if it were kinder to deceive than to shut them out? How many patrons, still half asleep and suffering from last night's hangover, will need to be reminded of their client's name a thousand times before he can repeat it while he overbearingly gives his client an arrogant kiss? Bear in mind that this miserable client broke his own slumbers so that he could wait around for his patron.

#208: A Client Complains of His Useless Effort

Martial, *Epigrams* 5.22
Late First Century AD

It was easy for a member of the upper classes to forget how important the *salutatio* could be for the poor. In this passage, Martial complains how he trudged across town to the house of his patron only to be told by the doorkeeper that his patron had cancelled the *salutatio* and had already left for the day.

If I had not wanted and deserved to see you at home this morning, Patron Paulus, then I might wish that your house on the Esquiline Hill might be farther away. My apartment is on the Quirinal Hill, very close to the Tiburtina column in the place where the temple of Flora faces the ancient temple of Jupiter. To get to your place, I must face the climb up the hill from the Subura by narrow alleys that twist up the hill. There is a stairway, too, that is never dry and is filled with broken cobblestones. I am barely able to find a path between the long lines of carts pulled by oxen and the blocks of marble transported down the street. Finally, after enduring a thousand trials, Paulus, I reach the door of your house. The slave at the door, however, says, "Sorry. He's not home to receive his clients this morning." That was the outcome of my vain labor. All I managed to get was a wet toga. If I had been able to see my patron it would have only barely been worth the trip. Why must dutiful clients have thoughtless patrons? You will not be able to be my patron unless you decide to sleep in.

#209: The Imperial Patron and Client

Juvenal, *Satires* 1.95–113, 117–126
Late First/Early Second Centuries AD

In his first satire, Juvenal recounts the cesspit of vice into which Rome has sunk. Among his complaints are numerous attacks on the patron–client relationship and the extent to which the *salutatio* had become a sham. In the first part of this quote,

Juvenal describes a poor client who is first treated with suspicion and then forced to wait when a rich freedman arrives and demands that he be allowed admittance first just because of his superior wealth.

Nowadays, a crowd of clients in their togas must sit at their patron's front door in the hopes of a little handout. The patron first gazes into the face of each client, afraid lest he be tricked and give his handout to an imposter under a false name. Only once you are recognized will you be eligible to receive your handout. Before you get your payment, however, the patron orders that some senatorial descendants of Trojans be admitted. They had been waiting just like the rest of us. The patron announces, "First the praetor then the tribune." A freedman, however, interrupts and says, "I was here first! Why should I be hesitant to defend my right by order of arrival? Yes I was born along the far-away Euphrates River. The little earring holes in my ears bear witness to my foreign origin, something I tried to deny for a long time. Now, that doesn't matter. I own five shops of my own which bring in a fortune of four hundred thousand *sestertii* every year. Senatorial status isn't worth what it used to be. One senator, Corvinus, hires himself out as a shepherd in Laurentum. My property worth is more than those famous wealthy freedmen Pallas and Licinius. Let the senatorial tribunes wait their turn. Wealth trumps all. Just because a person is supposedly of honorable status does not mean they are more important. Sure, it was only recently that I came to this city and my feet are still white from the slave market, but no deity is so deserving of worship as wealth..."

When it comes time at the end of the year to balance your checkbook, how much of a difference does the handout from your patron really make? What does it really add to your financial picture? What advantage is there for clients like me, who must, out of the handout, pay for our toga, nice shoes, bread, and fuel for the fire at home? Still, a thick pack of litters bearing clients arrives looking for their dollar-a-day. In some cases, a sick or pregnant wife follows her husband and makes the rounds, or else the man will, by a well-known trick, claim to have one with him. He points to the litter, empty and shut up, and says, "My Galla is in there. Come out quickly, woman. Why are you delaying? Stick out your head, Galla!" When there is no reply (how could there be?), he says, "Don't bother her. She must be asleep."

Chapter 13: Business and Occupations

It was necessary for the vast majority of Romans to work for a living. Commerce, industry, and trade were reserved, in large part, for the equestrian and lower classes. People lived and worked together in a diverse urban landscape in which the shopkeeper sold his goods next door to a house owned by an aristocrat. Because day-to-day occupations often did not attract the interest of our aristocratic authors (#210), it is difficult to know what life was like for a lower-class businessman or worker. The streets of Pompeii and Ostia, however, are rich with evidence for the commercial and industrial life of an ancient Roman city. Epigraphy, also, once again preserves the lives of a broader slice of the population.

#210: A Senator's View on the Nature of the Various Professions

Cicero, *On Duties* 1.42
Middle of the First Century BC

Although the Roman aristocrat was not ignorant about commercial activities, apparently he believed that such pursuits were unbecoming of someone of his social standing. In his book *On Duties* (*De Officiis*), Cicero outlines his opinion on different occupations and explains why he considers some to be degrading. Cicero's opinion betrays the aristocratic bias against lower-class occupations.

> We have generally the following opinion concerning which trades and occupations are to be considered honorable and which should be considered demeaning. In the first place, you should avoid those occupations that incur the hatred of humankind, for example, the tax collector and the loan shark. Also dishonorable are the sordid occupations of all workmen who are hired for their brawn rather than their skill. Their pay is essentially a contract for their servitude. Also to be considered demeaning are those who purchase goods from a merchant simply so they can turn around and sell them for a profit. My low opinion of this occupation comes from the fact that the merchant is unable to make a profit unless he lies to people, and there certainly is nothing more base than telling lies. All craftsmen, too, are employed in a sordid profession because there is nothing about a workshop that could be considered noble. The professions that win the least approval are those who cater to base pleasure, "fish sellers, butchers, cooks, people who raise poultry, and fishermen," as Terence says. Add to this number, if you please, perfume makers, dancers, and the whole entertainment industry.

Workers

Rome was naturally a city filled with shopkeepers, laborers, merchants, craftsmen, and builders. Because so many of these occupations employed the lower classes, little was recorded about the workers as individuals. The aristocratic literary texts only mention them in passing, and often with disdain. Among the ruins of towns like Ostia and Pompeii, we can still see where they worked. Without detailed records of life for members of the lower classes, however, we must examine the architectural remains of where they worked and the epigraphic records of the lives as reported on their often-short tombstone inscriptions. Included here is a sample of such inscriptions. There is a stone-engraver (#211), a fish seller (#212), a fruit seller (#213), a dealer in bronze and iron (#214), a pottery merchant (#215), a seller of embroidered clothing (#216), an assortment of merchants (#217), a chicken seller (#218), an importer of liquid goods (#219), some agricultural workers (#220), and a selection of artisans (#221). Also, a wax tablet from Dacia records a labor contract for a mine (#222).

#211: Diomedes the Engraver

CIL 6.9221 (Rome)
First to Third Centuries AD

Some of our best evidence for ancient occupations comes in the form of the tombstones workers left behind to commemorate their lives. Like the other tombstones encountered thus far, the inscriptions these people dedicated to themselves were meant to elicit a memory of the deceased. Most merely document the name and occupation of the deceased, but these texts nevertheless demonstrate the rich variety of workers who lived in the ancient world. Sometimes, the text includes a reference to where the person's shop was located to further aid the reader's memory. This inscription from Rome mentions a freedman who had his engraving shop on the *Via Sacra*, the road that ran across the length of the forum from near the Colosseum to the foot of the Capitoline Hill. This was prime real estate, especially as so much of the forum was occupied by public buildings. This freedman probably worked in silver or other precious metals.

> To Lucius Furius Diomedes, freedman of Lucius, engraver on the *Via Sacra*, dedicated this to his wife Cornelia Tertulla, the daughter of Lucius.

#212: Aurelia Nais the Fish Seller

CIL 6.9801 (Rome)
Second or Third Century AD

This text is another funerary inscription. It mentions a female fish seller (*piscatrix*). The warehouse of Galba was one of the important warehouses in the dock district

Figure 13.1 Tomb Epitaph of the Fish Seller (*Piscatrix*) Aurelia Nais (Terme Museum, Rome; Photograph by B. Harvey).

along the Tiber. This inscription is dedicated to a woman, Nais, thus showing how urban women of lower social status sometimes worked to supplement the family income (see Figure 13.1).

> To Aurelia Nais, freedwoman of Gaius, fish seller in the neighborhood of the warehouse of Galba; Gaius Aurelius Phileros, freedman of Gaius, her patron, and Lucius Valerius Secundus, freedman of Lucius, put this up to her.

#213: Epaphra, Fruit Seller in the Circus Maximus

CIL 6.9822 (Rome)
Second or Third Century AD

This tombstone commemorates a man who sold fruit in the Circus Maximus, Rome's premier chariot racetrack. Races were only held on holidays when normal business was prohibited. On workdays, however, large, clear spaces such as the giant Circus Maximus served as open-air markets. As Epaphra's inscription shows, marketers rented lots in these open spaces. Epaphra claims with pride that his was the lot in the track directly in front of the imperial box, where the emperor would watch the races. Epaphra would of course not be able to sell fruit on the racetrack itself on the race days, so his location does not indicate imperial patronage or even awareness.

To Gaius Julius Epaphra, seller of fruit in the Circus Maximus, in front of the imperial box, made this for himself and for his wife Venuleia Helena, freedwoman of the two people named Gnaeus.

#214: Dealer in Bronze and Iron

CIL 6.9664 (Rome)
First to Third Centuries AD

The following text is dedicated to a freedman. His tombstone not only gives Hermes' job but also his place of business. The monument itself seems to have also been in the shape of Hermes' shop. The two sons of Hermes and his wife Obellia Threpte were buried in the monument.

To the Spirits of the Dead; Lucius Lepidius Hermes, freedman of Lucius, dealer in bronze and iron in a shop near the temple of Fortune at the Fountain of Ares, and Obellia Threpte made this for Lucius Lepidius Hermeros, son of Lucius, of the Palatina tribe, who lived eight years, one month, and twenty-two days, and Lepidia Lucilla, daughter of Lucius, who lived five years and nine days, their sweetest and most devoted children as well as for their freedmen and freedwomen and their descendants. A building in the shape of my former shop is a guardian for our burial; neither the burial chamber nor the building monument should pass to the heir.

#215: Merchant of Imported Kitchenware in Gaul

CIL 13.1906 (Lugdunum, Gallia Lugdunensis)
First to Third Centuries AD

This inscription is dedicated to a man who owned a shop after his military service. The First Legion Minervia spent most of its history in Germania Inferior, and so was not that far from Felix' later home. Felix adds the interesting fact that many of the important events in his life all took place on Tuesdays.

To the Spirits of the Dead and eternal memory of Vitalinus Felix, veteran of the First Legion Minervia; he was a most wise and faithful man and merchant in Lugdunum of imported kitchenware; he lived fifty-nine years, five months, ten days; he was born on a Tuesday, enlisted in the army on a Tuesday, was honorably discharged from military service on a Tuesday, and died on a Tuesday; Vitalinius Felicissimus, his son, and Julia Nice, his wife, took care of constructing this monument and dedicated it while still under construction.

#216: Merchant of Embroidered Clothing

CIL 13.1945 (Lugdunum, Gallia Lugdunensis)
Third or Fourth Century AD

This tombstone honors another man from Lugdunum in Gaul. Aequalis, however, was a wealthy freedman and member of the Augustales, a kind of club open to freedmen. Because they were unable to run for political office no matter how wealthy they might be, they sought unofficial advancement through benefactions. Aequalis sold clothing that was embroidered with silver or gold threads and was himself German in origin.

To the Spirits of the Dead and eternal memory of Constantinus Aequalis, a merchant of embroidered clothing and member of the Augustales of the colony of Copia Claudia Augusta Lugdunum, originally from Germany; he lived forty-five years, three months, and twelve days; Pacatia Servana took care of paying for this monument to her dearest and incomparable husband as well as for herself; his sons Constantinus Servatus and Constantinus Aequalis and Constantinus Constantius also helped with the dedication to their most dutiful father; they dedicated this monument while it was still under construction.

#217: Selection of Inscriptions Dedicated to Merchants

CIL 3.5824; 6.9661, 25081; 14.3958; *ILS* 7614
First to Third Centuries AD

The following is an assortment of tomb inscriptions dedicated to a variety of merchants from the Roman Empire.

3.5824: To the Spirits of the Dead and perpetual security; Tiberius Claudius Euphras, member of the Augustales, merchant of goods made with purple dye, who lived seventy-six years, made this for his wife Senilia Lasciva and Claudius Fortunensis and Antogonus and Aper his sons; he made this while living for his still-living family members. [Augusta Vindelicorum, Raetia]

6.9961: To Ulpius Eutyches, merchant in the camp of the Praetorian Guard; Ulpia Secundina made this new monument for her husband along with his children Ulpius Secundinus and Ulpia Iulia and Ulpia Secundina and Ulpius Iustus in honor of their most dear father; they also made it for themselves and their family members and their freedmen, freedwomen, and their descendants. [Rome]

6.25081: To the Spirits of the Dead; to Marcus Licinius Moschus, merchant of poles, and Cornelia Procla, his wife; Pomponius Olympus, his brother, and Filumenus, Sotas, and Zosimus their freedmen and heirs made this. [Rome]

14.3958: Sacred to the Spirits of the Dead; to Marcus Livius Hermeros, clothes merchant in the neighborhood of the Warehouse of Agrippina; Claudia Moschis, daughter of Tiberius, made this for her dearest husband. [Nomentum, Italy]

ILS 7614: Lucius Flavius Celer, son of Lucius, of the Stellatina tribe, dealer of incense, member of the Augustales, ordered in his will that this monument be made for himself and for Petronia Salvia. [Augusta Taurinorum, Italy]

#218: A Seller of Chickens

CIL 6.9674 (Rome)
Third Century AD

This inscription commemorates a man who lived sixty-eight years and worked as a seller of chickens (*pullarius*). It is possible that these chickens were the sacred chickens used to take the auspices at religious festivals. The man's wife and three children dedicated the monument. Interestingly, the daughter, Septimia Euresis, gets her nomen from her mother rather than her father.

Sacred to the Spirits of the Dead; to Marcus Aurelius Euretus, dearest husband, who lived sixty-eight years and eight months; Septimia Felicissima, his wife, and his children, Marcus Aurelius Euretus, Septimia Euresis, and Aurelius Pudentianus, made this for their dearest, most loyal, and deserving father, who was also a seller of chickens.

#219: An Importer of Liquid Goods

CIL 6.29722 (Rome)
First to Third Centuries AD

Here we have the tombstone of a man of equestrian rank who had a business selling wine (probably from his native Lugdunum) and olive oil from Baetica, a province known for its olive oil. It is likely that the oil was imported by boat in large storage vessels called amphorae. He was a captain of a ship that sailed up and down the Arar River selling his wares. The Arar River (the Saône River) was a tributary of the Rhone and connected southern Gaul with the Rhine to the north). Lugdunum was one of the major cities in Gaul.

Sacred to the Spirits of the Dead; to Gaius Sentius Regulianus, a Roman *eques*, a trader of olive oil from Baetica and head of guild of traders of olive oil, trader of wine from Lugdunum based in an office the civilian settlement of the nearby military camp; president and patron of the guild of wine merchants; captain of a ship on the Arar River, patron of the guild and captains of ships, patron of the priests of the imperial cult based in Lugdunum. Lucius Silenius Reginus Aus[. . .] and Ulattia Metrodora along with his sons have ensured that this monument was erected.

#220: Selection of Agricultural Workers

CIL 6.9458, 9683, 33887, 37806 (Rome)
First to Third Centuries AD

These four tombstones commemorate workers associated with other agricultural pursuits. There is a vegetable farmer, a merchant of fruits and legumes, a seller of swine and sheep, and a cattle merchant. In some cases, these merchants may have also been the people who grew the produce or raised the animals and then took their goods to the city to sell to the people living there.

9458: Lucius Horatius, son of Lucius, of the Voturia tribe, vegetable farmer; Sextus Horatius, son of Lucius, of the Voturia tribe, the elder brother; this monument is [?] feet wide and twenty feet deep.

9683: To the Spirits of the Dead; to Abudia Megiste, freedwoman of Marcus; Marcus Abudius Luminaris, her former master and also husband, made this for her. She was well deserving and very dutiful. She was also a merchant of fruits and legumes by the middle staircase [in the market]; he also made this for himself and his freedmen and freedwomen and their descendants as well as for Marcus Abudius Saturninus, their son, and fellow resident on the Esquiline Hill; he lived eight years.

33887: To the Spirits of the Dead; to Marcus Antoninus Terens, son of Marcus, of the Claudia tribe, originally from the town of Misenum where he fulfilled all of the obligations and honors available in his hometown; he was a very famous seller of swine and sheep; his sons and heirs Marcus Antonius Teres and Marcus Antonius Proculus made this monument in accordance with his wishes.

37806: Quintus Brutius, son of Publius, of the Qurina tribe; while alive he was a cattle merchant in the marketplace; now he sleeps here in his tomb; he was frugal, upright, and lovable to all; Brutia Rufa, freedwoman of Quintus, dutifully made this for her former master before he died.

#221: Collection of Artisans

CIL 4.3130, 8505; 5.5919; 6.9402, 33914; 9.1719; 13.3700, 5154

The following is a selection of tombstones commemorating artisans. They demonstrate a high level of specialization. Many of the texts are quite short and include little more than the name of the deceased and their occupation.

4.3130: Marcus Vecilius Verecundus, clothing dealer. [Pompeii, Italy]

4.8505: Priscus, stone engraver, made this happily for Campanus, jeweler. [Pompeii, Italy]

5.5919: Gaius Atilius Iustus, son of Gaius, maker of army boots, provided in his will that this monument be put up for himself and for his wife Cornelia Exorata. [Mediolanum, Italy]

6.9402: To the Spirits of the Dead; to Lucius Licinius Statorianus, son of Lucius; Lucius Licinius Patroclus, freedman of Lucius, maker of glass eyes for statues, made this for his dearest brother. [Rome]

6.33914: To the Spirits of the Dead; Gaius Iulius Helius, cobbler whose shop was near the Porta Fontinalis [Gate in the Servian Wall in the Campus Martius near the Capitoline Hill], made this while still alive for himself and for his daughter Iulia Flacila, his freedman Iulius Onesimus, and his freedwomen, and their posterity. [Rome]

9.1719: To Marcus Lucilius Diocles, freedman of Marcus, player of the trumpet and the organ, and to his freedman and freedwomen; this monument was constructed at the decision of Marcus Ofillius Tertius. [Beneventum, Italy]

13.3700: To the Spirits of the Dead of Eugenia, deceased daughter; Iulius Victor, cooper and maker of bags, made this while still alive for her as well as for himself, his wife Acceptina and son Florentius. [Trier, Belgica]

13.5154: To the Spirits of the Dead; Camillius Polynices, from the country of Lydia, goldsmith [probably making gold decorations for woodwork] and a member of the builder's guild in which guild he held all of the offices available to him; he lived more than sixty years; he made this monument for himself and for his son Camillius Paulus who had the same profession and was a member of the same guild, who lived thirty-three years. [Amsoldingen, Germania Superior]

#222: Labor Contract from Dacia

CIL III, p. 948, X (Rosia Montana, Dacia)
May 20th, AD 164

This is a wax tablet from the province of Dacia recording a labor contract between the owner of a mine and a worker. It set the start and end date for the work, the pay rate, and the penalties if the worker tries to get out of the contract early.

On the fourteenth day before the Kalends of June while Macrinus and Celsus were consuls [May 20th, AD 164], I, Flavius Secundinus, wrote this at the request of Memmius, son of Asclepius, because Memmius said that he was not able to write on his own. This document shows that Memmius has hired out himself and his services in the gold mine of Aurelius Adiutor from this day until the upcoming Ides of November [November 13th] for seventy *denarii* plus money for board. He shall receive a portion of his wages at fixed intervals of time. Memmius will be obligated to provide himself as a strong and valuable worker to the above-mentioned contractor. If in the event Memmius should wish to leave his job or cease work against the wishes of the contractor, Memmius will be required to pay five *sestertii*, eight *aeres* per day to the contractor. If a flood should put a stop to the work, the contractor will be allowed to calculate a deduction based on the length of the work stoppage. If the contractor should delay payment to the worker for an extended period of time, he will be obligated to pay the same penalty of five *sestertii*, eight *aeres* (after a three-day grace period). This contract was made at Immenosus Maior. [Signed by:] Titus (also called Bradua), son of Beusans; Socratio, son of Socratio, and Memmius, son of Asclepius.

Shops and Workshops

Many shops lined the streets of an ancient Roman city. These shops appear in the surviving ruins as relatively large rooms that open directly onto the street through large entranceways. Sometimes the shops would have a small room attached to the back of the main room. Also in evidence within the shop or the back room were small wooden staircases that led up to a mezzanine level where the shop owner might live or keep his supplies. In buildings such as the atrium-style houses encountered in Pompeii, shops flanked the entrances to the grand, aristocratic houses where the long entrance hallway (*fauces*) leading to the atrium provided space for shops on the street. In the apartment buildings (such as the majority of buildings in Ostia and the Ara Coeli apartment building in Rome), shops generally occupied the ground floor with the residences on the upper floors (see for example the House of the *Lararium* in Ostia; #223). There were also specially designated structures in the city that served as open-air markets. The so-called *macellum* in the northeastern corner of Pompeii's forum was such a structure. Permanent shops lined the southern side of an open courtyard in which temporary stalls could be placed on market days.

Rome, always an unusual city due to its size, also had areas in town that had a strictly commercial function. The forum had long since ceased to be a marketplace. Instead, a variety of *macella* (such as the one at the Esquiline Gate in the northeastern part of Rome) served as market bazaars. The Markets of Trajan in Rome were an enclosed market with many shops. It is the closest we can come in the ancient world to a modern mall. Rome's enormous population, however, demanded more commercial space. When Trajan built his new forum, he built this large, multi-level market complex into the side of the Quirinal Hill overlooking the forum.

In addition to the many shops, a Roman city also featured workshops where goods were manufactured. Roman cities were more than just heavy consumers; they also produced a diverse range of goods. These goods were sold both locally and exported if production outstripped local demand. Many workshops of various types have been discovered in Ostia and Pompeii. The presence of tools, certain architectural features, and inscriptions are the primary means of identifying these workshops and distinguishing them from private residences.

#223: The House of the *Lararium*, Ostia

Many apartment buildings, including the Ara Coeli building, were constructed as hollow squares with an internal courtyard. Shops opened both onto this courtyard as well as onto any streets the building faced. The House of the *Lararium* (I.9.3) standing on the *decumanus* near the forum in Ostia is a good example of this type of commercial/residential structure because it is decently well preserved.

The name of the building comes from a niche on the northern side of the courtyard in which there was once a statue of the deity who presided over the building. Corridors lead into the courtyard from the streets on the southern and western sides of the building (see Figure 13.2, #1, 2). Numerous shops opened onto the streets outside as well as the courtyard. The courtyard was quite small, but it would have had at least provided natural light to the shops on the courtyard (see Figure 13.3). On the northern side of the courtyard, a staircase led to the upper floors, not unlike the Ara Coeli building (see Figure 13.2, #3). Many of the shops contain remnants of the internal staircases leading to the mezzanine level. In some cases, the travertine braces for the wooden floor of the mezzanine are still visible. The courtyard is cramped and irregularly shaped, but it reflects an inventive use of space.

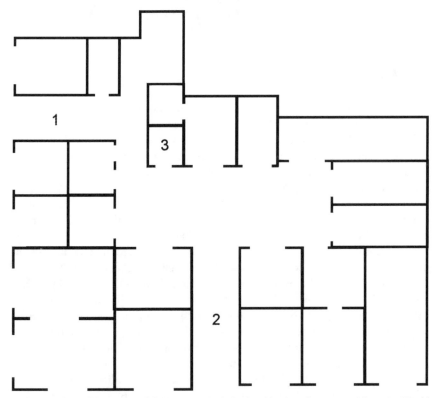

Figure 13.2 Plan of the House of the *Lararium*, Ostia (1: Corridor into the courtyard from the *Via del Larario*; 2: Corridor into the courtyard from the *decumanus*; 3: Staircase to the upper floor).

Figure 13.3 View from the *Decumanus* into the Courtyard of the House of the *Lararium*, Ostia (Photograph by B. Harvey).

The Fuller

The fullery (*fullonica*) was a common industry found in an ancient Roman city. Fullers, the term for the people who worked in a fullery, cleaned and bleached newly woven clothes and clothes dirtied from use (#225 gives a number of epigraphic examples of fullers). Fullery buildings are characterized by large basins for soaking and cleaning clothes. Other common artifacts associated with fulleries include "cleaning bowls," which were oval or circular basins, often made out of the lower half of large jars (#226 describes the so-called *Fullonica* of Stephanus from Pompeii). The fuller placed the clothes into these bowls and then added water and detergent (usually, human urine; #224). He then stepped, stomped, and danced over the clothes for hours to get them clean. Bowls were separated by short dividing walls that the fuller could use to steady himself while treading in the bowls. After washing, the clothes were pressed by beating them with sticks or by using a mechanical corkscrew press. They were then returned to the basins for a final rinse to remove the detergents. Next, the fullers spread the clothes in an open area. After they were dry, they brushed the clothes with a thistle or hedgehog-skin brush. The lint was caught and used for stuffing pillows and mattresses. The clothes were then spread over a curved wicker frame and a pot of sulfur was burned underneath. This step helped with the bleaching process. Finally, the cloth was rubbed down with absorbent clay called fuller's earth, to improve the texture and remove stains.

#224: Vespasian Collects "Dirty Money"

Suetonius, *Vespasian* 23
Written in the Early Second Century AD Describing
the Emperor Vespasian (AD 69–79)

The most important detergent used in the fullery process was animal or human urine because of its quality as a natural bleaching agent. Urine was collected from public urinals, small jars set in the streets around town. Urine was precious to the fullers, and their zealous use of it was one of the main reasons for their unpopular reputation as *personae non gratae* around town. The urine the fullers needed was so valuable, in fact, that the emperor Vespasian put a tax on its use. In the passage here, Suetonius reports a satirical scene related to Vespasian's collection of "dirty money."

When his son Titus criticized his father Vespasian for collecting a tax on urine, the emperor held a coin collected with the first payment under Titus' nose and asked if he was put off by the smell. When Titus said it smelled no different than any other coin, Vespasian replied, "Still, it comes from urine."

#225: Examples of Fullers

CIL 6.4336, 4445, 6287, 6289, 6290, 7281a, 9429 (Rome)
First to Third Centuries AD

Despite the bad reputation of those who worked in the trade, fulling was a thriving industry in the ancient city. Ostia had its own guild of fullers, the *corpus fontanorum*. Many were wealthy enough to provide a decent burial for themselves and their families. The following are some examples of fullers. Many are just names from small tomb epitaphs or cinerary urns. In one, Felix Germanicianus is said to have lived fifty years and was honored by a masseuse named Leonta, perhaps his wife.

4336: Felix Germanicianus, fuller, lived fifty years; Leonta, masseuse, made this.

4445: Gaius Claudius Eros, fuller.

6287: Donatus Tironianus, fuller.

6289: The bones of Hilarius the fuller are buried here.

6290: Fosporus, fuller.

7281a: Philomusus, fuller, officer in his guild; Daphnus, his accountant, and Hedylalus, his secretary, provided this monument for him.

9429: Lucius Autronius Stephanus, freedman of Lucius, fuller, and Autronia Tychene, freedwoman of Lucius, made these cinerary urns.

Figure 13.4 Bowls for Cleaning Cloths in the *Fullonica* of Stephanus (Photograph by B. Harvey).

#226: The *Fullonica* of Stephanus, Pompeii

The fullery of Stephanus on the busy *Via dell'Abbondanza* in Pompeii is one of the best examples of a fullery to survive from the ancient world. The building had once been a private atrium-style house, but, after the earthquake of AD 62, the house was converted into a fullery. A large cleaning facility was added to the back part of the ground floor of the building, where three oblong cleaning bowls were installed in the floor along the eastern wall (see Figure 13.4). A small vat nearby possibly held cleaning detergents, which would thus be conveniently located near the cleaning bowls. There were also three large basins. The basin in the rear of the building was the highest and received water directly from the public water supply. Pipes moved the water from this basin to the other two. The front part of the house was where most of the finishing work was done. Several metal combs and the iron frame of a press were found in this area. In the place of the normal *impluvium*, another large basin was added. It may have been used for washing in the later stages of the processing.

Chapter 14: Religion

The Romans worshiped a diverse pantheon of gods, each of which had her or his own realm of influence and personality. Indeed, Rome allowed the cults of the people they had conquered over the centuries to coexist with their own, provided the subject peoples of the empire included the Roman state cult in their own religious systems. The Romans used mandated participation in the state cult as a means of creating a unified cultural identity and solidifying their authority in newly acquired territories. While Rome's subjects were allowed to continue worshipping their own gods in a separate context, or syncretized with the state religious practices, failure to observe the state cult was a sign of social and political rebellion. The continuous insistence of Jews and Christians to worship their own deity and reject all other gods, including those of the Romans, alienated them from Roman society and led to their occasional persecution not only by the local and imperial authorities, but also their neighbors.

The Roman Gods

It would be impossible to discuss Roman religion without first mentioning the Roman pantheon. For the Romans, the state cult facilitated communication with the gods, which enabled the Romans to gain a sense of control over their world. In early Italy, the gods were the unseen powers who caused the seemingly uncontrollable phenomena of nature (#227 and #228). Each of these divine powers was a *numen*, with its own particular sphere of influence, such as the rain, a particular location, or activity (in #229, the Christian Augustine makes fun of the diversity of the Roman pantheon). The gods only assumed human shape when Rome began to interact with (and conquer) the Etruscans to the north and the Greek colonies in southern Italy in the fourth and third centuries BC, which led to the assimilation of many Greek anthropomorphic deities and their own *numina*.

#227: The Influence of the Gods on the Mortal World

Cicero, *On the Laws* 2.15
First Century BC

A core religious belief of the Romans was the conviction that the gods not only took an interest in, but also influenced events in the mortal realm. In the passage quoted here, the orator/philosopher Cicero sums up how this concept influenced the state's prerogative to establish religion amongst its subjects. This and similar texts show us that Roman religion inculcated the belief that the attitude and actions of mortals toward their deities affected whether the gods would treat them beneficently or cruelly. Belief in the gods and their powers, demonstrated by the correct performance of religious rites on their behalf, were the best ways to avoid the malevolency of the gods.

> Thus, then, we must from the beginning persuade the citizens that the gods are the lords and controllers of all things and that whatever happens is done with their plan and power (*numen*). It should also be established that the gods deserve the very best from humanity. Everyone should believe that the gods know what kind of person he is, what he does, what he believes about himself, and how he performs the rites in terms of his mental attitude and devotion (*pietas*). They should understand that the gods keep account of everyone, pious and impious alike.

#228: Deities in Nature

Seneca, *Letters* 41.3
First Century AD

For the Romans, there were gods all over nature. They preferred to see a multitude of gods presiding over narrow areas of influence to a single deity who controlled everything. In this passage, the philosopher Seneca describes how peculiar features of nature could be the result of the indwelling of a god.

> Have you ever come upon a grove full of very old trees that have grown to an unusual height? Perhaps the sky is not visible because of the thickness of the branches and the way in which those branches spread out as if trying to hide the sky. The height of the trees, seclusion of the spot, and unusual shadiness despite the grove being in a relatively open area should lead you to believe that the grove is, indeed, the home of a deity (*numen*). Perhaps you have seen a cave, cut deeply into the living rock beneath a high mountain. It was not made by human hands but rather was cut out naturally to create such a large open space underground. Once again perhaps your mind will be seized with the belief that a god is there. We worship the sources of mighty rivers. A place where a stream erupts suddenly from an underground source also is venerated with altars. Hot springs also are holy places. Sacred too are certain pools either because of their dark waters or tremendous depth.

#229: The Diverse Roman Pantheon

Augustine, *The City of God* 4.8
Early Fifth Century AD

The multitude of gods was a feature of Roman religion and was meant to reflect the wide variety of phenomena visible in nature. Christians, believing in a single god only, attacked this diversity as a sign of the weakness of the Roman gods in the face of the omnipotent Christian God. In the following passage, the Christian theologian Augustine tries to unmask the silly nature of the Roman gods by describing the extremely specialized roles of some of their minor deities associated with wheat.

How can I fully document the names of all of the gods and goddesses in this one book? Indeed, it would be very difficult to do so even in many large volumes if one were to include the narrow realms of influence for each individual deity. The Romans have, indeed, decided that the ground itself should not fall under the domain of one god only. Agricultural land is the domain of the goddess Rusina. The ridges of the mountain belong to Iugatinus. Collatina is the goddess of hills and Vallonia of valleys. Segetia is unable, in their eyes, to be the sole guardian of the wheat crop (*segetes*). Instead the goddess Seia is in charge of the seeds when they are still in the ground. Segetia only takes over when the stalk grows and begins to produce ears of wheat. Tutilina presides over after the grain that has been harvested and stored to keep it safe (*tuto*). Let us return to Segetia. Who would not think that she would be powerful enough to take care of the wheat from the point it sprouts until it is ready to harvest? Yet, she still does not seem to be powerful enough for a people who worship a multitude of gods. These people have looked down on the chaste embrace of the one true God and instead chosen to prostitute their miserable souls to a crowd of demons. As a result, they put Proserpina in charge of the ears of wheat when they first begin to sprout. The god Nodutus is in charge of the joints and knots of the stems. Volutina presides over the sheaths that wrap around the wheat itself. When the sheaths open, however, and the ears appear, the wheat is turned over to Patelana. When the stems are as long as the new ears, they belong to the goddess Hostilina (because the ancient Romans called this stage *hostire*). Flora is the goddess in charge when the wheat flowers (*flores*), Lacturnus when white substance drips from it like milk (*lactescentes*), and Matuta when the wheat is mature (*maturescentes*). When the wheat is taken out of the soil (*runcantur*), it is under the control of Runcina. Even after all of this, I cannot bring myself to mention all of the deities involved because it disgusts me, although it causes the Romans no shame.

Cult and Worship

Roman religion was practiced using two main cultic rituals: the performance of sacred rites (*sacra*) and the observance of omens to determine the will of the gods for the future (*auspicia*). Both were forms of communication between the human and divine realms. The *sacra* were requests to the gods for their assistance in human affairs using sacrifice and honorary festivals as offerings. The *auspicia*, often referred to as "taking the auspices," was a system of divination in which humans read prophetic signs from the gods, primarily by watching the

flight patterns of birds or examining the entrails of sacrificial animals (#230).
Major portents (*prodigia* or *monstra*) from the gods, such as three-headed calves,
signaled more extreme situations that demanded immediate religious interpretation and possibly appropriate action (such as a placatory animal sacrifice). In
order to achieve a successful outcome in either the *sacra* or the *auspicia*, the participant needed to be *pius*, i.e., be endowed with *pietas*. In the religious realm, *pietas*
toward the gods demanded the correct observance of the sacred rites (*sacra*) and
the willingness to accept the god's wishes when they were made known through
the *auspicia*. Observance of the *sacra* with *pietas* would placate the gods. Thus,
if the participants carried out their sacred rites with *pietas*, it was assumed that
their request would be granted. It would further create a state known as *felicitas*
(happiness/good fortune), wherein the gods worked in man's favor and provided
beneficia as a true patron would. Thus, *pietas* and *felicitas* went hand-in-hand. True
felicitas could only be achieved through *pietas* towards the gods (#231; see #232
for when something goes wrong).

#230: A Disagreement over the Auspices

Livy, *Histories*, 10.40
Written in the First Century BC Describing 343 BC

In the following passage, the historian Livy recounts an event during the Samnite
Wars in which there was a disagreement over the interpretation of *auspicia* before
the beginning of a battle.

> While the consul was busy with the preparations for the battle, a disagree-
> ment between the keepers of the sacred chickens arose over the interpreta-
> tion of the *auspicia* taken that day. A group of cavalry soldiers overheard the
> argument and thought that the situation should not be ignored and reported to
> Spurius Papirius, the consul's nephew, that there was uncertainty about inter-
> pretation of the signs. This young man, born in a time before children were
> taught to look down on the gods, investigated the situation so that he might
> be in possession of all of the facts and then brought it to the attention of the
> consul. When he had done so, the consul said to his nephew, "Very good. I
> applaud your virtue and diligence in this matter. However, it is the ones who
> take the *auspicia* who bear the burden of responsibility. If they make a false
> report, they will only bring the anger of the gods upon themselves. For my
> own part, I was told that the chickens ate the food eagerly. That is the most
> favorable omen for the Roman people and its army." The consul did give the
> centurions an order to position the keepers of the sacred chickens on the front
> line for the upcoming battle. Soon the battle began and the Samnites signaled
> the advance. The Roman line, in full regalia and armor, advanced as well and
> filled the enemy with awe. Before either side raised the shout and ran forward
> to the attack, a Samnite threw a javelin and struck and killed one of the keep-
> ers of the sacred chickens who was standing near the standards. When this

fact was announced to the consul, he replied, "The gods are participating in the battle. The guilty one has received his punishment." While the consul was saying this, a crow in front of the consul interrupted with a clear caw. The consul accepted this as a good omen and proclaimed that never before had the gods been more involved in human affairs. He then ordered the signal for the attack to be given.

#231: The Connection between *Pietas* and *Felicitas*

Panegyric 11(3).18 (Genethiliacus to Maximian Augustus)
Speech Originally Delivered in AD 290/291

In the passage here from a speech of praise (a panegyric) of the later emperor Maximian, the orator praises the emperor and the peace he has brought as a result of his *pietas*.

> In the present war you have taken vengeance on your enemies not with arms or an army, as you have done up until now, but rather, most fortunate emperors, you have conquered with *felicitas* alone. Is there anything Roman emperors are happier to hear about their own *felicitas* than to be told that the enemy is quiet, is idle, and cultivates peace? And yet how much happier and better it is when, on the subject of the prosperity of an emperor's reign, people go around saying, "The barbarians are under arms, but they are busy fighting with each other! The barbarians have won a battle but one over their own kinsmen!" Fortune has brought you so many novel successes over every kind of enemy that it is necessary for me to add to the universal praise lavished upon our emperors the comment I made at the beginning of my speech while I attempt to give an account of so many deeds: you deserve, oh best of emperors, that *felicitas* because of your *pietas*.

#232: When Things Go Wrong: The *Impietas* of Claudius Pulcher

Cicero, *On the Nature of the Gods* 2.7
Written in 45 BC Describing 249 BC

Because the rites had been prescribed by long-standing tradition, any variation, intentional or unintentional, could be used to explain away unexpected or negative results. Even a small mistake in the performance required that the participant restart the rite from the beginning. *Vitium* is the Latin term for an unintentional mistake in the performance of a rite. *Vitium* was a minor offense because the mistake was not done purposefully. Much more serious were occasions when a person intentionally did not perform the *sacra* exactly as tradition had passed them down or ignored the signs of the gods. The Latin term for this crime was *impietas*, the opposite of *pietas*. In the following passage, Cicero describes an event in 249 BC when the general Appius Claudius Pulcher, admiral of a Roman fleet in the First Punic War, ignored the negative result of the auspices and went into battle anyway.

> The recklessness of Publius Clodius during the First Punic War is an interesting case study for the negative effects of ignoring the signs from the gods. In fact, Clodius made a joke of the gods when he took the auspices before a naval battle. When released from their cages, the sacred chickens gave a bad omen when they did not eat their feed. Clodius ordered them to be thrown overboard and was heard to exclaim, "If they do not want to eat, let them drink!" His joke caused much grief when the fleet was defeated in the battle and inflicted a major disaster upon the Roman people. In the same year, Clodius' colleague in the consulship, Lucius Junius, also lost a fleet when he did not obey the signs from the auspices. As a result, Clodius was condemned in a public trial and Junius committed suicide.

Priests

Naturally, the burden of overseeing the correct observation of *pietas* fell primarily upon the priest, although every Roman was expected to show *pietas* through participation (active or passive) in religious ceremonies. In private cult, it was the *paterfamilias* who acted as the family priest by performing the *sacra* and representing his family before the gods. In the public state cult, the priest essentially represented the whole Roman state before the gods. The priest performed the *sacra* by leading the procession, directing the actions, and saying the prayer. Aristocrats rather than professionals served in the most important Roman priesthoods (#236). In Rome, these priesthoods were grouped into four major senatorial "colleges." The four colleges consisted of the pontiffs (the *pontifices*), the *augurs*, the fifteen men in charge of the sacred rites (*quindecimviri sacris faciundis*), and the seven men in charge of religious banquets (*septimviri epulonum*). Their chief member was the *pontifex maximus*, a post reserved exclusively for the emperor after Augustus took the office in 12 BC. The other *pontifices* presided over the state cult in general (#233). The *septimviri* organized the religious banquets during the major festivals. These two colleges were primarily concerned with the *sacra*. The other two were responsible for the *auspicia*. The *augurs* took the auspices by observing the flight of birds and other natural phenomena. The *quindecimviri* interpreted other portents (*prodigia*). To do this, they were the keepers of the so-called Sibylline Oracles, a book containing lists of *prodigia* and the rites necessary to counteract any divine unhappiness the *prodigia* might reveal. Also included in this section are two texts related to the important priestly college of the Vestal Virgins (#234 and #235).

#233: The *Pontifex*

Dionysius of Halicarnassus, *Roman Antiquities* 2.73.1–2
First Century BC

In the following passage, the Greek historian Dionysius of Halicarnassus describes the function of the *pontifices*.

The last category of priests set up by King Numa to be discussed here is composed of priests of the highest order who have the greatest religious power among the Romans. A priest of this category is called a *pontifex* in Latin because one of their duties involved the repair of the wooden bridges in the city (*pontes*). These priests are in charge of the most important affairs. They are the ones who serve as judges in religious cases involving private citizens, magistrates, and anyone involved with religious worship. It is they who decide whether some new observance or ritual without a basis in written law or custom should be added to religious tradition. It is also their duty to investigate the conduct of all of the priests, servants, and attendants who are used in the performance of sacred rites to make sure that no offences are made against sacred law. In the eyes of the private citizens, these are the priests who, as interpreters and teachers, understand the nuances of the worship of the gods and *numina*. If they learn that someone has not obeyed their commands, they inflict such punishment as fits their crime. They are exempt from trial and punishment and cannot be held accountable to the Senate and People of Rome for any action done in the realm of religious matters.

#234: The Vestal Virgins

Dionysius of Halicarnassus, *Roman Antiquities* 2.67
First Century BC

One of the most important minor priestly colleges was that of Vesta, an ancient goddess who presided over the hearth of the home. Long the object of private worship, the state adopted her as the protector of the metaphorical "hearth of the state," a fire kept perpetually burning in a round (and hence hearth-shaped) temple in the middle of the forum. Only virgin women were eligible to serve as priestesses of the cult of Vesta. The Vestal Virgins, always of senatorial descent, served a term of thirty years.

In ancient times, there were four virgins who kept the sacred rites of Vesta. It was the king who chose them according to the system established by King Numa. Later, because new rites and duties were added, their number was increased to six, and that remained the size of the college to our own time. The Vestals live in the precinct of the temple. No one wishing to enter their abode is prohibited from doing so during the daytime, but at night, it is against the law for any man to enter. The Vestals are required to remain in service for 30 years, during which time they must remain unpolluted by marriage and perform the sacred rites as regulated by religious law. They spend their first ten years of service learning their duties, their second ten years performing the sacred rites, and their final ten years teaching the new Vestals. Once their thirty years of service have ended, there is nothing preventing them from setting aside their priestly garb and other religious emblems and leaving Vesta's service to get married. There have been some, although very few, who have done just that, but the rest of these women's lives generally turned out to be quite unlucky. As a result, most of the others take the misfortunes of those who did leave as a warning and remain in Vesta's service until their deaths, after which new members are chosen by the *pontifices* to round out the required number.

#235: Statue Base of a Vestal Virgin

CIL 6.32408 (Rome)
Later Fourth Century AD

The so-called Atrium of Vesta, attached to her temple in the forum, was the home of the serving Vestal Virgins. In a large, open courtyard, the statues of numerous chief Vestals have been preserved. This inscription is preserved on the base of one of those statues. Coelia, in fact, was the last chief Vestal Virgin. The Christian emperors of the later fourth century AD closed the temple after which Coelia stepped down from her post and converted to Christianity.

> Coelia Concordia, chief Vestal Virgin; Fabia Paulina, daughter of Gaius, assumed the responsibility of paying for and placing this statue in recognition both of Coelia's remarkable chastity and noteworthy dedication concerning the religious rites of Vesta. She put up a statue to Fabia's husband Vettius Agorius Praetextatus, a man of senatorial background who was noteworthy in every way and was deserving of the honor granted him by the virgins and priestesses of this cult.

#236: Local Priest of Ostia

CIL 14.400 (Ostia)
AD 141

Municipal aristocrats in Ostia also presided over the prominent imperial cult (the cult of the emperor). The prestigious *flamen* of Rome and Augustus was not only in charge of the temple of Rome and Augustus in the forum but also acted as the head of the city's imperial cult. There were also individual *flamines* for the cult of each of the deified emperors. The chief *flamen* of Rome and Augustus was held for life by an aristocrat of high standing, while the *flamines* of the individual imperial cults were young aristocrats at the start of their public careers.

To Quintus Plotius Romanus, son of Quintus, of the Qurina tribe, who was honored with a horse at public expense by the divine emperor Hadrian; he served as aedile of Ostia and held the posts of *flamen* of Rome and Augustus and *flamen* of the Divine Titus. The town council decreed that a statue of him be put up at public expense. His father, Quintus Plotius Niger, assumed responsibility for the statue and provided the money for it from his own estate; the location for the statue was arranged by decree of the town council. It was dedicated on March 17th, while Titus Hoenius Severus and Marcus Peducaeus Priscinus were consuls [AD 141].

Temples

Most Roman temples were rectangular in shape and stood upon high podia. Their elevated position not only dominated the surrounding landscape, but also gave priests a better view of the sky for the purpose of taking the auspices. A deep porch fronted by one, two, or three rows of columns emphasized the entrance to the temple. The porch of a Roman temple was a significant departure from the Greek-style temple, which had columns all the way around the building, inviting the visitor to travel around to view its decorative elements. The entrance within the porch led to the main chamber of the temple, the *cella*. The cult statue of the god would generally be centrally placed at that back of the *cella*.

Religious rituals often took place in the vicinity of the temple dedicated to the god being worshipped. This is why altars are found in front of the temple rather than inside. In fact, the altar was generally in direct line with the entrance to the *cella* so that the deity could watch the sacrifice from inside the *cella*.

This section includes examples of several temples: the round temple in the Forum Boarium in Rome (#237) and the *capitolium* in Ostia (#238). Also included is a letter by Pliny the Younger describing his restoration of a temple of Ceres on one of his properties (#239) and additional inscriptions mentioning the construction of temples (#240).

#237: Round Temple in the Forum Boarium, Rome

In the middle Republic, while Rome's interaction with the Greeks increased, some Romans chose to adopt the characteristics of Greek temples for their own new constructions. In the Forum Boarium (see Figure 14.1), the small but well-preserved round temple, often associated with Hercules Victor (Hercules the Victorious) illustrates this assimilation of Greek architectural styles. Unlike Roman temples that were rectangular with columns only along the front porch, this round temple has

Figure 14.1 The Round Temple in the Forum Boarium, Rome (Photograph by B. Harvey).

columns completely surrounding its circular *cella*. This temple, constructed in the
later second century BC, when Rome was in the process of conquering the Greek
world, was the first in Rome to be built completely of marble.

#238: The *Capitolium* of Ostia

The most prominent and important temple in Rome was the temple dedicated
to the Capitoline Triad (Jupiter, Juno, and Minerva) on the Capitoline Hill (see
Figure 14.2). In imitation of Rome, cities across the empire built temples, called

Figure 14.2 Remains of the *Capitolium* in Ostia. The altar stands outside
the temple on the right side of the photograph (Photograph by B. Harvey).

capitolia, dedicated to the same Capitoline Triad in their forums. The *capitolium* of Ostia sat atop a high podium on the northern side of the forum. Much of the *cella* wall is preserved (although the marble that once faced its brick and concrete core were looted long ago). The remains of this temple now stand more than fifty feet tall, making it one of the most visible buildings in Ostia. The altar in front of the temple still has some of its marble frieze preserved.

#239: Pliny Restores a Temple of Ceres

Pliny the Younger, *Letters* 9.39.1–4
Early Second Century AD

The responsibility for building, renovating, and restoring temples fell to the aristocracy who were expected to help the state with their personal financial resources. In the following text, Pliny the Younger writes to a friend named Mustius that he is planning to restore a temple that stands on his property. He asks his friend for building materials to help him in his endeavor.

On the advice of the *haruspices*, a temple to Ceres that stands on my property must be rebuilt to improve both its appearance and size. It is indeed a very old temple but also too small seeing how crowded it gets on its festival day. On the Ides of September, a large number of people come from the whole region to the temple. At this festival, many rites are performed, vows are repaid, and new ones are made. There is, however, no refuge from the rain or the sun in the vicinity of the temple, so I think it would not be out of place for me to act generously and reverently with one act by building as beautiful of a temple as possible for the goddess and at the same time adding a portico in the area in front of the temple for the enjoyment of the people. Please buy for me four marble columns of whatever type seems to you to be appropriate. Please also purchase some additional marble for decorating the floor and walls. I must also make a new cult statue of the goddess. The original is very old and made of wood and has several pieces missing because of its age.

#240: Temple Construction Commemorations

There are numerous inscriptions commemorating construction of sacred structures by aristocrats. Some are in the form of statue bases or altars with inscriptions that commemorate a special event or ritual. Others are dedications of the temple itself or a renovation of it and originally stood over the main entrance of the temple. The inscriptions here commemorate the temple of Hercules the Victor by the man who sacked the City of Corinth in the Third Macedonian War, the building inscription from the Temple of Concord in Rome, and record of construction in a temple of Aesculapius in North Africa by a local aristocrat.

CIL 6.331 (Rome)
Second Century BC

Lucius Mummius, son of Lucius, consul. In the war conducted under his auspices and command he annexed the province of Achaia and sacked the city of Corinth. He returned to Rome and was granted a triumph for the successful campaign. During this war, he vowed this temple and statue of Hercules the Victor and dedicated them as the triumphant general. [Rome]

CIL 6.89 (Rome)
Early First Century AD

The Senate and People of Rome restored the Temple of Concord after it had fallen into a state of disrepair because of age and made it larger in the construction and more splendid in its decoration. [Rome]

AE 1968, 586 (Musti, Africa Proconsularis)
Reign of the Emperor Hadrian (AD 117–138)

Sacred to Augustan Aesculapius for the good health of the emperor Caesar Trajan Hadrian Parthicus Augustus, Father of his Country; Gaius Julius Placidus, son of Marcus, of the Cornelia tribe, promised ten thousand *sestertii* on the occasion of his election to the position of *flamen* for life and added a further two thousand *sestertii* from his own funds on the occasion of his election to *duovir* all for the construction of a temple of Pluto with three painted marble statues. He further provided that a ceremonial basin and pitcher be made from six pounds of silver. He dedicated the work with the support of a decree from the town council. [Musti, Africa Proconsularis]

Sacrifice and Ritual

Sacrifice was the most common and important Roman religious rite. In general, sacrifice consisted of an offering made to a particular god or gods upon an altar in front of a temple. Sacrifices were very crowded events. In addition to numerous observers, many participants were present including one or more priests. The potential for crowding was a primary reason for placing the altar outside the temple rather than in the *cella*, close to the cult statue. As Pliny the Elder indicates, prayer was a very important part of the ritual (#241; the Arval Hymn, #244, includes a very old example of a ritualistic prayer). I have also included some examples of rituals in literature and art. Cato the Elder describes a rustic harvest festival (#242).

The sacrifice scene from the altar in the Temple of Vespasian in Pompeii depicts a sacrificial scene (#243).

#241: The Power of Words in Ritual

Pliny the Elder, *Natural History* 28.10–11
First Century AD

In this passage, Pliny the Elder discusses the debate on whether words have power. He describes how there are individuals who disbelieve their power, but that, as a group, humankind seems to unconsciously think they do have power. The example he gives is the importance of the prayer to religious ritual.

Take, for example, sacrificial rites. If animals are sacrificed without an accompanying prayer, there is a general feeling that the gods have not been consulted correctly. Moreover there are prayers for particular occasions: one for seeking omens from the gods, another to protect against evil, another to recommend a course of action. We have seen that magistrates of the very highest ranks entreat the gods with prescribed prayers. They do this to make sure that not one word is omitted or uttered out of place. There is a person who writes the prayer down in a script beforehand. Another person is appointed as a kind of guard to oversee the recitation. Yet a third person demands silence from the crowd. While the prayer is recited, musicians play so that those in attendance hear nothing but the prayer. We have on record two types of problems that can occur in rituals during the prayer: sounds of bad omen that interrupt the prayer and speakers who make an error in the recitation. In times like that, it is not unusual for there to also be trouble with the omens of the animal itself. A part of the entrails or the heart will be missing or duplicate organs will spawn while the animal is still alive.

#242: A Rustic Religious Ritual

Cato, *On Agriculture* 134
Mid-Second Century BC

In this passage, the middle Republican author Cato describes in detail how to conduct a private ritual in preparation for the harvest. The instructions include not only the sacrifices and deities to be worshipped but also prayers to be spoken at the time of the sacrifice.

Before beginning the harvest, you should sacrifice a pig as a preliminary sacrifice in the following way. Sacrifice a sow to Ceres before you harvest the following crops: spelt, barley, wheat, beans, and seed products. Offer a prayer to Janus, Jupiter, and Juno along with incense and wine before sacrificing the pig. In the case of Janus, say the following while offering a sacrificial cake: "Janus, father, by offering this cake, I pray a good prayer asking that, if willing, you look favorably upon me, my children, my house, and my family." Offer a cake to Jupiter as well and say the following prayer: "Jupiter, by making this offering, I pray a good prayer asking that, if willing, you look favorably upon me, my children, my house, and my family." Next make an offering of wine to Janus and say the following: "Janus father, as you were pleased with the cake and wine, may you also be pleased with the wine I have offered to you." Only then should you sacrifice the pig. When the entrails have been removed, offer another cake to Janus and make another prayer as you did previously. Then do the same thing for Jupiter. Next, repeat the offering of wine to Janus and then to Jupiter in the same way that you had done for the offering of the cake. Finally, sacrifice the entrails from the pig and some wine to Ceres.

#243: The Altar from the Temple of Vespasian, Pompeii

First Century AD

Visual depictions of sacrifices in Roman art are quite plentiful and can tell us much about what would happen at these public events. The relief sculpture shown in Figure 14.3 comes from the front of the altar in the temple of Vespasian on the forum in Pompeii. It depicts the scene at the altar during a sacrifice. The priest (to the left of the altar in the center) pours wine onto the altar from a small bowl called a *patera*. The boy who stands on the far left holds the jug in which the wine had been brought. Religious attendants take care of the bull that is to be sacrificed. In the background is a musician playing a flute. As mentioned in the Pliny passage quoted above (#241), the musician would play throughout the whole ritual. The attendants (*victimarii*) would bring the sacrificial bull forward and sprinkle its head with water and a mixture of grain and salt called *mola salsa*. While the priest began to recite the prayer, a *victimarius* would hold the bull's head still while the *popa*, another attendant, knocked the bull on the head with a large mallet. The *victimarii* would catch the head of the bull as it fell, while another attendant, the *cultrarius*, struck the beast's neck with an axe to release the blood, which was caught in a basin. After the bull had been killed, it was butchered. Some parts of the body were set aside for sacrificing on the altar to the god. Some of the innards (most notably the heart and liver) were taken to the *haruspex* so that he might inspect them to ensure that the sacrifice was acceptable to the gods. If the *haruspex* found anything amiss in the animal, the sacrifice would need to be repeated. After the animal had been butchered, the priest, attendants, and crowd participated in a dinner with the god, whose statue was often placed upon a couch and positioned in a place of honor at one of the tables. While some of the meat was sacrificed on the altar, the vast majority, including the choicest cuts, was kept for the feast.

Figure 14.3 Sacrificial Scene on the Relief Sculpture on the Front of the Altar in the Temple of Vespasian in the Forum of Pompeii (Photograph by B. Harvey).

#244: The Arval Hymn

CIL 6.2104 (Rome)
May, AD 218

The traditional prayer recited during public religious rituals was often very old. By chance, the records of a priestly college called the Arval Brethren preserve the prayer spoken by their chief priest at the climax of the college's main festival to Dea Dia in May of AD 218. The language of the prayer is so antiquated that it is impossible to accurately translate it in modern times, and it is also highly unlikely that anyone in the third century AD who recited the prayer had a clear understanding of what it said. The prayer is not only a very old form of Latin, but most likely acquired errors as it was copied over the centuries by those who were unable to understand it.

Enos Lases iuvate, enos Lases iuvate, enos Lases iuvate! Neve lue rue Marmar sins in currere in pleores, neve lue rue Marmar sins in currere in pleores, neve lue rue Marmar sins incurrere in pleores! Satur fu, fere Mars! Limen Sali, sta berber! satur fu, fere Mars! Limen Sali, sta berber! Satur fu, fere Mars! Limen Sali, sta berber! Semunis alternei advocapit conctos, semunis alternei advocapit conctos, semunis alternei advocapit conctos! Enos Marmor iuvato, enos Marmor iuvato, enos Marmor iuvato! Triumpe, triumpe, triumpe, triumpe, triumpe!

The Growth of Christianity

The Christians did not participate in the Roman state cult. They refused to acknowledge any other gods other than their own. This brought them into conflict with the Roman authorities as well as their neighbors. Because they stood apart from the normal functions of the state religion, they were seen as antisocial and a detriment to the world's *felicitas* and so they became targets for persecutions (as under Nero in AD 64, #245). Despite the persecution that resulted from Christians' resistance to Roman traditions, Christianity grew in popularity. One important reason for this was Christianity's acceptance of people of all social statuses. In the fourth century AD, Christianity became the official state religion and some emperors, most notably Theodosius (AD 378–395), began persecuting paganism (#246).

#245: The First Christian Persecution

Tacitus, *Annals* 15.44
Written in the Early Second Century AD Describing Events of AD 64

The first state-sponsored persecution of Christians came during the reign of the emperor Nero. After a major fire burned a considerable part of Rome, Nero placed blame for the fire on the Christians in order to deflect accusations against him. In this passage, the historian Tacitus mentions the persecutions and alludes to the origins of Christianity.

> Nero had done everything he could think of. He tried generosity and appeasement of the gods. Even so, he could not silence the rumors that he had given the orders to start the fire. His next move was to accuse a group of people in Rome who called themselves "Christians." The people hated them for their offenses, and Nero used that anger as an excuse to inflict upon them the most exquisite punishments. The founder of this cult was a man named Christus who was executed by the procurator Pontius Pilatus while Tiberius was emperor. The death of this person only temporarily halted the spread of the cult, and it soon broke out again, not only in Judaea, the place of origin of the evil, but also in Rome, the place to which atrocities and shameful conduct from all directions flow and find a home. First, a number of people confessed to being Christians and were arrested. On their testimony, a huge multitude of others were also taken. Their convictions were the result not so much of the charge of arson but rather the general hatred of humankind. Mockery was added to the executions of the Christians. Some were covered with the skins of animals and torn apart by dogs. Others were crucified. Others were burned alive, used as torches when evening came. Because the amphitheater had been burned, Nero opened his private gardens for the event. He also simultaneously held chariot races in the circus at which he dressed as a charioteer and mingled with the crowd or stood on a miniature chariot. Nero's display gave rise to the notion that, although the condemned were guilty and deserved such novel

forms of execution, nevertheless people felt pity for them because they felt they were being sacrificed not for the public good but rather to appease Nero's savagery.

#246: The Ban on Pagan Sacrifice in the Fourth Century AD

Theodosius, *Code* 16.10.12
November 8th, AD 392

Despite persecution by the Romans, Christianity spread quickly, and had won over a substantial portion of the population by the beginning of the fourth century AD when Constantine converted. With state backing, Christianity quickly overtook the role of state cult. Eventually, the Roman gods were no longer worshipped, and their temples fell into disuse or, like the Pantheon, were converted into churches. The text here records a law passed by the Christian emperor Theodosius. It bans all forms of pagan sacrifice and illustrates how Christianity was now indeed the official religion of the Roman Empire.

The emperors Theodosius, Arcadius, and Honorius to Rufinus the Praetorian Prefect. Absolutely no one of any kind or class of people, including aristocrats, whether they be in a position of authority of holding political office, or they were born by chance into a powerful or humble family, shall in any place or any city sacrifice an innocent animal to a statue that has no sentient nature or worship a household god with a private propitiating sacrifice, or a protective deity with wine, or a god of the cupboard with incense, nor should they light altars, burn incense, or hang garlands for them.

If anyone should dare to sacrifice an animal or consult the entrails of a sacrificial animal, he shall be tried on the charge of treason. Any person can bring an accusation on this charge. The accused, if found guilty, will be punished as defined in the law on treason, even if the sacrifice was not made against the health and well-being of the emperors. All that is needed for an action to fall under this crime is to wish something to happen against the laws of nature, to inquire about the illegal, to reveal the hidden, to attempt the forbidden, to ask for the misfortune of another, or to have hope from the death of another person.

If anyone should worship with the burning of incense statues made by mortal hands, statues destined to decay with age, or suddenly in a silly way place wreaths in a tree or construct an altar out of turf. The builder may have thought that what he has made is divine, but they are truly empty. To honor such humble and powerless items is a serious offense to religion. He who does such a thing will be found guilty of the charge of violating religion and the house or property in which the superstitious rite was carried out will be confiscated. We decree that all places where it has been discovered that incense has been burned for cult purposes, if it can be proven that the accused is the owner of that property, must be confiscated to the imperial treasury.

If, however, anyone should try to perform the kind of sacrificial rite described here in a temple, public shrine, or building or property owned by someone else (provided it be established that the person performed the rite without the owner's knowledge), the person will be compelled to pay twenty-five pounds of gold as a fine. Also, anyone who turns a blind eye to this crime will also be punished in the same way as the one who actually performed the sacrifice.

We wish the judges, defense advocates, and town council members of the individual cities to prosecute this law as follows: any accusation they discover is to be immediately brought to trial and they should punish those found guilty of the charge. If those in authority should think that they can cover up any of these crimes out of partiality toward the accused or sweep the charges under the rug by neglecting their duty, they will be subjected to judicial indignation. If a judge should attempt to put off punishment through various forms of dissimulation once a guilty verdict is reached, he is to be fined thirty pounds of gold. The officials in his cabinet also will be subject to a similar fine. This pronouncement was made on November 8th, AD 392.

Chapter 15: The Army

Roman civilization was a militaristic one. The Romans aggressively expanded their empire throughout its history, and military victory was always an integral part of the legitimation of political power. The Roman people enjoyed the riches and sense of security conquest gave them. During the Republic, service in the army was a requirement of all Roman male citizens. During the civil wars of the late Republic, this citizen militia army was transformed into a professional fighting force in which volunteers recruited increasingly from the frontiers of the empire bore the burden of conquest and garrisoning the empire.

The Army of the Republic

The army of Rome's early history was primarily a militia force. Soldiers were recruited on an as-needed basis from the citizen body as a whole. For centuries, Rome's wars were not far from home and soldiers were recruited to serve, fight in the war, and still return home in time to harvest their crops. While non-citizens could fight in the army, the backbone of the army remained its heavy infantry citizen soldiers. Rome's willingness to co-opt conquered peoples into their citizenry gave them an abundant source of manpower for its legions. The four passages in this section come from Polybius' lengthy but very important discussion of the Roman army (#247 on the battle line, #248 on weapons and armor, #249 on the centurion, and #251 on the cavalry). I have also included a famous passage on the rivalry of Vorenus and Pullo, high-ranking centurions in the army of Julius Caesar in Gaul (#250).

#247: The Republican Battle Line

Polybius, *Histories* 6.21.6–10
Second Century BC

In his account on Roman Republican history, the Greek historian Polybius wrote a lengthy digression on the military institutions of the Romans. Writing for a primarily Greek audience, Polybius wished to explain how the Romans were so successful in their wars (they had already conquered much of the Hellenistic kingdoms of the east and shown their superiority to the Greek phalanx). In this passage, he describes how the line of battle was formed. Ancient armies fought primarily hand-to-hand and relied upon cohesive lines to provide stability and confidence to the soldiers in the line. These lines were not only wide to prevent an army from getting around their sides (outflank) but also deep so that men behind the front line could support and even replace the soldiers in the thick of the fray. As Polybius shows

here, a soldier's age and experience were the main ways of determining his position
in the line.

> In Rome, the tribunes administer the oath of allegiance and set a place and time
> on which each recruit will be required to assemble again without their equip-
> ment. The recruits are then sent away. On the appointed day, the men gather at
> the agreed-upon location. The youngest and poorest of them are assigned to the
> *velites*, lightly armed troops who skirmish in front of the line or on the flanks.
> Others from the youngest group also form the *hastati*. The men in the prime of
> life are assigned to the *principes*. The oldest men comprise the *triarii*. These are
> the names used by the Romans for the parts of the battle line in respect to their
> age and equipment. They arrange the members of each part of the line so that
> there are six hundred *triarii*, twelve hundred *principes*, and twelve hundred *has-
> tati*. Any other men beyond that number, namely the youngest, are in the body
> of *velites*. If more than four thousand men should be recruited into the legion,
> then additional men are added to the *principes* and *hastati* in equal proportion.
> The *triarii*, however, are always kept at six hundred men.

#248: Roman Republican Weapons and Armor

Polybius, *Histories* 6.22–23
Second Century BC

Following his description of the parts of the battle line, Polybius goes on to describe
the weapons and armor of the soldiers in the line. The basic soldier of the Roman
army was the heavy infantryman called the legionary (*legionarius* in Latin). The
legionary wore heavy iron armor to protect him from glancing blows. Because its
weight could impede the soldier's ability to fight, this armor required a great deal of
strength and endurance to wear in combat. The Romans used two types of weapons: a throwing javelin (*pilum*) and a short sword (*gladius*). The *pilum* was about six
feet long and had an iron shank attached to a wooden shaft. It was relatively light
and was designed to be thrown rather than thrust like the Greek spear. A soldier
would usually carry two javelins into battle. Generally, they would throw their javelins as they approached the enemy line in an attempt to disrupt their opponent's
formation. The main hand-to-hand weapon of the Roman soldier was the Spanish
short sword, the *gladius*. The *gladius* had two edges with a sharpened point. It was
mostly used as a stabbing weapon, but slashing was also possible. Generally, the
soldier would use his shield for cover and then make quick stabs at the enemy's
stomach from behind it with his *gladius*.

A Roman soldier's armor included a breastplate, helmet, shield, greaves for the
shins, and heavy military boots. The breastplate, or *lorica* in Latin, was made up of
multiple bands of metal connected together with leather straps that ran between
the bands on the inside of the breastplate. The leather straps were connected to the
metal bands with metal clasps. One advantage of this design was that rather than

having a single piece of metal that would not bend or flex, the so-called *lorica seg-mentata*, or segmented breastplate, allowed the soldier to move his arms quite effec-tively, allowing him to throw the *pilum* with his arm up and stab and thrust with the *gladius*. The rectangular shield (*scutum*) was designed to protect the soldier carrying the shield alone. In the Greek world, the large, round shield of the primary infantry soldier, the hoplite, covered part of the hoplite and afforded some protection to the soldier on his left. The shape tells us that a Greek soldier was not expected to fight outside of his formation. The Roman soldier also fought in a formation for pro-tection, but the shape of the shield documents how a soldier in the Roman army fought with more open space around him to better allow him to swing his swords and throw his javelins.

The youngest of the light-armed skirmishers (*velites*) are equipped with a sword, javelin, and small shield (*parma*). The *parma* is constructed to be strong and is large enough to provide the soldier protection. It has a diameter of three feet. They wear a plain helmet, but sometimes individuals would cover the helmet with a wolf skin or something similar not only for protection but also to make the soldier stand out from his comrades so that his officers can recognize him and know if he fights with courage or not. The javelin has a wooden shaft that is about two arm's lengths long and is as thick as a man's finger. The tip of the javelin is a piece of metal hammered out to a very thin edge so that it bends when it first hits its target. This is done so that the enemy cannot throw the javelin back with any effect. If this were not the case, the Roman javelin would be usable by both sides.

The second order of soldiers in order of seniority is the *hastati*. These sol-diers wear the full panoply. The first element of this panoply is the long, rect-angular shield (*scutum*). The *scutum* has a surface that curves inward on the edges. It is two and half feet wide and four feet tall. At the rim, it is as thick as a man's palm. The *scutum* is constructed with two boards that are glued together. The outer face is covered first with canvas and then finished with calf-skin leather. Both the upper and lower edges are reinforced with strips of iron that protect it from blows coming from above as well as damage when it is resting on the ground. In the center of its outer face is an iron boss which is strong enough to deflect strong blows from stones, heavy spears, and larger missile weapons. In addition to the shield, the *hastati* also carry a sword. This Spanish sword (*gladius*) hangs from the right thigh. The *gladius* is very effective as a thrusting weapon, but both edges also cut effectively as the blade is very strong. They also carry two *pila*, a bronze helmet, and greaves. They carry two types of *pila*: one heavy and one light. The heavy *pila* are round and as thick as a man's palm. The light *pila*, which they carry along with the heavy, are similar to medium-sized hunting spears. Both types are three arm's lengths long and have a barbed iron head that is half as long as the shaft of the spear. The metal that attaches the head to the shaft is very long and runs down a considerable part of the shaft with numerous rivets holding the metal and wood together. For this reason, the head is more likely to break than detach. The point at which the head connects to the wood is only a finger and a half thick. That is how firmly the Romans attach the head of the *pilum* to the shaft. They also wear a headdress containing three purple or black feathers of about an arm's length each. These feathers sticking out over all of the equipment has the effect of making the soldier look twice as tall as he actually is and presents a more frightful appearance to the enemy. The legionaries also wear a plate of bronze about five inches square. The soldier places it directly over the heart and calls it a *pectorale* ("chest protector"). More wealthy soldiers, whose property is valued at more than ten thousand *denarii*, wear a full breastplate (*lorica*). The *principes* and *triarii* wear very similar equipment with the exception that the *triarii* carry long spears (*hastae*) rather than *pila* since they stand at the back of the battle line.

#249: The Centurion

Polybius, *Histories* 6.24
Second Century BC

Each legion was divided into ten cohorts and each cohort had six centuries. At the highest levels, senatorial commanders and tribunes of the soldiers led the Roman army. These men owed their position more often to their political connections than to their leadership abilities or military experience. The day-to-day running of the army at the lower levels instead fell to the centurions, the officers in charge of individual centuries in the legion. Centurions were generally experienced soldiers who rose through the ranks and had a proven military record.

With the exception of the skirmishers (*velites*), the soldiers in each class elect ten officers according to ability. They then elect a second group of ten officers in each class. The Latin term for these officers is *centurio* ("centurion"). After their election, the centurions appoint an equal number of junior officers (*optiones*). Next, each class of soldiers in the legion (except the *velites*) is divided into ten units. Two from those who were elected as centurions and two *optiones* are put in charge of each of these units. For organizational purposes, the *velites* are divided equally into subunits. The Romans call these units *ordines*, maniples, or *vexilla* and their officers centurions. Within their maniples, the centurions choose two of the best and bravest soldiers to serve as standard bearers (*vexillarii*). It is only natural that the Romans preferred to appoint two centurions to each maniple rather than one. It is never certain how officers will behave or what may happen to them. The waging of war is not the time to listen to excuses and it is important that the maniples never be without their officers. If both centurions are still capable of leadership, then whichever of the two was elected first commands the more prestigious right side of the maniple while the other commands the left. If only one centurion remains then he commands the entire maniple. The Romans want their centurions to be not so much brave and fearless as good leaders with stable and relaxed natures. A centurion who is willing to lead the charge and start a battle is less qualified in the eyes of the Romans than one who can hold his ground and be ready to die when he is faced with a superior force or is being hit hard by the enemy.

#250: Rival Centurions in the Army of Julius Caesar

Julius Caesar, *The Gallic War* 5.44
Middle of the First Century BC

Over the course of almost a decade, Julius Caesar led an army in a war of conquest in Gaul (modern France). One reason for Caesar's overwhelming success was his ability to inspire in his soldiers loyalty to their general and a wish to impress him and earn his respect. Centurions, especially, strove to win Caesar's approval. Every centurion in the legion was ranked in order of seniority from the most junior centurion in the most junior maniple to the prestigious *primus pilus*, the chief centurion of the legion. Centurions could only advance when a position in a higher rank became available and, by the late Republic, it was the commanding officer who had the last word on promotions. The following passage is Caesar's own account of the rivalry between two high-ranking centurions: Titus Pullo and Lucius Vorenus. This story is one of the most dramatic in Caesar's narrative of the Gallic Wars and was the inspiration for the main characters in HBO's original series *Rome*.

In the legion there were two very brave centurions who were competing for the rank of *primus pilus*. Their names were Titus Pullo and Lucius Vorenus. These two were involved in a continuous rivalry over which of them would be chosen when it came time for the annual review of centurions eligible for promotion. During one particular battle, there was very intense fighting taking place in front of the fortifications of the camp. Pullo yelled out, "Vorenus, why are you hesitating? Do you think there will ever be a better opportunity for demonstrating your valor? I believe this day will determine the winner of our rivalry." When he had said this, Pullo moved outside of the protective fortifications and charged the enemy where they seemed to be the most numerous. Fearing what the other soldiers would think if he did not match Pullo's bravery, Vorenus also left the fortifications and followed Pullo. While there was still some distance between himself and the enemy, Pullo threw a javelin and struck one of the throng that was running toward him. The Gaul was wounded and died, but the others covered him with their shields and threw their javelins at Pullo. They began to maneuver around him to prevent him from any chance of escape. One enemy javelin went right through Pullo's shield and stuck into his belt. The force of the blow pushed his scabbard out of position so that when Pullo went to draw his *gladius*, he was unable to find it. The enemy poured around him now that he was at a disadvantage. Vorenus ran up and gave support to his struggling rival. All of the enemy soldiers immediately turned their attention from Pullo to Vorenus. It seems that the Gauls thought that Pullo had been killed by the spear. Vorenus fought hand-to-hand with the enemy and managed to drive them back after killing one of them. Vorenus was too eager to push his advantage and tripped over a depression in the ground. Now it was Pullo's turn to come to Vorenus' rescue. After killing numerous Gauls, both safely reached the Roman fortifications to the great praise of their fellow soldiers. Fortune took such a hand in their rivalry and struggle that each ended up being the source of help and safety to the other. Indeed, Caesar was unable to decide which of them was more deserving of promotion.

#251: The Cavalry of the Republic

Polybius, *Histories* 6.25
Second Century BC

The heavy infantry legionaries were not the only types of soldiers in the Roman army. The Romans also used light-armed cavalry. Heavy cavalry shock forces were extremely rare in the ancient world and, before the invention of stirrups and the modern saddle, were relatively ineffectual against heavy infantry. Like the *velites*, the cavalry would protect the flanks and skirmish with the other cavalry in hopes of gaining an advantage and perhaps provide an opportunity for the infantry to outflank the enemy army. If the Romans won the battle, the more mobile cavalry would pursue the fleeing enemy infantry and kill as many as they could catch. In this passage, Polybius continues his description of the Roman army of the Republic. Much of what he says continued to be the practice throughout Roman history.

As in the case of the infantry, the Romans divide their cavalry into ten units (*turmae*) and appoint three officers (*decuriones*) for each *turma* who then appoint three junior officers (*optiones*). The first *decurion* to be chosen is the senior and is in charge of the whole *turma* but all three are technically the same rank. If the chief *decurion* should be absent, the second to be chosen takes command of the *turma*. The Romans currently equip their cavalry in the same way as the Greeks. Originally, however, Roman cavalry wore no breastplate and only fought in very light garments to better allow them to mount and dismount their horses with speed and ease. Because they were nearly naked, however, this practice proved very dangerous in close combat with enemy infantry. Their javelins originally were not very useful for two reasons. First, they constructed them to be very light and bendable, but this caused them to be very difficult to aim. Also, the bobbing up and down of the horse caused many of the spears to break before they could be thrown and hit anything. Second, unlike infantry javelins, the cavalry's spears did not have a spike on the butt end, so they could only deliver one blow and, if the javelin broke, they were not completely useless. Their small shields were made of cow leather and were shaped like the round cakes used at religious sacrifices.

They were not of very strong construction so they could not be used reliably in combat. The rain would also often cause the leather to peel back from the core and rot causing a shield that was already quite useless to be completely so. Because the equipment of the cavalry did not stand up against the test of time, the Romans adopted the Greek type of armaments. Now, the construction of the javelins demonstrates much more strength and sturdiness and so the spear point is much easier to aim and flies with more impact. The same is true of the Greek shield, which is more solid and stronger and so can be used both for defense and offense. The Romans learned from their mistakes and quickly adopted Greek cavalry armaments. The Romans are, indeed, very good about adopting new practices and imitate what others do better than they do, even if those others are foreigners.

The Army of the Imperial Period

One of the most important and far-reaching changes instituted by Augustus after he came to power was his reforms to professionalize the army. The dominance of the army in the hands of ruthless generals had been a major reason for the political instability of the first century BC and had led to the collapse of the Republic.

As part of his efforts to professionalize the army, Augustus set the period of service and pay of the soldiers. He standardized armor and gear. He also established permanent garrisons of legions and non-citizen auxiliary forces on the frontiers (the *auxilia*). Passage #252 is the historian Tacitus' summary of the locations of the army in the first century AD. Like Polybius of the third century BC, the Jewish writer Josephus, in his account of the disastrous rebellion of Judaea under Nero, tries to explain to a foreign audience why the Roman army was so successful (#253 on military training, #255 on discipline, and #258 on their brutality). There is also a speech of the emperor Hadrian following a review of one of the legions in North Africa (#254). Tacitus' account of the military mutiny on the northern frontiers following the death of Augustus reveals more on the discipline of the army (#256). As examples of soldiers, I include a selection of tombstones from the legionary cemetery in Apamea, Syria (#257).

#252: The Frontier Garrisons

Tacitus, *Annals* 4.5
Written in the Early Second Century AD Describing
the Situation of the First Century AD

In the Republican period, the Romans recruited armies on an as-needed basis. When absolutely necessary, the Romans would leave soldiers under arms to garrison distant provinces or military zones but there was no set practice. Augustus greatly expanded the empire and kept a standing army in service at all times. When parts of this army were not at war, they were serving as garrisons along the frontiers.

There were a little fewer than thirty legions stationed at any given time in camps around the Roman Empire. In this passage, the historian Tacitus documents the location of the various legions during the reign of the emperor Tiberius.

> Two fleets, one at Misenum and the other at Ravenna, guard the seas on the two sides of Italy. Another fleet of warships (which Augustus had captured at the battle of Actium) he sent to Forum Iulium to guard the southern shore of Gaul. The strongest frontier garrison is certainly the eight legions on the Rhine River to protect against the Germans and Gauls. Spain, still only recently completely conquered, has three legions. The Romans had arranged for Mauretania to be ruled by a native king named Juba. Two legions are stationed in the other parts of Africa although Egypt has two legions of its own. Next, the very large territory between Syria to the Euphrates River is protected by four legions. In this area, we rely on client kings of the Hiberi, Albani, and others who would protect our interests against foreign powers. Thrace is also under the client king Rhoemetalces and the children of Cotys. There are additional legions on the Danube River: two in Pannonia, two in Moesia, and two in Dalmatia. Dalmatia is situated behind Pannonia and Moesia and is not very far away if Italy should suddenly need military aid. Rome itself, however, has its own garrison: three urban cohorts and nine praetorian cohorts. The soldiers in these elite forces are recruited mostly from Etruria, Umbria, old Latium, and the older Roman colonies. In addition, there are various allied fleets, and non-citizen auxiliary cavalry and infantry (the *auxilia*) positioned in key locations. These troops are almost as numerous as the citizen legionaries. It would be confusing, however, to try to document the location of all of these troops since they tend to move from place to place as the situation demands. Their number also tends to increase and diminish.

#253: Military Training

Josephus, *The Jewish War* 3.72–76
First Century AD

In the section translated here, Josephus touches on the training regimen of the Roman army. It was important for the professional army of the empire to be prepared for war. It was also advantageous to keep the army busy while serving garrison duty.

> War is not the first time a Roman soldier uses his military equipment. Their hands are not idle in peace only to answer the call when there is need. Instead, the Romans, as if they were born with their weapons as part of their bodies, never take a break from training and do not wait for there to be a need to begin their military exercises. In fact, their training is just as vigorous as war itself. Every soldier works very hard at his daily military training and treats drills no differently than war itself. For this reason, a Roman soldier is able to better withstand

the pressure of battle. Confusion does not cause the battle line to lose cohesion. The soldiers do not freeze with fear. They do not weary easily from their labors. Because their opponents cannot match their abilities, victory is a guaranteed certainty. I do not think that I would be wrong to say that their training exercises are like bloodless battles and their battles are like bloody training exercises.

#254: Hadrian Reviews a Training Exercise in North Africa

CIL 8.18042 (Lambaesis, Numidia)
AD 128

The emperor Hadrian spent much of his reign traveling around the empire inspecting the frontier military garrisons. In AD 128, he traveled to North Africa to the legionary fortress of the Legion III Augusta in Lambaesis, Numidia. During his visit, the legion put on a display of military exercises. Afterward, Hadrian gave a speech before the assembled soldiers to congratulate them on their abilities. After the emperor left, the legion put up a dedicatory monument on which they copied the text of the emperor's speech.

The emperor Caesar Trajan Hadrian Augustus addressed the Legion III Augusta after watching their military exercises. What is written below is the text of that speech given on July 1st while Torquatus (for the second time) and Libo were consuls [128 BC].

To the chief centurions of each cohort: my friend the legionary commander Catullinus has pleaded in your defense and described all of the things that might have hindered you from giving a perfect performance. I understand that one of the legion's cohorts is away performing its annual service with the proconsul of North Africa. I also understand that three years ago a cohort and four men from each century went to reinforce your comrades in the third legion in the east. I also have taken into account how your responsibility to watch over so many scattered stations along the African frontier keeps you separated. I would also add that in my own memory you have not only changed fortresses twice but have also built the new fortresses. All of these excuses would have been acceptable if your military exercises had not been as good as they should have been, but the truth is that your performance was so good that there is no need to make any excuse at all...

To the legionary cavalry: Military training exercises have their own set of rules. If someone should add or remove something from these rules, either the exercise becomes trivial or too difficult. The more difficult the exercise, the less pleasant it is to watch. In your exercises, however, you performed one of the most difficult maneuvers: throwing a javelin from horseback while wearing a breastplate.... Fortifications that other soldiers might take several days to complete you finished in a single day. This work included a long wall of the type that is normally only seen in more permanent winter camps and you did it in the time that it would take to construct a wall of turf. In a turf wall, the earthen building blocks are cut and transported easily and can be put into place without difficulty owing to the fact that they are soft and have straight edges. Your wall, however, was made of large and heavy stones with irregular shapes. It is impossible that such materials can be transported, carried, and placed in such a way that their irregularities are not visible in the construction. You also cut a ditch through ground that was hard and rough with gravel. You even made the surface smooth by pounding out the earth. Once your officers approved of your work, you re-entered the camp and had a quick lunch, took your equipment, and followed the cavalry who had already been sent out ahead of you...

[To another unit:] I praise your commander for having you do that training exercise. It had the appearance of actual combat and does an excellent job of preparing you for war. I would also like to praise Cornelianus your camp prefect who has done such a fine job of carrying out his duties.

On July 13th to the first cavalry auxiliary regiment of the Pannonians: you have done all your exercises well. You filled the field with your cavalry maneuvers. You threw your spears quite well despite the fact that you were using short and inflexible weapons. Many of you are very skillful with missile weapons. You mounted your horses with great agility and swiftness both today and yesterday. I was watching very closely and if something was not done correctly I would have noticed. I would have pointed out any glaring mistakes in any part of the exercise. My friend the legionary legate Catullinus, a man of senatorial background, has demonstrated equal concern for all of his responsibilities...

To the cavalry of the sixth auxiliary cohort of Commageni: it is difficult for cavalry attached to an infantry auxiliary unit to put on a good show even on your own without the presence of the infantry after watching the training exercises of an exclusively cavalry auxiliary unit. They have the advantage of covering a larger part of the field and have more soldiers throwing javelins. They were able to perform the Cantabrian maneuver in close formation. The quality of their horses and equipment is in keeping with their higher level pay. Nevertheless, you did not shy away from the heat and kept our attention by vigorously doing what you needed to do. You also fired stones from your slings and performed mock battles with your javelins. You all mounted your horses quickly. The exemplary abilities of my friend the legionary legate Catullinus is clear from the fact he has soldiers like you under his command...

#255: The Discipline of the Roman Army

Josephus, *The Jewish War* 3.102–107
First Century AD

The Roman army's discipline was certainly one of the major reasons for its success over the centuries. As the text from Lambaesis demonstrates, the professional army spent a good deal of its time performing training exercises. In the following passage from his description of the Roman army, Josephus shows that training was only part of Roman discipline. Fear and respect, too, were important. Soldiers needed to follow the orders of their officers in dangerous situations. The Romans believed that soldiers should fear their officers more than the enemy. In keeping with the tradition of brutal and exemplary justice, the Romans dealt with insubordination with the utmost harshness.

Training exercises are useful for instilling *virtus* in not only the bodies of the soldiers but also their spirits. Fear, however, should also be included under the heading of training. There are rules in the Roman army that inflict the death penalty not only for desertion but also seemingly trivial neglect of duty. It is their aim to make the soldiers more afraid of their officers than the rules. They give the highest honors to the brave and proportionally punish those who fail in their duties. The soldiers' great obedience to their officers makes them a useful presence in peacetime and in war causes the whole army to act as if it were one body. Their ranks are tight. Their movement is exceptionally sharp even when wheeling around. Their ears listen attentively for their orders. Their eyes watch for their signals. Their hands are constantly ready to do what needs to be done. As quickly as they are ready to do their duty, so also are they slow to give in to their hardships. There has never been a time when a Roman army was clearly bested by numbers, trickery, unfavorable ground, or even by luck. They are more certain of victory than luck. When deeds follow a sound plan of attack and an army is so eager to carry out that plan, it is not surprising that the Roman Empire extends to the Euphrates River in the east, the Ocean in the west, the fertile regions of Libya in the south, and the Ister and Rhine Rivers in the north. I believe it is proper to say that the empire is great but its soldiers are greater still.

#256: A Military Mutiny

Tacitus, *Annals* 1.17, 20, 23
Written in the Early Second Century AD Describing Events of AD 14

After the death of Augustus in AD 14, the armies on the Rhine and Danube Rivers attempted a mutiny. The times were uncertain and many soldiers felt that the conditions of their service had become worse over time. Many of the soldiers also had completed their terms but were still awaiting formal discharge. For our purposes here, this passage reflects how the superior discipline of the Roman army could become a serious burden in the eyes of the soldiers.

The leader of the mutiny saw that there were more soldiers who were on the verge of joining the insurrection. He addressed them like a political demagogue and said, "Why are you willing to obey like a bunch of slaves the orders of a few centurions and even fewer tribunes. When are you going to demand some relief? There is no time to voice your complaints or begin armed resistance than when the emperor is new and still uncertain in his throne. We have wandered enough like sheep these long years. In some cases that service has gone on for thirty or even forty years and left us old men. Most of us bear serious scars from our war wounds. Not even discharge is an end to our military service. Instead, we must continue in those same duties only under another name. If anyone does manage to survive all of the misfortunes of service, then he is dragged off to some remote part of the world where he has been given for his discharge bonus a tract of land (if a swamp or overgrown goat path on the side of some mountain could be called 'land'). Military service is difficult and unprofitable. We sell our bodies and souls for a mere ten bronze coins a day and out of that we have to pay for our clothing, equipment, and tents. That is also all the money we have for bribes to keep back the savagery of the centurions and exemption from camp duties. My goodness, think of the hardships: beatings and wounds, harsh winters, unbearable summers, not to mention the harsh realities of war itself and even peace, a time that brings no end to our suffering. There is no way to fix our situation unless the government should agree to changes to our terms of service: a pay raise to sixteen coins per day, a length of service no longer than sixteen years after which we should not be retained as continuing soldiers in the individual units of the army but rather as camp fellows who are paid a salary."

[The mutiny intensifies and violence breaks out] The mutineers attacked the centurions who tried to control the soldiers first with ridicule and insults and then with beatings. The soldiers were especially angry at the camp prefect Aufidienus Rufus. They grabbed him and tied him to the front of a cart used to transport the baggage. They then made him drag his load at the front of the line and asked him wither he could stand the heavy load and long marches. Rufus had come up through the ranks. He began as a common soldier and was later promoted to centurion and eventually camp prefect. He tried to revive traditional military discipline. He was accustomed to toil and labor and was all the less lenient because he had been able to endure…

[Additional outrages to the officers] They threw the tribunes and camp prefect out of the camp and pillaged their personal belongings. They even killed the centurion Lucilius. To this man, the soldiers had given the joke name "Give Me Another" because once he had broken the centurion's cane he carried with him on the back of a soldier he was disciplining and had then asked in a loud voice "give me another one."

#257: A Legionary Cemetery in Syria

AE 1987, 955; 1991, 1572; 1992, 1686; 1993, 1573, 1574, 1575, 1577, 1579, 1581, 1584, 1585, 1595, 1597 (Apamea, Syria)

The city of Apamea in Syria in the east was the location of winter quarters of the Legion II Parthica during part of the first half of the third century AD. The emperor Septimius Severus created the legion and based it in Italy, but he and subsequent emperors frequently relocated it to the east for invasions of the Parthian Empire. During these campaigns, the legion would spend the winter in Apamea. It was in the east for the Parthian war of Caracalla when Macrinus murdered Cara-calla and usurped the throne. The following year, the legion sided with Elagabalus who successfully overthrew the emperor Macrinus and claimed the throne for himself. The legion returned to the east again for wars under Alexander Severus (AD 222–235) and Gallus (AD 251–253). The inscriptions given here come from a legionary cemetery at Apamea. They document a number of soldiers from the II Parthica and some related auxiliary units. The soldiers frequently refer to their century and cohort number. The centuries (and the centurions who commanded them) were ranked in order of importance. The first cohort of the first century (commanded by the *primus pilus*, the chief centurion of the whole legion) was the most important and the sixth century of the tenth cohort was the least prestigious.

AD 1987, 955: To Aurelius Bassus, who was once the standard bearer of the First Ulpian cavalry unit of lance bearers; he served eight years and lived twenty-nine years. This inscription was placed on April 21st, AD 252 by Marcius Cotus, the *decurio* of the cavalry unit of Roman citizens.

AE 1991, 1572: To the Spirits of the Dead; Felsoniuis Verus, eagle standard bearer of the Legion II Parthica Gordian Loyal and Faithful Forever, he was in the first century of the first cohort; he served eleven years; he was born in Thuscia; he lived thirty-one years; his wife Flavia Magna placed this honor of the memory of her well-deserving husband.

AD 1992, 1686: To the Spirits of the Dead; to Petronius Proculus, adjutant of the tribune of the Legion II Parthica of Alexander Severus Loyal, Faithful, and Lucky Forever; he was in the second century of the ninth cohort; he lived thirty-seven years, eight months; he served eighteen years; his daughter and heir Petronia Procla and his brother and secondary heir Petronius Primus took care to erect this monument to him, well-deserving.

AE 1993, 1573: To the Spirits of the Dead; Aurelius Zoilus, soldier of the Legion II Parthica of Antoninus, Loyal, Faithful, and Lucky Forever; he enlisted at the age of twenty; he served twenty years; he died at the age of forty; Aurelius Dionysius and Aurelius Longinus, soldiers in the same legion, his heirs, made this to him well-deserving.

AE 1993, 1574: To the Spirits of the Dead; Lucius Septimius Viator, who served sixteen years in the *lanciarii* [light armed soldier who skirmished in front of the line] of the Legion II Parthica; he was born in Pannonia; he lived thirty-five years; his heir made this for him well-deserving.

AE 1993, 1575: To the Spirits of the Dead of Aurelius Mucianus; he was in training for the *lanciarii* of the Legion II Parthica; he served in the first century of the ninth cohort for ten years; he lived thirty years; Septimius, a recipient of double pay in the same legion and in the [. . .] century of the eighth cohort made this for a superb and well-deserving fellow soldier.

AE 1993, 1577: To the Spirits of the Dead; Aelius Verecundinus, centurion of a fifth century in the Legion Fourth Scythica; he was born in Dacia near the legionary camp where the Batavians served; he served twenty-one years; he was first promoted to serve as bookkeeper of the detachment in charge of the grain supply; he was later as a re-enlisted man an intelligence officer of centurion rank and after that he served a centurion in the detachment in charge of the grain supply; he lived thirty-six years; Aelius Rufinus, his freedman, made this out of funds from Verecundinus' estate.

AE 1993, 1579: To the Spirits of the Dead; Aurelius Mucianus, soldier of the Legion II Parthica Loyal, Lucky and Faithful Forever in the fourth century of the third cohort; he lived thirty years and served ten; Aurelius Dizza his heir put this up to him well-deserving.

AE 1993, 1581: To the Spirits of the Dead; to Aelius Longinus, soldier of the Second Legion Parthica of Severus in the third century of the fifth cohort; he served twelve years and lived thirty years, five months; his heir Licinius Priscinus, cavalry soldier in the same legion put this up to him well-deserving.

AE 1993, 1584: Baebius Severus, artillery soldier exempt from physical duties in the Legion II Parthica of Severus, Loyal, Lucky, and Faithful Forever, in the second century of the fifth cohort; he lived thirty years, three months and served twelve years; he was originally from the town of Perusia; his primary heir Valerius Respectus made this for him well-deserving.

AE 1993, 1585: To the Spirits of the Dead; to Aurelius Celsus, soldier in charge of the watchword in the Legion II Parthica of Severus, in the second century of the fourth cohort; his wife and heir Clodia Felicissima and his second heir Aurelius Celer put this up.

AE 1993, 1595: Aurelius Disas, trumpeter in the First Flavia cavalry unit from Britain; he served eleven years and lived thirty-two; his secondary heir Aurelius Romietalca put this inscription up to his colleague.

AE 1993, 1597: To Antonia Kara, who lived twenty-eight years, four months; Probius Sanctus, centurion in the Second Legion Parthica, made this for his incomparable and well-deserving wife.

#258: Roman Brutality in War

Josephus, *The Jewish War* 6.403–406, 414–419
First Century AD

Although Roman discipline and ability were in many ways unparalleled, the Roman army was not above using terror to their advantage. Any enemy willing to engage in battle had to be prepared for heavy losses in the retreat that was likely to come after they had lost. Resistance to Roman conquest or any attempt to rebel was also treated very harshly. Captured cities were often sacked and pillaged and the bloodshed was usually not limited to soldiers but spread to the civilian population as well.

In AD 66, the province of Judaea rebelled from Roman control. The emperor Nero responded by sending the general Vespasian to quell the uprising. Vespasian moved methodically through the province and eventually besieged the last remnants of the Jewish rebels in Jerusalem. The siege lasted more than a year as the

Romans took one wall after another. Finally, the Romans gained entrance to the heart of the city and the last bastion of the rebels and townspeople. Once inside, the Roman soldiers began a wholesale killing of the inhabitants. Titus, the son of Vespasian and commanding general at the time of the capture of Jerusalem, allowed the soldiers to act so brutally in part because the sacking of cities was one of the rewards for a victorious Roman army. Vespasian also saw the act as justified owing to the resistance that the insurgents had mounted against the Romans. The following is the Jewish historian Josephus' eyewitness account of the sack of Jerusalem.

> After they had gained control of the walls, the Romans placed their standards on the towers and with applause and joy they sang their war song in honor of victory. This was in part because they had found the end of the war to be easier than the beginning. They had climbed the last wall without meeting resistance and without bloodshed and even now they were shocked that no one came out to oppose them. They drew their swords and ran down the streets, killing everyone that they came upon. Some people fled into their homes and locked the doors, so the Romans burned the houses with the people still inside. In some cases, soldiers entered houses to search for loot but found inside the bodies of families dead and rooms filled with people who had died from starvation during the siege. The sight made them sick and they left the houses empty-handed. Although the soldiers showed a kind of pity to those already dead, they had no similar feeling for those people still alive. They killed every person they found alive until the streets were full of bodies and the city ran with the blood of the victims. Indeed, the blood and gore extinguished some of the fires...
>
> Since the soldiers were getting tired of the slaughter, although there were still a great many survivors that were being found, Titus ordered that the soldiers kill only those people carrying weapons or offering resistance but to make the rest prisoners of war. The soldiers did as they were ordered with the exception that, in addition to any hostile survivors, they also killed the old and weak. Everyone in the prime of life or otherwise useful they gathered together and put in the Court of Women to await their fate. Titus placed one of his freedmen in charge of the prisoners. He also charged his friend Fronto to act as judge and decide their fate. He executed all of the revolutionaries and brigands based on information that the prisoners gave against one another. He also set aside the tallest and best looking of the prisoners for the triumph that would eventually be held in Rome. Any that were over seventeen years old he sent to work at hard labor in Egypt. A large number were also sent to amphitheaters across the empire to be killed by wild beasts and in mock battles. The children under seventeen years old were sold into slavery. Fronto spent several days reaching his decision. During that time, eleven thousand of the prisoners died from starvation not only because the guards would not give food to the prisoners out of anger but also because some of the prisoners refused to eat when food was offered. In any case, there were not enough provisions for such a large throng of people.

Chapter 16: Life in the Country

Most of the inhabitants of the Roman Empire were farmers. The economy was in large part based on agriculture. Unfortunately, much of our evidence for the Roman world comes from literary sources of the upper classes and has a very urban focus. As the poorest members of society, farmers, even those of freeborn, citizen descent, left little trace of their existence. It is therefore necessary to turn to descriptions of country life in the literary works of the aristocracy. The members of the senatorial aristocracy were required by law to base their wealth in agriculture. As a result, they owned large farms spread out across Italy and the empire.

As primarily city dwellers, many of these aristocratic farm owners saw their farms more as luxury villas than agricultural production facilities. Many of these sources also idealize country living as more wholesome and pure than city living. As a result, our surviving sources tend to reflect pastoral ideals more than reality. There are several Roman aristocratic authors who wrote handbooks on farming that have survived. Even these works, however, sometimes are more literary endeavors than practical guides.

Glimpses of Country Life

There is a considerable range of texts that describe life in the Roman country-side. The Roman government tended to focus on urban life in its method of rule, and the emperor or members of the urban aristocratic elite (the so-called *lati-fundia*; #264) owned a large part of the agricultural land in the Roman Empire. Aristocratic owners often saw their farms as little more than producers of income and country retreats (#263; owning farms was also a handy way for aristocrats to show their connection to the ideal traditional Roman farmer; #259). They also tended to look down on or ignore members of the lower classes, so they do not give much thought to the tenant farmers (or in some cases slaves) that worked on their farms. The result is an often-skewed view of country life that, like so much other ancient literature, fails to take into account viewpoints other than the writer's own. Horace describes the differences between urban and rural life through the story of the city mouse and the country mouse (#260). Pliny the Younger's letter describing his daily routine in the country (#265) differs greatly from the life of the simple farmer described in the Appendix Vergiliana (#266). As for the actual work on a farm, a calendar from Rome gives agricultural information (#261). Pliny the Elder describes the act of plowing the fields (#262).

#259: The Farmer as the Ideal Roman

Cato, *On Agriculture*, Introduction to Book 1
Mid-Second Century BC

The legal requirement that all senatorial aristocratic wealth be based in agriculture was an attempt to maintain connection with an idealized past in which, like the early Republican statesman Cincinnatus, self-sufficient Romans both grew their own food on small farms and served their country with honor and courage. The passage translated here comes from the second century BC agricultural treatise of Cato the Elder. Although the audience of his treatise is aristocratic landowners, he still, in his introduction, reflects the traditional view that the independent farmer with his own small farm was the ideal Roman.

Sometimes people seek to make a profit through trade, but it is a risky proposition. Money lending is another method, but it is not very honorable. Our ancestors knew the latter to be true and wrote it into the laws. When found guilty, a thief is fined double the property that he stole, but a moneylender is fined quadruple. From this we can see that a moneylender is considered to be a worse person than a thief. In the old days, when a person was to be praised, it took this form: "He was a good farmer and a good land owner." Indeed, this was the highest praise a man could receive. I believe the merchant is vigorous and eager in his pursuit of wealth, but, as I said already, his profit comes only with risk and the potential to lose everything. The bravest men and most vigorous soldiers, however, derive from the farming class. Their profession is viewed as the most patriotic and stable and is looked down upon the least of all professions. People tend not to think badly of someone employed in farming.

#260: The City Mouse and the Country Mouse

Horace, *Satires* 2.6.79–117
Mid-First Century BC

In this passage, the Augustan poet Horace tells the Roman fairy tale of the city mouse and the country mouse. The story of how the two mice envy the life of the other is still told today and illuminates some of the differences between city and country living in the Roman world.

Once upon a time, a country mouse received as a guest in his poor mouse hole a city mouse. The two were old friends. The country mouse was uncultivated and thrifty in spending money, but he nevertheless loosened his purse strings in the name of hospitality. To make a long story short, the country mouse willingly offered his friend chickpeas from his private reserve as well as long-grained oats. He also retrieved from his stores some dried fruit and a morsel of half-eaten bacon and gave them to the city mouse. The country mouse was hoping that by offering a wide variety of foods he could overcome the hesitation of the city mouse to eat any of the food that was being offered to him. The owner of the house reclined on a couch of fresh straw ate some spelt and darnel, but left the very best pieces for his friend. At last, the city mouse exclaimed, "My friend, how can you actually like living on the ridge of a steep forest? Don't you think you would prefer people and the city to all these trees? Trust me, you should hit the road and come back to the city with me. It is the fate of all inhabitants of earth to have mortal souls. No one, great or small, is able to escape their fate. While you still have the option, my friend, you should live a happier life and enjoy pleasures." These words convinced the country mouse and he capriciously decided to leave home. Both set out on their agreed journey and planned to enter the city at night by crawling under the walls.

The moon was already high in the sky when the two mice came to a grand aristocratic house. There was a room with ivory couches covered with sheets dyed red and purple. There were many leftovers from a grand dinner party the night before sitting in baskets. The city mouse placed his country friend on a purple couch and, like a household slave, he ran about to gather up and offer a non-stop feast of courses. The city mouse took small tastes from each of the items he gave to the country mouse. The country mouse, reclining on his couch, was enjoying his new lifestyle and expressed his pleasure with the fine meal. Suddenly, there was a loud bang at the door and both mice were thrown off their couches. Terrified, they ran across the wide-open space of the dining room. They became even more frightened when they heard the barking of Molossian hunting dogs resounding through the house. The country mouse said to his friend, "This is certainly not the life for me. I must say good-bye. My forest and cave, safe from dangers like these, will be enough for me."

#261: A Farmer's Calendar

CIL 6.32503 (Rome)
First Century BC

The following text is an inscription in the form of a calendar that was found in Rome. It lists all of the months and gives details on the major days. The Romans numbered their days based on the three key days of the month: the Kalends (always on the first of the month), the Nones (early in the month) and the Ides (the middle of the month). For each month, the inscription includes information relevant for farmers.

January has thirty-one days. The Nones falls on the fifth. The day lasts nine and three quarter hours and the night fourteen and one quarter hours. The sun is in the constellation of Capricorn. The month is under the protection of the goddess Juno. Farmers should sharpen their stakes and cut back the willow reeds. Sacrifices are made to the gods of the household (Penates).

February has twenty-eight days. The Nones fall on the fifth. The day lasts ten and three quarters hours and the night thirteen and one quarter hours. The sun is in the constellation of Aquarius. The month is under the protection of Neptune. Farmers should weed their wheat fields, cultivate the part of the grapevines that appear aboveground, and burn the reeds. During this month are the festivals of the Parentalia, Lupercalia, the Dear Relatives, and the Terminalia.

March has thirty-one days. The Nones fall on the seventh. The day lasts twelve hours and the night twelve hours; the equinox itself is on the twenty-fifth of the month. The sun is in Pisces. The month is under the protection of Minerva. The vines should be propped up and pruned. The spring wheat should be planted. This is the month in which the sacred ship of Isis is offered. Sacrifices are made to Mamurius, and festivals include the Liberalia, the Quinquatria, and the Washing.

April has thirty days. The Nones are on the fifth. The day lasts thirteen and a half hours and the night ten and a half hours. The sun is in Ares. The month is under the protection of Venus. Lambing takes place in this month. There are festivals to Isis of Egypt as well as Serapis.

May has thirty-one days. The Nones is on the seventh. The day lasts fourteen and a half hours and the night nine and a half hours. The sun is in Taurus. The month is under the protection of Apollo. The wheat fields should be weeded. The sheep should be shorn and the wool cleaned. The young oxen should be trained for plowing. The vetch that will be used for animal fodder should be cut. There are sacrifices to Mercury and Flora.

June has thirty days. The Nones is on the fifth. The day lasts fifteen hours and the night nine hours. The summer solstice falls on the twenty-fourth of the month. The sun is in Gemini. The month is under the protection of Mercury. The hay is cut down and the vines are cultivated. There are rites in honor of Hercules, Bravery, and Fortune.

July has thirty-one days. The Nones fall on the seventh. The day lasts fourteen and one quarter hours and the night nine and three quarters hours. The sun is in Cancer. The month is under the protection of Jupiter. Barley and beans should be harvested. Festivals include those of the Apollinaria and the Neptunalia.

August has thirty-one days. The Nones fall on the fifth. The day lasts thirteen hours and the night eleven hours. The sun is in the constellation of Leo. The month is under the protection of Ceres. Farmers should prepare the stakes and harvest the rest of the crops, including the wheat. The stalks still in the field should be burned. There are rites in honor of Hope, Good Health, and Diana. This is also the month of the Volcanalia.

September has thirty days. The Nones fall on the fifth. The day lasts twelve hours and so does the night. The equinox is on the twenty-fourth day. The sun is in Virgo. The month is under the protection of Vulcan. The inside of the storage vessels should be coated with pitch. All of the fruit should be picked. The dirt around the fruit trees should be aerated. The sacred feast in honor of Minerva is during this month.

October has thirty-one days. The Nones fall on the seventh. The day lasts ten and three quarters hours and the night thirteen and one quarter hours. The sun is in Libra. The month is under the protection of Mars. Farmers should harvest the grapes. There is a sacrifice in honor of Bacchus.

November has thirty days. The Nones fall on the fifth. The day lasts nine and a half hours and the night fourteen and a half hours. The sun is in Scorpio. The month is under the protection of Diana. The wheat and barley should be harvested. Dig the trenches for the trees. There is a sacred feast to Jupiter in this month. It is also the time of the Discover festival.

December has thirty-one days. The Nones is on the fifth. The day lasts nine hours and the night fifteen hours. The sun is in Sagittarius. The month is under the protection of Vesta. The beginning of winter is in this month (at the winter solstice). Farmers should spread manure on the vines, plant beans, cut wood, and gather and sell olives. This is the month of the Saturnalia.

#262: Plowing the Fields

Pliny the Elder, *Natural History* 18.174–175
First Century AD

The planting, care, and harvesting of grain crops were some of the most important duties on a Roman farm. In this passage, the natural historian Pliny the Elder discusses the importance of plowing and gives advice on how it should be done. Much of our surviving agricultural evidence is in the form of advice to farmers. Because there are so many factors that go into a good harvest, just like in modern times, it seems that everyone has their own ideas of what is the best plan.

Farmers absolutely must follow the hallowed advice of Cato when it comes to plowing. He said "what makes for good agriculture? Good plowing. What is the second most important thing? Plowing. What is third? Spreading manure." He also said, "Plow in a nice straight line" and "Plow at the right time of year." I would add the following advice. In warmer regions, start plowing in the middle of winter, but in colder places, plow no earlier than the spring equinox. Plowing should also be done earlier in dry soil than in wet. So also you should plow dense soil should before loose and rich before less fertile. If your summers tend to be drier and hotter and the ground is more chalky and thinner, it is better to plow between the summer solstice and fall equinox. If you have milder summer heat with more frequent rain and a rich and grassy soil, however, it is advisable to plow when it is hot. Heavier soil should be plowed even during the winter-time, but thin and dry earth should only be plowed just before planting.

#263: Cicero on the Pleasures of Farming

Cicero, *On Old Age* 15.51
Mid-First Century BC

In this passage, the orator Cicero describes his delight in farm life in his old age. He demonstrates once again the belief of the aristocracy in the honorable profession of farming. Like the other authors we have seen here, however, Cicero alludes to the idealized version of country life of the detached senatorial aristocratic landowner who owned numerous country farming estates and would only visit sporadically. These wealthy owners did not work the land themselves every day. Most of the time, these owners entrusted the management of their estates to slave or freedman bailiffs (*vilici*). It was the tenant farmers or slaves who did the vast majority of the laborious physical chores.

> I now turn to the pleasures of farming, in which I take incredible delight. There is nothing that bars the old man from participating in these pleasures. Indeed, in my opinion, country life comes closest to my idea of the life of the wise. It is as if farmers have a business agreement with the earth. The earth never refuses what it has been ordered to do. It makes a return on anything the farmer chooses to invest. Sometimes the profit is not very extensive, but most of the time it is considerable. It is not only the crops that interest me, but also the power and nature of the soil itself. The earth accepts in its softened and overturned bosom the seeds the farmer plants. At first, it keeps locked away the hidden seed (indeed, the act of turning over the soil during planting is called "harrowing," a word that means to hide). Later, the seed is heated by the natural warmth of the earth's embrace and it begins to grow. The plant begins to sprout and its leafy greenness appears above ground. Springing up from its roots, the plant grows little by little and eventually stands tall on its jointed stalk. The fruit-producing part of the plant, however, still remains hidden in its sheath as it matures. Finally the plant emerges from its sheath and produces its fruit. Then the crops can be seen in long rows. They are protected from the pecking of birds by a row of spikes.

#264: The Appearance of Large Aristocratic Estates

Pliny the Elder, *Natural History* 18.7.35
First Century AD

Although the ideal Roman was the small independent farmer, because the senatorial aristocracy was required to have their wealth based in agriculture, a major trend of the Republic was the growth of large aristocratic agricultural estates at the expense of the small independent farmer. In this passage, Pliny the Elder laments how these estates (called *latifundia* in Latin) have ruined Italy and how much of the empire's arable land has come under the control of an increasingly small number of people.

> The ancients believed that it was of primary importance that farms remain small. Their advice was that it was better to plant less and to plow more. I know that Ver-gil believed in this maxim. It cannot be denied, in fact, that the large agricultural estates owned by the rich (*latifundia*) are ruining Italy as well as the provinces. At one time, six people owned half of the landmass of the province of Africa. Then the emperor Nero killed those six owners and took their property and made it his own. The Republican general Pompey is called the Great and indeed he lived up to that name with his practice of never buying land that joined any property that he already owned. The author Mago claimed rather harshly that if someone should buy a country estate that he should at the same time sell his house in town. That is the statement that begins his collection of advice. If nothing else, this statement does ask people to exercise moderation in their property purchases.

#265: A Day in Pliny's Country Life

Pliny the Younger, *Letters* 9.36
Early Second Century AD

Like his fellow senators, Pliny the Younger owned numerous country estates across Italy. Although his political and legal career kept him in Rome most of the time, the summer months usually had enough free time to allow him to escape for a holiday in the country. One of his favorite destinations was his estate in Tuscany. The villa was close enough to Rome to be easily reachable but yet was far enough to be remote from urban life. In this letter, he answers his friend Fuscus' request for a detailed summary of his daily activities in the summer at his estate. It should be noted that Pliny's country life was not one dedicated to farming but rather the pur-suit of literary interests and bears closer resemblance to a holiday than a work visit.

> You have asked how I spend my days at my Tuscan estate in the summer. I wake up whenever I want to. Usually that is around the first hour of the day, sometimes earlier but rarely later. My windows remain shut. It is amazing how the silence and darkness isolate me from the normal pressures of life, and so I am left to myself. In this way, I am free to visualize what I am thinking rather than allowing what I am thinking to be dictated by what I see. This phenom-enon can only take place, however, when there are no visual distractions to cause your eyes to take precedence over your mind. If I am currently working on a piece of writing, I ponder it. In this environment, I am able to work on it word for word as if I were writing or editing the work directly. Sometimes I can get through more, sometimes less, depending on how difficult the material is

that I am working on. I find that I am able to compose easily in this way and my mind is able to remember what I do. After that, I call in my secretary and open the window to let the sunlight in. I dictate what I have composed to the secretary. After a while, I send the secretary away, compose some more, call him back again, and then have him leave.

When the fourth or fifth hour has arrived (I don't keep to a tight schedule when I am in the country), depending on the weather, I will go to my patio or covered porch to think some more about my composition and dictate it to the secretary. I then get in my cart and take a ride. I continue writing, however, just as if I were taking a walk or reclining back in the house. I find that the mind is refreshed by such a change in physical activity. Later, I take a short nap and then go for a walk. Then I read aloud a speech in Greek or Latin. I do so clearly and with vocal intonation, not so much for the sake of my voice but rather for my digestion. In any case, both are strengthened by the exercise. Next, I take another walk, I bathe, I take some exercise, and then visit my private baths. If I have my dinner with my wife or a few of my friends, a book is read to me. After dinner, we watch a comic actor or listen to a musician. I then take a walk with my domestic staff, in whose number I have some educated persons. In this way, the evening is spent in various forms of conversation. Although summer days are the longest, nevertheless, they seem to go by quickly.

There are some occasions on which I will change elements of my daily routine. If I stay in bed later or take a longer walk, I will forgo the ride in the cart after my nap and take a ride on horseback instead because it is faster and takes less time. Sometimes friends from the neighboring towns will come to visit and they take up a part of the day. In many cases, the interruption can come at just the right time to give me a break. Sometimes I go hunting. Even then, however, I am not without my writing utensils to allow me to get some writing done. In that way, even if I don't catch any game, at least I won't come back empty-handed. I need to spend some time with the requests of my tenant farmers as well (although if you ask them, they would say that I don't spend enough time with them). I find that their rustic complaints make me think higher of my literary pursuits and the joys of an urban lifestyle. Good-bye.

#266: The Life of Simple Farmer

Appendix Vergiliana, the *Moretum*
First Century AD

The following text is the first part of a poem describing how a simple farmer began his day. His house and furniture are simple. Wheat seems to have been his primary crop.

It was the tenth hour of the night and the watchful rooster had crowed at the coming day when Simulus, farmer of a small plot of land, shuddering at the thought of the sorrowful hunger that would come with the arrival of daylight, lifts his arms and gradually climbs out of his squalid bed. His tired hand feels around in the lifeless shadows to find the hearth. At last his weary hand comes upon it. A tiny spark remained in a charred piece of wood and the ashes hid the light of the embers they covered. He bends his head over the coals and brings his lamp up to them. With a needle, he pulls out the dried wick. After a great deal of puffing he manages to get the flame going again. At last, he gets the fire going again and moves away. He takes his key and opens the front door of his home. He shields the fire from the wind from outside. On the ground was spread a meager pile of grain. From this, he picks up as much as he can carry, which amounts to sixteen pounds. Next he goes and sits at the mill and puts his lamp on the small shelf attached to the wall specifically for that purpose. He then pulls both of his arms out of his shirt and does his work wearing only a shaggy goatskin. He begins by sweeping with a broom the stones and interior of the mill. He then puts both of his hands to work, one for each part of the task. The left hand feeds the wheat into the mill while the right pushes the grinding stone over the grain to crush it. He moves the stone around and around in a circle. The grain, now crushed into flour, passes through the mill as the stone grinds it down quickly. Sometimes, he brings his left hand over to support his weary right hand and sometimes the right relieves the left. Once in a while, he sings a country song and makes his work lighter with his rustic voice.

The Rustic Labor Force

Although most agricultural land was owned by the aristocracy, it was poor farmers like Simulus (see #266) who worked the land. In early Roman times, independent farmers worked their own land, but as the *latifundia* grew, the aristocracy turned to hired hands and tenant farmers to serve as their workforce (as did Pliny the Younger, #268, and the emperor, #269). Slave labor figures prominently in Roman agricultural manuals such as those by Cato the Elder (second century BC) and Columella (first century BC). These authors were writing at a time, however, when constant warfare was flooding the market with slaves of all kinds. Cato mentions food and clothing allowances to slaves (#267).

#267: Food and Clothing Allowances to Slaves

Cato, *On Agriculture* 56–59
Mid-Second Century BC

The following text comes from the early agricultural manual written by Cato. The passage outlines the amount of food, wine, spreads for bread, and clothing that Cato recommends giving to farm hands and slaves to support them in their work on a large agricultural estate. The unit of grain measure used by the Romans was the *modius*, a unit equivalent to a little more than a peck or almost nine liters. The units for liquids described here are the *congius* (a little more than three liters) and the *sextarius* (about half a liter).

This is the recommendation for food for the *familia*. Those who do manual labor: four *modii* of grain in winter, four and a half in the summer. For the estate steward (*vilicus*), his wife, the overseer, and herdsman: three *modii*. For slaves kept in chains: four pounds of bread in the winter but they should receive five pounds from the time when they begin to cultivate the grapevines until the fig crop is harvested after which they should receive four pounds again.

This is the recommendation for wine for the *familia*. During the grape harvest, they should drink the *lora* wine (weak wine made from the grape skins) for three months. In the fourth month they should receive a half *sextarius* per day, that is two and a half *congii*. In the fifth, sixth, seventh, and eighth months: five *congii* per month, so about a *sextarius* per day. In the ninth, tenth, eleventh, and twelfth winter months, they should receive one and a half *sextarii* per day, so about an *amphora* per month (forty-eight *sextarii*/ eight *congii*). They should receive an additional allowance of three and a half *congii* combined for the Saturnalia and Compitalia festivals in December. Therefore, the total wine each person receives each year is equal to seven *amphorae* (fifty-six *congii*). For the chained slaves, a certain portion of wine is added to the rations listed above according to the amount of work they are doing at that time of the year. Ten *amphorae* per year is not too much for any one of them to drink.

This is the recommendation for bread spreads for the *familia*. First, keep any olives that have fallen from the trees as much as possible. Later, use the ripe olives as they yield the least amount of oil in the processing. Take care that these reserves last as long as possible. When they have eaten these olive stores, give them fish sauce and vinegar. Give each person one and a half *modii* of olives per month. A single *modius* of salt per person will be enough for the whole year.

This is the recommendation for clothing for the *familia*. Give them a tunic weighing three and a half pounds and a cloak every other year. When you give someone a new tunic or cloak, be sure to get their old one back as you can use the material to make hats. You should give them new wooden shoes every other year.

#268: Pliny and His Tenant Farmers

Pliny the Younger, *Letters* 9.37
Early Second Century AD

Freeborn tenant farmers who worked the land for their aristocratic owners were probably the most common type of agricultural laborers by the end of the first century AD. The use of such dependent farmers prevailed in the large, mostly imperial estates outside of Italy, but even in Italy, the more self-sufficient tenant farmers began to replace slaves whose food, clothing, and care were the responsibility of the master. In the passage here, Pliny the Younger mentions the tenant farmers (*coloni*) that worked on his estates.

I am currently unable to return to the city because I need to arrange the longer-lasting leases on my agricultural estate. There have been problems recently and I need to create a whole new method of doing the leases. Over the past lease period, many of the tenant farmers have been unable to meet their financial obligations and so have fallen into debt even after I relaxed their lease agreements. Many of them have given up trying to lessen their debt out of the belief that they will never be able to pay it off completely. Others have begun taking all of the crops for themselves and using it as they see fit because they have gotten it into their heads that there is no use in meeting their obligations to the owner of their land. I must therefore face the growing problem and come up with a solution. One possible remedy I am considering is to stop requiring the tenant farmers to pay their leases in coin but instead to allow them to pay by turning over a percentage of their crops. I would then have to allocate people from my staff as overseers of the harvest and guards for the crops. There is no fairer kind of revenue than what is produced by the earth, the weather, and the season. The drawbacks include the trust I will have to put in the tenants, the need for their overseers to watch the situation carefully, and the larger number of people I will have to allocate to this method in general. I must attempt this solution, however. When it comes to finding a cure for a disease that has lasted so long, nothing must be left untried.

#269: Imperial Response to the Complaints of Tenant Farmers

CIL 8.14464 (Bagradas, North Africa)
Reign of the Emperor Commodus (AD 180–192)

The following text comes from the province of North Africa, one of the most important wheat producers in the empire. The emperor owned much of the province. The territory was divided into districts and farmed almost exclusively by tenant farmers with imperial agents of equestrian status overseeing each district (called procurators). This text from the reign of the emperor Commodus is a letter to the emperor outlining how those agents had been mistreating the tenant farmers. Also included is the emperor's short response to the letter. The stone is badly carved and preserved so it is difficult to understand what is happening in places.

[The top of the text is missing] ... You should know of the plot that your procurator has hatched not only with our enemy Allius Maximus but also of almost all of the other agents working under him. They act not only against what is right but are also destructive to your financial pursuits in the area and go beyond what could be considered fair treatment. You should also realize that over the past several years he has not allowed us to come before him with our petitions or to send you a commission to ask for your assistance. He has given orders to his contractor Allius Maximus (with whom he enjoys a close personal friendship) to send soldiers to our district the Saltus Burunitanus. There, he has had some of the tenant farmers arrested, others beaten up, yet more chained up and has ordered that a few, Roman citizens even, be beaten with canes and clubs. In truth, all that we had done to deserve such treatment was that we had decided to send you a letter asking for your help in the face of such severe mistreatment and our own inability to do anything in our own meager power. On the basis of such clear evidence, Caesar, the judgment can easily be made that... [unintelligible section]... This fact has forced us, most wretched of humanity that we are, to ask for your divine help. Specifically, we request, most sacred emperor, that as it reads in the heading of the law of the emperor Hadrian which we included in our petition that neither the procurator nor his contractors be given the power to the detriment of the tenant farmers to increase the rents or the amount of work required. Instead, let them adhere to the stipulations in the letter sent to the procurators which is in the records office in the district of Carthage that every man be obligated to provide no more than two days of plowing, two of planting, and two of harvesting every year. These rents should not be in dispute since they are inscribed in bronze and are the rents that have been in force for all time up until the present day in all of the districts neighboring our own. They are also the rents dictated in the letter to the procurators mentioned above. Please come to our aid. We are but poor farmers who must achieve everything by the toil of our hands. We are no match for this contractor who has managed to ingratiate himself with your procurators through generous bribes and by giving large kickbacks through the changing of the lease policies they have with us. Have pity on us and send a response that requires us to provide no more than is stipulated in the law of Hadrian and the letters of your procurators, that is, three periods of time in which each man must work two days. We ask that you do this so that, through the benefaction of your majesty, we your farmers, born and raised on your country estates, may no longer be harassed by the contractors of the agricultural estates owned by you and live in peace.

The emperor Caesar Marcus Aurelius Commodus Antoninus Augustus Sarmaticus Germanicus Maximus to Lurius Lucullus and the other procurators associated with him: in keeping with fair practices I institute that each man be put under obligation of work no more than the usual three-day period of two days work each. Anything more that you require is wrong and against the established practice.

Chapter 17: The Baths

Visiting a public or privately owned bathhouse was one of the most popular activities in the Roman city after the workday was over. Bath buildings (in Latin, *balnea* or *thermae*) were a common feature of the urban landscape. Because only the richest citizens could afford indoor plumbing, it was necessary for the majority of the population to go outside the home to clean themselves. A visit to the baths could be a long process involving multiple pools with water of varying temperatures; exercise; and, perhaps most importantly, socializing (#271). Not surprisingly, the Romans considered the baths to be one of the pleasures of life (#270).

#270: The Pleasures of Life

CIL 6.15258 (Rome)
First or Second Century AD

Because of their costly and sumptuous nature, baths gained a reputation for immorality and excess. While cleanliness was valued, overindulgence and the lack of moderation when it came to visiting the baths were considered to be excessive. The following is a first century funerary inscription put up by a woman in honor of a man she calls her *contubernalis*, a term from the military meaning "tent mate." Slaves were not allowed to legally marry, so this term is often used instead of "husband" and "wife" in servile contexts.

> He lived 52 years. To the Spirits of the Dead of Tiberius Claudius Secundus. He has everything with him here in his tomb. Baths, wine, and sex corrupt our bodies, but baths, wine, and sex make life worth living. Merope, slave of the emperor, made this for her dear slave husband [*contubernalis*] as well as for herself and their descendants.

#271: A Day in the Life of the Baths

Seneca, *Letters* 56.1–2
First Century AD

In this passage, the author Seneca presents a humorous vignette of the noise from a bath complex located in the lower floors of his apartment building. Seneca here mentions a number of activities that took place in the baths. In addition to bathing and relaxing in pools, people could exercise, get massages, or be groomed. The baths were also a popular hangout for petty criminals who hoped to rob people's unattended clothes. There were even people selling food and drink. The noise coming from the baths, so odious to Seneca, was characteristic of a busy Roman bathhouse.

> I am done for if silence is as necessary as it seems for someone looking for quiet time for his literary pursuits. See how a cacophony of sound bombards me from every side. This is because I live upstairs from a bathhouse. Imagine now for yourself all the different voices that can cause your ears to prick in anger. The muscle men work out and throw around lead weights with their hands. I hear their groans as they exert all their effort (or pretend to do so). Every time they release their pent-up breath, I can hear their hissing and become extremely annoyed with their grunts. So too I can hear the smack of a masseur's hand as he slaps them on the shoulders of some lazy guy, content to be massaged with a cheap rubdown. The sound changes depending on whether the masseur's hand is opened or cupped. It is all over for my train of thought if a ball player shows up and begins to keep score aloud. Add now I hear the brawler, the thief who has been caught, and the man who loves the echo of his own voice in the bathhouse. Add now those who jump into the pool with a great splash. All of these people are annoying, but, if nothing else, at least they have normal voices. Notice the man with the armpits plucked clean of hair. I can hear him chattering now and then with his thin and high-pitched voice as he tries to get noticed. He never keeps himself quiet until he plucks someone else's armpits and makes them scream instead of him. Now I can hear the shouts of numerous sellers of drinks, sausages, and pastries and all the hucksters at the food stands selling their goods each with his own conspicuous melody.

The Bath Complex

A visit to the baths included a wide variety of activities. As a result, the bath building included multiple rooms. Because the bathing process involved water of various temperatures, the building had to be arranged to keep the rooms with the hotter water and saunas closer to the furnaces while colder rooms were kept farther away (Lucan mentions the variety of rooms in his description of a bath complex; #272). As the passage from Seneca quoted above (#271) illustrates, there were also areas designated for changing, exercising, eating, reading, socializing, and so on. As a result, bath buildings were complex and often large structures. The rich sometimes installed bath complexes in their own houses. The House of the Faun in Pompeii is an example of a house with its own bathing facility.

The most common type of bathing facility was the *balneum*, a privately owned bath building. These were relatively small and catered often to a restricted clientele and charged an admission fee. The much large public baths (*thermae*) were either free or charged a very small admission fee. These baths were open to the general public and were provided by the munificence of local aristocrats or the emperor (#279 gives some examples of bath construction inscriptions). The Forum Baths in Pompeii (#273), the Baths of Neptune in Ostia (#274 and #275), the bath complexes of

Agrippa (#276), and Diocletian (#277) in Rome fall into this category. These baths were made to be luxurious and were richly decorated with expensive materials and works of art (#278).

#272: Description of a Bath Complex

Lucian, *The Baths* 5–8
Second Century AD

In this passage, Lucian describes a fancy set of baths. He mentions all of the rooms and demonstrates how the heating would differ from one room to the next.

The building has a very tall door. The staircase leading up to the door has steps that are longer than they are tall to make it easier to climb them. The first room you come to is an entrance hall. It is very large and has plenty of room for the slaves and attendants. To the left of this room are some cubicles in which people can relax. They are perfectly suited to a bath building. They are nicely decorated and well lit. Next there is a corridor. It is larger than is really necessary, but the size is necessary for the rich clientele the *balneum* wishes to attract. Next, on either side of the building, there are changing rooms (*apodyteria*) in which people can undress. Between them runs a hall with a high ceiling and lots of light (*frigidarium*). Inside this hall there are three swimming pools with cold water (*piscina*). This hall is decorated with Laconian marble and contains two statues done in ancient style: one of the goddess Health and one of Aesculapius.

After leaving this hall you come into another hall that is a little warmer (*tepidarium*). In this way, the bather is not met with the hottest air from the furnaces but can ease into the warmth gradually. It is shaped like a wide oval and has a niche on each end of the room. To the right of this hall is the massage parlor. It has two entrances, the doors of which are decorated with marble from Phrygia. One entrance leads from the bathing hall and the other from the exercise yard (*palaestra*). Next is a hall that I think is the most beautiful in the entire world. Here, a visitor can sit or stand comfortably as long as he wishes without any danger or take a stroll to improve his health. This room is also decorated right to the roof with marble from Phrygia. Next is the fully heated *caldarium*. It is decorated with marble from Numidia. The next hall is very beautiful and is also well lit. It is decorated with purple decorations. It contains three tubs filled with hot water. After finishing in this room, the bather does not need to retrace his steps but can return directly to the cold room through a connecting corridor with warm air.

The entire complex is lit with natural light from windows. Every room is as high as it should be and the width is proportionate to the length. The complex has been decorated beautifully and everywhere one finds loveliness. As Pindar said, "Everything you construct should have a beautiful appearance." One of the main reasons for this is the amount of light that comes in from the abundant windows. The builder, Hippias, was clearly intelligent as demonstrated by the fact that he placed the cold rooms on the northern side of the building (though these rooms still have some exposure to the south) and the warmer rooms on the southern, eastern, and western sides. I do not need to mention how the exercise area and changing rooms are all connected and easily reached from the rooms for bathing, making everything convenient and without risk.

#273: The Forum Baths in Pompeii

First Century AD

The plan in Figure 17.1 shows the layout of the forum baths in Pompeii. There are two suites of rooms: one for men and one for women. The baths themselves are on the interior of the block and are accessed from doors on the left side of the plan. Shops surround most of the exterior of the block. One of the most important features for understanding the function of the various rooms is the location of the furnaces. In the forum baths, there is one large furnace (marked with a "U" on the plan). In order to distribute the hot air through the baths, the floor of rooms needing heat were lifted up onto brick or masonry piers, allowing air circulation beneath the room. This system, called a hypocaust, is visible in most existing Roman bath complexes. The room in each suite that is closest to the furnaces would then be the *caldarium* with

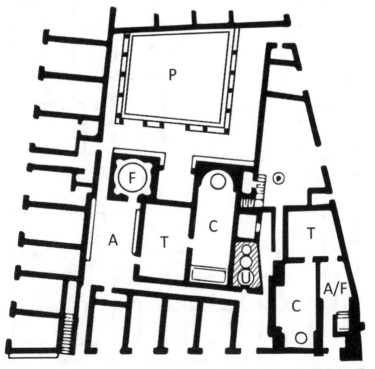

Figure 17.1 Plan of the Forum Baths of Pompeii (A: *Apodyterium*; F: *Frigidarium*; T: *Tepidarium*; C: *Caldarium*; U: Furnaces; P: *Palaestra*).

the hot water since the air in the hypocaust will be hotter ("C" on the plan). Farther away from the furnace is the *tepidarium*, or warm room ("T" on the plan). The *frigidaria* ("F" on the plan) are the farthest away. The entrances from the street open onto the *apodyterium* in each suite ("A" on the plan). In the men's plan, the *frigidarium* and *tepidarium* are both accessed from the *apodyterium*, but the *caldarium* is only accessible from the *tepidarium*. The *palaestra* ("P" on the plan) may have been for men only as it is accessible only through the *apodyterium* on the men's side.

#274: The Baths of Neptune

Second Century AD

The Baths of Neptune in Ostia stand in the northeastern part of the city north of the *decumanus*. Their construction was a joint effort by the emperors Hadrian and Antoninus Pius in the first half of the second century AD although they did replace an earlier, first century AD set of baths. People accessed the baths through the entrance on the right side of the plan (see Figure 17.2). From the *fauces*, the visitor

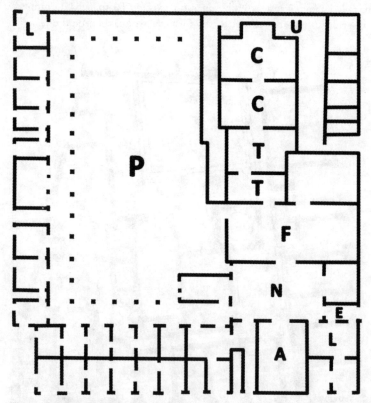

Figure 17.2 Plan of the Baths of Neptune of Ostia (E: Entrance; A: *Apodyterium*; N: Hall with the Mosaic of Neptune; F: *Frigidarium*; T: *Tepidaria*; C: *Caldaria*; U: Furnaces; P: *Palaestra*; L: Latrine) (Plan after R. Meiggs, *Roman Ostia* [Oxford], p. 412).

Figure 17.3 The *Frigidarium* of the Baths of Neptune, Ostia (Photograph by B. Harvey).

could go directly to a large public latrine or the central hall, which contains the large mosaic of Neptune and his retinue from which these baths got their modern name. The *apodyterium* opens off the central hall, as does the *frigidarium* (see Figure 17.3). The furnaces are in the upper right hand corner of the plan. These baths also have a doubling of rooms like the Forum Baths in Pompeii, but the rooms are ordered sequentially, so the division seems more to allow for a higher capacity rather than the separation of genders. As public baths, there were probably different times for men and women to bathe. The *caldaria* are closer to the furnaces. They are followed by the *tepidaria*. The large *frigidarium* is the farthest from the furnaces. These baths have a very large *palaestra* beyond the indoor complex.

#275: Dedicatory Inscription from the Baths of Neptune, Ostia

CIL 14.98 (Ostia)
AD 118

The Baths of Neptune in Ostia were constructed in the second century AD. The following inscription discovered in Ostia is generally believed to be the dedicatory inscription from the baths. The biography of Antoninus Pius in the *Historia Augusta* refers to that emperor's construction of a bath complex in Ostia (*Historia Augusta, Antoninus Pius* 8.3) and it seems those baths and the ones mentioned here are the same. The inscription here tells how Antoninus Pius continued work begun under his predecessor Hadrian.

The emperor Caesar Titus Aelius Hadrianus Antoninus Augustus Pius, Pontifex Maximus, holding the tribunician power for the second time, consul, son of the divine Hadrian, grandson of the divine Trajan Parthicus, great-grandson of the divine Nerva completed these baths. For their original construction, the emperor's divine father promised two million *sestertii*. The emperor added as much additional funding as was needed as well as more money so that the baths could be completely decorated in marble.

#276: Public Baths in Rome: The Baths of Agrippa

Dio Cassius, *History* 53.27.1 and 54.29.4
Written in the Early Third Century AD Describing the First Century BC

The baths built in the later first century BC by Augustus' general and close friend Agrippa were the largest and grandest in Rome at the time. Agrippa also constructed a new aqueduct to supply the baths with water, the *Aqua Virgo*, which was dedicated in 19 BC. These two passages from the *History* of the third century AD historian Dio Cassius refer to the early history of those baths. In the first passage, Dio documents the building projects of Agrippa. The second passage mentions how, after his death in 12 BC, Agrippa bequeathed his baths to public ownership and eliminated the admission fee. These became the first public baths (*thermae*), which were maintained at the expense of the emperor Augustus.

Agrippa spent his own money to beautify the city of Rome. In honor of his victories at sea, he constructed the Basilica of Neptune. He adorned this building with a painting of Jason and the Argonauts. He also built a new heated sauna that he called "Laconian" because at that time the Spartans were renowned above all others for their love of stripping naked, rubbing themselves down with oil, and exercising.

Agrippa was generous while he was alive. Even after his death, he remained a benefactor. In his will, he left to the people his gardens and the baths named after him. So that the people might use these baths without an admission fee, Agrippa left Augustus some agricultural estates, the profit from which would pay for the upkeep of the baths. Augustus did as Agrippa wished and even distributed to the people a gift of 400 *sestertii* per person and said that it was done as Agrippa himself had wished.

#277: Dedicatory Inscription from the Baths of Diocletian in Rome

CIL 6.31242 (Rome)
AD 299

Succeeding emperors continued to emulate Agrippa's act of beneficence to the Roman people by building larger and grander public bath structures. Nero built new baths in the Campus Martius, not far from those of Agrippa. Titus and then Trajan built baths on the slope of the Esquiline Hill overlooking the Colosseum. In the early third century, the emperor Caracalla built massive baths on a hill overlooking the *Via Appia* in the southeastern corner of the city. The last imperial public baths in Rome were those of Diocletian of the late third/early fourth centuries AD on the Viminal Hill, near the modern Termini train station. The church of Santa Maria degli Angeli, the Piazza della Repubblica, and the Museo Nazionale of Rome are built inside the shell of the ruins.

This fragmentary inscription documents the construction of those baths. Construction of the baths began in AD 299 and was completed just before the death of Constantius in AD 306.

> Our lords Diocletian and Maximian, unconquered senior emperors, fathers of emperors and Caesars, and our lords Constantius and Maximian (Galerius), unconquered emperors, and Severus and Maximinus, most noble Caesars, built these fortunate Baths of Diocletian. The emperor Maximian in person arranged the funding and gave the order for their construction after his return from Africa [AD 299]. He dedicated the baths in the name of his brother the emperor Diocletian. Existing structures in the area were purchased to make room for construction. The baths were constructed with every refinement as demanded by the greatness of the building and were given as a gift to the Roman people.

#278: Lysippus' Statue in the Baths of Agrippa

Pliny the Elder, *Natural History* 34.62 and 35.26
Written in the First Century AD Describing the Reigns
of Augustus and Tiberius (27 BC–AD 37)

Baths became synonymous with luxury. The baths, especially the great imperial *thermae*, were richly decorated with marble, columns, and artwork. In the following two passages, Pliny the Elder remarks how the Greek Lysippus' Apoxyomenos statue stood in front of the Baths of Agrippa. Indeed, such famous statues as the Laocoon, the Farnese Bull, and the Boxer were removed from the ruins of the baths of Caracalla in Rome during the Renaissance.

> Marcus Agrippa placed Lysippus' statue of the man anointing himself (the Apoxyomenos) in front of his baths. The emperor Tiberius liked the statue very much. At the beginning of his reign, although he generally was restrained in his exercise of power, nevertheless in the case of this statue he could not resist the temptation and moved the statue from the Baths of Agrippa to his bedroom. He put another statue up in its place, but the people became so angry that one day in the theater they chanted, "Give us back our Apoxyomenos." Tiberius, although he loved the statue very much, was obligated to return the statue to its original location.

#279: Texts Commemorating Baths Construction

As was the case of other examples of public construction we have seen so far, it was the private funds of the aristocracy that paid for public baths. Such acts of generosity made the benefactor stand out and earned him the approval of the people of his town. The following is a collection of texts commemorating newly constructed baths and the people who paid for them. The first mentions reconstruction of baths by the emperor Hadrian in Cyrene in North Africa. The second inscription commemorates new construction and renovation of existing baths in another town in North Africa. The third inscription comes from the Stabian Baths in Pompeii and documents work done in those baths by the year's *duoviri* in the first century BC.

AE 1928, 2

AD 118

The emperor Caesar Trajan Hadrian Augustus Pontifex Maximus, holding the tribunician power for the third time, consul for the third time, son of the divine Trajan Parthicus, grandson of the divine Nerva, ordered that the baths be restored for the city of the people of Cyrene along with the porticos, ball courts, and all nearby structures which had been thrown down and burned during the uprising of the Jews. (Cyrene, Cyrenaica)

CIL 8.23964

Second or Third Century AD

[Statues of] the Magniliani; Quintus Vetulenius Urbanus Herennianus, *flamen* for life, controller of city finances, built from the ground up a new *apodyterium* in the baths to the right as you leave the baths, two swimming pools, and other restored parts of the baths. He added marble statues, paintings, columns to the entrances of the various rooms, as well as other forms of decoration, all at his own expense in conjunction with his son Magnilianus, a most promising and prudent youth. At the dedication of the construction, he provided to all of the people of town a banquet lasting for three days along with some theatrical performances. (Boucha, Africa Proconsularis)

CIL 10.1635

First Century BC

Gaius Vulius, son of Gaius, and Publius Aninius, son of Gaius, *duoviri* with legal jurisdiction, saw to the construction of a new sauna and rubdown room and the restoration of the portico and *palaestra*. This work was down by decree of the town council out of the money that in the town charter was required to spend on games or in public construction. They began the work and oversaw the construction. (Pompeii, Italy)

The Bathing Ritual

A trip to the baths was generally considered to be a pre-dinner activity, and thus would fall between the end of the workday or the siesta and dinner (between the sixth and the ninth hours). The hot, warm, and cold rooms and the varied activities available meant that it was easy for a visitor to spend a considerable amount of time in the baths. In one of his letters, Seneca describes how the process had become significantly more complex since the early days of Rome's history (#280). Many saw the baths (and their overuse) as a symbol of the decadence of imperial Rome (#281).

Upon arriving at the baths, the customer would pay a small entrance fee if the establishment was under private ownership. Near the entrance was the changing room, the *apodyterium* (#282). The *apodyterium* had niches or cupboards high off the floor for holding the clothes of the bathers (guarded by the *capsarius*; #283). Complete nudity in the baths seems to have been the standard. While robes might have been used sometimes while exercising in the *palaestra*, even these would have been discarded when entering the bathing area.

Although surprising to modern sensibilities, mixed bathing of men and women was not uncommon in the Roman world of the first century AD. During the Republican period, either the women were prevented from using the baths or were compelled to use them at a different time from the men (#284; see #285 for Juvenal's criticism of a woman bather).

After undressing, the visitor of the baths would rub oil all over their body (or have a slave do it for him or her). The oil, it was believed, absorbed the dirt and grime, promoted greater opening of the pores, and encouraged sweating. Actual cleaning of the body, however, was not done in a pool, but involved scraping off the oil using an item called a strigil, a curved piece of metal with a wooden handle (#286).

An important part of many visitors' time at the baths was exercise in the open-air exercise yard, the *palaestra*. Although Greek-style athletics such as wrestling and boxing are attested, especially on mosaics from the baths, ball games were one of the most popular forms of exercise (#287). The famous Roman medical doctor Galen wrote an entire treatise on the advantages of exercising "with the small ball." Coming just before dinner, some people used the baths to get an invitation to a rich person's dinner party (#289). Also included is an inscription commemorating a young boy who drowned in a pool in the baths (#288).

#280: Evolution of the Bathing Process

Seneca, *Letters* 86.4–11
First Century AD

In this passage, Seneca describes his visit to the house of the historical hero of Rome, Scipio Africanus. While there, he sees the bath complex in the house. The simplicity of Scipio's baths gives Seneca an opportunity to contrast the baths in Scipio's day with those of his own time. In the process, Seneca reveals much about the Roman bathing ritual and how it had changed over time.

On my visit, I saw a villa built with large, carved stones. The wall encloses a forest of trees and towers erected on both sides to defend the villa. The water cistern is hidden away among the buildings and gardens but is large enough to supply water to an army. The villa had a tiny, narrow bath complex. It was a dark area in accordance with the belief of our ancestors that a person should not bathe in hot water except in the dark. It filled me with tremendous pleasure to compare Scipio's bathing ritual with our own. In this little niche the "Horror of Carthage," the man who saved Rome by keeping it from being captured by the enemy, would wash his body weary from its farm work. Indeed, Scipio engaged in agricultural pursuits (as was common for our ancestors). In my visit, I could not help but think how that great man once stood under this thatched roof. He once walked on this dirt floor. Nowadays, who would be able to endure bathing in such poor conditions? We think ourselves poor and disadvantaged if the walls of our baths do not shine with large and valuable mirrors, if the Egyptian marble is not contrasted nicely with Numidian mosaics, if the edges of those mosaics are not marked with elaborate designs like a painting, if the ceiling is not decorated with faience, if our swimming pools are not faced with stone from Thasos (once a rare sight one would only see in temples; now we jump into these pools with our bodies still wet with sweat), and if the water does not come out of silver faucets. The modern conveniences of which I speak are those found in the establishments of the common people. What could I say about the baths of freedmen? There you would see so many statues, so many columns that support nothing but are placed just for decoration and because they are expensive. Think also of the huge amounts of water that pours from one level of the baths to the one below with a crash. We have sunk to such a level of extravagance that we are not willing to walk on anything except precious gems.

These baths of Scipio have cuts in the wall that are more cracks than windows. These allow the light to get in but do not diminish the strength of the walls. In the present, however, people say that baths are only good for moths if they are not built so that very large windows allow in sunlight throughout the whole day. Modern Romans want to wash themselves and get a suntan at the same time. They also expect to be able to look from their tub across fields and seas. That is how fashion works. When something is new, it attracts crowds and their admiration. When luxury devises some new way of expressing itself, the old baths are tossed aside as an antique. In the old days, there were not many bath complexes and the ones that did exist were not adorned with much decoration. Our ancestors would have thought it too extravagant to use something that was more valuable than useful. People of those days did not have water poured over them nor did they always have fresh water running as if from a hot spring. "What do I care if the water is clean or not? I am just going to leave my dirt in it anyway." Good heavens, how refreshing it was to enter those baths even though they were so badly lit and covered with a rustic roof. I could just imagine the aedile, perhaps Cato or Fabius Maximus or one of the Cornelii themselves, checking the temperature of the water with his hands. In those days, the magistrates, even those from the noblest of families, had the duty of entering public baths and checking their cleanliness, usefulness, and healthy water temperature. In modern times, bath water in those places is like an inferno. In fact, the water is so hot nowadays that it would not be out of place to condemn a slave convicted of a crime to be bathed alive rather than burned. There seems to be no difference between saying that a bath is boiling hot and that it is warm.

Many people today criticize Scipio as a country bumpkin because he let sunlight into his hot baths through tiny windows and because he did not try to get a tan in all the sunlight and because he did not cook himself in his bath water. "Such a pitiful fool! He did not know how to live" people may say, "His water is not filtered. It is often cloudy and is almost muddy after a hard rain." Scipio wouldn't have cared what people were saying about his bathing habits. He would have told them that he went to the baths to wash off the sweat, not to anoint himself with expensive ointments.

#281: Excessive Use of the Baths

Juvenal, *Satires* 11.204–207
Late First/Early Second Centuries AD

As Seneca claimed in the previous passage, the baths had begun as a sign of the value Romans placed upon cleanliness but slowly evolved into another avenue for the pursuit of luxury. In this passage, Juvenal comments on how many people visited the baths earlier in the day than was customary. He adds the criticism that excessive bathing, even in the pursuit of luxury, would eventually lead to boredom. The biography of the infamous emperor Commodus in the *Historia Augusta* disparagingly describes him as taking seven or eight baths a day (*Historia Augusta, Commodus* 11.5).

These days, people do not blush when they go to the baths, even if it is still early, even a whole hour before noon. You would not be able to do so five days in a row, however. Such excess would just lead to boredom. Pleasure is more keenly felt if the experience is a rarer one.

#282: The *Apodyterium*

Martial, *Epigrams* 12.87
Late First Century AD

The baths had a reputation as a hangout for petty thieves who took advantage of the long absence of the patrons from the *apodyterium* to steal people's clothes. In this passage, one patron of the baths has come up with a cunning way to avoid losing his shoes.

Cotta complains that he has twice lost his shoes at the baths but yet he only brings a solitary slave with him. Unfortunately, this slave is not very good at paying attention. This poor slave must take the place of a whole crowd of servants, but Cotta is just a poor man. Although poor, Cotta is a sharp and cunning character. He came up with a way to avoid losing his shoes again. He decided to give up shoes altogether in the evening, even if it means going to dinner without them.

#283: The *Capsarius*

CIL 6.9232 (Rome)
Third or Fourth Century AD

Although the evidence is scanty, it seems that some baths posted guards in the *apodyterium* to prevent people stealing unattended belongings. The inscription here commemorates one of these guards (called a *capsarius* in Latin) from the Baths of Caracalla (the Antonine Baths) and his wife.

Cucumio and Victoria made this tomb for themselves while still alive. He was a *capsarius* in the Antonine Baths.

#284: Mixed Bathing

Pliny the Elder, *Natural History* 33.153
First Century AD

In the passage translated here, Pliny the Elder complains how Fabricius, a great general of the Republic, would frown to see the mixed bathing common in Pliny's day. Apparently, to accommodate this problem, two of the earliest baths in Pompeii, the Stabian and Forum Baths, had two sets of bath suites, one for women and one for men. The majority of the later, imperial baths, however, had no such provision. Either the genders had separate bathing hours, or mixed bathing was allowed.

What would the great Fabricius say if he were to see the women of our own time visiting baths coated in silver decoration from floor to ceiling and bathing at the same time as the men? In his day, Fabricius would allow no general of the Roman army to have more silver in his possession than a sacrificial bowl of saltshaker. He would cringe to see how the rewards of military courage are luxury items like these or the rewards are melted down to make such objects. Oh the morals of our times! Certainly Fabricius would be ashamed of us.

#285: A Woman Bather

Juvenal, *Satires* 6.419–429
Late First/Early Second Centuries AD

In this passage, Juvenal criticizes a woman for her brash bathing habits. She visits the sauna, exercises with weights, and gets a rubdown. All the while, her guests have been made to wait. When she finally does arrive, she makes a very negative impression as a result of overdoing it at the baths.

> She goes to the baths at night. It is only after she is done bathing that she orders her toiletries and army of attendants to make her up for the day. She just loves to sweat amidst all the hustle and bustle of the place. After her arms fall, weary from lifting heavy weights, a skillful masseur presses his fingers to her private parts and makes the upper thigh of his mistress smack with his hand. In the meantime, her miserable dinner guests are overcome with weariness and hunger. Finally she arrives, her face flush and thirsty enough to drink a whole tub of wine herself. A full urn of wine is brought up and placed before her feet. She drinks two full pints out of this before dinner and says it is to give her an appetite as if it were some kind of dainty aperitif. It is too much, however, and she soon brings it all up again and leaves the contents of her stomach on the floor.

#286: The Strigil

Historia Augusta, Life of Hadrian 17.5–7
Written Possibly in the Fourth Century AD Describing
the Emperor Hadrian (AD 117–138)

This passage is a humorous anecdote from the biography of the emperor Hadrian in which the one old man benefits from the kindness of the emperor.

> Hadrian frequently bathed in public, even with every class of society. From this practice, the following humorous anecdote of the baths began to circulate. One time, Hadrian saw a certain ex-soldier whom he had known from his days in the army. This man was rubbing his back and other parts of his body against a wall. Noticing this, Hadrian asked him why he was scraping himself against the wall rather than with a strigil. When the man told the emperor that he had to scrape himself this way because he did not own a slave, Hadrian gave the man

slaves and the money for their upkeep. The next day, however, when Hadrian returned, he saw several old men rubbing themselves against the wall in order to inspire a similar generous gesture from him. The emperor therefore ordered them to come away from the wall and take turns scraping each other instead.

#287: Trimalchio Plays Ball

Petronius, *Satyricon* 27–28
First Century AD

In the passage quoted here from the novel *Satyricon*, the author Petronius describes an odd ballgame played by the gaudy freedman Trimalchio. He and some of the other characters from the novel had gone to the baths before the dinner party Trimalchio was holding at his house. Like with so many of his activities, Trimalchio wanted to advertise his wealth but instead showed his lack of good taste.

While waiting for dinnertime and dressed in our finest, we began to wander. We dawdled for a time and then went toward the ball court. Suddenly, we saw a bald old man wearing only a red tunic. He was playing ball with a group of boys with long hair. It was not the boys that caught our attention (although they certainly deserved a second look) but rather the old man. He was wearing his slippers and exercising with a green ball. Every time the ball fell to the ground he would not go to fetch it himself, but a slave with a full bag of balls would supply a new ball to the group as they played their game. We noticed a few other innovations in their game as well. Two eunuchs were standing in different parts of the court. One of them was holding a chamber pot. The other was keeping score. The score he was keeping, however, was not of the number of times that the ball passed from the hand of one player to another but rather how many times a person missed the ball. While in awe we were watching this display of extravagance, our friend Menelaus ran up and said, "This is the man with whom you will be having dinner. Indeed, what you are witnessing is the opening act of his dinner show." As soon as Menelaus had finished speaking, Trimalchio snapped his fingers. At this signal, the eunuch with the chamber pot ran up to him. Without stopping the game, Trimalchio emptied his bladder into the pot and asked for water to wash his hands. He put a little water on his fingers and ran them through the hair of one of the boys.

It would take too long to go over all of the details, so I will be brief. We entered the baths. We stayed in the sauna until we started to sweat and then entered the *frigidarium*. By now, Trimalchio had been oiled up and was being rubbed down, not with linen rags but with expensive cloth made from the softest wool. Three masseurs were drinking valuable Falernian wine in front of him. They began to argue and a large quantity of the wine was spilt. Trimalchio saw it and said that they were drinking to his health. Finally, he was dressed in a scarlet cloak and put into a litter. Four runners wearing metal ornaments went before his litter to clear the path. Trimalchio's pet slave had his own little cart. This boy had an ugly face like an old man and his eyes were runny. Indeed, he was uglier than his master Trimalchio. While Trimalchio was making his way through town in this way, a musician walked behind him with a tiny flute. The man played this instrument the whole journey right into the ear of Trimalchio as if he were telling him a secret.

#288: An Accident at the Baths

CIL 6.16740 (Rome)
First to Third Centuries AD

The baths could be a dangerous place. The following text commemorates a young boy who drowned in a swimming pool.

Daphnus and Chryseis, freedmen of Laco, put this up to their little boy Fortunatus. He lived eight years. He drowned in the swimming pool at the baths of Mars.

#289: Fishing for a Dinner Invitation

Martial, *Epigrams* 12.82
Late First Century AD

Many people, like Trimalchio, used the baths as a precursor to dinner. In the passage translated here, some people use their trip to the baths as an opportunity to score a dinner invitation for themselves from a friend or acquaintance.

It is not possible to escape Menogenen in the public or private baths. You can try every trick in the book, but it won't work. In the middle of a game of catch with the small ball, he will stand behind you and vigorously catch in his left and right hands any of the balls you miss so that you can score more points. If you miss any of the large balls, he will go and get them out of the dust and bring them back to you even if he has already washed and is wearing his shoes. If you pick up your towel, he will say it is whiter than snow, even if it is more soiled than a baby's dirty diaper. While you comb what little is left of your hair, he will say that you are arranging hair as full as that of Achilles. He will bring you a glass of wine from the dregs of a smoky cask and continuously wipe the sweat from your forehead. He will constantly praise everything that you do. He will express his admiration as well. Finally, wearied by his incessant attention, you say, "come to dinner."

Chapter 18: Dinner Parties

The last event of the day's activities was dinner (*cena*). The *cena* was the largest of the day's meals. Indeed, most Romans had not eaten anything substantial since they had awoken that morning. Although some dinner parties could go on late into the night, the customary dinner time (a few hours before sunset, the eighth or ninth hour) allowed people to finish eating and be ready for bed by sundown.

Dinner was also the most communal of meals, as it tended to be the one meal the whole family would enjoy together. Frequently, dinner was shared also with friends, clients, or acquaintances. Dinners ranged from small, intimate affairs to grandiose events.

Because the houses of poorer families were small and rarely had kitchens, dinner was either purchased from a local eatery or cooked in a portable brazier. Aristocratic houses, however, had their own kitchens and often a specialized servile household staff, which could include butchers, chefs, bakers, servers, and entertainers.

The *Triclinium*

The largest room in the house, whether it be the large, well-lit room at the end of the central hall in a *medianum*-style apartment or one of the spacious rooms off the peristyle in an atrium-style house generally served the purpose of a dining room. Although many people sat on chairs at tables to eat the *cena* (particularly the lower classes), those with the means and desire could purchase the required dining-room furniture for what was called a *triclinium*. *Triclinium* literally meant "three couches" in Latin. In this arrangement, three couches were set up around a table in a "U"-shape pattern with the heads toward the center and the feet toward the outside. Each couch was wide enough to accommodate three diners side-by-side. A small table placed in the center was therefore accessible to all three couches. The servants could reach the table from the side without a couch.

Because dinner parties were one of the most important social functions held within an aristocratic house, a great deal of effort was put into the decoration and location of the dining room so as to create a suitable environment not only for comfort but also to delight the guests and impress them with the refinement of the host. Creating a sense of an open, natural environment was frequently the decorative goal within a *triclinium*. In *atrium* and courtyard-style houses, most *triclinia* were located off the peristyle so that the garden would serve as a backdrop to the dinner party (#290). In the House of the Vettii in Pompeii, the main *triclinium* sits on axis with the center of the peristyle. The large dining room of the House of Fortuna Annonaria in Ostia (equipped with an apse in a much later, fourth century AD renovation) was similarly located along the long axis of the courtyard.

Outdoor dining rooms were quite common as shown by the excavations of Pompeii. These *triclinia* were frequently placed in gardens under an awning, often near outdoor shrines or fountains. In city houses, the closeness of the neighboring houses forced dining rooms to be resourceful with wall painting and other decorative elements to create artificial scenes of nature. In country villas, however, dining rooms frequently looked outward toward the countryside (#291 describes Pliny the Younger's *triclinium* in his villa in Tuscany).

#290: The Location of the *Triclinium*

Vitruvius, *On Architecture* 6.4
First Century BC

In this passage, Vitruvius describes the theory behind the placement of the *triclinium* inside of the house. It was common in aristocratic houses for there to be numerous *triclinia*, including ones designated as summer and winter dining rooms. The first would take advantage of the summer breezes to cool the dining room. The winter *triclinium* was generally more sheltered and warmer.

> Next I will discuss the specific characteristics of type of rooms as applies to their function and their relationship to the weather and season. Winter *triclinia* and baths should face the sun as it sets during the winter so that it can benefit from the sunlight in the late afternoon and more importantly to receive the light from the setting sun which in turn warms these rooms in the evening when they are being used. *Cubicula* and libraries ought to face the east because these rooms benefit most from light in the morning. The books in the library are less likely to get moldy as well because rooms that face the south and west are more likely to have problems with worms and dampness due to the moist winds that foster vermin and cause the books to get wet and spoil. Spring and autumn *triclinia* should face the east. As long as the windows are kept closed until the afternoon, they can stay cool until the time of day when they are used. Summer *tricilinia* should face north because with that orientation they do not receive heat during the summer solstice. Turned away from the rays of the sun, they are always cool and healthy and provide the greatest enjoyment during the hot months of the year.

#291: The *Triclinium* in Pliny's Villa in Tuscany

Pliny the Younger, *Letters* 5.6.19
Early Second Century AD

In this passage, Pliny describes the situation of one of the *triclinia* in his villa in Tuscany. This dining room took advantage of the peristyle setting and the villa's natural surroundings. As Pliny's description exemplifies, the mixture of open meadows and wooded groves added to the appeal of the vista. In the description of his villa at Laurentum translated earlier, Pliny says how his summer *triclinium* directly over-looked the sea.

> At the primary end of the portico stands a *triclinium*. From here is visible through folding doors the far end of the courtyard and, beyond that, a meadow and a good deal of the countryside. From the windows of this room one can see the side of the courtyard and the section of the villa that sticks out from the main part of the building. Also visible are the groves and trees that surround the nearby hippodrome.

Invitations to Aristocratic Dinners

Dinner invitations were exchanged between members of the aristocracy as favors and marks of prestige and political connection. Patrons might invite clients as a reward for faithful service. A more prestigious host might invite a protégé to allow him to interact with other important people (#295 from Juvenal's satires describes the mistreatment of social inferiors at a dinner party; in #296, Pliny the Younger warns hosts against such treatment). A client or protégé could also invite his patron to dinner in order to curry favor and try to improve his position in the eyes of his patron (although if the disparity in prestige between host and prospective guest was too great, the invitation was usually declined). Often, a person would invite to dinner his social equal, more akin to a true "friend" in the modern sense, with the expectation that his friend would return the favor and invite him to dinner in the near future. Dinner parties were popular settings in Roman literature. As such, literary invitations to dinner are quite common in surviving authors (#292, Martial; #293, Catullus; #294, Pliny the Younger).

#292: The Promise of a Good Dinner

Martial, *Epigrams* 5.78
Late First Century AD

Dinner parties were popular settings in Roman literature. In the poem here, the poet Martial invites his friend Toranius to dinner. He promises a variety of simpler types of food, drink, and entertainment. This poem includes a long list of foods, an often-appearing element in the literary motif of invitations to a dinner party.

> If you hate the thought of a dreary dinner in your own home, Toranius, you can come and be hungry with me. If it is an appetizer that you want, you will find on my table some cheap Cappadocian lettuce, plain leeks, and bits of young tuna fish hidden away in eggs cut in half. Green cabbage sprouts freshly picked from the chilly garden will be served on a black serving platter for you to eat with your oily fingers. There will also be little sausages in white porridge

and pale beans with red bacon. If you ask for a second course, you will be served some dried grapes and pears of the variety called "Syrian" and roasted chestnuts produced in cultured Naples. The wine I will serve you will recommend by drinking it. After all of this, if the wine has made you hungry again, I will serve some high quality olives that only recently still hung on the branch in Picenum. You will also get some hot chickpeas and heated lupines. No one can deny that this is merely a light snack. When you have dinner with me, however, you can be yourself. You will not be told any lies and you can recline at the table without having to worry about acting a certain way. Your host will not pull out his unedited magnum opus and read it aloud to you nor will lecherous girls from immoral Gades shake their lascivious arms and legs during a dance they have practiced to perfection. The pipes of my slave Condylus will play a tune that is light and pleasant. Such is my little dinner. My guest Claudia will recline in the highest position. You will recline below her. Whom would you like to invite to recline above me?

#293: Catullus' "Invitation" to Dinner

Catullus, *Poems* 13
First Century BC

Catullus, the first century BC love poet, wrote a similar poem addressed to his friend Fabullus. In the poem, Catullus pleads poverty but still promises a good experience.

If the gods favor you, my friend Fabullus, you will dine well in my house in just a few days' time. Just make sure to bring a good and sizable meal with you. Remember also to not arrive without a good-looking girl and some wine, salt, and all of the jokes you can muster. If you will bring all of that, my charming friend, you will dine well. You see, the wallet of your comrade Catullus is full of cobwebs. In return for your generosity, you will receive my undying love or whatever you would consider to be sweeter or more refined. I will also give you some perfume, which Venus and Cupid gave to my girlfriend. Indeed, when you smell it, Fabullus, you will ask the gods to make you all nose.

#294: An Invitation Refused

Pliny the Younger, *Letters* 1.15
Early Second Century AD

In this letter addressed to the equestrian Septicius Clarus, the man to whom he dedicated his published letter, Pliny the Younger plays with the traditional literary motif of the dinner invitation to criticize his friend for refusing his dinner invitation. The letter is filled with mock anger as Pliny complains that Clarus refused only because he preferred to dine at the house of someone who was offering rare, gourmet delicacies, treats too expensive for Pliny to afford.

Hey! You promised to come to dinner, but you did not come! I have come to a verdict and here is your punishment: you will repay me down to the last penny for the expense (and that isn't small). For each of us I had prepared courses that included one head of lettuce, three snails, two eggs, and fish soup with mead and snow. Indeed, the first step in your punishment will be to pay recompense for the snow, because it melts in the dish. There were also olives, beets, gourds, onions, and a thousand other things no less refined. You would have heard a comic actor; a reading; a lyre player; or, as is characteristic of my generosity, all of them. You, however, preferred the oysters, sow's wombs, sea urchins, and Spanish dancers in the house of someone else.

#295: Treatment of a Social Inferior at Dinner

Juvenal, *Satires* 5.12–25, 30–37, 80–91
Late First/Early Second Centuries AD

Not all of the guests at dinner parties were of such close social status. At times, patrons would invite their lower-class clients. Such an invitation was undoubtedly a rare delight for the client, who was given the opportunity to eat the delicacies and enjoy the entertainments usually reserved for those of higher social standing. All too often, however, it seems, the pleasure of such occasions was tempered in that the host used the dinner to remind the client of his lowly status. In the passage translated here, Juvenal contrasts the experience of the client and his less-than-generous patron at such a dinner. Because one of the most important aspects of throwing a dinner party was to impress the guest, some hosts thought it unnecessary to impress guests of lower status.

Imagine this scene first. You have been invited to come to dinner and your first thought is that it is repayment for your long-time good service to your patron. It is true; the food you receive is the profit gained from your relationship with him. Indeed he does reckon your invitation as repayment. The invitation is a rare event indeed, but he still counts it against you. "This guy has been my client for two months" he thinks to himself, "so I will invite him since I haven't invited him before. Besides, I don't have anyone else to fill the third couch." And so, at the end of the day, he says "come to dinner with me," and you think that this is an answer to your prayers. What more could you want? At last you have your reward for all those days you woke up in the middle of the night to go to your patron's *salutatio* in a rush with your sandals falling off because you are afraid that he and the mob of his other clients may have already left the patron's house to go on the day's rounds in town. You must do this even while the stars are just beginning to disappear in the light of dawn and you can see the winter constellation of Bootes in the sky above you. Then, once you are at dinner, you come to realize the reality of your invitation. The wine you are given is so bad that even a sponge refuses to soak it up. Your patron is a different story. He drinks wine that was bottled in the days when consuls still grew their hair long. The grapes in his cup were crushed 150 years earlier. He is stingy with that vintage though. He would never even send a cup to an ailing friend. Tomorrow he will drink a wine produced in the Alban Hills or in the town of Sentina in north Italian wine country. The age and place of origin of these wines will be difficult to read because the dust has eroded the labels. This is the kind of wine that the stoics Thrasea Paetus and Helvidius Priscus used to drink the toast on the birthdays of Cassius and the two Brutuses who assassinated Julius Caesar.

A lobster is brought out to the host. See how its long body adorns the platter. It is surrounded on all sides by asparagus. With its long tail it looks down upon the other diners from on high as a tall slave brings it in to give to the host alone. All you get is a crab garnished with half an egg, the kind of dinner you would expect at a funeral. Your host pours over his fish expensive olive oil from Venafrum. All the miserable client gets are some pale stems of lettuce that smells like an oil lamp. Everything that you have been served was brought to Rome in a rowboat from North Africa. In Rome, that smell prevents everyone from wanting to be in the same bath complex as one of those boatmen, but at least it keeps away poisonous snakes.

#296: Warning Against Class Distinction at Dinner

Pliny the Younger, *Letters* 2.6.1–5
Early Second Century AD

While surely an exaggeration, it would seem that dinner parties with a mixture of social classes would often include methods to maintain decorum and remind people of their social position. Like in the baths, the more humble guests could see how the "other half" lived, yet were kept at a suitable distance. Pliny the Younger, ever trying to set himself up as the paragon of aristocratic moderation, frowned upon the kind of overt differentiation between dinner guests that Juvenal described in his satire.

It would take too long to explain (nor does it really matter) how I came to have dinner at the home of a certain man with whom I only have a passing acquaintance. This man seemed in his own eyes to be refined yet frugal. To me, however, he seemed rather vulgar and extravagant. At dinner, he served very rich meals to himself and a few others. To the rest of the diners, however, he served cheap meals with small portions. Wine was served in three small bottles with each bottle containing a different quality of wine. The reason for this was not to give the guests the luxury of choosing what they would like to drink but rather to remove any chance of refusing what was given to each person. To himself and to some of us he gave one type of wine. His lesser friends got another kind (even his friends are graded) and the third kind was given to our freedmen. The man reclining next to me also saw what was happening and asked whether I approved. I told him I didn't. "What do you do about people of different social statuses at your dinner parties then?" he asked. I replied, "I serve everyone the same food and wine. I invite people to eat dinner, not to be discriminated socially. I make all my guests equal in all things." "Even the freedmen?" the man asked. "Even them," I replied, "I consider them my fellow diners rather than freedmen when they eat with me." The man said, "that must cost you a lot of money." "Not at all," I replied. "How is that possible?" he asked. "Because my freedmen do not drink the same wine I would usually drink, but rather when I dine with them, I drink the kind of wine my freedmen would drink." Look. It is like this. If you can moderate your tastes, it is not a difficult thing to share with many other people what you yourself enjoy. It is your tastes that must be restrained. It is your tastes that must be kept in line, so to speak. If you want to save money, then you should consider tempering your tastes a little before resorting to being rude to your dinner guests.

Luxurious Dinner Parties

Much like the rest of aristocratic life, dinner parties were a time for the rich to advertise their wealth and power. A great deal of time, effort, and money went into preparing for the event. Roman literature is littered with accounts of extravagant dinner parties. Plutarch says that in the late Republic, the senator Lucullus held a dinner party costing two hundred thousand *sestertii*. Of course, it should be kept in mind that in the first century AD, a family of four could live at subsistence level for a *year* for a mere eight hundred *sestertii*. Such expenditure, even by the aristocracy, was unusual and generally only merited mention because it was so exceptional and extravagant even in the realm of aristocratic self-promotion. This section includes some examples of extravagant dinner parties and criticisms of them. Seneca complains of the emperor Caligula's excessive dinner parties (#297). The *Historia Augusta* includes spending on dinner parties as one of Lucius Verus' vices (#298). On the other hand, Suetonius says that Augustus was much less extravagant (#299). Finally, I have included some excerpts from the infamous Dinner of Trimalchio scene in Petronius' novel, *Satyricon* (#300).

#297: Extravagance at Dinner

Seneca, *Consolation to Helvia* 10.2–4
First Century AD

In this passage, Seneca complains about luxurious dinner parties. Because dinner parties were one of the most important ways for an aristocrat to express his wealth and power, it was only natural for the host to attempt to outdo his peers with tasty treats and luxury. As a result, aristocratic competition sometimes led to escalating displays of extravagance. In another passage (*Letters* 95.41), Seneca puts the expense of these dinner parties into perspective and claims that some aristocrats were spending the equivalent of the property qualification for entrance into the equestrian order (two hundred fifty thousand *sestertii*) or even into the senate (one million *sestertii*). Emperors naturally set a new standard of luxury. In this passage, Seneca tells of Caligula's excessiveness.

It is not necessary to scour the whole sea, to weigh down the belly with piles of dead animals, or to dig up shellfish from some unknown shore on the most distant sea. May the gods and goddesses curse those people whose reputation for luxury already extends beyond the boundaries of an empire already envied! They wish to bring to their kitchens game from beyond the Phasis River in the far east. They are not even ashamed to import birds from Parthia, a nation on which we have not exacted full vengeance for past military disasters. They bring from everywhere every food that has ever been known just to feed their demanding appetites. Of course, their stomachs, weakened from their delicacies, are barely able to keep down what is brought from the farthest ocean. Indeed, they vomit so they can eat, and eat so they can vomit. The dishes for which they scour the whole world they think unworthy to be digested.... It seems that nature produced the emperor Gaius Caesar merely to demonstrate how supreme vice could follow supreme power. On one dinner party alone he once spent ten million *sestertii*. Everyone in his court exercised their talents to find ways to spend all that money at once, but even so he found it difficult to spend the equivalent of the tribute of three provinces on one meal. How unfortunate are those people whose palate is stirred by nothing except the most costly of foods!

#298: An Extravagant Dinner of Lucius Verus

Historia Augusta, Life of Lucius Verus 5.1–6
Written Possibly in the Fourth Century AD Describing
the Emperor Lucius Verus (AD 161–169)

This passage describes one especially extravagant dinner held by Lucius Verus, the co-emperor of Marcus Aurelius. The author of the *Historia Augusta* often contrasts the virtuous Marcus Aurelius with the decadent Lucius Verus. In the case of this passage, Lucius Verus' extravagance is in direct contrast to Marcus' frugality.

One of the dinner parties of Lucius Verus is especially notorious. This was the first time that twelve people sat in a single *triclinium*, despite the fact that there is a well-known maxim about dinner parties that says, "the presence of seven people makes a dinner party but nine just makes a lot of noise." The handsome boys that were doing the serving he gave as gifts to the diners. Meat carvers and serving platters were also given out to the guests as well as live animals both wild and tame and both bird and land animals of the types that had been served as food during the course of the meal. He also gave out as party favors drinking cups made of myrrh and crystal from Alexandria. Each guest received one every time he drained his cup. He also gave out gold, silver, and gemmed bowls. The guests received garlands woven with golden ribbons and containing flowers that were out of season. Guest also received golden vases in the shape of perfume boxes containing various ointments. There were even gifts of carriages with silver harnesses that included the mules and drivers to allow the diners to return home in style. The cost of this dinner party has been estimated at six million *sestertii*. When Marcus heard about this party, he is said to have groaned and wept for the fate of the world.

#299: Augustus' Eating Habits

Suetonius, *Augustus* 76–77
Written in the Early Second Century AD Describing
the Emperor Augustus (27 BC–AD 14)

Not every emperor was a glutton or wasteful with his money. In this passage from Suetonius' biography of the emperor Augustus, we learn that Augustus was quite restrained with his expenditure on his own dietary needs.

Augustus preferred to eat only light and cheap meals. He preferred second-rate bread, small fish, buffalo cheese pressed by hand, and green figs from the second harvest. He would eat also before dinner time whenever and wherever he felt hungry. I have found some phrases of his in his letters: "We ate some bread and dates in the carriage" and "While I was coming home in a litter from the forum, I ate a piece of bread and a few grapes with tough skins" and "Not even a Jew refrains from eating on the Sabbath as much as I did today, my dear Tiberius. I ate only two mouthfuls and that was only after the first hour of the night while I was in the baths and about to be rubbed down with oil." His own need to eat does not seem to have preoccupied his thoughts. He often would eat dinner alone either before the beginning of a dinner party or after it was over. During the dinner itself, he would often not eat anything at all. He was by nature very moderate in his drinking of wine. The writer Cornelius Nepos reports that while he was on military campaign at Mutina during the civil wars he was in the habit of drinking no more than three cups of wine during dinner. Even later when he was emperor and was indulging himself most, he never drank more than a full measure. If he did drink more, then he would throw it up again. He was most fond of wine from Raetia but he rarely drank anything during the day. Usually, if he was thirsty, he would soak some bread in cold water or eat a slice of cucumber, some lettuce leaves, or a tart apple that was either fresh or dried.

#300: The Dinner of Trimalchio

Petronius, *Satyricon* 31, 34, 35, 49, 53
First Century AD

The primary example of an opulent dinner party is the narrative in Petronius' *Satyricon* of the dinner hosted by the freedman Trimalchio. As a former slave who had earned his vast wealth through business, Trimalchio embodies everything the old aristocracy found distasteful in the freedmen *nouveau riche*. Trimalchio's wealth allows him to compete with the sumptuous spreads of the aristocracy, and his conscious effort to outdo them causes him to commit uncouth social *faux pas*. The following are some excerpts of Petronius' account of the fictional dinner party.

Finally we took our places in the *triclinium*. Boys from Alexandria poured water cooled with snow over our hands. Other boys followed them and removed hangnails from our feet with the greatest skill. Even in this unpleasant task the boys were not silent but kept singing while going about their business. I wanted to find out whether the whole *familia* of slaves could sing, so I asked for a drink. The slave with the wine jug answered my request with a song no less shrill. Every slave that was asked to do anything also sang. You would think you were at a theater performance rather than in the house of a private family. Some very refined hors d'oeuvres were brought out. Everyone had taken his or her place at the table except for Trimalchio himself. In a reversal of custom, the first place was being reserved for him instead of the most important guest. The figure of a donkey made of Corinthian bronze with twin saddlebags was brought out on a serving tray. It had white olives in one bag and black olives in the other. Two silver dishes were on the back of the donkey. On the edges of these dishes was inscribed the name of Trimalchio and their weight. Little bridges glued to the dishes held dormice dipped in honey and poppy seeds. There were also sausages placed over a hot grate and plums from Syria and pomegranate seeds beneath the grate...

Next, glass jars covered with gypsum were brought to the table. On the necks was fixed a label that read "Falernian wine from the consulship of Opimius; 100 years old." While we were reading the label, Trimalchio clapped his hands and said, "Look! This wine has lived longer than a pitiful human being. So let us drink and be merry. Wine is life. I present to you a real wine from the consulship of Opimius. The stuff I put out yesterday was not as good and I was dining with people of much higher status." As we were drinking and marveling at the delicacies with our full attention, a slave brought in a skeleton made of silver. It was constructed in such a way that the backbone was flexible and every part of it could be bent...

The next dish to be brought out was not as large as I expected it to be, but the novelty did catch everyone's attention. The round serving tray had the twelve signs of the zodiac arranged in a circle. Over each sign the artist had placed food that was proper and fitting to the sign. There were ram chickpeas over Ares, pieces of beef over Taurus, testicles and kidneys over Gemini, a crown over Cancer, an African fig for Leo, a sow's uterus over Virgo, a scale holding a pastry on one side and a cake on the other side for Libra, a small fish from the ocean over Scorpio, a crab over Sagittarius, a marine lobster over Capricorn, a goose over Aquarius, and two mullets over Pisces. In the middle of the plate was a tuft of sod with grass growing over it holding a honeycomb. A boy from Egypt was carrying bread around the table in a silver breadbasket...

Trimalchio had not yet finished saying everything he had planned to say when a serving tray with a huge pig was placed on the table. We began to marvel at the speed with which the pig had been cooked [they had chosen the pig only a short time earlier]. We swore that not even chicken can be cooked so quickly. We were all the more suspicious because the pig on the platter seemed to be much larger than the boar we had seen just a short time ago. Trimalchio repeatedly looked at the pig and said, "What? This pig is not even gutted? By god! It isn't. Get the cook out here right now!" A cook with a sorry look on his face was brought to the table. He admitted that he had forgotten to gut the pig. "How could you forget such a thing?" Trimalchio exclaimed, "From the way he speaks you would think he had merely forgotten to season the beast. Prepare this man for a good beating!" Without delay, the cook had been stripped of his clothing and stood frowning between two torturers. Everyone began to intercede on the cook's behalf saying, "Mistakes happen. Please forgive the man. If he does the same thing again, none of us will speak on his behalf." My idea of severity tends toward cruelty and I was not able to restrain myself, so I leaned over and whispered into the ear of Agamemnon, "Certainly this cook is a worthless slave. What kind of cook would forget to gut a pig? By god, I would not forgive him even if he had merely forgotten to gut a fish." Trimalchio's expression by this time had softened into a smile. He said, "Therefore, since your memory is so bad, gut the pig right here in front of us." The cook put his clothes back on and pulled out a knife. He cut the belly of the pig from one end to the other with a trembling hand. Without delay, the slit widened from the pressure and sausages and black puddings poured out...

Finally the acrobats arrived. A mindless simpleton stood holding a ladder and called out to a boy to climb the rungs and dance a jig on the very top. Then he jumped through burning hoops and finally held up in the air an amphora with only his teeth. Only Trimalchio was impressed by this display, and he claimed that acrobats were artists that never got the praise they deserve. "There are only two things in all of human existence," he said, "that really please me to watch: acrobats and horn players. Everything else, including animals and plays, is sheer nonsense. I once bought a comedy troupe, but I preferred them to do Atellan plays. I also ordered my flute player to play only songs in Latin."

Chapter 19: Bars and Inns

Dinner parties were a wonderful way to spend an evening in town for the small percentage of Romans who were either wealthy enough to host a *cena* or sufficiently well connected to receive an invitation. The lower-class poor who chose not to spend a quiet evening at home, however, had other options in the city. A stroll through the ruins of Ostia or, especially, Pompeii reveals numerous public eateries. These special shops were characterized by the ubiquitous bar counter facing the street. These counters had large jars set into them so that the lip of the jar just reached over the countertop. In these jars, wine, hot and cold water, as well as stews and sauces were stored for sale to customers. These establishments ranged in size from tiny street-side stands with few options to large restaurants, with several rooms and sometimes internal gardens in which customers could dine in comfort.

Eating and Drinking Establishments

Popina was the term for a restaurant that only offered drinks and food but not lodgings. The lack of sleeping accommodations for the traveler was what separated a *popina* from a *caupona*, an inn.

Popinae were usually located along busy streets. They did business during the day by providing quick lunches to hungry workers on their way to their afternoon activities. Their most important business, however, came in the evening when people might stop in for wine, company, or a more substantial meal (see #304 for wine).

Because the upper classes would generally dine at their own home or a friend's dinner party, the *popinae* focused on attracting the lower classes. Because of this, bars were often depicted in upper-class literature as having a bad reputation (#307 and #308). The presence of gambling did not help their reputation (#309). Graffiti from Pompeii's bars reflect some of the more candid statements from the town's inhabitants and visitors (#301). The barmaid was a stereotypical fixture of the *popina* (#302 and #303). This section includes a few examples of bars: the bar near the Forum Baths in Pompeii (#305) and the House of the Thermopolium in Ostia (#306).

#301: Bar Graffiti

CIL 4.1679, 3494, 8475
First Century AD

The following are some examples of graffiti reflecting life in a bar. The first gives prices for different qualities of wine. An *aes* (plural *aeres*) was equivalent to a quarter of a *sestertius*. Other sources indicate that a day laborer in Pompeii might expect to make four *sestertii* per day.

Falernian was considered the best Roman wine. It was made from grapes grown in northern Campania, some distance south of Rome in one of Italy's most important ancient wine making regions.

1679: Hedone says: You can get a drink here for only one *aes*. You can drink better wine for two *aeres*. You can drink premium Falernian wine for four *aeres*.

3494: [Picture of a woman holding a pitcher] Whoever wants to get his own drink can go on and drink from the sea.

8475: [Drawing of a woman] Palmyra, the thirst-quencher.

#302: The Barmaid

Appendix Vergiliana, the Copa lines 1–8 and 29–33
First Century AD

The following passage from a poem by an unknown author entitled the *Copa* ("Barmaid") describes the kind of sights and sounds one would expect to experience in a restaurant. In this passage, the barmaid attracts potential customers into her establishment with her sensuous dancing and promise of a dining room set in an interior garden, reminiscent of the garden *triclinia* of the upper classes. As she seeks to attract customers, she promises music, dancing, and an abundance of wine.

The barmaid Syrisca's ["the Syrian woman"] head is wreathed with a Greek headdress. Trained to move her gyrating hips to the music of the castanet, she sensuously and drunkenly dances in the smoky tavern and shakes the rustling reeds on her elbows. She says, "What good is it for a weary man to be off somewhere in the hot dust rather than reclining here on the drinking couch? Here there are landscape paintings, drinking cups, roses, flutes, guitars, and a cool terrace roofed with shadowing reeds.... Recline and drink from your cups of warm wine. Lift your ever-refilled cups. Come here, weary one, and rest under the shadow of the vines. Crown your head with a garland of roses. Snatch a kiss from the pretty lips of a youthful girl."

#303: The Barmaid Amemone from Tibur

CIL 14.3709 (Tibur, Italy)
Second or Third Century AD

The following is the tombstone of a famous barmaid from Tibur, the modern town of Tivoli, not far from Rome. Her husband put the inscription up in her memory.

Amemone, a sweet woman and dear to her husband, lies in this tomb. She was a sweet barmaid whose reputation extended beyond her hometown and attracted many people to visit Tibur. Now the most powerful deity has taken away her fragile life and kindly light has received her soul into the heavens. I, Philotechnus, made this inscription for my chaste wife. It is right that her name survive for all eternity.

#304: Drinking Wine

Martial, *Epigrams* 1.18 and 3.57
Late First Century AD

One important aspect of ancient Roman wine consumption was that it was rarely drunk straight. The Romans considered drinking undiluted wine to be too intoxicating and those who did so were scorned as immoderate barbarians. Very often, the water used to dilute the wine was heated in a bowl placed over a stove. The hot water (*calida*) was then added to wine so as to make a warm or hot drink. The stoves used to heat the *calida* created a smoky atmosphere inside the *popina*. Another popular drink was *conditum*, a spiced wine. In some bars in Ostia, mortars (grinding stones) were found, testifying to the grinding of pepper and other spices for making *conditum*.

In the passages translated here, Martial complains first of mixing high quality Falernian wine with inferior wines. In the second passage, he tells how he recently received straight wine when he asked for it mixed with water.

What good does it do you, Tucca, to mix young wine stored in cheap Vatican jars with aged Falernian wine? What good have the worst wines ever done you? What harm have the best wines caused you? It is of little consequence what the mixture would do to your guests. The real crime is how you strangle the Falernian and pollute a good wine from Campania with such a noxious poison. Maybe your dinner guests deserve to die, but such a costly bottle of wine certainly does not.

A crafty tavern keeper in Ravenna recently cheated me. I asked for wine mixed with water but he gave it to me straight.

#305: Bar Near the Forum Baths, Pompeii

First Century AD

Popina counters were very common along the excavated portion of Pompeii. One excellent example (in Building VI.8.8; see Figure 19.1) was located on prime real estate across the street from the main entrance of the Forum Baths. Its large,

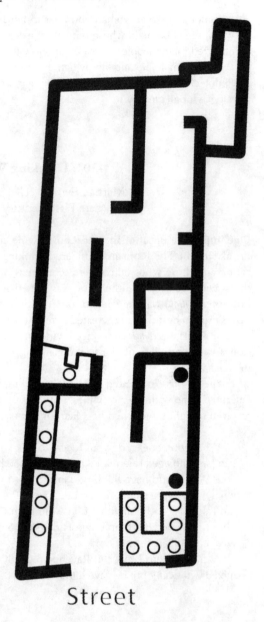

Figure 19.1 Plan of the *Popina* in
Building VI.8.8 in Pompeii (1: Room
with the submerged jar; 2: Room with
the counters; 3: Seating area; 4: Outdoor Garden Area).

Street

U-shaped counter pressed against the eastern wall and faced the street (see Figure
19.2). Six jars and an oven were inserted into the counter. Another large jar was
partially submerged next to one end of the counter. Another counter with six more
jars was placed along the western wall beneath the sloping ceiling created by an
external staircase to upstairs apartments. Additional rooms inside the establishment
provided living quarters for the owner, a kitchen, a latrine in a small room in the
very back, and seating space for customers (including a *triclinium*).

Figure 19.2 Counter in the *Popina* in Building VI.8.8 in Pompeii (Photograph by B. Harvey).

#306: The House of the Thermopolium in Ostia (Building I.2.5)

Second Century AD with Modifications in the Third and Fourth Centuries

Numerous *popinae* have been preserved in Ostia as well. One of the best examples is the so-called House of the Thermopolium (Building I.2.5; see Figure 19.3). This *popina* occupied the northeastern corner of a courtyard-style multipurpose mercantile/apartment building, resembling the House of the *Lararium* described earlier. The *popina* has three rooms opening directly onto the *Via di Diana*. There is also an open courtyard behind the easternmost room. The middle room contains the typical bar counter and masonry shelves. Further south, shelves line the wall (see Figure 19.4). Above the shelves a fresco depicts fruits and vegetables.

The western room was probably used for the preparation of the food and drinks. A submerged jar with a capacity of at least two hundred gallons probably held the bar's wine. A stove for heating the *calida* was also found here.

The eastern room is probably where customers sat. It has easy access to the bar area in the central room, and is the most distant from the smoky oven in the western room. More seating would have been available in the courtyard south of this room. The courtyard has a small fountain and a long masonry bench along the eastern wall. A small, partially submerged room in the courtyard might have been a pantry.

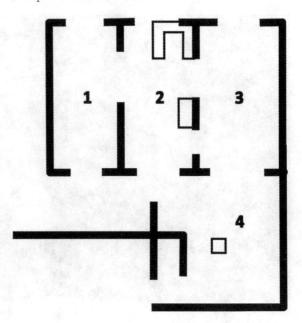

Figure 19.3 Plan of the House of the Thermopolium, Ostia (1: Room with the submerged jar; 2: Room with the counters; 3: Seating area; 4: Outdoor garden area).

Figure 19.4 Central Room and Shelving in the House of the Thermopolium, Ostia (Photograph by B. Harvey).

#307: The Bad Reputation of Bars

Juvenal, *Satires* 8.171–178
Late First/Early Second Centuries AD

Despite the fact that the *popinae* and drinking *tabernae* were popular replacements for the upper-class dinner party, it is very common for our sources to disparage these establishments as low class and magnets for criminals.

In the following passage, the satirist Juvenal pokes fun at a senatorial aristocrat who spends his time in a low-class *popina* in Ostia. This passage is part of a longer discussion of activities that might be allowable for a young man but not a respected senator. Visiting a *popina* was considered to be vulgar behavior for this governor who apparently preferred the atmosphere of an Ostian *popina* to completing his official duties. With typical satiric exaggeration, Juvenal describes how *popinae* are full of criminals and people with the basest of jobs. Unlike the baths and dinner parties, however, where social distinctions were important, everyone was treated equally in the *popina*.

> Send someone to Ostia, Caesar, to find your provincial governor, but start your search in some large *popina* there. You will find him reclining next to some assassin. He'll be nestled in a crowd of sailors, thieves, and fugitive slaves. He'll be there amongst executioners, the builders of cheap coffins, and the eunuch priests of Cybele who have finally stopped beating their drums only because they have passed out. There are no class distinctions in a place like that. The drinks are shared; there are no private couches at the table; no one is closer to the table than anyone else.

#308: The Attractions of the City

Horace, *Satires* 1.14.21–26
Mid-First Century BC

In the aristocratic literature, the *popina*, as a thoroughly lower-class establishment, became symbolic of uncouth behavior and therefore was shunned by the upper-class citizens of good upbringing. In the following passage, Horace criticizes the freedman manager of one of his country estates for his desire to be in Rome. Horace contrasts his own desire for solitude in the country with his manager's desire for the *popina*.

> I see how the brothel and greasy *popina* instill in you this desire for the city. Your little hut here provides pepper and spice faster than wine. There is no bar nearby to supply you with wine. There is no flute player who doubles as a prostitute to whose playing you can dance upon the earthen floor.

#309: Augustus' Gambling Habit

Suetonius, *Augustus* 71
Written in the Early Second Century AD Describing
the Emperor Augustus (27 BC–AD 14)

Gambling, an activity that was frequently associated with bars and contributed to their bad reputation, was illegal (with the exception of during the Saturnalia festival in December). That didn't seem to stop people from gambling, however. Dice are frequently found in archaeological digs. In the following passage from his biography of Augustus, Suetonius describes Augustus' love of gambling and even quotes a letter to the future emperor Tiberius about one particular event at which he and his dinner guests played dice.

Augustus in no way worried about his reputation for playing with dice. He played openly in public for the sake of enjoyment. He did so even as an old man and not only in the month of December when, during the Saturnalia, gambling was allowed, but also on holidays and work days. This habit of his is verified by a letter in his handwriting that I have seen. In it, he says, "I had dinner, my dear Tiberius, with some friends of mine. Vinicius and the elder Silius were present. We played dice like old men during dinner both yesterday and today. We were playing with the rules that anyone who threw the dog or a six would put a *denarius* into the pot and whoever threw Venus would win the pot."

In another letter he says, "We spent the Festival of Minerva very pleasantly. We played dice the whole day and kept the game board warm. As we played, your brother kept shouting about his luck. He did not lose much in the long run. In fact, he gradually made up his heavy losses to the point where he came out considerably ahead. I, however, lost twenty thousand *sestertii* but only because I was especially generous in the way I played, as is usual for me. If I had kept all of the winnings to which I was entitled and kept all the money that I gave to others to keep the game going then I would have come out fifty thousand *sestertii* ahead. I prefer things this way, though, because my generosity lifts me to a higher level of status."

To his daughter Julia he wrote the following, "I have enclosed two hundred fifty thousand *denarii*, the sum which I gave each of my dinner guests in case they wished to play at dice or the game of odds and evens during dinner."

Inns

The Roman inn (*caupona* in Latin), not only served food and drinks like the *popina* but also offered lodging to travelers. The *caupona* had a bar with a long counter like the *popinae*, but also included guestrooms, and other rooms like a *triclinium* and sitting rooms. Many establishments also had stables for horses or oxen. Like the

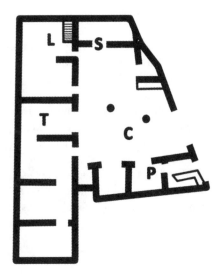

Figure 19.5 Plan of the Inn of Albinus, Pompeii (C: Courtyard, P: *Popina*, S: Stable; T: Triclinium; L: Room with a staircase to the upper floor).

popinae, the *caupona* tended to house people of lesser means. The wealthy preferred to stop at houses or villas owned by themselves or one of their friends.

The Inn of Albinus in Pompeii is a good example of a *caupona* (#310). Also included in this section are three texts to illustrate life in a town inn: the inscription of an innkeeper from Aesernia (#311), some graffiti from Pompeii (#312) and Herculaneum (#313) documenting people's happiness or disappointment with their service.

#310: The Inn of Albinus in Pompeii

First Century AD

The Inn of Albinus in Pompeii (*Insula Occidentalis* 1–2; see Figure 19.5), located just inside the Herculaneum Gate, had a large courtyard into which animals and carts could be brought through the large opening from the street. The stable itself was on the northern side of the courtyard. A loft above the stables possibly sheltered the hired cart drivers. Most of the guest rooms were on the second floor and were entered via a balcony that ran around the courtyard. Food and drink could be purchased from the attached *popina* in the southeastern corner of the *caupona*. A *triclinium* with a nearby kitchen opened onto the western side of the courtyard.

#311: Inscription of the Innkeeper Eroticus

CIL 9.2689 (Aesernia, Italy)
First to Third Centuries AD

The following inscription from Aesernia in Italy includes a fictitious bill from a *caupona*. While it is not completely certain, it seems that Eroticus was the innkeeper and Voluptas his wife. The quote at the end of the inscription seems to be an anecdote from Eroticus' life.

The inscription was found along with a relief sculpture of a man in a hood leading a donkey and giving money to a man, probably Eroticus. Lodgings were not included on the bill, but the mention of the cost of fodder would suggest the presence of a stable.

Prostitution was common in *popinae* and, especially in the larger *cauponae*. Even the names of the innkeeper (Eroticus, "lover") and his wife (Voluptas, "pleasure") seem so appropriate for the *caupona* that they may be fictional or nicknames.

> Lucius Calidius Eroticus made this for himself and for Fannia Voluptas. "Let us calculate the bill for the innkeeper. The glass of wine cost one *aes*; the vegetable plate two *aeres*; the girl comes to eight *aeres*; fodder for the mule comes to two *aeres*. That mule will be the end of me."

#312: Complaints on the Service in Inns in Pompeii

CIL 4.3498, 4957, 8075
First Century AD

The following three graffiti from Pompeii record witty criticisms of service people received while visiting Pompeii. Rooms could be small or lacking in expected amenities. The food and wine served might not always be good.

The first graffito comes from outside a *caupona* in the northern part of Pompeii, a block from the *Strada del Vesuvio*. The second was found on a wall near a *caupona* in the vicinity of the House of the Vettii. The third appears in the atrium of a house across the *Via dell'Abbondanza* from a small *popina*.

> 3498: What a lot of tricks you use to deceive, innkeeper. You sell water but privately drink unmixed wine.
> 4957: We have wet the bed, innkeeper. I confess we have done wrong. If you want to know why, there was no chamber pot in the room.
> 8075: The finance officer of the emperor Nero says the food here is poison.

#313: Two Brothers Document Their Visit to Herculaneum

CIL 4.10674, 10675, 10677, 10678
First Century AD

The following four texts were all found in a small room near the entrance to the Maritime Baths in Herculaneum, one of the cities on the Bay of Naples buried in the eruption of Vesuvius. The first looks like a tab of food purchases. The final two record what Apelles Mus, the chamberlain of the emperor and his brother Dexter did in town. It is likely that the two companions in the second text were the same Apelles and Dexter.

10674: . . . Some nuts . . .[?] coins; drinks: fourteen coins; lard: two coins; bread: three coins; three meat cutlets: twelve coins; three sausages: eight coins. Total: fifty-one coins.

10675: Two companions were here. While they were, they had bad service in every way from a guy named Epaphroditus. They dismissed him and most agreeably spent on whores the 105 and half *sestertii* they would have spent on his service.

10677: Apelles the chamberlain with Dexter, chamberlain of Caesar, ate here most agreeably and had sex with a girl during his visit.

10678: Apelles Mus and his brother Dexter each pleasurably had sex with two girls twice.

Chapter 20: Public Entertainment:
The Theater and Circus

Public entertainment in Rome began as a component of religious holidays. The Latin word *ludi* not only indicated a religious festival but also the entertainment associated with it. The earliest form of festival entertainment was the *ludi circenses*, chariot races. Later, when Rome began to interact with the Greek colonies in southern Italy, the Romans added theatrical performances (the *ludi scaenici*).

While the Greeks preferred to hold amateur athletic and theatrical competitions in their religious festivals (such as at the ancient Olympic games), the Romans relied upon professional entertainers, usually of servile or freed status. Because the games required professional entertainers, putting on games was expensive. In the Roman Empire, the duty of paying for the games fell to the aristocracy. Although a financial burden, putting on games was also politically advantageous, as it allowed an ambitious aristocrat to develop popularity among the lower classes and hopefully win votes for election to higher office. After the creation of the Empire, the emperor assumed much of the financial burden for holding games within the city of Rome. Outside of Rome, wealthy aristocratic sponsors paid for these public entertainments.

The Theater

The *ludi scaenici* in Rome were modeled on the Greek tradition, and they continued to reflect their Greek origin during the imperial period. The earliest plays were Greek tragedies and comedies that had been translated into Latin (Valerius Maximus describes the origins of theatrical performances in Rome; #314; see also his discussion of the lack of seating at the earliest events; #315). Later, plays with more Roman themes and settings began to be written, some by Greek-born authors and others by native Romans. The first permanent theater building in Rome was that constructed by Pompey in the first century BC (#316). As an example of a theater, #317 describes the large theater in Pompeii. I have also included a passage from Vitruvius describing optimal theater construction (#318).

Our evidence indicates that the Romans preferred comedic productions in their theaters to tragic drama. The earliest comedies were primarily translated or adapted from Greek plays. Shorter and more coarse in language and content were the Italian *atellanae*, developed in the Campanian town of Atella around the second century BC. The actors in these performances were called *histriones* and were generally freed and servile professionals who worked in troupes. The head *histrio* acted as their manager and arranged performances, with wealthy benefactors paying for the performances.

By the end of the first century BC, the professionalism of the performances and participants had increased, as did the cost of hiring the actors and staging the productions. Also at this time the pantomime became popular. Pantomime featured a male actor who performed completely on his own (the famous pantomime Apolaustus appears in #319). He would not speak or sing but would dance to the accompaniment of musical instruments and choral singing. The art form was considered to be one of the most technically demanding. Not only did the actor need to tell the story with gestures only, but he also played all the parts himself. Mimes were also popular beginning in the first century BC (#320). Unlike pantomime actors, mimes worked together in troupes of seven. The *archimimus* was the name of the leader and manager of a mime troupe. Unlike other forms of theatrical performances, both men and women could be mimes (in traditional theater, men played all the parts, including female characters). Despite their enormous popularity, mimes were rather notorious for their immoral performances and lewd behavior (#321).

#314: The Origin of Theatrical Performances

Valerius Maximus, *Memorable Deeds and Sayings* 2.4.4
Written in the Early First Century AD Describing Events of 361 BC

In this passage, Valerius Maximus outlines the origins of the performance of plays in Rome and describes the earliest actors.

> Now I will discuss the reasons for the institution of the *ludi*. When Gaius Sulpicius Peticus and Gaius Licinius Stolo were consuls [361 BC], a terribly virulent plague broke out. The pestilence forced the city to turn its attention from military affairs to concern for its own domestic and internal problems. At that time, it seemed that their efforts should be put toward some new and unusual religious practice rather than any human endeavor. So, the Romans began to listen to songs designed to please heavenly powers. Until that time, they had been content with the chariot races only. Romulus had been the first to offer chariot racing in Rome. Indeed, it was at a chariot festival called the Consualia that the Romans abducted the Sabine women. Because it is normal human behavior to follow up such small beginnings with eager application, some of the young men watching began to add simple and unprofessional dances to the words addressed to the deities. Soon, they hired a professional dancer from Etruria to perform a dance. The skillful agility of this dancer followed the practices of Crete and Lydia in the east (regions from which the Etruscans claim their origin). This dancer pleased the eyes of the Romans with his novel grace. Because the Etruscan word for dancer is "hister," the term for dancers in the *ludi scaenici* are called *histriones*. Slowly, the performing arts adopted the meter of the *saturae*. Livius was the first poet to attract spectators to the story lines of his plays. Livius acted in his own productions. Once when he lost his voice because he had given too many encores, he began to perform his dance in silence to the accompaniment of a young flute player.

#315: Prohibition on Sitting at Theatrical Performances

Valerius Maximus, *Memorable Deeds and Sayings* 2.4.2
Written in the Early First Century AD Describing
Events of the Second Century BC

In the earliest days of Roman history, the *ludi scaenici* were performed on temporary wooden stages built out in the open. No seating was provided. In the passage
quoted here, Valerius Maximus reports that in the second century BC, the senate
passed a law prohibiting the construction of seating at theatrical events. This conservative law, however, quickly fell out of use.

> The Romans passed a senatorial decree that prohibited the construction of
> seating in Rome or within a mile of Rome or for people to even sit at the
> games. This certainly comes from the belief that the relaxation of the mind
> goes together with the virility that comes from standing. This belief is charac-
> teristic of the Romans.

#316: The Theater of Pompey

Tertullian, *On Spectacles* 10
End of the Second/Beginning of the Third Century AD

Due to intense political competition in Rome itself, the senate prohibited the
construction of any permanent entertainment building within the city. The senators feared that the person who paid for such a building would gain an unfair
advantage in popularity with the lower classes. In the mid-first century BC, the
senatorial general and statesman Pompey built Rome's first permanent, stone
theater. It stood in the Campus Martius, between the Capitoline Hill and the
Tiber. According the Christian author Tertullian, Pompey circumvented the law
against such structures by constructing a small temple dedicated to Venus above
the upper tier of seats, and then claiming the building was a "temple" rather than
a "theater." Tertullian has a negative view on the games in general, so his description is rather harsh.

> When Pompey the Great, a person inferior only to the theater he built, finished
> construction of that theater dedicated to every wickedness, he was afraid that
> there would be public outrage of his memory and so built a temple of Venus
> on top of his theater. When it came time for the dedication of the building, he
> announced by edict that he was summoning them to a temple of Venus and not
> a theater. He added that he had placed seats for watching the performances
> beneath the temple. So he dressed up a building that was illegal and deserved
> to be illegal to look like a temple and overstepped the whole issue of legality
> with religious superstition.

Figure 20.1 The Large Theater in Pompeii (Photograph by B. Harvey).

#317: The Large Theater in Pompeii

First Century BC

Although law restricted their construction in Rome, theaters on the Greek model sprung up in other cities across Italy. Nestled amongst the Greek colonies of *Magna Graecia*, Pompeii had two theaters before Pompey built his in Rome: a traditional Greek-style theater constructed in the second century BC (see Figure 20.1) and a smaller, indoor theater (*odeon*) from the first half of the first century BC, shortly after the creation of the veteran colony under Sulla.

A theater building had two major components: the stage (*scaena*) and the seating (*cavea*). The stage was a long, rectangular platform. At the back was generally a large edifice with columns on numerous tiers to create a backdrop with scenery for the performance. The seating radiated outward and upward from the stage in a semicircular pattern in wedges (*cunei*) with aisles between each wedge. The semicircular space between the first row of the *cavea* and the stage was called the orchestra. In Greek theaters, the orchestra was where the chorus would perform while the action took place on-stage. In a Roman theater, however, it was reserved for elite spectators. Not only did it give the best view of the play, but also made these particular audience members more visible to those in attendance.

#318: Healthy Theater Construction

Vitruvius, *On Architecture* 5.3.1–4
First Century BC

This passage from Vitruvius describes some of the architectural features to consider when constructing a theater in a town.

After the forum has been situated, a location must be chosen for the theater that will be used during the holidays dedicated to the immortal gods. The location should be very healthy, preferably in the wholesome zone along the city walls as I described in the first book of this work. While the spectators with their wives and children sit during the performances and their attention is on the show, their bodies, stationary in their preoccupation, have pores that are wide open so as to allow the air to pass through easily. If that air comes from a marshy area or some other dirty place, it will infuse the body with harmful vapors. If the location of the theater is chosen with more care, such problems can be avoided.

Provision must also be made that the theater does not face south. If the sun is allowed to shine directly into the theater, the air will get locked in by the curvature of the structure and the building will get hot because the air is not able to circulate. The heat then will burn and dry out the body and impair the humors. For these reasons, harmful areas should be avoided and healthy locations chosen.

The design of the foundation of the theater will be easier if it should be placed on a hill. If it is absolutely necessary to place it in an open field or in a marsh, the piers and substructures should be built following the method outlined for the foundations of temples to the gods in book three of this work. The substructures sit on top of the foundation and tiers for the seating made of stone and marble are placed on top of the substructures.

The number of levels of passages beneath the seating should be determined by the height of the theater. The passages themselves should also not be taller than they are wide. Taller passages block the sound of the human voice and keep it from reaching the seats located above the passages and important elements of the words will be lost in the air. In short, the building must be designed so that a line drawn from the lowest to the highest tier should touch the tip of every seat on the angle of the interior of the theater.

#319: The Pantomime Apolaustus

CIL 14.4254 (Tivoli, Italy)
Later Second Century AD

In the inscription given here, the town of Tivoli honors a pantomime actor named Lucius Aurelius Apolaustus Memphius, a freedman of the emperor Lucius Verus. Apolaustus is described as a superior actor and was even granted honorary membership amongst the decurions, the town councilors. As a freedman, he could not be admitted to the town council itself, but it was common to bestow honorary membership upon freedmen benefactors.

To Lucius Aurelius Apolaustus Memphius, freedman of the emperors, pantomime, winner of the sacred games three times, and most important actor of his time. He was nominated to the college of the Augustales of Hercules. The

Senate and People of Tivoli also honored him with honorary membership in their town council.

#320: The Acclaimed Mime Bassilla

G. Kaibel, *Epigrammata Graeca* 609 (Aquileia, Italy)
Third Century AD

This Greek inscription honoring a female mime named Bassilla was discovered in the amphitheater in the northern Italian city of Aquileia.

In earlier days, she won glory among many peoples and many cities as she performed on the stage every type of theatrical show in mime, choruses, and also frequently in dance. Even so, this tenth muse has died but is not gone. I am Heracleides, a mime-actor, and I know what I am talking about as I inscribe her epitaph. She may be only a corpse now, but she has won the same glory as she did in life when she would cause her body to fall to the ground as a part of a performance. The other actors in your troupe also wish to say "Farewell Bassilla; no one is immortal."

#321: The Notorious Reputation of Mimes

Pliny the Younger, *Letters* 7.24
Early Second Century AD

The following passage from a letter of Pliny the Younger notes the death of Ummidia Quadratilla, an elderly aristocratic woman who had never remarried after the death of her husband. Pliny comments how she kept a troupe of freedmen mimes in her house. Implied in his critique of this practice was the immoral reputation of such entertainers. Pliny, however, praises Ummidia (who was seventy-nine when she died) because she never allowed her grandson, a budding aristocrat, to view the private performances these mimes would put on for his grandmother.

Ummidius Quadratus lived in the house of his grandmother Ummidia Quadratilla. She was a woman given over most fervently to pleasure, but she did not allow her interests to become a problem. She kept pantomimes in her house and was a fan perhaps more than was fitting for a woman of her status. Quadratus never watched the performances of these pantomimes either in the theater or at home, nor did Quadratilla compel him to do so. She told me when she was entrusting her grandson's education to me that, in the life of leisure that her gender compelled her to have, she liked to relax by playing board games and watching her pantomimes perform. She also told me that when she was about to engage in either activity, she would tell her grandson to leave and work on his studies. I think she would do this out of a combination of respect for him as well as love.

You will be surprised (I know I was) by what happened later. At the most recent *ludi scaenici* held by the priests in town, pantomimes were included on the program. After it was over, Quadratus and I happened to leave at the same time and ran into each other. Quadratus said to me, "You should know that today was the first time I have ever seen my grandmother's pantomime's perform." I would say this to describe the honor of the grandson. Other men of the basest sort would try to give honor to Quadratilla (something that shames me to even mention) by rushing to the theater in order to fulfill their obligations to fawn over her. They would give standing ovations, clap their hands, and act as if it was the best performance they had ever seen. They would watch Quadratilla carefully so that they could copy every one of her gestures she used to praise her troupe. These men were looking to receive sizable inheritances from Quadratilla after her death, but she only left them a very small legacy: that of a great theatrical performance. Even the performance they had to accept as part of the generosity of an heir (Quadratus) who had never even watched the pantomimes perform before.

The Circus and Chariot Racing

The *ludi circenses*, or chariot races, were one of the most popular components of the spectacle entertainments associated with religious holidays (see #322 for Caligula's obsession with the circus; even the horses could be popular—#323). The chariot races originated in the early Republic and lasted long into the era of the Christian empire. They were held within an open structure called a *circus*, meaning "round" or "track."

The circus building itself was a racetrack with two long, parallel legs with an ornamental barrier (*spina*) that ran down the center. At either end of the *spina*, at the point where the chariots would make the turn to go down the other side of the track, were turning posts (*metae*). The *metae* were three cones tall enough for the charioteers to see from a distance down the track. Tiered seating rose from all sides of the track. The starting gates stood at one end of the structure. The first and most famous circus in the Roman world was the Circus Maximus in the valley between the Palatine and Aventine hills (#324).

Like theatrical performers, charioteers were trained professionals of low (often slave) social status. Individual charioteers belonged to an organization known as a faction; the factions would compete against one another. Rome (and towns following the Roman model) had only four factions, each designated by a color: red, green, blue, and white (see #325 for a chariot faction roster). The evidence indicates that people tended to favor a particular team rather than individual charioteers (#326). The races themselves featured twelve teams, four from each faction (see #327 for drawing of a mosaic depicting a chariot race). The inscription survives of one of the most successful charioteers of history, a man named Diocles (#328). To further illustrate the popularity of the games, I have included a curse tablet against a charioteer (#329) and Ovid's account of a date with a girl at the chariot races (#330).

#322: Caligula as a Fan of the Circus

Suetonius, *Caligula* 55
Written in the Early Second Century AD Describing
the Emperor Caligula (AD 37–41)

Chariot racing was wildly popular. Whether out of a genuine affinity for the races or a desire to appeal to the circus' multitude of fans, emperors often publicized their preferred chariot faction. In the passage quoted here, the biographer Suetonius reports the emperor Caligula's incredible passion for the circus.

> Caligula was such a fan of the green faction that he would frequently dine in their faction stable and would even spend the night. At one drinking party with the faction, among his other handouts, he gave the charioteer Eutychus two million *sestertii*. On the day before a race, he would compel silence in the neighborhood of the stables by posting soldiers there so that his favorite horse Incitatus would not be disturbed. In addition, he gave Incitatus a marble stable box, an ivory manger, purple blankets, and a collar made of out jewels. He even gave the horse a house complete with household staff and furniture. In the horse's name, guests would be invited to dine with considerable elegance. It is even stated that Caligula had reserved a consulship for Incitatus.

#323: Inscription Dedicated to a Charioteer and His Horses

CIL 6.10069 (Rome)
Second or Third Century AD

Successful charioteers could be immensely popular. Paintings were hung about town depicting the most famous professional charioteers. As Suetonius' description of Incitatus indicates, even the individual horses from successful teams could become famous. An inscription in the Capitoline Museum in Rome (see Figure 20.2) dedicated to the leader of the red faction includes pictures of two horses: Aquilo and Hirpinus. The inscription gives their pedigree and even lists the number of victories.

> Aquilo, black in color, foal of Aquilo, won 130 races, came in second 88 times, came in third 37 times.
> Hirpinus, black in color, foal of Aquilo, won 114 times, came in second 66 times, came in third 56 times.

Figure 20.2 The Inscription of a Charioteer and His Horses in the Capitoline Museum, Rome (Photograph by B. Harvey).

> To the Spirits of the Dead; Claudia Helice made this for Lucius Avillius Dionysius, manager of the red faction and her most worthy husband.

#324: The Circus Building

Chariot racing began as early as the regal period, but the first permanent seating was only added in the late Republic. By the time of the renovations and seating enlargements of Trajan and later Caracalla, the Circus Maximus could have held as many as two hundred fifty thousand spectators. Unfortunately, very little is left of the Circus Maximus today, but its outline is still visible (see Figure 20.3).

The Circus of Maxentius a few miles from the *Via Appia* is much better preserved. It is possible to see there the remnants of the starting gates; the shell of the *spina*; and the structure of the seating, including the imperial box. Other circuses were constructed in major cities, but their enormous size and expense precluded their construction in smaller towns like Ostia and Pompeii.

#325: A Chariot Faction

CIL 6.10046 (Rome)
First Century AD

The inscription here is a roster for a chariot faction in Rome. The estimated date puts the inscription in the very early empire, before the full development of the four factions.

Figure 20.3 Remains of the Circus Maximus in Rome (Photograph by B. Harvey).

The charioteer organization of Titus Ateius Capito of the swallow-colored faction, while Chrestus was the financial officer. The following people, divided into organizational decurions, were given oil for lamps: Marcus Vipsanius Migio [owner]; Docimus, manager; Chrestus, head of the stables; Epaphra, quartermaster; Menander, charioteer; Apollonius, charioteer; Cerdo, charioteer; Liccaeus, charioteer; Helles, assistant to head of the stables; Publius Quinctius Primus; Hyllus, physician; Anteros, operator of the starting gates; Antiochus, cobbler; Parnacus, operator of the starting gates; Marcus Vipsanius Calamo; Marcus Vipsanius Dareo; Eros, operator of the starting gates; Marcus Vipsanius Faustus; Hilarus, charioteer; Nicander, charioteer; Epigonus, charioteer; Alexander, charioteer; Nicephorus, thrower of water; Alexio, delayer; [. . .], publicist.

#326: Pliny's Disenchantment with the Circus

Pliny the Younger, *Letters* 9.6
Early Second Century AD

Not everyone liked the circus races. Many aristocrats felt contempt for any type of entertainment that they associated with the vulgar mob. In this letter, Pliny reveals his upper-class bias in his opinion of the circus and its fans. For him, chariot racing is repetitive and pointless. Pliny seems disdainful that fans favored a faction rather than appreciating the skill of individual charioteers.

I am not captivated by chariot racing in the least. In it, there is nothing new, nothing various, nothing that would not suffice to see just once. How amazed I am that so many thousands of people wish childishly again and again to watch horses running and men standing in their chariots. If they were captivated by the speed of the horses or the skill of the men, at least that would be something. But, in truth, they are fans of their team color; they love their team color. Indeed, if on the track itself, in the middle of the race, charioteers should exchange their jersey, the crowd's zeal and favor will change with it. Suddenly, they will abandon those charioteers and horses that they were watching from a distance and whose names they were shouting. There is such popularity, such authority in one extremely cheap tunic [with the faction color]. I do not have to mention how the vulgar crowd is obsessed with their teams (the common people are just as worthless as the faction jersey). What I do find surprising is how many aristocrats are fascinated with the races. When I think of those people, I take a certain amount of pleasure in the fact that I am not distracted by that spectacle.

#327: A Typical Chariot Race

Each chariot race had twelve teams, three from each of the four factions. The most common chariot team was the *quadriga*, a four-horse chariot. Novices might use teams of only two horses (*biga*); very advanced charioteers might compete in novelty events with as many as six or even eight horses.

Roman circus starting gates were very similar to modern horse racing starting gates. The teams waited in boxes for the gates to open to begin the race. The gates were spring-loaded like mini catapults and were all connected to a single lever so as to assure a fair start. The person paying for the games (the *editor* or *munerarius*) would signal the start by dropping a white cloth (*mappa*). When the cloth hit the ground, a person would pull the lever and the gates would spring open.

There were seven laps in a race. The turns were always the most dangerous, and the best opportunity for a good charioteer to take or extend the lead. The *spina* was only about five meters wide, so turns could be very tight; if the charioteer decided to take a wide turn in the interest of safety, he lost valuable time. The race ended at the finish line in front of the box of the presiding magistrate. The winner received a victory palm frond to carry around the track and some prize money. There were typically twenty-four races a day. Figure 20.4 is a drawing based on a mosaic depicting a chariot race. The drawing shows the *spina* and its associated monuments, four chariots (one for each of the four factions), and a crash (on the far left, partially lost in a break in the mosaic).

Figure 20.4 Drawing of a Mosaic Depicting a Chariot Race (H. Bender, *Rom und Römisches Leben in Altertum* [Tübingen, 1898], p. 315).

#328: The Famous Charioteer Diocles

CIL 6.10048 (Rome)
Third Century AD

The funerary inscription of one of the most successful charioteers in Roman history, Diocles, has been preserved. On his tombstone, Diocles records his complete career statistics. He lived forty-two years and began racing at the age of eighteen. He seems to have continued racing until his death and changed factions several times. In all, he raced 4,257 times and won 1,462 times, collecting a tremendous amount of prize money. It is especially interesting to note how he compares his own career with that of other prominent charioteers from Roman history. It is clear that detailed records and statistics were kept of charioteer careers.

Gaius Appuleius Diocles, Charioteer of the Red Faction, Spanish by nationality from the province of Lusitania. He lived forty-two years, seven months, twenty-two days. He raced for the first time in the white faction when Acilius Aviola and Corellius Pansa were consuls [AD 122]. He won his first race while a member of the same faction when Acilius Glabrio and Gaius Bellicius Torquatus were consuls [AD 124]. He began racing for the Green Faction when Torquatus Asprenas for the second time and Annius Libo were consuls [AD 128]. His first win with the Red Faction came when Laenas Pontianus and Antonius Rufinus were consuls [AD 131]. His racing career lasted twenty-four years. During that time, he started in 4,257 races and won 1,462 times. In the prestigious first race after the inaugural procession, he won 110 times. In individual races [one chariot from each faction], he won 1,064 times. He won ninety-two major prizes: thirty-two of thirty thousand *sestertii* (three of which were with six-horse teams), twenty-eight of forty thousand *sestertii* (two with six-horse teams), twenty-nine of fifty thousand *sestertii* (one with seven-horse teams), and three of sixty thousand *sestertii*.

In doubles [races with two teams from each faction instead of four], he won 347 times (three of which were with three-horse teams for prizes of fifteen thousand *sestertii*). In triples [races with three teams from each faction], he won fifty-one times. In total, he came in first or placed 2,900 times, second 861 times, third 576 times, fourth 1 time (for one thousand *sestertii*). He lost 1,351 times. He tied a blue charioteer ten times, and a white ninety-one times (two of which were for prizes of thirty thousand *sestertii*. He won a total of 35,863,120 *sestertii*. Also, three times he won races of two-horse chariots with prizes of one thousand *sestertii* each. In these, he tied a white charioteer once and a green charioteer twice.

He took the lead from the start and won 815 times. He came from behind and won sixty-seven times. He won in other ways forty-two times. He stole the victory late in the race 502 times: 216 times against green charioteers, 205 times against blues, and 81 times against whites. He made nine of his horses winners of one hundred races and one horse was used in two hundred of his wins.

His accomplishments include two wins in the first year he began to race with four-horse chariots. Both of those wins he took the lead late in the race. In the public records, Avilius Terens is said to have been the first of his faction to win 1,011 times. In the year that Terens won 100 times, Diocles won 103 times (83 of them were in singles [races with only one team, probably a champion, from each faction]). He increased the glory of his career when he surpassed the record of Thallus, another charioteer of the red faction, by winning 134 times with a lead horse that was not his own (118 in singles events). This record also beat that of the charioteers of all of the other factions who ever participated in the *ludi circenses*. It is noted with deserved admiration that in a single year with a lead horse other than his own and with the horses Cotynus and Pompeianus as his yoke horses that he won ninety-nine times, winning prizes of sixty thousand *sestertii* once, fifty thousand *sestertii* four times, forty thousand *sestertii* once, and thirty thousand *sestertii* twice. [. . .?. . .] of the green faction won 1,025 races, the first of all charioteers to do so in all of Roman history. He was also the first to win fifty thousand *sestertii* seven times. Diocles has him beat. With three horses on the yoke (Abigeius, Lucidus, and Paratus), he won fifty thousand *sestertii* eight times. He also has beaten Communis, Venustus, and Epaphroditus, three charioteers of the blue faction who had each won one thousand races. They also, combined, had won eleven races with prizes of fifty thousand *sestertii* each. Diocles, with the horses Pompeianus and Lucidus in his team, won fifty thousand *sestertii* [twelve?] times. [. . .?. . .] of the green faction winner of 1,025 races, Flavius Scorpus winner of 2,048 races, and Pompeius Musclosus winner of 3,559 races won a combined 6,632 races and prizes of fifty thousand *sestertii* twenty-nine times. Diocles, most famous of all charioteers, won 1,462 races and fifty thousand *sestertii* twenty-nine times. Diocles' career stands out above all of them. Fortunatus of the green faction with his horse Tuscus won 386 races and prizes of fifty thousand *sestertii* nine times. Diocles with his horse Pompeianus won 152 times and prizes of fifty thousand *sestertii* ten times and sixty thousand *sestertii* once.

Diocles also stands out among all recorded charioteer careers with his novel prizes. On a single day, he won forty thousand *sestertii* twice, both in races of six-horse chariots. To add to this feat, he raced in a specialty contest with seven horses yoked to the same chariot, a spectacle never seen before. He won this race and took away the prize of fifty thousand *sestertii*. In the race, Abigeius was his lead horse. He also won races in which the charioteers were not allowed to use a whip for prizes of thirty thousand *sestertii* [. . .?. . .] times. For such novel feats, he deserves twice the glory. Pontius Epaphroditus appears as pre-eminent among the charioteers with at least one thousand wins because during the reign of Antoninus Pius he won 1,467 times (911 in singles races). Diocles still has his record beaten with his 1,462 wins (1,064 in singles races). Also during those days, Pontius Epaphroditus pulled ahead late in the race and won 457 times, but Diocles did the same thing 502 times. In the same year that Diocles won 127 races, he was the winner 103 times with the horses Abigeius, Lucidus, and Pompeianus in his team. Among those charioteers who used African horses, Pontius Epaphroditus of the blue faction won 134 races with his horse Bubalus. Pompeius Musclosus of the green faction won 115 races with his horse named [. . .?. . .]. Diocles again surpasses these charioteers with his 152 wins with the horse Pompeianus (144 in singles). His career was further enhanced with his horses Cotynus, Galata, Abigeius, Lucidus, and Pompeianus who won a total of 445 times (397 in singles).

#329: A Curse Tablet against a Charioteer

AE 1902, 55 (Hadrumetum, Africa Proconsularis)
Third or Fourth Century AD

Many people took chariot racing very seriously. Like modern horse racing, betting was extremely common. Factions competed for fans as well as victories. This enthusiasm led to drastic measures in some cases. Many curse tablets have been found invoking the death and destruction of rival charioteers. The following example from the later empire is a good example of the kind of texts that were written for someone to gain what they thought was an edge in an upcoming race.

I urge you by oath, demon, whoever you may be, and I demand from this hour, from this day, from this moment even that you shatter and kill the horses of the green and white factions and that you kill and crash the charioteers Clarus, Felix, Primulus, and Romanus. Steal the breath from their bodies. I ask this from you by him who has released you at this time: the god of the sea and air. [list of deities/magic words] Iao, Iasdao; cuigeu, censeu cinbeu perfleu diarunco deasta bescu berebescu aurara; Noctivagus, Tiber, Ocean; antmoaraito.

#330: A Date at the Chariot Races

Ovid, *The Loves* 3.2.1–14, 63–84
Late First Century BC

In his *Amores* (*The Loves*), the Augustan poet Ovid recounts his relationships in mock epic fashion. In the passage translated here, he describes a day at the chariot races in the company of a woman.

I am not sitting here in the circus because I am a big fan of the races. My only prayer is that your favorite charioteer will win. I only came so that I could talk with you, sit with you. I want to make sure that you recognize my love for you. While you watch the races, I am watching you. We both are able to watch what we want to watch, and both of us have plenty for our eyes to feast upon. Is that your favorite charioteer? He really is a lucky guy. What is it about him that makes you care for him so? Would you look at me that way if I made the jump from the hallowed starting gates to be carried bravely behind my horses? I would not fail to whip my horses on and mark their backs with scars. I would cut the corner at the turning post very sharply. As fast as I may be going, I would have no choice but to stop if I were to catch sight of you in the middle of the race. The reins would fall out of my hands...

Oh wait. Your feet are dangling. If it would help, you could put your toes in the grating in front of you. Now the magistrate has given the signal for the most important event of the day: the races with the four-horse chariots out of the fair starting gates. I can see your favorite charioteer now. Whoever he may be, may he win. Even the horses seem to know that you are a fan. Oh no! He has taken too wide a turn! What are you doing? The charioteer in second place has pulled inside and threatens to pass by hugging the barrier with his inner wheel. What are you doing, you fool? You are threatening to dash the hopes and prayers of my girl. Apply the lash more strongly with your left hand! It seems that we are cheering for an idiot. Come on, spectators, call for a false start! Indicate your wish by swinging your toga in the air. Look! They are signaling a false start! Your charioteer will get another chance. Be careful that those swinging togas don't mess up your hair. Why don't you put your head down into the folds of my toga to keep it safe?

Soon, the starting gates are released and the doors swing open once again. The four faction colors are a blur as the horses dart off. This time get a good lead and increase it in the open stretch before the first turn. Fulfill my vows, and, most importantly, those of my girlfriend. In fact, however, a chariot racing victory is really the vow of only my girlfriend. My true prayer is yet to be fulfilled. My girl's favorite charioteer has won his race, but my race has yet to be finished. She looks at me and giggles in glee. It seems like she is making promises with her eyes. That is enough of this story. I am going to leave the rest for another day.

Chapter 21: Public Entertainment: The Amphitheater

Gladiatorial combat in the Roman amphitheater is one of the most enduring images of ancient Rome, and also one of the most misunderstood. Like the Romans' reputation for decadence and luxury, which is based on exaggerated descriptions of atypical aristocrats and emperors, gladiatorial combat has given the Romans a reputation as bloodthirsty and cruel. It is vital, however, to understand the context of the games and carefully examine gladiatorial combat before passing moral judgment upon the Romans.

The History of Amphitheatrical Games

Gladiatorial combat was associated originally not with religious holidays like the *ludi circenses* and *scaenici*, but rather with funeral ceremonies (#331). The term for these games was *munus* (plural *munera*), which connoted a duty or obligation as well as a gift. This memorial tribute to the deceased became something the crowd expected to be included in the usual funeral ceremonies.

By the late Republic, the *munera* had become very popular with the lower classes, a fact not lost upon the aristocrats. As a result, the games lost their connection with aristocratic funerals and became another facet of the aristocratic competition for honor and support (#332 describes the games given by Julius Caesar). During the imperial period, the games tended to celebrate the emperor and his family and were often held on important imperial anniversaries or birthdays.

The origins of the *munera* in funeral ceremony have led to a great deal of confusion regarding the purpose of gladiatorial combat (#333). The reality, however, would seem to be that gladiators were not a form of human sacrifice, even in their origins. Instead, gladiatorial combat originated as a violent, sometimes deadly, re-enactment of the deceased's battle prowess (#334). I have also included, as evidence for the popularity of the games, a painted advertisement from Pompeii for an upcoming gladiator show (#335) and an inscription dedicated to a municipal aristocrat mentioning the games he put on (#336).

#331: The First Gladiatorial Games in Rome

Valerius Maximus, *Memorable Deeds and Sayings* 2.4.7
Written in the Early First Century AD Describing Events of 264 BC

The passage here from Valerius Maximus describes how two brothers put on the first gladiatorial show at the funeral of their senatorial father in 264 BC. Similar

shows were held on an ad hoc basis throughout the middle Republic when someone wanted to embellish the funeral of an illustrious person.

The first gladiator show in Rome was given in the Forum Boarium in the consulship of Appius Claudius and Quintus Fulvius [264 BC]. Marcus and Decimus, the sons of Brutus Pera, gave the games to honor their father's ashes
with a funeral memorial. An athletic contest was held at the same time at the
expense of Marcus Scaurus.

#332: The Games of Julius Caesar in Honor of His Daughter Julia

Suetonius, *Julius Caesar* 26
Written in the Early Second Century AD Describing 50 BC

In 50 BC, Caesar, stretching the applicability of the *munera*, gave a show in honor
of his daughter Julia, who had died several years earlier. Caesar's games came at an
important political time: his invasion of Italy and the beginning of civil war with
Pompey. Indeed, these games won him vital popular support at a politically unstable
time.

Julius Caesar announced a gladiator show for the people as well as a public banquet in the memory of his daughter Julia. No one had ever done this
before. Several things raised people's expectations, but some rumors about the
banquet got the most attention. It was circulated that supplies for the dinner
were being arranged by Caesar's own household.

#333: Tertullian on the Origins of the *Munera*

Tertullian, *On Spectacles* 12.1–4
End of the Second/Beginning of the Third Century AD

In the passage quoted here, the Christian author Tertullian, who was opposed to
violent amphitheatrical events, claims that the battles were blood offerings to the
gods of the underworld. This misconception has endured into the modern era,
bringing with it the idea that gladiators were relics of ritualized human sacrifice.

It remains for me to discuss that most notable and popular of spectacles. It
is called a *munus* because it is derived from official duty. Therefore, it can
be called an official duty or a *munus*. Our ancestors thought that with this
spectacle they were fulfilling their duties to the dead. It was only later that
they spoiled the *munus* with a kind of civilized atrocity. At one time, because

there was a belief that the souls of the departed were appeased with human sacrifice, the Romans would sacrifice prisoners of war or slaves of bad character as part of the funeral rites. Later, they thought they could cover up the wickedness of the act by calling it entertainment. The people they furnished for these entertainments they trained to fight as best they could. Really, however, they were only learning how best to die. On the appointed day of the funeral, they served this purpose next to the tomb of the deceased. In conclusion, they took consolation in death through murder. This is the origin of the *munus*. Gradually, these "games" grew in sophistication to match their cruelty. Such beastly people could find no pleasure in entertainment unless they could view humans torn apart by beasts.

#334: The Military Connection of the *Munera*

Historia Augusta, Maximus and Balbinus 8.7–8
Written Possibly in the Fourth Century AD

In the following passage, the late imperial pagan work known as the *Historia Augusta* reflects some of the debate regarding the origin of the *munera* and voices disapproval of the belief that gladiatorial combat originated as human sacrifice. The connection of the games with the military might also hint at gladiatorial combat as an inspirational battle spectacle for a warlike society.

Many authors, including some older sources, say that the giving of gladiatorial shows before going out to war was a ritual made against the enemy so that Nemesis (that is, the avenging power of fortune) would satiate herself with the blood of citizens being spilled in something that is reminiscent of battle. Others say in their works something that I believe is closer to the truth, that the Romans before going to war thought that it was a good idea to see battle, wounds, iron, and naked bodies struggling against one another so that in actual battle they would not be so afraid of the armed enemy or wounds and blood.

#335: Advertisement for Games in Pompeii

CIL 4.3884
Middle of the First Century AD

The abundance of gladiatorial graffiti from Pompeii reflects the enormous popularity of the gladiatorial shows in that city. Extant graffiti include drawings of gladiators and gladiatorial combat; poems describing gladiators; and, perhaps most importantly, advertisements put up by aristocrats paying for the games. The following is an example of a gladiatorial advertisement from Pompeii. In addition to naming the person paying for the games (the *munerarius*) and the number of gladiators to appear, the document also mentions how a morning beast show will be included and awnings to provide shelter from the sun.

> Thirty pairs of gladiators belonging to Decimus Lucretius Satrius Valens, priest for life of Nero, son of the emperor, and ten pairs belonging to his son Decimus Lucretius Valens will fight at Pompeii on April 8th–13th. There will be a beast hunt and awnings. Aemilius Celer wrote this alone by the light of the moon.

#336: A Municipal Aristocrat Gives Games

AE 1975, 255 (Paestum, Italy)
Second or Third Century AD

Games were clearly an important way for aristocrats to earn popularity in their hometown. This inscription comes from the tomb of an aristocrat from the town of Paestum in southern Italy. It commemorates money he spent on games for his town.

> To Marcus Egnius Fortunatianus, son of Marcus, of the Maecia tribe, *duovir* with censorial powers for the second time; the most splendid order of the town council, at the request of the people, decreed a statue to him to be put up because of his special and significant munificence to his city, namely that, after the state had given him twenty-five thousand *sestertii* to hire gladiators for the *munera*, he added another twenty-five thousand to hire even better gladiators. He also added some bears of amazing size as well as criminals along with all of the required apparatus and amenities. His preparations made the day memorable.

The Amphitheater

The amphitheater was the specific location of the *munera*. The amphitheater was oval in shape with an arena in the center and seating on all sides. The term "arena" is derived from the word for the sand (*harena*), which covered the wooden floor of the amphitheater. Before the prohibition on permanent entertainment buildings had been lifted, the *munera* in Rome were held in wooden structures in the forum or Campus Martius. The oldest extant amphitheater, in fact, is not in Rome, but in Pompeii (#337; see #339 for the riot in the Pompeii amphitheater in AD 59). The largest and most magnificent amphitheater of the ancient world, however, was the Colosseum (#338).

#337: The Pompeii Amphitheater

CIL 10.852 (Pompeii)
First Century BC

Like the small, covered theater in town, the amphitheater of Pompeii (see Figure 21.1) was constructed in the first century BC, shortly after Sulla founded the veteran's colony in the town. The builders constructed the amphitheater against the angle in the city wall in the southeastern corner of town, which enabled them to use the existing masonry as support for tiers of seating. The arena was also partially sunk into the ground so that some seating could be constructed at ground level. An additional tier of seating was created, however, with ramps leading from the exterior ground level up to the top of the amphitheater seating. The following is the dedicatory inscription from the two entrances into the amphitheater.

> Gaius Quinctius Valgus, son of Gaius, and Marcus Porcius, son of Marcus, the *duoviri* with censorial powers, for the sake of bringing honor to the colony of Pompeii, saw to the construction of this entertainment building with their own money and gave it as a gift to the townspeople forever.

Figure 21.1 Interior of the Amphitheater at Pompeii (Photograph by B. Harvey).

#338: The Colosseum

Martial, *On Spectacles* 1–2
Late First Century AD

The Flavian emperors built the Colosseum after their victory in the civil war of AD 69 on ground that Nero had appropriated for his new private palace, the Golden House. The structure resembles closely that of the Augustan Theater of Marcellus, with seating on artificial tiers supported by impressive Roman style columned arcades and vaults (see Figure 21.2). While the Theater of Marcellus only had two tiers, the Colosseum had three. Some entrances led to the prestigious seats in the lower levels, while staircases led to the upper floors and galleries. It has been estimated that the Colosseum could have held between fifty thousand and eighty thousand spectators. The wooden floor of the Colosseum has long since disappeared to expose the substructures that housed the various professionals and animals awaiting their turn before the crowds (see Figure 21.3). In the passages quoted here, the poet Martial celebrates the grandeur of the new amphitheater and is eager to point out how the land had once been in the private ownership of the emperor Nero.

[Poem 1] Let Egyptian Memphis stop talking about the wonder of the Pyramids. The Assyrians should not boast about their efforts with the city of Babylon. Don't praise the Ionians for their temple of Diana of the Three Ways. The altar with all the decoration should not be the main attraction on the island of Delos. The Carians should not immodestly brag to the stars about the tomb of Mausolus as it hangs in the empty air. All of these fall short of the glory of the new amphitheater the emperor has built. History will only remember this one magnificent work and forget the rest.

[Poem 2] This is the place where the lofty colossus looks at the stars up close and tall scaffolding rises in the middle of the road. The enviable Golden House of that nasty emperor Nero used to be the jewel of this part of town (in fact reconstruction efforts after the fire made this the only house still standing in the whole city). This place where once was the artificial lake of Nero is now where construction of the magnificent spectacle of the new amphitheater is going up. We can also see new baths being constructed here, gifts from our emperors. At one time, the emperor Nero tore down private houses here to build a haughty private resort in the middle of town. The colonnade of the terrace of Claudius is where once stood the farthest entrance of the Golden House. Rome is back in the hands of the Romans. While you have been in power, Caesar, what was once the private resort of a tyrant is now a delight for the people.

Figure 21.2 Exterior of the Colosseum, Rome (Photograph by B. Harvey).

Figure 21.3 Seating and Substructures of the Interior of the Colosseum (Photograph by B. Harvey).

#339: Riot in the Pompeii Amphitheater

Tacitus, *Annals* 14.17
Written in the Early Second Century AD Describing Events of AD 59

In AD 59, a riot broke out during shows in the Pompeii amphitheater between the townspeople and visitors from nearby Nuceria. When Nero in Rome investigated, he punished the local magistrates and the man responsible for holding the games during which the riot occurred. He also banned the holding of games in Pompeii for ten years. It is possible that a painting found in a house in Pompeii (currently in the National Museum in nearby Naples) depicts the riot.

> Around the same time, a violent event between the townspeople of Nuceria and Pompeii occurred over trivial matters. The bloodshed took place during a gladiatorial show that Livineius Regulus had given. As I have already mentioned, this Regulus had been thrown out of the senate in Rome. The competitive spirits of the people of the towns began with jeers but then turned to the throwing of rocks and eventually the seizing of weapons. In the battle that followed, the Pompeians had the advantage because the spectacle had taken place in their town. The mutilated bodies of many of the dead Nucerians were sent to Rome. Many mourned the loss of their parents or children. The emperor referred decision on the matter to the senate. The senate turned it over to the consuls. After decision was again turned over to the senate, it was decided that the people of Pompeii would not be allowed to meet in groups publicly for ten years and any organization that was created contrary to this law would be dissolved. Livineius and the others who had been behind the disturbance were exiled as a punishment.

Gladiators

Like other professional Roman entertainers, gladiators were of the lowest social standing simply by virtue of their profession (equivalent to slaves). Despite their low social status, however, gladiators were often extremely popular. The chance for popularity attracted even freeborn people to the profession. Such persons of non-servile status wishing to fight as gladiators were required to swear an oath to the *munerarius* saying that their bodies and lives were at his discretion in an act that essentially brought the low status of a slave upon themselves. Even aristocrats would stoop to this level in search of fame (#340).

One of the attractions of gladiatorial combat was the variety of types of combatants with different weapons and armor (#341 gives examples of the different types of gladiators). The *secutor*, *murmillo*, and *thrax* all used different varieties of swords and shields. The *hoplomachus* used a long spear and small round shield. The *retiarius* fought with a net, trident, and very little armor. The *eques* fought from horseback. *Essedarii* entered the arena on a chariot and perhaps opened the battle with some maneuvers similar to jousting before dismounting and fighting hand-to-hand. While the *eques* or *essedarius* usually fought against each other, usually combat took place between gladiators of different types. One of the most popular was a fight between the heavily armed *secutor* and lightly armed *retiarius*. I have also included the tombstone inscription of a comic gladiator who claims to have lived ninety-eight years (#342).

#340: Prohibition of Aristocrats from Performing in the Games

AE 1995. 354 (Larinum, Italy)
AD 19

The text quoted here is a law from the reign of Tiberius preserved in the town of Larinum, Italy. It documents penalties for members of the upper classes who sullied the prestige of their class by hiring themselves out as entertainers.

The following is a senatorial decree created on the Palatine Hill, in the portico that is next to the temple of Apollo. Present at the writing were Gaius Ateius Capito (son of Lucius), Sextus Pompeius Octavius (son of Sextus), Octavius Fronto (son of Gaius), Marcus Asinius Mamilianus (son of Curtius), the quaestor Gaius Gavius Macer (son of Gaius), the quaestor Aulus Didius Gallus. Text of the decree: the consuls Marcus Silanus and Lucius Norbanus Balbus have stated that they have composed a memo in accordance with the business assigned to them about matters pertaining to the license of some women and to certain aristocrats who, contrary to the dignity of their order, have displayed themselves in the theater or amphitheater or promised that they would. In earlier years, senatorial decrees had prohibited such action because such performances diminish the majesty of the senate. On this matter, the senate decreed that no son, daughter, grandson, granddaughter, great-grandson, or great-granddaughter or any male whose father or grandfather (maternal or paternal) or brother had ever received the privilege of watching the games from the seats of the equestrians or any female whose father or grandfather (maternal or paternal) or brother had reached the same status, all of such people are prohibited from performing on the stage, promising to do so, [. . . fighting in the arena?. . .], taking up the equipment of a gladiator, serving as a trainer, and doing anything of a similar kind. It is also hereby illegal for anyone to hire such a person for those purposes. People also may not hire themselves out. For this reason, the senate thought it best to take preventive measures in the case of people with the right of sitting in the seats at the games reserved for the equestrians who continue down this dangerous path and in so doing make a mockery of their social status. There are some who accepted such public disgrace or who were condemned for their ruined reputation by pledging themselves as gladiators or performing on the stage and only afterward claimed that they had given up their aristocratic standing of their own free will. It is also decreed that if any of the persons listed above act contrary to the dignity of their social status in this way, they will be prohibited from proper burial after death. The exception to this law is any a person who previously appeared on the stage; fought as a gladiator; or is the son or daughter of an actor, gladiator, gladiatorial agent (*lanista*), or pimp. There was an earlier senatorial decree from the consulship of Manius Lepidus and Titus Statilius Taurus [AD 11] that stated that no woman of free birth under the age of twenty and no freeborn man under the age of twenty-five may appear on the stage or fight as a gladiator without the consent of the emperor Augustus or the emperor Tiberius Caesar Augustus. The current decree upholds that legislation with the exception that . . . [text broken at this point]

#341: Types of Gladiators

First to Third Centuries AD

The following are funerary inscriptions for dead gladiators. On their tombstones, the inscription always mentions the specific type of gladiator they were. Also note that, on many of these inscriptions, wives or other family members are mentioned.

CIL 6.10167 (Rome)

To the spirits of the dead; to Publicia Aromate, dearest wife; Albanus, a veteran *eques* in the *Ludus Magnus* put this up. She lived twenty-two years, five months, eight days. Size of the burial plot: three feet wide, eight feet deep.

CIL 12.3323 (Nemausus, Gaul)

Beryllus, *essedarius*, freedman, fought twenty times; Greek by nationality, lived twenty-five years; Nomas, his wife, made this for her well-deserving husband.

CIL 6.33977 (Rome)

To the spirits of the dead of Marcus Ulpius Felix, veteran *murmillo*, who lived forty-five years, from the nation of the Tungri; Ulpia Syntyche, freedwoman, to her sweetest and well-deserving husband, and Iustus, their son, put this up.

AE 1962, 52 (Corduba, Baetica)

Actius, *murmillo*, won six times, lived twenty-one years. He is buried here. May the earth rest lightly upon you. His wife put this up to her husband with her own money. Whatever anyone of you might wish for me, now dead, may the gods always grant to you, living and dead.

AE 1934, 284 (Salonae, Dalmatia)

To the spirits of the dead; to Thelonicus, a man from the countryside; once, while a *retiarius*, he was freed with the *rudis* by the generosity of the people; Xystus, his friend, and Pepticius, his companion, put this up.

CIL 3.8830 (Salonae, Dalmatia)

To Maximianus (stage name Aureus), *secutor*, lived twenty-two years, fought in five fights, deceived by bandits. His brother put this up to his dearest brother. His wife, Maximiana, put this up for her most desirable husband.

CIL 6.10190 (Rome)

To the spirits of the dead; to Superbus, *secutor*; Tiberius Claudius Vitalio made this for his well-deserving friend.

CIL 6.10197 (Rome)

To the spirits of the dead; to Macedon, who, as a new recruit *thrax* from Alexandria, died in his first fight; the whole class of *thraces* from his school put this up for him, well-deserving, having lived twenty years, eight months, twelve days.

#342: A Comic Gladiator

CIL 6.10168 (Rome)
First to Third Centuries AD

This inscription commemorates a man named Secundus who is described as a *paegniarius*, probably some kind of comic gladiator who would perform between the bouts of the real gladiators. He belonged to the *Ludus Magnus*, the premier gladiator school in Rome. His inscription claims that he lived more than ninety-eight years.

> To the spirits of the dead; to Secundus, the "gnat," *paegniarius*, of the *Ludus Magnus*; this well-deserving man lived ninety-eight years, eight months, eighteen days; his gladiatorial *familia* willingly put this up in his honor.

Gladiatorial Combat

Gladiatorial combat was a one-on-one contest in which the combatants were expected to put on a good show of skill (#343). Death was not the point of the contest. Gladiators of similar skill were pitted against one another. When one of the gladiators realized that he was beaten, he threw away his shield; raised his index finger; or, preferably, both, in order to indicate to the referee that he wished to yield and end the contest. The referee then immediately jumped in to restrain the victorious gladiator from dealing a mortal blow to his vanquished and now unprotected opponent. It was then the *munerarius* who decided if the life of the defeated gladiator should be spared. It was also traditional for the *munerarius* to look to the crowd for help in making this decision. Death was not the typical outcome of a gladiatorial combat (despite the very unusual admonishment of the gladiator Urbicus in #344; see also #348 for examples of people who died in the arena). Because the contest was meant to be a show of skill, death was reserved for the defeated gladiator who did not measure up to the expectations of the *munerarius* or the crowd; death would thus naturally follow a cowardly or otherwise disgraceful performance (see #345 for the evidence for the "thumbs-up" gesture). It is very likely that a defeated gladiator would be spared and released (*missio* in Latin; #346; see also fights *sine missione* in #347).

#343: Gladiatorial Combat

Seneca, *On Providence* 3.3–4
First Century AD

Gladiatorial combat was a one-on-one contest in which the combatants were expected to put on a good show of skill. Death was not the point of the contest. Gladiators of similar skill were pitted against one another. In the passage quoted here, Seneca says that it was disgraceful for a gladiator to be matched with an obviously inferior opponent.

> Our friend Demetrius has many magnificent maxims. This is one that I heard him say recently and it is still rattling around in my head. "In my opinion, nothing is more unfortunate than a man who has never had to face difficulty." It is not right that a man never has the opportunity to see what he is capable of. The gods, in truth, condemn him if they give him everything he wants (even before he knows he wants it). Someone would look at such a person and consider

him unworthy because he has never had luck turn against him. After all, fortune of all kinds tends to keep its distance from cowards. To apply this maxim to gladiatorial combat, a gladiator might say, "What should I do? Do I really want such a fortuneless person to be my opponent? He is likely to surrender immediately. There will be no need to use all my power against him. He will flee at the slightest threat. I doubt he will even be able to look me in the face. I had better wait for someone else to fight. I would be ashamed to do battle with a man who is just waiting to be beaten." A gladiator thinks it a disgrace to be matched with a lesser man and knows that to win without danger is to win without glory. Fortune is the same. It seeks the bravest people who are its equals. Anyone else it passes over with disdain.

#344: The End of a Gladiatorial Fight

CIL 5.5933 (Milan, Italy)
Second or Third Century AD

The funerary inscription from Florence translated here commemorates a gladiator named Urbicus. The end of the text includes the unusual advice that a gladiator should kill any opponent that he defeats. In a recent article, M. J. Carter hypothesizes that this might reflect an unwritten code of conduct during gladiatorial combat in which gladiators expected each other to fight bravely in order to win the contest but not to fight in such a way to inflict serious injury or death upon their opponent. Urbicus may have spared his opponent only not to receive the same treatment later (probably from the same person he had spared).[1]

To the Spirits of the Dead; to Urbicus, top-ranked *secutor* in his school, from Florence; he fought thirteen times and lived to be twenty-two years old; Olympias his daughter, who was only five months old when he died, and his other daughter Fortuensis and his wife Lauricia made this for her well-deserving father and husband. Urbicus and Lauricia were married for seven years. I warn my fellow gladiators to kill anyone they have defeated. His fans will honor his memory.

#345: The Decision of Life and Death

Juvenal, *Satires* 3.34–38
Late First/Early Second Centuries AD

This small selection from the third satire of Juvenal is our only evidence for the hand gesture used to indicate a decision for death. Contrary to common modern

---

1. M. J. Carter, "Gladiatorial Combat: the Rules of Engagement," *The Classical Journal* 102 (2006/2007), pp. 97–114.

belief, choosing to spare the gladiator's life was not signaled by "thumbs up" and giving him death by "thumbs down." Juvenal refers only to how the mob would order the death of a gladiator "with a turned thumb" (*vetere pollicem*). He does not specify whether the thumb was turned up or down. It is most likely that the person making the signal would turn his thumb and jab it toward his own throat. This is because they would simultaneously shout "*iugula*" ("throat") while making this gesture.

At one time, these people were low-class trumpeters and frequent spectators at the amphitheatrical events in the local towns. Their horn blowing was known in those little towns. Now they are rich and give games of their own. In their effort to win popular support, they give the sentence of death to any gladiator the people ask with the turn of their thumb. After making a show of themselves at their games, they return to doing their contract work for public latrines.

#346: Fighting to a Draw

CIL 10.7297 (Sicily [Possibly Palermo])
First or Second Century AD

This inscription documenting an experienced gladiator from Sicily includes wins, losses, and draws. The Latin term for a draw is *stans missus*, "released standing." If the battle went on for some time, it was customary to declare a draw with no clear winner. In that case, both gladiators were *stantes missi*.

Flamma the *secutor* lived thirty years, fought thirty-four times, won twenty-one times, fought to a draw nine times, received *missio* four times, from Syria; Delicatus, his companion-in-arms, made this for him.

#347: Fights *Sine Missione*

Martial, *On Spectacles* 29
Late First Century AD

While a battle between two well-matched gladiators that resulted in both being *stantes missi* may have given a great show, the lack of a winner was undoubtedly disappointing to many spectators. The result was a kind of battle called *sine missione*, "without release." Sometimes, this term has been interpreted as a battle to the death in which the defeated gladiator would die without an appeal for life or death. In fact, however, the term referred simply to a contest from which there must be a clear winner; a draw was not a possible outcome. In the poem translated here from the collection of poems called *On Spectacles*, a short book describing games in the Colosseum during the Flavian emperors, the poet Martial describes a battle between Priscus and Verus that had been set as *sine missione*.

> While Priscus and Verus drew out their contest and the battle raged for a long time equally for both of them, the people shouted loudly for both men to be given *missio*. Caesar, however, obeyed his own rule. Indeed, the rule was: "the fight must continue until the finger is raised and the shield thrown away." The emperor even tried to entice one or the other to surrender by frequently offering platters of money and other gifts. At last, they found a fitting end to their equal contest. They fought as equals and they conceded as equals. Caesar gave both of them the palm of victory and even added the *rudis* and their freedom. This was the prize for their natural battle prowess. It is fitting that it happened in no reign other than yours that two men fought but both were winners.

#348: Death in the Arena

First to Third Centuries AD

Death did sometimes take place in the arena. Gladiatorial battles were violent and sometimes punished a lack of performance with death. "Deceived" commonly appears on gladiatorial tomb inscriptions as a euphemism for death. It is interesting that many of these types of inscriptions attribute gladiators' failure in the arena to being "deceived by fate."

CIL 11.1070 (Parma, Italy)

> To the spirits of the dead of Vitalis, unbeaten *retiarius*, Batavian by nationality; he died here along with his adversary as they fought with equal *virtus*; he was fast and a veteran of three fights; [. . .]n, his co-victor, put this up to him.

CIL 3.14644 (Salona, Dalmatia)

> Amabalis, *secutor*, born in Dacia, fought thirteen times; deceived by fate, not by his opponent.

Glossary

aedile: one of the major Roman senatorial magistracies that supervised public works.

aes: the small copper coin in the Roman monetary system; there were four *aeres* per *sestertius*, sixteen per *denarius,* and four hundred per *aureus.*

ala: "wing"; an auxiliary cavalry division; in an atrium-style house, can also refer to small adjunct rooms on one or both sides of the far end of the atrium.

alieni iuris: term for a person who is legally dependent on someone else (for example, a child is dependent on the *paterfamilias*).

amicitia: the bonds of official friendship between two Romans.

amphitheater: large, oval building in which gladiatorial *munera* were held.

apodyterium: a changing room in which people could dress or undress in a Roman bath complex.

aqueduct: a piping system that carried water by gravity from a water source at higher elevation to a town at lower elevation.

Ara Pacis: the "Altar of Peace"; an altar dedicated by the Senate in honor of the peace that Augustus brought to the state after a century of civil war.

archimimus: the leader and manager of a mime troupe.

atrium: the entrance hall in an atrium-style house.

augur: a religious official who watched the flight of birds as a form of *auspicia*.

Aurelian Wall: the wall built by the Emperor Aurelian (AD 270–275) that ran around the city of Rome.

aureus: the valuable gold coin in the Roman monetary system.

auspicia: the observance of religious omens and signs to determine the will of the gods about the future.

auxilia: auxiliary units in the Roman army; *auxilia* were cavalry and infantry units of only five hundred or one thousand men each and so were smaller (and less prestigious) than the legions; service in the *auxilia* was also open to non-Roman citizens (with the promise of citizenship after their term of service).

Aventine Hill: one of the major hills of Rome; in the south part of the city; location of a major temple dedicated to Diana.

balneum: a smaller, often privately owned bath complex; they were often open to the public for an admission fee.

basilica: a law court.

beneficia: acts of kindness between social allies.

biga: a two-horse chariot raced in the circus.

caldarium: a room with pools or basins of hot water in a Roman bath complex.

calida: hot water that was added to wine to make a hot or warm drink.

Campania: region of southern Italy; location of the Bay of Naples, Mount Vesuvius, and Pompeii.

Campus Martius: the "Field of Mars"; the open space northwest of the Roman forum; originally the practice field for the Roman army; later it became filled with public buildings and monuments.

Capitoline Hill: one of the major hills of Rome; location of the major temple to Jupiter Optimus Maximus; overlooks the Roman Forum.

capitolium: dedicated to the so-called Capitoline Triad (Jupiter, Juno, and Minerva), Rome's three chief deities.

capsarius: slave in a Roman bath complex who guarded the clothing left in the *apodyterium*.

carcer: a prison.

cardo: the north–south-running road in a roman town.

caritas: female virtue referring to a wife's love for her husband.

castitas: female virtue referring to sexual fidelity.

caupona: an inn; usually also had the ability to serve food and drinks.

cavea: the seating in a theater.

cena: the evening meal, dinner; the largest meal of the day.

census: a review of the list of citizens in the Roman Empire.

centuria: a century in the Roman army; composed of sixty to eighty men; commanded by a *centurio* (centurion).

centurion: military commander of a *centuria* (century), about sixty to eighty men.

circus: a large, open structure in which chariot races were held.

Circus Maximus: the major circus building in Rome; in the hollow between the Palatine and Aventine hills.

clementia: male virtue meaning "clemency," the treatment of others better than they deserved.

Cloaca Maxima: the major sewer in Rome; originally built to drain the excess water from the low area between the Palatine, Esquiline, and Capitoline hills (what would eventually become the forum).

colonus: literally, a colonist, someone sent out to live in a *colonia* of Roman citizens; later, it often referred to a tenant farmer who works the land of a farm owned by someone else.

Colosseum: the Flavian amphitheater; a large arena for amphitheatrical events built during the first century AD.

compitia: a crossroad.

compluvium: the hole in the roof of the atrium in an atrium-style house.

concordia: female virtue referring to marital concord.

conditum: a spiced wine that was usually heated before drunk; a popular drink.

coniubium: the right of marriage; a component of a citizen's right to legal marriage was that the children of the union take the status of their father and are in his *potestas*.

consul: one of the senatorial magistracies; there were two consuls each year who served as the head of the senate and chief executive magistrate in the state.

crudelitas: (the opposite of *severitas*); a vice ("cruelty") that meant savage or cruel behavior; in the area of law, *crudelitas* referred to punishments that exceeded what was allowable under the law.

cubiculum: a small room in an atrium-style house.

curia: the building where the senate met in Rome; also the term used for the building in Roman towns in which the town council met.

decumanus: the east–west-running road in a Roman town.

decurio: a member of a local aristocracy; generally analogous to a senator in the city of Rome.

denarius: the silver coin in the Roman monetary system; there were twenty-five *denarii* per *aureus*.

dictator: A dictator was a temporary magistrate for emergency situations. The dictator had supreme power in the state but only held office for six months.

duovir: the two chief magistrates of a Roman town; analogous to the two consuls in Rome.

editor: the person who paid for games in the circus or amphitheater.

eques: type of gladiator that fought from horseback.

Equestrian Order (*equites*): an aristocratic class that ranked below the senatorial order; they generally focused on trade endeavors and government contracts; during the Empire, they also had a wide range of political and military positions available to them.

Esquiline Hill: one of the major hills of Rome; it was located northeast of the center of town.

essedarii: type of gladiator that at least started the fight in a chariot.

Etruscans: people living in Etruria north of Rome and Latium; they were one of Rome's early adversaries.

exedra: term for a larger room in an atrium-style house.

familia: "family"; included all persons and property that fell under the power (*potestas*) of the *paterfamilias*, "father of the family."

fauces: "jaws": the doorway of an atrium-style house; the "jaws" refers to how the entranceway was usually a narrow corridor created by shops that were built into the façade of the house.

fecunditas: female virtue referring to fertility.

felicitas: good fortune that comes as a result of the happiness of the gods.

fortitudo: male virtue meaning "bravery."

forum: an open space in the middle of a Roman town; the location of the most important civil and religious buildings in a town.

frigidarium: a room with pools or basins of cold water in a Roman bath complex.

fullonica: a fullery; a business that dyed or cleaned clothing.

gladius: the short, Spanish sword used in the Roman army.

groma: a surveyor's tool.

harena: sand; also the term for the arena of an amphitheater.

haruspex: a religious official who examined the entrails of animals as a form of *auspicia*.

Herculaneum: city on the Bay of Naples that was destroyed in the eruption of Mount Vesuvius in AD 79.

hilaritas: female virtue referring to cheerfulness.

hoplomachus: type of gladiator that fought with a long spear and small round shield.

horrea: a warehouse.

Ides: one of the three major divisions of a Roman month; it fell on the 13th or 15th, depending on the length of the month.

impietas: a major religious offense caused by a mistake that was done purposefully.

impluvium: a shallow pool, which caught rainwater in an atrium-style house.

Janiculum Hill: One of the hills of Rome; it is on the other side of the Tiber River from the main part of town.

Kalends: the first day of the month on the Roman calendar.

laetitia: female virtue referring to happiness.

lares: guardian spirit of a person, place, or thing.

lares compitales: guardian spirits of crossroads.

latifundia: large agricultural estates owned by the very wealthy.

Latium: region of Italy in which Rome is located.

legion: the basic unit in the Roman army; made up of Roman citizens; the majority of soldiers in a legion were heavy infantry; for most of its history, a legion was composed of five thousand to six thousand men.

legionarius: a legionary; the heavily armed infantry of the Roman army.

lex: a law that had been passed through the voting assemblies.

libertus: a freedman; a slave who has received his manumission.

lictor: a lesser official who attended and guarded a Roman magistrate; they carried the *fasces*, bundles of rods attached to an axe.

litterator: an elementary school teacher.

ludi: a religious festival that included some form of entertainment (*ludi scaenici* with theatrical performances and *ludi circenses* that included chariot races).

ludus: training school for performers who appeared in amphitheatrical *munera*.

macellum: a market.

magister: a trainer or instructor.

mancipium: "ownership"; possessions that are held in the "hand" (*manus*).

manumission: "sending from the hand"; the liberation of a person (usually a slave or child) from the *potestas* of the *paterfamilias* or master.

manus: "hand"; similar to *patria potestas*; refers to a husband's control (or lack thereof) of his wife.

manus marriage: a marriage in which the wife was legally transferred to the family of her husband.

mappa: the white cloth dropped by the *editor/munerarius* to signal the start of a chariot race.

medianum: the central hall of a *medianum*-style apartment.

mensor: official who measured grain coming in to the port at Ostia.

metae: the turning posts at each end of the *spina* in a Roman circus.

mime: actors who performed in troupes (usually of seven).

missio: decision at the end of a gladiator fight in which the loser is allowed to live.

moderatio: male virtue meaning "moderation."

modestia: female virtue referring to modesty.

modius: measuring device used to measure imported wheat.

munera: amphitheatrical games; also the term for a duty or obligation as well as a gift.

munerarius: the person who paid for games in the circus or amphitheater.

murmillo: type of gladiator that fought with a sword and shield.

nomen: the second part of the Roman name; the family name.

Nones: the day between the Kalends (the 1st) and the Ides (the 13th or 15th) of a month in the Roman calendar; fell on the 5th or 7th, depending on the length of the month.

numen: the divine spark that inhabited a place, person or thing.

nutrix: wet nurse.

odeon: a small, covered theater.

orchestra: the semicircular space between the first row of the *cavea* and the stage in a theater.

ornatrix: a hairdresser/cosmetician; usually a slave who attended an aristocratic woman.

Ostia: the port city of Rome positioned at the point where the Tiber River meets the Mediterranean.

paedagogus: a slave who attended the child of an aristocrat.

palaestra: an exercise yard as seen frequently in a Roman bath complex.

Palatine Hill: one of the major hills of Rome; many rich aristocrats had their houses there in the Republic; in the Empire, it was the location of the imperial palace.

Pantheon: Temple dedicated to "all of the gods"; a small temple that stood in the Campus Martius; one of the most famous monuments still surviving today.

pantomime: a male actor who performed scenes completely on his own.

Parthia: major empire in the east (successor of the original Persian Empire) that gave Rome many problems from the first century BC to the third century AD.

paterfamilias: "father of the family"; the oldest living male in a Roman family; he owned all property in the family and everyone was under his *patria potestas*, "fatherly power."

patria: "fatherland"; can refer to one's native country, town, or city.

patria potestas: "fatherly power"; the power the *paterfamilias* had over the property and members of the family.

patrician: a category of Roman citizens based on birth; people from patrician families were generally older and more prestigious.

peristyle: an open courtyard in the back part of an atrium-style house.

pietas: Roman virtue meaning that a person correctly performs sacred religious rites; it also describes a person who observes the natural hierarchy of society.

pilum: throwing javelin of the Roman army.

piscina: a swimming pool with cold water in a Roman bath complex.

plebeian: a category of Roman citizens based on birth; all families who were not from patrician origins were plebeian.

Pompeii: city on the Bay of Naples that was destroyed in the eruption of Mount Vesuvius in AD 79.

popina: a restaurant or bar that offered drinks and food but not lodgings.

portico: a covered colonnade with columns on one or both sides.

Portus: "Harbor"; the city that grew up in the second and third centuries AD around the harbors built by Claudius and Trajan north of Ostia.

praenomen: the first part of the Roman name; the personal name.

praetor: one of the major Roman senatorial magistracies that oversaw the law courts.

Praetorian Guard: the personal bodyguard of the Roman emperor.

prefect: general term for a person who is put in charge of something.

primus pilus: "first spear"; the centurion in charge of the first century of the first cohort of a Roman legion; the highest-ranking centurion in a legion.

probitas: female virtue referring to goodness.

procurator: an equestrian administrator, usually associated with some kind of property (often that owned by the emperor).

province: administrative region of the Roman Empire in which Roman magistrates exercised their jurisdiction.

pudicitia: female virtue referring to a sense of decency.

pulchritudo: female virtue referring to beauty.

quadriga: a four-horse chariot raced in the circus.

quaestor: one of the major Roman senatorial magistracies that oversaw the state finances.

regio: region within a Roman city. Rome had 14 *regiones*.

Res Gestae: "things done"; the name of the document the first Roman emperor Augustus wrote describing his life and deeds.

retiarius: type of gladiator that fought with a net, trident, and very little armor.

sacra: general term for all types of sacred religious rites.

salutatio: the official meeting and greeting of an influential person with his clients of lower social status or standing.

scaena: the stage of a theater.

scutum: the rectangular shield used in the Roman army.

secutor: type of gladiator that fought with a sword and shield.

senate: the legislative body of Roman government composed of men who had held magistracies.

Senatus Consultum: a senatorial decree; an official pronouncement made by the senate; did not technically have the same force as a *lex* (law), but still carried great weight.

sestertius: the bronze coin in the Roman monetary system; there were four *sestertii* per *denarius* and one hundred per *aureus*.

severitas: a male virtue meaning "severity"; the fair treatment of others under the law especially where punishments were concerned.

sine manu marriage: a marriage in which the wife remained a legal member of her original family rather than that of her husband; the most common type of marriage during the Empire.

sine missione: a type of gladiator fight in which there must be a clear winner; fights to a draw (*stans missus*) were not allowed.

socius: a social, military, or political ally.

spina: the ornamental barrier that ran down the center of a circus.

stans missus: a gladiator fight in which the two combatants were so well matched that a draw was declared.

strigil: a curved piece of metal with a wooden handle used to scrape the oil used to clean the body during the bathing ritual.

Subura: the poor section of the city of Rome in the valley along the road that led from the forum up the Esquiline Hill toward the Esquiline gate.

sui iuris: term for a person who is legally independent.

taberna: a tavern or bar.

tablinum: the room at the opposite end of the atrium from the *fauces*; room in which the owner would sit to meet his clients during the *salutation*.

tepidarium: a room with pools or basins of lukewarm water in a Roman bath complex.

thermae: the larger, publicly owned bath complexes; they were open to the public, and, often, had free admission.

thermopolium: term for a popina (restaurant/bar) that had a counter opening onto the street where food and drinks could be heated and served.

thrax: type of gladiator that fought with a sword and shield.

Tiber River: the river that runs through the city of Rome.

toga: the complex outer wool garment worn by Roman men.

tonsor: a barber.

Transtiberim: the district of Rome that was "across the Tiber."

tribe: a division of Roman citizens originally determined geographically; one method of voting was done by tribe.

tribune (military): military officer; in the Empire, there were six tribunes per legion; tribunes were drawn from a mixture of young, aspiring senators and equestrians at various points in their career.

tribune of the plebs: magistracy of the Roman senate that was originally created to protect the interests of the common people.

triclinium: the dining room in a Roman house; also the term for the three couches set up around a table in a "U"-shape pattern with the heads toward the center and the feet toward the outside.

triumph: a procession through the streets of Rome awarded to a Roman general after a significant military victory.

triumvir: board comprised of three men.

Twelve Tables: the first written law code in Rome from the middle of the fifth century BC.

velites: lightly armed skirmishers in the Roman army of the Republic.

Vesuvius: volcano that erupted in AD 79.

Via Appia: the "Appian Way"; the road built during the third century BC running from Rome to Brundisium in the south.

Via Sacra: the "Sacred Way"; major road that runs through the middle of the forum.

vicomagister: magistrate in charge of a Roman *vicus*.

vicus: neighborhood within a Roman city.

vigiles: "watchmen"; usually refers to the fire brigade.

virtus: virtue referring to manly courage, especially as it refers to courage on the battlefield but could also refer more generally to any "virtue."

vitium: a minor religious offense caused by a mistake that was not done purposefully.

Works Quoted

Ammianus Marcellinus: a fourth-century AD Roman historian. His wrote a history that covered the period from the accession of Nerva (AD 96) to the Battle of Adrianople (AD 378), thus covering the period after that written about by the historian Tacitus. Only eighteen of the more than thirty original volumes have survived. These preserved volumes recount the period from 353 to 378 and volumes are especially interesting because they describe events during Ammianus' own lifetime. Ammianus was also an army officer who served in the army of the emperor Constantius II.

***L'Année épigraphique* (AE):** a French journal published annually that seeks to collect all of the newly discovered inscriptions from ancient Rome. The journal was first published in 1888. Entries are arranged geographically and chronologically.

***Appendix Vergiliana*:** a collection of poems that are ascribed to the great Roman poet Vergil. Most scholars agree now, however, that these poems were written by a variety of authors during the first century AD. Portions of two of these poems appear in this collection: the *Copa* (about a barmaid) and the *Moretum* (describing a poor farmer cooking a meal).

Apuleius: a second-century philosopher and novelist from the province of Numidia in North Africa. His most famous work is the *Metamorphoses* (also known by the title *The Golden Ass*), a fanciful novel recounting the exploits of an aristocrat named Lucius who is turned into a donkey through magic. Throughout the novel, Apuleius interrupts the plot with various stories, the most famous (and lengthy) of which is the story of the romance between the mortal woman Psyche and the god Cupid.

Augustine (St.): a fourth/fifth-century AD Christian theologian and author from North Africa. His most famous work (and the one quoted in this book) is *City of God*, a philosophical work that explained how Rome's decline was not caused by the adoption of Christianity.

Augustus: Roman emperor from 27 BC to AD 14. At the end of his life, he composed an account of his life generally known today as the *Res Gestae* ("things done"). This work is very important for understanding Augustus' political position and the way he advertised that position to the people of the empire.

Aulus Gellius: a second-century AD author from the city of Rome. His book, entitled *Attic Nights* (named thus because he began writing the work while spending the winter in the region of Attica in Greece) is a collection of trivia and antiquarian stories.

Cato the Elder: a politician and historian of the third/second century BC. Of plebeian descent, the traditionalist Cato held the most important magistracies of the senate. Although he wrote many books, the only one to survive in its entirety is his *On Agriculture*, a manual on how to run a farm.

Catullus: love poet of the first century BC. He was born to an equestrian family in northern Italy. One hundred and sixteen of his poems have been preserved. His poems were heavily influenced by the poetry of the Greek Hellenistic poets, most notably the school of poets from Alexandria in Egypt. In turn, Catullus influenced later generations of Latin poets, most notably Ovid, Vergil, and Horace.

Cicero: Roman statesman from the first century BC. He was born to an equestrian family in central Italy but won election to the senate and eventually rose to the consulship in 63 BC. He also acted as a defense attorney and prosecutor in many high-profile cases. Many of his speeches from these cases he edited and published. He also wrote many works of philosophy. Cicero was outspoken against the triumvir Antony and met his end in the proscriptions of 43 BC. This book includes quotes from his speech in defense of Murena against a charge of bribery; his speeches against Antony (the Philippics); letters to his friends; and philosophical works on old age, the laws, duties and moral obligations, the nature of the gods, and the republic.

Claudian (Claudius Claudianus): poet of the late fourth/early fifth century AD. Originally from Alexandria in Egypt, he became the court poet to the western Roman emperor Honorius. This book includes a quotation from his poem *On the Consulship of Stilicho*. Stilicho was a very important general of Honorius.

***Corpus Inscriptionum Latinarum* (CIL):** a multi-volume set of books seeking to collect and publish all ancient Latin inscriptions. The work began in 1847 under a committee headed by the great German epigrapher and historian Theodor Mommsen. Volumes continue to be published today. Volumes are arranged geographically.

Cornelius Fronto: a senator and author of the second century AD. The emperor Antoninus Pius appointed him as tutor for his adoptive sons (and future emperors) Marcus Aurelius and Lucius Verus. A number of letters between Fronto and Marcus Aurelius have been preserved. The book includes a quote from one of those letters describing the loss of his children.

Dio Cassius: Roman senator of the late second/early third century AD. He was born in Nicaea in the province of Bithynia. He wrote a history of the Roman Empire in eighty volumes that covered everything from the arrival of Aeneas in Italy to his own times. The vast majority of this history is only preserved in epitome, a condensed version created by the eleventh-century monk Xiphilinus.

Dionysius of Halicarnassus: Greek historian of the first century BC. His major work, *Roman Antiquities*, tried to explain the Romans and their success to the Greek peoples of the east. Originally twenty volumes, *Roman Antiquities* covered Roman history from the foundation of Rome to the start of the First Punic War. About the first half is preserved in its entirety, but the later volumes are only preserved in a Byzantine abridgement.

Florus: historian from the later first/early second centuries AD. He was originally from Africa. He wrote a short history of the Roman Empire based heavily on the much larger history of Livy. It covered Roman history from the foundation of the city to the closing of the Temple of Janus by the emperor Augustus in 25 BC.

Frontinus (Julius): Roman senator of later first century AD. His most important work, *On the Aqueduct System of the City of Rome*, comes from his appointment as Caretaker of the Water Supply by the emperor Nerva in AD 97. It describes in great detail the water that was coming into the city of Rome via the aqueducts.

Gaius: Roman legal writer of the second century AD. His most important work, the *Institutes*, is a four-book introduction to Roman legal institutions. This book includes quotes from the first book of this work, which covers people and social status.

***Historia Augusta* (also known as the *Scriptores Historiae Augustae*):** a collection of imperial biographies spanning the period between Hadrian (AD 117–138) and the rise of Diocletian (AD 284). The work claims to be the effort of multiple historians writing during the reigns of Diocletian and Constantine. This, however, seems to be false and is instead the work of one man writing perhaps a century later, in the fourth century AD. The contents of these biographies are of dubious authenticity, but the *Historia Augusta* is often our only existing history describing the lives of some of these emperors. It is also likely that the author drew much of his material from good historians that have since been lost.

Horace: Roman poet of the first century BC. He was one of the court poets of the emperor Augustus. His works exhibit a great deal of influence from the Greek Hellenistic poets. This book includes quotes from his *Satires*, his first published work.

Josephus: Jewish historian of the first century AD. He served as the commander of the Jewish rebel army of Galilee in the Jewish rebellion during the reign of the emperor Nero. He was captured alive by the commanding general (and future emperor) Vespasian and joined his entourage. He went to Rome and wrote a number of books, most notably a history of the Jews (the *Antiquities of the Jews*) and an account of the rebellion in which he took part (*The Jewish War*).

Julius Caesar: Roman senator of the first century BC. One of the most important figures of the late Republic, Julius Caesar rose to the dictatorship of Rome before he was assassinated on the Ides of March, 44 BC. He wrote accounts of his two major military achievements: his conquest of Gaul (*The Gallic War*) and his victory in the civil war against Pompey the Great (the *Civil War*).

Justinian: Eastern Roman emperor from AD 527 to 565. He sponsored a complete codification and revision of the Roman law code (the *Corpus Iuris Civilis*). Although this source is quite late, it is based heavily on earlier legislation and precedent. The most important components of his legal works were the *Digest*, *Institutes*, and *Codex*.

Juvenal: satirical poet of the late first/early second century AD. Sixteen of his satires have been preserved. These satires poke fun at a variety of topics involving daily life. They also engage in a great deal of exaggeration for comic effect, which makes it difficult to take anything Juvenal says absolutely literally.

Livy: Roman historian of the first century BC/first century AD. He composed a mammoth history of Rome covering everything from the foundation of Rome to his own times. Originally 142 volumes long, only volumes 1–10 and 21–45 are preserved mostly intact. There are summaries of some of the other volumes as well.

Lucian: philosopher, orator, and novelist of the second century AD. He wrote many books on a wide range of topics. This book includes quotations from his work *The Baths*, which describes an opulent Roman bath complex.

Martial: poet of the first century AD. He was originally from the Roman province of Spain. He wrote a collection of epigrams in twelve volumes. Martial's epigrams are mostly short, satirical looks at his friends, life in Rome, and his own character.

Ovid: poet of the first century BC/first century AD. He was born to an equestrian family in the town of Sulmo, east of Rome. Although he started a public career, he gave it up early to pursue the writing of poetry. This book contains quotes from two of his works: *The Loves*, a collection of three volumes of love poems, and *The Art of Love*, a didactic poem, also in three volumes, teaching men how to woo, seduce, and keep lovers. Both books discuss affairs with married women. In AD 8, Ovid was exiled to the town of Tomis on the Black Sea. While these works went against Augustus' moral legislation, it is debated whether they were the cause of his exile. Ovid died in AD 17 or 18 while still in exile.

Paulus: an eminent lawyer and legal writer of the second/third century AD. Active during the Severan emperors, Paulus became one of the chief legal advisors of Alexander Severus (AD 222–235). The work entitled *Pauli Sententiae*, the "Viewpoints of Paulus" is attributed to him, although the compilation may include numerous other legal writers in addition to Paulus.

Petronius: a senator of the first century AD and friend and courtier of the emperor Nero (AD 54–68). He is described as the *elegentiae arbiter* ("judge of elegance") in the court of Nero. He reached the consulship in AD 62. He committed suicide in AD 65 when his political enemies accused him of treason. The partially preserved novel *Satyricon* is generally attributed to him. The *Satyricon* tells the story of the man Encolpius as he tries to keep his slave boy and lover Giton faithful to him.

Plautus: comic playwright of the third century/second century BC. While some of his plays are original, most are adaptations of original Greek plays for a Roman audience. The one play quoted in this book is the *Rudens* ("the Rope"), the story of a girl who was stolen from home as a baby by pirates only to be re-united with her family later.

Pliny the Elder: equestrian official of the first century AD. Pliny the Elder was a very active man who wrote many books and served in many official positions and was personal friends with the emperor Vespasian. His most famous literary work is the *Natural History*, a thirty-seven-book encyclopedia of human knowledge. While serving as admiral of the navy in Misenum on the Bay of Naples, Pliny went to investigate more closely the eruption of Mount Vesuvius in AD 79 and was killed.

Pliny the Younger: senator of the first/second century AD. He was the nephew and adoptive son of Pliny the Elder. Born into an equestrian family, he was elected to the quaestorship in the late 80s AD and so entered the senatorial order. He became consul in AD 100 and died while serving as governor of Pontus and Bithynia in 110 or 111. Two of his works have been preserved: his speech of praise of the emperor Trajan (panegyric) on the occasion of his consulship, and ten volumes of his published letters.

Plutarch: a historian and philosopher of the first/second century AD. He was born in Greece and wrote many books, the most famous of which is his *Parallel Lives*, a collection of biographies comparing individuals from the Greek and Roman worlds.

Polybius: a Greek historian of the second century BC. He was taken to Rome during the wars with the Greek East of the second century BC and became the tutor of the children of the Roman general Aemilius Paulus (the victor at the Battle of Pydna against Macedonia). He wrote a history that described Rome's rise to prominence in the Mediterranean, covering the years 264–146 BC. In his history, he described, to a Greek audience, Roman institutions and the reasons for Rome's success.

Quintilian: Roman orator of the first century AD. Originally from Spain, Quintilian studied rhetoric in Rome during the reign of Nero. After the rise of the Flavian dynasty, he opened a school of oratory in Rome. He wrote a book, *On Oratory*, in twelve volumes. In this book, he described the practice of oratory. He also extensively discusses education as well.

Sallust: historian of the first century BC. He was also a member of the senatorial order and eventually reached the rank of praetor. He was a supporter of Julius Caesar in the civil war. He wrote several works of history. This book includes quotes from his *The War against Catiline*, a description of the conspiracy of the senator Catiline against the state.

Seneca (the Younger): philosopher and author of the first century AD. Born in Spain, Seneca studied oratory in Rome from an early age. He was one of the two major advisors to the young emperor Nero (along with the praetorian prefect Antistius Burrus). He died in AD 65 when Nero forced him to commit suicide after the discovery of the conspiracy of Calpurnius Piso. He wrote numerous books. Quoted in this book are his *Letters* (moral essays sent as letters to Lucilius), *Consolation to Helvia* (letter consoling his mother during his exile in the reign of Claudius), *On Clemency* (essay addressed to the young Nero on the virtue of *clementia*), *On Providence* (short essay in the form of a Platonic dialogue discussing the Stoic notion of providence), *On the Constancy of the Wise Man* (on the virtue of *constantia*), *On the*

Happy Life (essay on the pursuit of happiness), *On the Shortness of Life* (essay explaining how life is long enough for a person who pursues wisdom), *On the Tranquility of the Mind* (essay addressed to his friend Annaeus Serenus explaining how to compose his mind in the face of troubles), and *On Wrath* (addressed to his brother and telling him how to control one's anger).

Strabo: first century BC/first century AD Greek geographer. Born in Pontus, Strabo spent much of his life traveling around the Mediterranean. In 44 BC, he moved to Rome. His most famous work is his *Geography*, an extensive collection of geographical information in seventeen volumes.

Suetonius: first/second century AD biographer. As a member of the equestrian order, Suetonius enjoyed a short but prestigious career. He was friends with the senator Pliny the Younger and enjoyed the patronage of the emperors Trajan and Hadrian. He was in charge of the imperial archives under Trajan and became one of the imperial secretaries under Hadrian. He was dismissed from this post, however, in AD 119, perhaps because of misconduct with the empress Vibia Sabina. His most famous work is his *Twelve Caesars*, a collection of biographies of the emperors (as well as Julius Caesar) through the Flavian dynasty.

Tacitus: senator and historian of the first/second century AD. He was born in northern Italy to an equestrian family but rose to the rank of senator and even became consul in AD 97. He wrote several works, including the *Annals*, a history of the Julio-Claudian emperors from the death of Augustus to the death of Nero. Earlier, he had written a history of the Flavian dynasty (the *Histories*), although only the first part of it survives (describing the chaotic year AD 69, the "Year of the Four Emperors").

Tertullian: first/second century AD Christian author from Carthage, North Africa. He wrote a number of books describing the Christian faith as well as engaging in theological discussion. This book includes quotes from *On Spectacles*, a work that examines the moral dangers involved with attending events at the theater, circus, and amphitheater.

Theodosius II: Roman emperor from 408 to 450. He was the son of the eastern emperor Arcadius. In 429, he created a commission to collect all of the legal pronouncements of emperors since 312. In 438, the commission completed their work and published the *Theodosian Code*. This collection would be important for Justinian in the sixth century when he created his legal works.

Ulpian: legal writer of the second/third centuries AD. He was an influential courtier and magistrate under the Severan emperors. He wrote numerous legal works, most of which have been lost or only preserved in fragment or in quotes in other legal sources. This book includes quotes from his *Rules*, a collection of legal pronouncements on a number of subjects.

Valerius Maximus: author and orator of the first century BC/first century AD. His *Memorable Deeds and Sayings* in nine volumes is a catalog of historical anecdotes arranged according to subject. His subjects tend to be virtues, vices, and other guidelines for positive and negative behavior.

Varro: author of the second/first century BC. He was born in Italy to an equestrian family. He sided with Pompey the Great in the civil war with Julius Caesar, but Caesar pardoned him after Pompey was defeated. He wrote numerous books, most of which are now lost. This book includes a quote from his full-preserved *On Agriculture*, a manual on running a successful agricultural estate.

Vitruvius: engineer and architect of the first century BC. It is possible that he served in the military as an artillery engineer. He wrote the book *On Architecture* in ten volumes. Within this book, he covers town planning, building materials, public buildings (such as temples), private houses, aqueducts and the water supply, and the science and technology of architecture.

Bibliography

Aicher, P., *Guide to the Aqueducts of Ancient Rome*, Wauconda: Bolchazy-Carducci, 1995.

Bauman, R., *Crime and Punishment in Ancient Rome*, London: Routledge, 1996.

Birley, A., *Marcus Aurelius: A Biography*, New Haven: Yale, 1987.

Bodel, J., "Dealing with the Dead: Undertakers, Executioners, and Potter's Fields in Ancient Rome" in *Death and Disease in the Ancient City* (E. Marshall and V. Hope, eds.), London: Routledge, 2011, pp. 128–51.

Bodson, L., "Motivations for Pet-Keeping in Ancient Greece and Rome: A Preliminary Survey" in *Companion Animals and Us: Exploring the Relationship Between People and Pets* (A.L. Podberseck, E.S. Paul, J.A. Serpell, eds.), Cambridge: Cambridge University Press, 2000, pp. 27–41.

Bradley, K., "Children and Dreams" in *Childhood, Class and Kin in the Roman World* (S. Dixon, ed.), London: Routledge, 2001, pp. 43–51.

Bradley, K., "Remarriage and the Structure of the Upper-Class Roman Family" in *Marriage, Divorce, and Children in Ancient Rome* (B. Rawson ed.), Oxford: Clarendon, 1996, pp. 79–98.

Bradley, K., *Slavery and Society at Rome*, Cambridge: Cambridge University Press, 1994.

Bradley, K., "The Sentimental Education of the Roman Child: the Role of Pet-Keeping," *Latomus* 57 (1998), pp. 523–57.

Bradley, M., "'It all Comes out in the Wash': Looking Harder at the Roman *Fullonica*," *Journal of Roman Studies* 15 (2002), pp. 20–44.

Campbell, B., *The Roman Army: 31 B.C.–A.D. 337: A Sourcebook*, London: Routledge, 1994.

Carter, M. J., "Gladiatorial Combat: The Rules of Engagement," *The Classical Journal* 102 (2006/2007), pp. 97–114.

Champlin, E., *Final Judgments: Duty and Emotion in Roman Wills 200 BC–AD 250*, Berkeley: University of California Press, 1991.

Clarke, J., *Roman Sex: 100 BC–AD 250*, New York: Harry N. Abrams, 2003.

Corbier, M., "Child Exposure and Abandonment" in *Childhood, Class and Kin in the Roman World* (S. Dixon, ed.), London: Routledge, 2001, pp. 52–73.

Corbier, M., "Divorce and Adoption as Familial Strategies" in *Marriage, Divorce, and Children in Ancient Rome* (B. Rawson, ed.), Oxford: Clarendon, 1996, pp. 47–78.

Crook, J., "Women in Roman Succession" in *The Family in Ancient Rome: New Perspectives* (B. Rawson, ed.), Ithaca: Cornell University Press, 1987, pp. 58–82.

Cruse, A., *Roman Medicine*, Stroud: Tempus, 2003.

D'Ambra, E., *Roman Women*, Cambridge: Cambridge University Press, 2006.

DeFelice, J., *Roman Hospitality: the Professional Women of Pompeii*, Warren Center: Shangri La Publications, 2001.

Dixon, S., *Reading Roman Women*, London: Bristol Classical Press, 2001.

Dixon, S., *The Roman Family*, Baltimore: Johns Hopkins University Press, 1992.

Dixon, S., "Sex and the Married Woman in Ancient Rome" in *Early Christian Families in Context: An Interdisciplinary Dialogue* (D. Balch and C. Osied, eds.), Grand Rapids: William B. Eerdmans, 2003, pp. 111–29.

Evans, H., *Water Distribution in Ancient Rome: The Evidence of Frontinus*, Ann Arbor: University of Michigan Press, 1994.

Everett, A., *Cicero: The Life and Times of Rome's Greatest Politician*, New York: Random House, 2003.

Fagan, G., *Bathing in Public in the Roman World*, Ann Arbor: University of Michigan Press, 1999.

Fantham, E., Foley, H., et al., *Women in the Classical World*, Oxford: Oxford University Press, 1995.

Finley, M., "The Silent Women of Rome" in *Sexuality and Gender in the Classical World* (L. K. McClure, ed.), Oxford: Blackwell, 2002, pp. 147–56.

Flower, H., *Ancestor Masks and Aristocratic Power in Roman Culture*, Oxford: Oxford University Press, 2000.

Frier, B. and McGinn, T., *A Casebook on Roman Family Law*, Oxford: Oxford University Press, 2003.

Garnsey, P., *Social Status and Legal Privilege in the Roman Empire*, Oxford: Oxford University Press, 1970.

Garnsey, P., and Saller, R., *The Roman Empire: Economy, Society, and Culture*, Berkeley, University of California, 2014.

Goldsworthy, A., *The Complete Roman Army*, London: Thames and Hudson, 2003.

Goldsworthy, A., *The Roman Army at War, 100 B.C.–A.D. 200*, Oxford: Oxford University Press, 1996.

Gradel, I., *Emperor Worship and Roman Religion*, Oxford: Oxford University Press, 2002.

Greene, K., *The Archaeology of the Roman Economy*, Berkeley: University of California Press, 1990.

Harlow, M., and Laurence, R., *Growing Up and Growing Old in Ancient Rome: A Life Course Approach*, London: Routledge, 2001.

Hermansen, G., *Ostia: Aspects of Roman City Life*, Edmonton: University of Alberta, 1981.

Higginbotham, J., *Piscinae: Artificial Fishponds in Roman Italy*, Chapel Hill: University of North Carolina, 1997.

Holland, R., *Nero: the Man Behind the Myth*, Glocestershire: Sutton Publishing, 1998.

Hopkins, K., *Conquerors and Slaves*, Cambridge, Cambridge University Press, 1978.

Humphrey, J., *Roman Circuses: Arenas for Chariot Racing*, Berkeley: University of California Press, 1986.

Jackson, R., *Doctors and Diseases in the Roman Empire*, Tulsa: University of Oklahoma Press, 1988.

Jennison, G., *Animals for Show and Pleasure in Ancient Rome,* Philadelphia: University of Pennsylvania Press, 2005.

Koch, G., *Roman Funerary Sculpture: Catalogue of the Collections,* Malibu: J. Paul
    Getty Museum, 1988.

Laes, C., "Desperately Different? *Delicia* Children in the Roman Household" in
    Early Christian Families in Context: An Interdisciplinary Dialogue (D. Balch and C.
    Osiek, eds.), Grand Rapids: William B. Eerdmans, 2003, pp. 298–324.

Laidlaw, A., *The First Style in Pompeii: Painting and Architecture,* Rome: G.
    Bretschneider, 1985.

Laurence, R., *Roman Pompeii: Space and Society,* London: Routledge, 2007.

Le Bohec, Y., *The Imperial Roman Army,* London: Hippocrene Books, 1994.

Lindsay, H. "Adoption and its Function in Cross-Cultrual Contexts" in *Childhood,
    Class and Kin in the Roman World* (S. Dixon, ed.), London: Routledge, 2001,
    pp. 190–204.

McWilliam, J., "Children among the Dead: The Influence of Urban Life on the
    Commemoration of Children on Tombstone Inscriptions" in *Childhood,
    Class and Kin in the Roman World* (S. Dixon, ed.), London: Routledge, 2001,
    pp. 74–98.

Meiggs, R., *Roman Ostia,* Oxford: Oxford University Press, 1973.

Moeller, W., *The Wool Trade of Ancient Pompeii,* Leiden: Brill Academic Publishers, 1976.

Musurillo, H., *Acts of the Christian Martyrs,* Oxford: Oxford University Press, 1972.

Nordh, A., *Libellus de Regionibus Urbis Romae,* Lund: G.W.K. Gleerup, 1949.

Osiek, C., "Female Slaves, *Porneia,* and the Limits of Obedience" in *Early Christian
    Families in Context: An Interdisciplinary Dialogue* (D. Balch and C. Osiek, eds.),
    Grand Rapids: William B. Eerdmans, 2003, pp. 255–74.

Packer, J., *The Insulae of Imperial Ostia, The Memoirs of the American School in Rome,*
    Rome: American Academy in Rome, 1971.

Potter, D., and Mattingly, D., eds., *Life, Death and Entertainment in the Roman
    Empire,* Ann Arbor: University of Michigan Press, 1999.

Rawson, B., *Children and Childhood in Roman Italy,* Oxford: Oxford University
    Press, 2003.

Rawson, B., "Death, Burial, and Commemoration of Children in Roman Italy" in
    Early Christian Families in Context: An Interdisciplinary Dialogue (D. Balch and C.
    Osiek, eds.), Grand Rapids: William B. Eerdmans, 2003, pp. 277–97.

Richlin, A., "Pliny's Brassiere" in *Sexuality and Gender in the Classical World*
    (L. McClure, ed.), Oxford: Wiley-Blackwell, 2002, pp. 225–52.

Robinson, O., *The Criminal Law of Ancient Rome,* Baltimore: Johns Hopkins
    University Press, 1995.

Saller, R., *Patriarchy, Property and Death in the Roman Family,* Cambridge:
    Cambridge University Press, 1994.

Saller, R., "Women, Slaves, and the Economy of the Roman Household" in *Early
    Christian Families in Context: An Interdisciplinary Dialogue* (D. Balch and C.
    Osiek, editors), Grand Rapids: William B. Eerdmans, 2003, pp. 185–204.

Shanks, H., "The Puzzling Channels in Ancient Latrines," *Biblical Archaeology
    Review* 28 (2002), pp. 49–51.

Stambaugh, J., *The Ancient Roman City,* Baltimore: Johns Hopkins University Press,
    1988.

Thylander, H., *Inscriptions du Port D'Ostie*, Lund: G.W.K. Gleerup, 1952.

Toynbee, J. M., *Death and Burial in the Roman World*, Ithaca: Cornell University Press, 1971.

Treggiari, S., "Divorce Roman Style: How Easy and How Frequent Was It?" in *Marriage, Divorce, and Children in Ancient Rome* (B. Rawson, ed.), Oxford: Clarendon, 1991, pp. 31–46.

Wallace-Hadrill, A., "Emperors and Houses in Rome" in *Childhood, Class and Kin in the Roman World* (S. Dixon, ed.), London: Routledge, 2001, pp. 128–43.

Wallace-Hadrill, A., "*Domus* and *Insula* in Rome: Families and Housefuls" in *Early Christian Families in Context: An Interdisciplinary Dialogue* (D. Balch and C. Osiek, eds.), Grand Rapids: William B. Eerdmans, 2003, pp. 3–18.

Wallace-Hadrill, A., *Houses and Society in Pompeii and Herculaneum*, Princeton: Princeton University Press, 1994.

Weaver, P., "Children of Freedmen (and Freedwomen)" in *Marriage, Divorce, and Children in Ancient Rome* (B. Rawson, ed.), Oxford: Clarendon, 1991, pp. 166–90.

Weaver, P., *Familia Caesaris: A Social Study of the Emperor's Freedmen and Slaves*, Cambridge: Cambridge University Press, 1972.

White, K., *Agricultural Implements of the Roman World*, Cambridge: Cambridge University Press, 1967.

White, K., *Roman Farming*, Ithaca: Cornell University Press, 1970.

Zanker, P., *Pompeii: Public and Private Life*, Cambridge: Harvard University Press, 1999.

Index